"We mustn't forget the terrifyi⌐ policies foreign and domestic th⌐ such a bloody hell for so ma⌐. But Brandon Gauthier in this meticulously researched, compellingly written, highly accessible volume shows why we need to remember them less as monstrous aberrations, more as human beings who ended up demonstrating the capability of our species for evil."

> — **Bradley K. Martin, author of** *Under the Loving Care of the Fatherly Leader: North Korea and the Kim Dynasty*

PRAISE FOR *BEFORE EVIL*

"Brandon Gauthier has written a powerful investigation into the myriad influences that created six of the most evil men in modern history. *Before Evil* deftly explains in stunning detail how Lenin, Hitler, Stalin Mao, Mussolini and Kim slowly turned from unremarkable children into authoritarian adults whose choices affected the course of the entire world. By asking readers to grapple with the humanity of men who are widely abhorred, Gauthier provides a fresh way to understand why these six leaders were able to wield power—and how dictators could use those same tactics to rise again."

> — **Beth Knobel, Associate Professor of Communication and Media Studies, Fordham University**

"*Before Evil* opens a compelling window into the humanity of some of the most tyrannical despots of the modern era. At times poignant, powerful, erudite, and even humorous, it reminds us that those we consider truly evil are still truly human, and that the lines between good and evil are not as simple as we might like to believe."

> — **Mitchell Lerner, Professor of History and Director of the East Asian Studies Center at The Ohio State University**

BEFORE EVIL

BEFORE EVIL

Young Lenin, Hitler, Stalin, Mussolini, Mao, and Kim

Brandon K. Gauthier

Tortoise Books
Chicago, IL

FOR PHOEBE, HADLEY, AND EMMELINE

Table of Contents

INTRODUCTION

N. *Here's your manuscript. I have read it all the way through.*

R. *All the way through? I see: you expect few will do the same?*

N. *Vel duo, vel nemo. [Perhaps two, perhaps none.]*

R. *Turpe et miserabile. [Disgrace and misery.] But I want a straightforward judgment.*

N. *I dare not.*

R. *You have dared everything with that single word. Explain yourself.*

N. *My judgment depends on the answer you are going to give. Is this...real, or is it a fiction?*

R. *I don't see that it matters. To say whether a Book is good or bad, how does it matter how it came to be written?*

N. *It matters a great deal for this one. A Portrait always has some value provided it is a good likeness, however strange the Original. But in a Tableau based on imagination, each human figure must possess features common to mankind, or else the Tableau is worthless. Even if we allow that both are good, there remains a difference, which is that the Portrait is of interest to few People; the Tableau alone can please the Public....*

R. *...I see the turn your curiosity is taking....Do you know how vastly men differ from each other? How opposite characters can be? To what degree morals, prejudices vary with the times, places, eras? Who is daring enough to assign exact limits to Nature, and assert: Here is as far as Man can go, and no further?*

N. *With such fine reasoning, unheard-of Monsters, Giants, Pygmies, fantasies of all kinds, anything could be specifically included in nature: everything would be disfigured; we would no longer have any common model! I repeat, in Tableaux of humankind, Man must be recognizable to everyone.*

\-   Jean-Jacques Rousseau, "Second Preface" to
Julie, or The New Héloïse

THIS IS ABOUT US

Adolf Hitler, Joseph Stalin, Vladimir Lenin, Mao Zedong, Benito Mussolini, and Kim Il-sung all believed with great conviction in the righteousness of their causes. From a young age, they moved into the future convinced they had discerned an ultimate pattern in daily reality—that they knew what had to be done, and would do it. Humility was for those they would murder.

Yet these heinous men—we must remind ourselves—were once relatable human beings. Flesh and blood, they emerged from the womb; and breathed; and cried; and drank breast milk; and slept; and crawled; and toddled; and walked; and bathed; and played with siblings; and made friends; and learned to read; and sang; and went to school; and wrote papers; and enjoyed certain kinds of food; and laughed; and wept; and encountered bullies; and earned good (and bad) grades; and got into trouble; and told jokes; and went through puberty; and got pimples; and had crushes; and masturbated; and made out with girls (for the most part); and listened to music; and clashed with Dad; and adored Mom; and went to church; and considered whether God existed; and fell in love with books; and dreamed; and wondered what they would be when they grew up (A teacher? A priest? An artist?); and worried; and behaved benevolently; and acted callously; and danced; and enjoyed nature; and fell in love; and lost their virginity; and suffered tragedies; and grappled with the complexities of an unforgiving world; and *realized that they too would die someday*. Monsters aren't real. Humans are.

The worst dictators of the 20th century—like us—had the capacity for both love and cruelty from a young age. That perspective is anathema to our need to believe that we're entirely different from these mass-murderers; we, who try to live ethical lives and treat others with dignity and respect. But that narrative is problematic. Thinking of ourselves as a distinct species from these men diminishes our ability to grapple with a conundrum we all share: that the line between individuals doing awful things *convinced they are just* and people doing awful things *knowing they are wrong* is not always so clear.[1] At what point can we ourselves become villains without realizing it? How can we guard against as much? The answers begin with considering what we have in common with "monsters" themselves.

◆ ◆ ◆

Human beings often dehumanize "others." A noxious belief system like racism, as Hannah Arendt observes in *The Origins of Totalitarianism*, represents an "emergency explanation of human beings" to the humanity of people they do not understand—what Arendt describes as "fright of something like oneself that still under no circumstances ought to be like oneself."[2] Odious ideologies in history—from Nazism to Stalinism—have denigrated the shared humanity of men and women everywhere by suggesting that given ethical values, and thus moral obligations, didn't apply to certain groups. Crimes against humanity followed as cruel tropes impeded nuanced discussions about human similarities and differences. Empathy became a defect.[3]

In the present, we risk continuing this trend by dehumanizing evildoers as demons unworthy of feelings except disgust. This reductive tendency distances atrocious individuals from ourselves. It offers comfort but undermines our ability to make sense of their actions as explicable phenomena.[4] We must avoid this in examining the worst propagators of ideological terror in the 20th century. Put differently, we must not envision ghouls in the place of living, breathing humans who committed unthinkable crimes with righteous dogmatism.[5] As we honor the memory of victims who suffered unimaginable tragedies—as we stand up for the dignity of men and women—we should examine all historical actors as real people and express sorrow at the lives of the monstrous. Doing so offers no mitigation of their guilt. It instead heightens their culpability by reminding us that they became who they became not in spite of their humanity, but because of it.[6] Their own agency ultimately drove their embrace of murderous belief systems. Yes, they swam along with countless others in an expansive ocean, pushed and pulled by currents beyond their control, struggling in one direction or another based on what seemed right at the time. Their existence, beginning with their youths, blurred the boundaries of "before-and-after-moments" amid a progression of evolving structural conditions. *But their individual choices mattered, and made the fundamental difference in the immense suffering they would cause.* Straight line paths to breathless inhumanity are not inevitable. Events could have unfolded differently.

Countless scholars have humanized these dictators, charting the intersection of their personal agency with social, economic, and political factors in a maze of historical causality. The works of a writer like Simon Sebag Montefiore make Stalin come alive. That despot was—as historian Stephen Kotkin stresses—"a human being....[who] collected watches....played skittles and billiards...loved gardening and Russian steam baths."[7] (Hitler in power was "given to uncontrolled farting," Kotkin also notes, for whatever it's worth.) Such facts, alongside a broader analysis of these dictators' times, are included in biographies of Hitler by Alan Bullock, John Toland, Joachim Fest, and Ian Kershaw; books on Stalin by Robert Tucker, Montefiore, Kotkin, and Ronald G. Suny; studies of Lenin (as well as Stalin and Trotsky) by

Robert Service and Isaac Deutscher; portrayals of Mao by Philip Short, Alexander V. Pantsov, and Frank Dikötter; works on Mussolini by R.J.B. Bosworth and Denis Mack Smith; and Dae-Sook Suh's scholarship on Kim Il-sung.[8] The historiography is immense, full of scholarly brilliance and encyclopedic detail enriching our understanding of these human beings.

Too often, however, these works don't make us *feel* for tyrants in a way that challenges our historical perspective about ourselves. Putting down Peter Longerich's excellent study of Hitler and the Third Reich does not give us any inkling that we ourselves might be capable of the dogmatism and callousness that came to define that Nazi dictator's life.[9] Instead, such scholarly biographies leave us cold, inhabiting a separate universe, grateful that we seem to share so little in common with mass-murderers. We are comforted by the (naïve) thought that these men are dead, unique specimens of twisted logic banished to hell. We might easily conclude that horrific acts committed by and against others have nothing to do with *us* per se. Evil, what psychologist Gilbert Gustave summarized as an absence of empathy, becomes something beyond our existence—that is, until it comes to terrorize us directly, *or we ourselves become it*.[10]

There is more to be written about despots before evil actions came to define them, when they were capable of different futures, both altruistic and mundane. We can feel disgust, sadness, and even sympathy for these bastards—and recognize that doing so is the antithesis of their tyranny, rather than the height of complicity. Rousseau was right when he stated: "It is by the activity of the passions that our reason improves itself."[11] A degree of *feeling* can encourage deeper thought through fostering emotional investment—the type of personal connection that makes critical thinking more experiential and meaningful.[12] Wollstonecraft put it more cogently: "We reason deeply, when we forcibly feel."[13] Grapple, then, with the humanity of those whom we abhor. Identify with them on a personal level by focusing on a time when they were young and anonymous and struggling with personal circumstances beyond their control. Feel revulsion at doing as much, and ponder your own susceptibility to dogma and self-righteousness leading to cruelty. Feel the human dignity of the very worst people in history as a means of affirming your own.

◆ ◆ ◆

Before Evil humanizes monstrous despots, in turn, to undermine their cults of personality. Recognizing that tyrants like Mussolini carefully cultivated their public image to appear superhuman—he even forbade photos of himself smiling for a time—the coming chapters highlight personal details that challenge their constructed personas. I agree with historian Heike Görtemaker that portraying Hitler as a "nonperson" or as an outright monster only "risk[s] succumbing to Hitler's own self-presentation, according to which his individuality was of secondary importance."[14] Describing Hitler's humanity is a rejection of the "Führer" pedestal itself—an assault on his cult. With that same purpose, the chapters call each dictator by their first name or a youthful nickname. (Joseph Stalin, for instance, becomes Soso; Kim Il-sung is Song-ju). The narrative rejects personas of oppression. Declining to use their surnames also encourages the recognition that their youths would always remain part of their identity. Evil alone did not define them.

Part One begins with each dictator's death and provides an overview of their time in power, personalities, and crimes against humanity. Part Two examines their families and early education. Part Three details how close relationships and personal struggles intersected with their evolving self-identities in the first years of adulthood. Positive trends in their youths, I argue throughout, made possible their later rise to power. First, each dictator had at least one good, loving parent who valued their education from an early age and enabled them to think about the world through the lenses of ideas. Books, particularly novels, inspired an early passion for myth-making stories that informed their own conceptions of personal destiny. In that regard, the narrative emphasizes a point generally underappreciated in our understanding of these men—that their early years reflect good fortune in addition to trauma. For too long, popular conceptions have assumed that tragedy drove who they would become. To the contrary, parents (especially adoring mothers) made the critical difference in their lives. Parental dedication to education in particular ensured that each learned to read, write, and speak effectively—fundamental skills for constructing ideologies and attracting followers later in life. The study of taboo works followed before long, and *learning became their first acts of rebellion*, to employ Ronald G. Suny's words about young Stalin.[15] (Note: radical intellectuals—not illiterate cobblers—led the Bolshevik Party to power in Russia in 1917.)[16]

Second, each of these future despots increasingly came to believe that they had something profound to do in life. The power of self-belief emerged from a young age and helped give rise to their determination to move the world. Growing faith in the meaning of their own will fueled their later desire to attain political power in service of an ideological cause. The origins of their "careers"—if not necessarily their later crimes—can be traced to youths in pursuit of self-fulfilling prophecies.[17] None of this is to diminish the centrality of innumerable structural conditions that help us analyze why macro-historical events—like the victory of the Chinese Communist Party in 1949—unfolded the way they did. It is not to over-exaggerate the role of any one individual in effecting larger sea changes in history. It *is* intended, however, to reiterate the power of self-belief as a historical variable—the construction of one's place in the world as an ideology in its own right. Self-conviction (the "so what?" of personal meaning) mattered tremendously for who these men became and their ensuing crimes. It still does for us today, for better and for worse.

◆ ◆ ◆

To make clear what this book is not intended to do, three caveats are in order. Caveat One: no humanizing details about these dictators, no degree of feeling we conjure up for them, matters when compared with their later crimes. Who cares that Hitler loved his mother—you might ask—before the specter of the Holocaust? Why read about Mussolini as a sex-obsessed adolescent, or Mao's love of classic Chinese novels? Rather than talking about teenage Lenin's grief over losing his father, shouldn't we be talking about the victims of war communism during the Russian Civil War? [How about the time in November 1918 when the Bolshevik dictator gave the following order: "....hang (hang without fail, so that the public sees) at least 100 notorious kulaks, the rich, and the bloodsuckers....People for hundreds of miles around will see, tremble, know and scream out: let's choke and strangle those blood-sucking kulaks."[18]] These arguments resonate deeply. Part One of this book describes who these men were as adults, highlighting their vast human rights abuses, precisely so we can prevent any misunderstanding.

Caveat Two: nothing in this work can offer any revelation that helps us definitively understand the later monstrosity of these men. If the coming chapters frequently interrogate each dictator's thoughts and feelings—real as supported by historical evidence, and presumed as suggested by immediate circumstances—resulting reflections about education and the power of self-belief do not pretend to have uncovered the cause of political evil. As Ian Kershaw wrote of the humanizing film *Downfall* about Hitler's last days: "His life has been scrutinised [*sic*] as scarcely no one else's, but an inner core is still unfathomable...[and]

will always remain in some senses an enigma."[19] Stephen Kotkin notes quite rightly that nothing in Stalin's childhood explains his crimes against humanity—there was no single moment that sent him down the path to mass murder. Youthful experiences cannot explain these despots' crimes. Nor can anything in their childhoods diminish the horror of their actions and their personal responsibility for them. No new biography—not the following chapters—can provide a certain formula for how such men come to be and how we might avoid them in the future. Apologies.

Caveat Three: this is not psychohistory. Although writers have argued that the personalities of Hitler, Mao, and Stalin reflect clear psychopathic tendencies and narcissistic traits, the fact remains that no psychiatrist can resurrect these criminals from the dead, interview them at length, and make diagnoses that explain their actions. Neither can we.[20] Second-hand psychological analysis reminds us of their explicability, but risks reducing their lives to the definition of a mental disorder that would have existed on a spectrum of human ambiguity. (Psychopathic tendencies, by the way, are not only found in those who commit grave crimes; high-functioning individuals who excel under extremely stressful conditions—neurosurgeons, for example—can reflect many of the same traits.[21]) The same goes for childhood trauma.[22] Early trauma and the loss of loved ones absolutely affected these men—I emphasize as much. But we cannot blame the Great Terror in the Soviet Union on Stalin's abusive father. Innumerable individuals (of course!) suffered far, far worse childhoods in history and yet lived ethical, productive lives thereafter.

◆ ◆ ◆

The style of this work is intended to engage wide-ranging audiences and bridge the popular/academic divide. It's meant to be in the vein of Blind Lemon Jefferson playing a one-string guitar with a broken bottle for slide. (I leave it to Longerich, Kotkin, Bosworth, et al., to perform Beethoven's 9th symphony.) In other words, my emphasis is not on sweeping surveys of structural conditions, new archival evidence, or all-encompassing erudition. Instead, this book, as a whole, emphasizes the personal experiences of these men based on existing primary and secondary sources. The *stories* in Part Two and Part Three focus on young people before their future crimes earned our enmity. There is little to no discussion in those sections of the larger historical circumstances that shaped their youths and countries before they came to power. Microhistory results, encouraging reflection on what we all have in common.

The tone weaves the earthiness of daily existence with analytical reflection, employing jarring language and, on occasion, contemporary cultural touchstones. The purpose is not to trivialize the grave subjects in question, but to heighten reader engagement. Intimate details, moreover, help us consider the blood-and-bones actuality of these men for the reasons listed above. (Mao's personal doctor notes that the Chinese leader enjoyed recalling his first sexual encounter as a teenager in his home village. "He was remarkably preoccupied with sex," recorded the physician.)[23] Scholarly works too often reject such gristle as inedible, leaving readers hungry.

History should never be stale. Life rarely is.

Finally, this book was written to the sounds of ambient music and orchestral soundtracks. The creativity and feeling of such music drove my exploration of these men's lives to deeper levels. For those who enjoy listening to instrumental music while reading, I recommend listening to the playlist and artists included in this endnote.[24] Doing so will create a richer reading experience, one that incites greater emotion and contemplation on the sublimity of the human experience in history. Whether it is the cacophony of established musicians such as

Greenwood and Reznor or the smooth tones of Loscil and Hauschildt, such art remains something for which to be grateful as we look towards the dawn of a new day.

◆ ◆ ◆

The historian Jonathan Spence has struggled with whether we should humanize grotesque dictators, asking "why historians should feel that they ought to be fair even to pathological monsters?" His answer helped inspire this work. "Without some attempt at fairness," Spence states, "...there is no nuance, no sense of light and dark. The monster, acute and deadly, just shambles on....No conscience, no meaningful vision of a different world except one where he is supreme."[25] Such an approach to studying deplorable dictators, Spence concludes, offers very little to learn—"*and that is a conclusion that, across the ages, historians have always tried to resist.*"[26] Examining the lives of such individuals as only tales of evil in the making overshadows a more difficult story about who we are as *homo sapiens*.[27] The search for answers to the unknowns all around us—full of joys, sorrows, frustrations, and horrors—should bind us *all* together and inspire empathy. Seeing monsters in the place of living and breathing people is to society's peril, now and in the future, as we grapple with new human-made tragedies that shape the daily lives of so many.

This is a story about us.

PRIMARY HISTORICAL ACTORS

Volodia (Vladimir Lenin)

Maria	- Maria Ulyanova (Volodia's mother)
Ilya	- Ilya Ulyanov (Volodia's father)
Sasha	- Alexander Ulyanov (Volodia's big brother)
Anna	- Anna Ulyanova (Volodia's older sister)
Nadia	- Nadezhda Krupskaya (Volodia's wife)

Benito (Benito Mussolini)

Alessandro	- Alessandro Mussolini (Benito's father)
Rosa	- Rosa Maltoni (Benito's mother)
Angelica	- Angelica Balabanoff (communist activist and early political ally of Benito)
Rachele	- Rachele Mussolini (Benito's wife)
Claretta	- Claretta Petacci (Benito's final mistress)

Adolf (Adolf Hitler)

Klara	- Klara Hitler (Adolf's mother)
Alois	- Alois Hitler (Adolf's father)
Paula	- Paula Hitler (Adolf's younger sister)
Gustl	- August Kubizek (childhood friend of Adolf)
Stefanie	- Stefanie Rabatsch (Adolf's first "girlfriend")
Eva	- Eva Braun (Adolf's girlfriend/wife)

Soso (Joseph Stalin)

Keke	- Ekaterine "Keke" Geladze (Soso's mother)
Beso	- Beso Jughashvili (Soso's father)
Koba	- Yakov Egnatashvili (Soso's patron as a boy)
Kato	- Ekaterine "Kato" Svanidze (Soso's first wife)

Kamo	- Simon Arshaki Ter-Petrosian (Soso's enforcer)
Sashiko	- Aleksandra Svanidze (Kato's older sister)
Svetlana	- Svetlana Alliluyeva (Soso's daughter)
Nadya	- Nadezhda Alliluyeva (Soso's second wife)

Renzhi (Mao Zedong)

Yichang	- Mao Yichang (Renzhi's father)
Qimei	- Wen Qimei (Renzhi's mother)
Xiaoyu	- Xiao Zisheng (Renzhi's friend and future political enemy)
Yang Changji	- (Renzhi's teacher at First Normal School)
Kaihui	- Yang Kaihui (Renzhi's first wife and Yang Changji's daughter)

Song-ju (Kim Il-sung)

Hyong-jik	- Kim Hyong-jik (Song-ju's father)
Pan-sok	- Kim Pan-sok (Song-ju's mother)
Shang Yue	- (Song-ju's teacher at Yuwen Middle School)
Sohn Jong-do	- (Christian minister, whose family aids Song-ju)
Zhengmin	- Wei Zhengmin (Song-ju's commanding officer in guerilla struggle against Japan)
Jong-suk	- Kim Jong-suk (female revolutionary, Kim's wife, and mother of Kim Jong-il)
Jong-il	- Kim Jong-il

PART ONE

KNOW THIS

Dawn came on us like a betrayer; it seemed as though the new sun rose as an ally of our enemies to assist in our destruction.

- Primo Levi

CHAPTER ONE
WHAT VOLODIA LOST

The founder of the world's first communist state asked for cyanide. Just after overseeing the creation of the Bolshevik regime, with so much remaining to be done, there was now little he could do, minus one last loss of consciousness. No more articles to write. No more books to read. No more revolutions to lead. Peak zenith preceding decay. Explosions fading into silence. Compelling as ever, "this dying life (shall I call it?) or this living death," as St. Augustine once put it.[1]

Volodia hadn't wanted it to end this way. He'd wanted to guide his newfound communist state into the future. What would happen to his visions of global revolution when he was no longer alive to dream them? What would become of his Bolsheviks when he was no longer around to guide them? His ability to grapple with such questions, he knew, was finite. Illness would gradually diminish his mind. His brain was the problem. Headaches, dizzy spells, blackouts, strokes. He would increasingly struggle to function—to read, write, speak. *The star student no more*. It was the end of his ability to define reality. Poison offered protest. And he had always liked certain answers.[2]

◆ ◆ ◆

Extraordinary exertion defined Volodia's "career" from April 1917 until his incapacitation in 1922.[3] After a popular revolution overthrew Russia's Tsar Nicholas II in February 1917, Volodia (with German help) raced home as soon as possible. At the height of the First World War, the moment he had waited for had arrived—and so had he.

At Finland Station in St. Petersburg on April 16, 1917, radical and utterly self-confident, Volodia stepped off a train to soldiers presenting arms and a Bolshevik delegation greeting him. A band played *La Marseillaise* as a celebratory roar rang out into the late evening. Banners hung across the station platform in welcome, with almost every conceivable revolutionary slogan. A ranking Bolshevik hollered to the crowd: "Please, Comrades, please! Make way."[4]

Volodia, clad in a bowler hat and a serious expression, moved at almost a running pace. He came face-to-face in the waiting room with a delegation from the Petrograd Soviet—a congress of socialist parties, of which Volodia's aptly named Bolsheviks [translation: *majority*] were a minority. They welcomed him with a request for unity and cooperation. Volodia took no interest—looking away, eyeing the ceiling, toying with flowers he had just received.[5] When the words ceased, the Bolshevik leader turned to address the room:

> Dear Comrades, soldiers, sailors and workers, I am happy to greet you in the name of the victorious Russian Revolution, to greet you as the advance guard of the international proletarian army....The piratical imperialist war [the First World War] is the beginning of civil war throughout Europe....The world-wide Socialist revolution has already dawned....The Russian Revolution achieved by you has prepared the way and opened a new epoch. Long live the worldwide socialist revolution![6]

A thronging crowd outside banged on the building's glass door, yearning for Volodia. Amid another rendition of *La Marseillaise*, the Bolshevik leader tried to leave through the main entrance and get into a waiting car, but onlookers' thunder made him think better of it, and he climbed onto the car's hood and shouted about "shameful imperialist slaughter" and "capitalist pirates." Then, preceded by a marching band, soldiers, and flags, his car departed. Masses eager to see him inspired impromptu speeches along the way. "Those who have not lived through the revolution cannot imagine its grand solemn beauty," his wife, Nadia, would recall.[7]

Only three months earlier, Volodia had conceded that he might not see the revolution in his lifetime. But now his dream was finally coming true.[8] The future swept forward like a heavy wind, and he *believed* that what he said and did mattered for humanity. His words wrote history in the air.

◆ ◆ ◆

Volodia would not tolerate fellow Bolsheviks who cooperated with the country's new democratic provisional government. Socialists in the Petrograd Soviet who worked with "bourgeois" parties disgusted him. His political misanthropy and his abhorrence of heresy were boundless. There could be no sharing of power; only a [communist] dictatorship of the proletariat was acceptable.[9] But what kind of political party—asked a socialist rival in June 1917—would actually want the challenge of ruling Russia? What organization would take over a country on the brink of defeat in the First World War, grappling with extreme economic problems and widespread unrest? Volodia's response: **THERE IS SUCH A PARTY**.[10] His ideological faith left him unafraid to face the lions.

The subsequent chaos of July 1917—including a premature Bolshevik uprising by his supporters—forced Volodia into hiding to avoid arrest by the provisional government. He found safety in nearby Finland. There, his radicalism fermented sour fears. The party's central committee, he worried, lacked the courage to act in his absence. The opportunity to seize power might slip away. Especially after a military coup nearly overthrew the provisional government in August, Volodia demanded his party seize control on behalf of the workers, soldiers, peasants. His impassioned letters from Finland mounted in intensity in September and October as the Bolsheviks hesitated. ("History will not forgive us if we do not assume power now."[11]) Dissenting voices warned that the Bolsheviks would not last long in power.[12] Such fears rankled Volodia! ("O wise men! They, perhaps, would be willing to reconcile themselves to revolution if only the 'situation' were not 'exceptionally complicated.'"[13]) Failure to act, he fired back, would "mean a total collapse of the internationalist proletarian movement....Delay would be fatal."[14] Break down the door to the future.[15]

Wearing a ridiculous wig and glasses—but no beard—Volodia returned to St. Petersburg on October 10 to confront the party's central committee. During ten hours of discussion (with breaks for tea and sausage) Volodia convinced his colleagues to take action. By dawn on October 11, the Bolshevik leader emerged victorious into the early morning rain, vindicated by a 10-2 vote in favor of a coup.[16] "The situation," Volodia emphasized, "is plain: either a Kornilovite [conservative military] dictatorship or a dictatorship of the proletariat and the poorest strata of the peasantry."[17] He carried the day, irascible and unyielding.[18]

But when no coup occurred by October 24, Volodia boiled over. His mind pounded like a bass drum. ("We must not wait! We may lose everything!....The government is tottering. It must be *given the deathblow* at all costs. To delay action is fatal!"[19]) He argued for a move <u>that very evening</u>. And then—largely as a product of his fervent demands—it happened. In a nearly bloodless coup, the Bolsheviks easily overthrew the provisional government. They did so in the name of the Petrograd Soviet, as if all the socialist parties in the capital had backed the action. (That clever move lent a veneer of popular legitimacy.)[20]

When the Petrograd Soviet convened on October 25, Volodia entered the room like a Bolshevik rock star. Rapturous applause resounded. American journalist John Reed bore witness, describing the revolutionary leader as follows:

> A short, stocky figure, with a big head set down in his shoulders, bald and bulging. Little eyes, a snubbish nose, wide, generous mouth, and heavy chin; clean-shaven now, but already beginning to bristle with the well-known beard of his past and future. Dressed in shabby clothes, his trousers much too long for him. Unimpressive, to be the idol of a mob, loved and revered as perhaps few leaders in history have been. A strange popular leader—a leader purely by virtue of

intellect; colourless, humourless, uncompromising and detached, without picturesque idiosyncrasies—but with the power of explaining profound ideas in simple terms, of analysing a concrete situation. And combined with shrewdness, the greatest intellectual audacity.[21]

This man, the middle-class son of a noble family, now established the world's first communist dictatorship. It was a self-fulfilled prophecy of socialist revolution made possible, in part, by his unyielding will. In October 1917—prior theories of historical materialism be damned— Volodia had accomplished what seemed the unlikeliest of outcomes. He was the black swan of history personified.[22]

◆ ◆ ◆

The Bolsheviks quickly repressed all other parties, socialist and conservative alike. To the dustbin of history with all who disagreed.[23] Volodia's new regime confronted unfathomable challenges. They initially controlled only St. Petersburg and Moscow in a land of over six million square miles—a tenth of all territory on the planet. Industrial workers—whom his party particularly claimed to represent—were but a small fraction of a population consisting largely of rural peasants. The First World War was still ongoing—some two million Russians had perished since 1914—and soldiers deserted in droves.[24] Peasants raged in the countryside. Factories stood at a standstill. The transportation system was a disaster. Cities starved. The Bolsheviks would all be dead or in exile within six months—so it seemed.

An extraordinarily complex civil war ensued. Volodia's forces battled overlapping factions of seemingly everyone: well-armed "reactionary" generals in the west and east; loyalists to the Romanov dynasty; liberals; competing socialist parties; peasants wanting to be left alone; and foreign troops from Britain, France, Japan, and the United

States, among other countries, eager to help destroy the world's first communist state. In the midst of *this situation*, the Bolsheviks had to build the Red Army; gain control of the country; end Russia's involvement in the First World War; modernize a rural, impoverished society[25]; and translate Karl Marx's dense theories into a functioning communist reality.[26]

Extreme force offered solutions.[27] There was no such thing as a revolution without firing squads, Volodia argued.[28] Only unrelenting terror would ensure victory. (The Bolshevik leader subjected dissenters in his regime to punishing mockery: "There are, pardon the expression, 'revolutionaries' who imagine we should complete the revolution in love and kindness. Yes? Where did they go to school? What do they understand by dictatorship? What will become of a dictatorship if one is a weakling?'"[29]) Cornered, Volodia's party obeyed. Defeat meant doom—for themselves and their global socialist cause. "We have only one way out: victory or death," Volodia reiterated before a factory crowd on August 30, 1918—imploring the audience members to "smash" their enemies.[30] An assassin nearly killed him on his way out, shooting him twice in the left shoulder.[31]

The nascent Red Army conscripted recruits and fought bitterly against the Whites, whose disunity helped the Bolsheviks. Meanwhile, Volodia—almost single-handedly—forced his party to accept a humiliating peace treaty with Germany. Marauding Bolsheviks seized grain from peasants to feed the cities. Volodia's secret police (the Cheka) used hostage-taking, torture, rape, and mass murder against perceived enemies. They burned people alive. Foes responded in kind. War and famine consumed lives like kindling in a fire. Thirteen million died. Adults ate children. Hell on Earth.[32]

For the deposed monarch Tsar Nicholas II, things turned out just as Rasputin had warned in 1914—that the First World War would end his family and bring boundless sorrow. (The depraved prophet:

"Woe, disaster, suffering without end....Night....Not one star...a sea of tears....So much blood.")[33] Volodia had Nicholas, along with his wife and five children, murdered in a basement on July 17, 1918. ("If in such a cultured country as England"—Volodia had written, referencing the execution of Charles I in 1649— "it is necessary to behead one crowned criminal...then in Russia, it is necessary to behead at least one hundred Romanovs."[34]) And so it was done. Ten Bolshevik minions shot Nicholas over and over in the chest while his family screamed. Then they shot his wife, Alexandra, in the head as she made the sign of the cross repeatedly. The murderers, struggling to see through the gunfire smoke, shot and stabbed the kids—Alexei, Anastasia, Maria, Tatiana, and Olga, ages thirteen to twenty-two—in a ghoulish frenzy. (Anastasia fought desperately before succumbing to a bullet in the head.)[35] In this atrocity, as in so many, Volodia and his followers betrayed their humanity for power.

Volodia did this, coldly sending orders from his Kremlin office. Mass murder from an individual of extraordinary erudition, an intellectual whose collected works ultimately numbered fifty-four volumes, some thirty-five thousand pages. This was a brilliant man— yet one who believed gross human rights abuses ethical, a matter of course for the supposed salvation of the world. ("The supersession of the bourgeois state by the proletarian state," he wrote dryly in August 1917, "is impossible without a violent revolution."[36]) Heinous means for Marxist ends. No guilt.[37]

◆ ◆ ◆

The stress of holding the Bolshevik regime together took its toll. Determined to work at full tilt, Volodia suffered headaches and insomnia. Walks around the Kremlin and hunting in the countryside offered relief, but by 1920 he began to feel tension in his chest and sharp aches in his legs, forcing him to rest more often.[38] The grave suddenly loomed by age fifty-one (his own father had gone in the ground at fifty-four). Fatalistic urgency reinforced his determination to see the Bolshevik regime survive its tumultuous childhood. He would not be around for its adolescence. *And Volodia knew it was hard to lose your father young.*

Mounting unrest, the Bolshevik leader realized in early 1921, endangered his regime. Famine was on the rise. Pitiless grain seizures had wrought disaster on food production. (Why grow crops if the government will seize them?) Dogmatist turned pragmatist, Volodia advocated a return to limited capitalism and pushed through economic reforms in February—the beginning of the New Economic Policy. These changes allowed peasants to trade in private markets; small businesses could exist again. Behold flabbergasted Bolsheviks. Capitalistic reforms?![39]

Volodia prevailed again. But the stress ruined him. His headaches, heart problems, and insomnia all worsened.[40] He tried to keep working vigorously, but long days became unsustainable by June 1921. Rest in the countryside was a necessity, and Volodia found himself in exile anew. Physically removed from the halls of power, grappling with his own mortality, anxiety surged. Neuroses mounted. Efforts to defy his growing illness only brought on blackouts. Self-preservation and mental exhaustion demanded extended rest—no more than an hour of work a day. Listless, reluctant to look at newspapers, Volodia faced a new struggle: the fight to no longer fight. Daunting in the extreme, the languor of losers.[41] The experience shook his sanity.[42] He bore witness to his own extinction—like a sea captain saying goodbye to the sun as his head drifted beneath the surface. *This living death.*[43]

Volodia considered suicide with quiet urgency. He asked Soso—successor-to-be—for help. Soso demurred, unable to end the life of the one man he loved.[44] Experiencing moments of numbness in his body, instances when he could not speak, Volodia made final preparations nonetheless, ensuring Soso's appointment to a position of immense power in the Party.[45] A severe stroke struck him down not long after on May 25, 1922, leaving him unable to write legibly or do basic math. His short-term memory was vastly diminished. The medical cause became clearer—a lack of blood flow to the brain.[46]

Denied euthanasia, Volodia fought back. His will, he hoped, might reverse mental decline. Like a diligent ten-year-old, the Bolshevik leader returned to his studies. (He had always excelled at school.)[47] If he could no longer multiply twelve times seven, he could find the sum through addition, *and did so over three hours*.[48] Wrestling with math problems, he timed himself for evidence to refer back to in coming months. He grappled with newspapers, though reading would sometimes provoke involuntary facial spasms—a civil war of the countenance. Some days he supposedly seemed like his old self again, albeit after not sleeping for a night.[49]

Periods of joy remained. His wife, Nadia, recalled that Volodia laughed and joked—and broke into song on occasion. (Picture him singing "The Internationale," the end looming in the background.) He took an interest in the well-being of peasants, workers, and painters around his country refuge—bowing to them. He also showed affectionate attention to his young nephews, watching as they listened to fairy tales, his eyes surely glistening at their innocence. (Much to Volodia's pleasure, a Christmas tree—a family tradition from his youth—was set up for local children at one point; the patient refused to let aides hush those boisterous kids.)[50] Volodia himself was not above playing elementary games. He once scampered off from his wife and orderlies during a summer stroll in the woods. (Did he giggle as they asked where he possibly could have gone?) Volodia adored the forest.[51]

◆ ◆ ◆

On November 20, 1922, the Bolshevik leader delivered the last of his public speeches, including one in German for more than an hour. Yet his speaking style had become different, and he lost his place at times.[52] By the end of the year, he could no longer touch his finger to the tip of his nose. He became more unpredictable. Volodia, recognizing that his role was spent, dictated a sort of political last testament to his wife, pointing out the weaknesses of his potential successors. The document caused problems for Soso, warning that he had become too powerful.[53] ("I am not sure whether he will always be capable of using that authority with sufficient caution.")[54] Volodia also prepared what would prove his final article, declaring that "the complete victory of socialism is fully and absolutely assured."[55] Confidence unshaken.[56]

A third major stroke on March 10, 1923 left him unable to form words and paralyzed his right side. Nadia interpreted his grunting. He couldn't tell a pen from eyeglasses. Comprehension faded.[57] Communists weren't supposed to cry, but Nadia wept anyway. The dying man offered her a handkerchief with his left hand.[58]

Volodia made clear again that he wanted cyanide. Soso still declined. ("I do not have the strength to fulfill the request," the successor-to-be confessed to other Bolsheviks.)[59] The patient continued to resist his decline regardless—learning to write with his left hand, scratching out "mama" and "papa," his vocabulary advancing like a toddler's from gibberish to a few spoken words.[60] Nadia's presence brought him joy.[61] He gripped her hand. Husband and wife. Woman and little boy. Sitting in serene silence, speaking "without words about different things which…have no names," as Nadia remembered.[62] Her affection was a monument to Chaucer's epiphany that the only thing better than wisdom is woman. "And what is better than a good woman? Nothing."[63]

Fleeting reminders of who Volodia was remained, instances when he sought to take account of his life, what he would leave behind. Early departure was beyond his control, but at least he could say goodbye. In October 1923, he insisted on being driven to the Kremlin—the final visit. Nadia tried to stop him. ("...they won't let you into the Kremlin: you haven't got an entrance card.")[64] Volodia, grunting in good humor, was adamant. They drove to Moscow and—indeed!—the guards initially denied him access to the Kremlin, prompting mirth from Volodia, assuredly amused at the irony.[65]

Undeterred, the leader reached his old apartment and the halls of power. He looked forlornly at the meeting room where he had led his regime through the desperate civil war. Emotion took hold of him, and he struggled to continue the visit. The immensity of the prior years hovered. Triumphant nostalgia tinged with sadness, acceptance of mortality betraying a life at its peak.[66] A bittersweet farewell. And no regrets at the mayhem.

On January 21, 1924 Volodia gulped down coffee and broth—hunger unsatisfied. Then a final stroke conquered him.[67]

CHAPTER TWO
BENITO'S EXTINCTION

It was raining on a cold spring morning. Wrapped in a blanket, Benito wore a German helmet—pulled down low—as he rode in the truck past Lake Como and surrounding green hills.[1] The dictator was haggard, almost skinny. He might have pondered what was to come, consoling himself with a well-worn line—"I don't rule out the possibility of a final day of sunshine."[2] Or maybe he just closed his eyes and put his head back, resigned. April 27, 1945.[3]

The roadblock loomed in the distance like a tombstone. Firing broke out with surrounding partisans but didn't last long. The fleeing vehicles had nowhere to go. A massive tree trunk, along with rocks and debris, blocked their path. A standoff ensued. More partisans flocked to the area. The Germans, eager to save themselves, allowed a closer look at their cargo.[4] "We've got big-head," shouted a partisan, finding

Benito.[5] (German protests that he was only an ordinary, drunk soldier fooled no one.) The dictator offered no resistance until he tried to tell his side of the story later that day, hopeful his lungs might save him yet. But the time to speak was over.[6]

◆ ◆ ◆

Benito was a confounding contradiction. He was a shameless opportunist who invented an ideology.[7] A warmonger who proclaimed peace. A philanderer who supposedly loved his wife ("...you have been for me the only woman whom I have really loved," he wrote to her, *just before dying with his mistress*).[8] A passionate bibliophile who ignored basic facts. A loving father who spent little time with his kids.[9] A tyrant who slept well as his world disintegrated.[10] Death should have taken him on many prior occasions.[11] He had survived an ugly wound from friendly fire in the First World War[12]; violent sword-duels (including one in 1921 when he nearly killed a newspaper editor[13]); car and airplane crashes ("We are falling," he realized as his plane plummeted 150 feet to the ground)[14]; and numerous assassination attempts.[15] He was both cautious and reckless—a man who "combined the 'ferocity of the tyrant' with the hesitations of a child," an individual who bragged his skull was bullet-proof (it wasn't!) yet feared injections at the doctor's office.[16] A fascist who sought to create a totalitarian regime in Italy—a war criminal responsible for a million deaths—but also a tragic buffoon who became lost in a dream until its consequences shook him awake.[17] *War was a stern teacher after all.*[18]

Fascism had germinated in Benito's brain throughout the First World War.[19] After the conflict's conclusion, Benito was thirty-six years old—an ex-socialist, rabble-rouser, newspaper editor, and veteran. He surrounded himself with former soldiers and formed a new party in March 1919: Italian Fasces of Combat, later renamed the

National Fascist Party. Nationalism, militarism, hatred of socialism, street violence, and crass opportunism defined what quickly became a militarized popular movement.[20] Fascism, Benito argued, would "discipline" the Italian people. War would offer national salvation.[21]

His newspaper *Il Popolo d'Italia* promised power for veterans while castigating those who had questioned Italy's participation in the war.[22] He wrote in typewriter bursts that punched the face, spilling ink to inspire the shedding of blood:

> ...innumerable heroes that wanted the war, knowing to want war; who went to war knowing what was war; who went to death knowing what it meant to go to death...you thousands and thousands of others that form the superb constellation of Italian heroism— don't you feel that the pack of jackals is trying to rummage your bones? Do they want to scrape the earth that was soaked with your blood and to spit on your sacrifice. Fear nothing, glorious spirits! Our task has just begun....We shall defend you.[23]

This Fascist movement, Benito wrote in October 1919, was "not a party, but rather an anti-party"—not republican, socialist, democratic, conservative, or nationalist. It was something distinctly new, a combination of all of the above. "Fascism rejects all parties yet completes them," argued Benito, meaning nothing and everything.[24] Potential converts could make of the specifics what they wanted.

After socialists trounced Benito's Fascists in November 1919 elections, the dictator-to-be swung to the far-right. Italy, he preached to nationalists, could have a vast empire again—Rome reborn! His fascist gangs (*Squadristi*) beat and tortured socialists, forcing castor oil down throats ("Fascist medicine"), sometimes leaving nude victims bound to trees without genitals.[25] Such savage violence fueled Benito's rise in the spring of 1921, plunging parts of Italy into anarchy that verged on civil war, leaving the public desperate for the order the

Fascists swore to restore. The ruse: Benito's movement extorted its way into power by precipitating the very chaos it pledged to end.[26]

The subsequent "March on Rome" in October 1922 with fewer than 30,000 Fascist militia brought Benito to power in a faux insurrection.[27] ("What a character," his wife, Rachele, supposedly remarked after hearing the news.[28]) The Italian legislature, in turn, gave Benito and his newly formed coalition cabinet ruling authority to see what it might achieve.[29] The murder of prominent leftist Giacomo Matteotti by Fascists on June 10, 1924 nearly threatened Benito's hold on power, proving too much for the political establishment. But Benito defused the crisis by accepting responsibility before the Italian parliament.[30] "If Fascism," he declared, "has only been castor oil or a club, and not a proud passion of the best Italian youth, the blame is on me!"[31] The regime would create peace and stability "with love, if that be possible, *or with strength, if that be necessary.*"[32] The situation necessitated more authoritarian measures—at least from Benito's perspective.

After surviving an assassination attempt on November 4, 1925, Benito went full-on dictator, banning all opposition parties and newspapers.[33] The Italian king and parliament did nothing. (Fascist thugs assaulted legislators who made trouble, as happened when some challenged the reimposition of the death penalty in 1926.)[34] The dictator's ensuing centralization of power was a disaster. He took the titles of prime minister, minister of foreign affairs, minister of war, minister of the navy, and minister of aviation.[35] On his 43rd birthday on July 29, 1926, he also named himself minister of corporations before later grabbing minister of the interior, minister of colonies, and minister of public works.[36] By promoting flunkies, and reserving the final word on seemingly everything, Benito caused rot in the ranks and paralyzed subordinates who could make no major decisions without him.[37]

Endless decrees flowed from his desk. Benito banned shaking hands (the Fascist salute was more hygienic)[38]; eliminated jazz from the radio (his youngest son, Romano, later became an acclaimed jazz musician!)[39]; outlawed shorts for women[40]; put a tax on "unjustified celibacy" and criminalized the distribution of contraceptives[41]; outlawed "obscene publications" and swearing in public[42]; and demanded unsuccessfully that children only play with Italian-made toys ("...toys must be at the service of the state," one Fascist writer exclaimed in 1937).[43] On issues of significance, Benito delivered mostly bluster—not substance.[44] He was "the biggest bluff in Europe," as Hemingway derided him. (Benito had already told Hemingway that the author was banned from ever living in Italy again.)[45]

Yet dissidents faced real oppression. The regime—if vastly less brutal than Berlin or Moscow—utilized the death penalty and island prison colonies.[46] Italy under fascism, Benito emphasized, was a *totalitarian* state—individuals did not exist outside their subordination to the regime. ("Freedom, of which democracies speak, is but a verbal illusion, offered intermittently to the naïve," Benito explained.[47]) His supreme will supposedly dominated. Fascism—he noted in that vein, invoking Nietzsche, probably paraphrasing Trotsky (who apocryphally referred to the Italian dictator as "his best student")—asked its people to take pleasure in obedience.[48] But can a dictator be loved?—an interviewer asked Benito. Yes, the tyrant responded: "Provided that the masses fear him at the same time."[49] Happiness in slavery.

◆ ◆ ◆

Benito's behavior as a leader was both a charade and an expression of who he was—an energetic man eager to affirm his own intelligence and vitality (to himself as well as his people).[50] He was, to be sure, a brilliant public speaker. His speeches energized frenzied crowds and demonstrated talent in playing large groups of people to his advantage.[51] Whether clad in a suit or a fascist military uniform, he knew the importance of looking the part. His theatrical ferocity (head arched back, eyes bulging, lower jaw jutting out, hands on hips, legs spread apart) had an intensity that suggested he might eat you. This was the type of leader who jogged down a line of soldiers as they presented arms for inspection.[52] His office in the cavernous Palazzo Venezia—the *Sala del Mappamondo*—required visitors to walk some sixty-feet (in a room with forty-foot-high ceilings and 14th century frescoes) to reach his desk.[53] He later made ministers run the distance.[54] There, his stare burrowed into your skull. It overwhelmed you.[55] He was obsessed with looking tough, lest others recognize vulnerabilities that would diminish his supposed greatness. By the mid-1930s, photographs of him depicted a hardened warrior ("the human machine") clad in a steel helmet. His stone-faced image, *all glower, no smiles*, became inescapable in daily life.[56]

Outside the office, Benito personified the multifaceted vitality of fascism as he dreamed it. He played violin; rode horses; drove fast cars; fenced; swam in the ocean; flew planes; played soccer—you name it.[57] He loved animals, particularly cats, and kept a female lion cub (named Italia) in his apartment for a time, driving around Rome with her as his co-passenger.[58] (The "strange man…caused some comment" in doing so, recorded a British ambassador.[59]) He cared little about money.[60] He ate simply.[61] He took his shirt off for the cameras too easily.[62]

Intellectually, Benito was a wannabe savant who showed off. Encountering him, even until the end, one would find volumes of Goethe or Plato nearby. He might brazenly lie to you about his ability to read Greek while standing in front of bookshelves lined with works by Kant, Aristotle, Homer, etc.[63] If one could dismiss him as a charlatan (as Hemingway did when catching him concentrating on an English-

French dictionary *held upside down* [!]), such conclusions ignore the extent to which Benito lived up to his intellectual aspirations.[64] He was a genuine bibliophile who spent too much money on books (as his wife complained early on).[65] He adored reading and writing—his complete works *Opera Omnia di Benito*... would stretch to thirty-two volumes. He took pleasure in translating texts from Italian to German, even if his abilities in the latter were never as good as he pretended.[66]

Study often went hand-in-hand with sexual infidelity. Even as Benito deplored the notion of independent women, and loathed female politicians, he had intimate relationships with female intellectuals who were brilliant (if homely).[67] "Let's read Nietzsche and the Quran together," he purred in a letter to the writer Leda Rafanelli before asking for a tryst: "'I am free every afternoon. Write to me when I can come, and I shall be there punctual and discreet'"[68] Long-time lovers like Margherita Sarfatti—an Italian-Jew with whom Benito was involved for over twenty years—were collaborators as well as sexual companions.[69] He felt comfortable revealing his true self in bed, physically and intellectually, exploring who he might still be. The same would prove true of his final girlfriend, Claretta Petacci.[70] More broadly, to say Benito had myriad sexual partners is an extraordinary understatement.[71] He was a promiscuous beast, not known for romance, whose sexuality was criminal at times.[72] ("He doesn't even take his breeches off," his last mistress supposedly complained.)[73] He was nothing if not "the Great Ejaculator."[74]

Then there was this man's poor wife. Rachele. Involved with Benito since 1910—formally married in 1915—she raised his five legitimate children: Edda, Vittorio, Bruno, Romano, Anna Maria. (Outside marriage, <u>Benito fathered at least nine other children with eight women</u>.[75]) Rachele was a hardy country woman who preferred rural Romagna to Rome.[76] Benito's prolonged extramarital affairs of the body and mind hurt her. ("Of all of your father's women," Rachele told her son, Romano, "I was jealous only of those who had a place in his mind."[77]) Yet his wife—who did not read books and lacked an intellectual connection with her husband—was a tough woman who apparently scared him. (Their eldest daughter, Edda, joked that Benito pursued power as a means of escaping her.[78]) When Rachele discovered his last mistress, Claretta, living nearby in October 1944, she boldly confronted her. Hearing of the exchange, Benito declined to go home—"fearing," as one biographer put it colorfully, "that Rachele...would be waiting for him behind the door with a rolling-pin."[79] Rachele, to the contrary, drank bleach—but didn't die. Benito returned to her (after asking permission to do so), holding her hand, kissing her, begging forgiveness.[80]

◆◆◆

In the 1930s, when he was an all-powerful dictator, Benito's imperial visions vastly outpaced Italy's military capabilities. The Mediterranean, he dreamed, would become an Italian lake (*Mare nostrum*—our sea.)[81] Only through war could the Fascist regime realize a new Roman empire and harden the Italian people once more. ("War is to men what maternity is to women," said Benito.)[82] War crimes made initial progress possible. Italian forces maintained a colony in Libya at the price of a hundred thousand Libyan lives. They conquered Ethiopia in 1935 using chemical weapons and massacres, eventually killing well over a quarter-million Ethiopians.[83] Within Europe itself, Benito sent Italian troops to fight in Spain with Franco's Fascist forces in 1936. He drew closer to Nazi Germany. In April 1939, Italian troops seized Albania as a protectorate—greedily eying Greece in the background—before embracing a formal alliance with Berlin.[84]

Joining Germany in its war against England and France in the spring of 1940 proved a harder decision for Benito. Italy was totally unprepared. ("Suicide"—that's how an Italian general described the likely results of entering the conflict.[85]) War readiness be damned, "the prospect of an imminent clash in which he might remain an outsider"— Benito's son-in-law-turned-foreign minister, Galeazzo Ciano, wrote in the moment—"disturbs him and, to use his words, humiliates him."[86] Believing that "a few thousand dead" would give Italy a say in the peace settlement, Benito fatefully chose war.[87] Witnessing rapid German victories, he thought it would all be over in days.[88]

This grave miscalculation threw the Italian people into a cauldron of horror. Squaring off with British forces in North Africa; invading Greece (disastrously!); participating in the Nazi attack on the Soviet Union; declaring war on the United States—all of these decisions marked the beginning of Italian Fascism's end. With the country's ill-equipped and poorly-led troops achieving few successes, German forces soon took the lead on every front. And Benito, once a role model of sorts for Adolf, became the German dictator's "rearlight" in a genocidal world war—including in the destruction of the Jews.[89]

Italy faced calamity by December 1942, and Benito sought solace in self-pity. Five days before Christmas, listening to Beethoven's 7th symphony, he actually sobbed—"crying in great gulps, lying stretched out on the ground, with his eyes covered in the dark," as his mistress Claretta recorded in her diary. The dictator recounted the August 1941 death of his son Bruno—a battle-hardened pilot whose plane had crashed—and stressed about saving Rome from Allied bombing raids.[90]

Reality's roar sounded when Allied air strikes devastated Italian cities over the next six months (and eventually killed sixty thousand men, women, and children by 1945).[91] Support for the regime plummeted. Benito's fascist enablers could take no more by July 25, 1943.[92] Members of the "Grand Council of Fascism"—including the son-in-law Ciano—demanded Benito give up power. [93] Some brought hand grenades in case of trouble.[94] But when a non-binding vote went against Benito, he merely complained that his underlings had created a crisis. Failing to comprehend the situation, he decided against having everyone arrested. Indeed he went to work the next morning as if nothing had occurred, even showing up for an appointment with the Italian king that afternoon.[95] ("Don't go," warned his wife, Rachele, "...he'll throw you overboard."[96]) It was a trap.

The announcement of Benito's arrest and the creation of a new Italian government precipitated widespread celebration. Italians pulled down Benito's statues and portraits (desecrating the latter with "everything the human body contained in the way of refuse and excrement," as one writer observed.[97]) Mothers who had lost sons cursed him. Benito, in the process, became "a bag of bones and muscle in a state of organic decay," as his own sister put it.[98] But Adolf pulled him out of the grave when German forces rescued the Italian despot on September 12, 1943.[99] Only the night before, Benito had theatrically slashed at his wrists with a razor blade, threatening suicide.[100]

Berlin installed Benito to run a puppet regime on the northern half of the peninsula—the Italian Social Republic (*Repubblica Sociale Italiana*)—while he wrote a self-justifying book on the betrayals of July 1943. Death sentences, at the insistence of Nazis and fanatical Fascists, followed for those who had voted against Benito in the grand council, including for his son-in-law. Though the dictator's oldest daughter Edda—with whom he was especially close—sent feverish demands for clemency, Benito did nothing. A firing squad shot her husband in the back on January 11, 1944. Three of Benito's grandchildren, like so many kids in those years, lost their father.[101] *When Grandpa had Daddy shot*—that's how Edda's son put it.[102]

By then Benito had become a ghost haunting a dictator's body, his power an obscene charade. He still reviewed Italian troops in front of the cameras, fantasizing that new German weapons might save them.[103] ("Stick to it, boys, we've won the war!"[104]) But the Nazis called the shots—charting a course to doom—and SS guards were always nearby.[105] When the end approached in April 1945, Benito visited Cardinal Ildefonso Schuster, the Archbishop of Milan, to sound out local partisans on a potential surrender deal. (Perhaps life in prison rather than a firing squad?) Benito, recorded Cardinal Schuster, "entered…with such a dejected look…a man nearly benumbed by an immense catastrophe."[106] He was ready for the end.

The scholarly archbishop offered Benito a book he had written on St. Benedict—"so that it might give him comfort in the sad days which lay before him." He told the dictator to consider his suffering "an expiation before God, just and merciful." Benito gripped the cardinal's hand at those words—*a fleeting flash of feeling*. But then he announced his intention to head into the mountains with thousands of fascist fighters before surrendering. A few hundred men at most might join, replied the Cardinal.

"I have no illusions," conceded the fallen dictator.[107]

◆ ◆ ◆

After partisans captured Benito at Lake Como, they allowed his lover Claretta to join him at a peasant house in the hills that night. Benito slept. His mistress cried.[108] Soldiers hastily arrived the next day promising rescue. (Claretta couldn't find her underpants in the hurry out the door but managed to put on black leather high-heels.[109]) This ruse brought Benito and his lover to the scene of their deaths—to the left of the gates of Villa Belmonte. The former dictator, facing gun barrels, supposedly summoned one last show of bravado, eyes bulging, pulling open his jacket, and commanding his executioners to strike him in the heart.[110] But this was no martyrdom, and the flash of light that followed was not "the fire of divine love" that Cardinal Schuster described as consuming the lives of the saints; it was a cold personal extinction brought on by Benito's own crimes.[111] (Execution was justice; mercy would have proved sacred.[112]) After the partisans dumped his body in Milan's Piazzale Loreto with Claretta's and others, women urinated on his corpse.[113] And the bodies ultimately hung upside down from a gas station roof, arms reaching for Earth, targets for spittle and invective. Benito's final page.[114]

CHAPTER THREE
ADOLF, DOOM, AND DRUGS

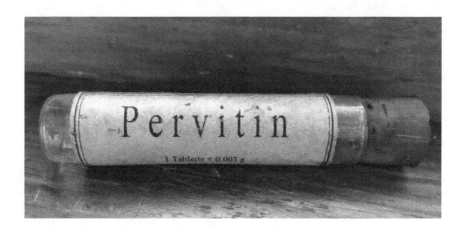

The doctor injected Adolf with hard drugs. A nasty mix of uppers and downers coursed through his veins. Small red holes in his arm floated in bruises—flags of surrender hidden from the enemy. The holier-than-thou nonsmoker vegetarian let his doctor shoot him up with concoctions of animal hormones, organ goo, and opiates.[1] Anything to stay in control. He was a decrepit man in his mid-fifties—stooped over, limbs trembling.[2]

Drug use notwithstanding, Adolf's personal valet said he remained open-eyed. ("Up to that final moment...he was Adolf...one hundred percent *compos mentis*."[3]) Knowing he would soon put a gun to his right temple, going out the way he insisted commanders should, he grappled with defeat. Daydreams of victory held sway at times, but the end was nigh. And he knew it. ("If only I had done that sooner..."[4]) Injections of Eukodal (oxycodone) and cocaine eyedrops—not to mention Pervitin pills (methamphetamine)—reinforced his uncompromising belief that he was a heroic genius. As enemy troops closed in, the drugs offered chemically-reinforced delusions of grandeur, another way of ignoring the reality that his life was an epic disaster with few rivals in history.[5]

He expressed no guilt. Ruminating, hiding in self-justification, Adolf wished he'd been harsher after 1933 in purging those of questionable loyalty. He insisted that the wider European conflict wasn't his fault: Britain and France had declared war on Germany—not the other way around. He still could not fathom how Churchill—no William Pitt!—refused his offer that Britain could keep its empire abroad in exchange for German control of eastern Europe. As for the Soviet Union, from his perspective he had no choice *but* to attack; Germany would not have won a defensive war when Moscow inevitably invaded.[6] He offered no remorse about the Holocaust either—to the contrary, he lauded himself for having "made a start in wiping out Jewry."[7] A glowing coal on the verge of ash, emitting noxious fumes, the mass murderer *was more himself than ever*, convinced of the same ideas that had caused misery on a satanic scale.[8]

◆ ◆ ◆

Adolf had become the chancellor of Germany as a result of democratic elections.[9] The early 1930s saw his party—the National Socialist German Workers' Party (NSDAP)—engaged in grassroots organizing as its thugs attacked political opponents in the streets. From above, Adolf delivered stirring campaign speeches. He promised a return to national greatness; and roaring cheers lent credibility to his supposed magnificence. He politicked relentlessly in 1932, traveling by road until his party hired a plane. Then Adolf crisscrossed the country with arresting energy, speaking in twenty cities in six days. He often delivered three speeches a day, with audiences in big cities numbering up to thirty thousand people.[10] He was everywhere at once, seen by voters unlike any other candidate before in Germany.[11] Supporters mobbed him in streets and villages. Many, who had waited hours to hear him speak, simply called him "the Führer." One eyewitness described a rally:

> The hours passed...expectation mounted...'The Führer's coming!' A thrill goes through the masses....There stood...[Adolf]...in a simple black coat, looking expectantly over the crowd. A forest of swastika banners rustled upwards....His voice was hoarse from speaking so much in previous days. When the speech was over, there were roars of jubilation and applause....How many look to him in touching faith as the helper, saviour, the redeemer from overgreat distress.[12]

So many at these rallies became complicit in the NSDAP's ideological evil, its virulent anti-Semitism.[13] But Adolf himself largely left out anti-Semitic remarks in the 1932 campaigns, calling instead for national unity beyond class differences and castigating the country's democratic system. In the haze of the Great Depression, his bombast convinced Germans of diverse backgrounds that he offered salvation.[14]

Mounting economic problems and fears of communism strengthened his hand.[15] Industrial production in Germany had plummeted by 42% since 1929. By the fall of 1932, some 8.7 million— close to half the working population—were unemployed or partially employed.[16] Significant electoral support for the German Communist Party unnerved middle-class men and women—teachers, small businessmen, doctors, lawyers—who looked to the political right for solutions. If many Germans found the party's heinous propaganda towards Jews disturbing, huge numbers voted for it regardless. Anti-Semitism was not a disqualifying factor.[17]

Throughout the summer and fall of 1932, Adolf failed to become chancellor. Reich President Paul von Hindenburg, eighty-five years old and a famed World War I general, refused to allow it. (Hindenburg told him: "a presidential cabinet led by you would develop necessarily into a party dictatorship with all its consequences for an extraordinary accentuation of the conflicts in the German people."[18]) Yet the cooperation of former German Chancellor Franz von Papen, a wealthy conservative, delivered Adolf's breakthrough on January 30, 1933.[19] Adolf would become chancellor, von Papen agreed in negotiations with the NSDAP, if conservative parties could gain control of important ministries in his cabinet; von Papen himself would become vice chancellor.[20] Conservatives—von Papen argued, in one of the worst mistakes in political history—could control Adolf. (*This will end with you running away from your ministry at night, clad only in your underwear, to avoid arrest*—went one scorching riposte.[21]) Von Papen helped persuade President Hindenburg to agree.[22]

Thus, on February 10, 1933, Adolf, now chancellor of Germany, spoke at the Berlin Sportpalast to the nation. (His propaganda stooge delivered a horrifying opening, threatening the country's so-called "Jewish press."[23]) Adolf declared that a "decisive phase in the fight for the German resurrection" had started, a struggle born of defeat in the World War. "The people's will," Adolf stated (after condemning Marxism as a betrayal of the working class), had lifted him into power. He claimed no interest in money or rewards— only the country's salvation with its citizenry's help. "German people," he demanded, "give us four years, then judge and sentence us....I swear that as we and I entered this office, I will then be willing to go."[24] It would take twelve years—a second world war, the murder of six million European Jews, and the destruction of large parts of Europe— before judgment arrived.

◆ ◆ ◆

Adolf sought to appear godlike, but was ordinary in many ways. He had a private life.[25] Architecture was a lifelong passion.[26] He enjoyed operas, performances, and movies (*King Kong*!).[27] He had an extensive record collection (even if he mostly played Wagner and Beethoven).[28] He had a favorite restaurant—the Osteria Bavaria in Munich—with a regular table where he devoured ravioli with a guilty conscience. ("What's good today? Ravioli? If only you didn't make it so delicious. It's too tempting!"[29]) This "passionate cake lover"—to use his valet's words—fretted about gaining weight. No such thing as a fat Führer; this, of all things, was unconscionable to him.[30]

Fears of weight gain aside, Adolf exercised little beyond walking.[31] Sports were a source of potential humiliation.[32] "People sometimes ask me why I play no games," said Adolf in August 1942. "The answer is simple—I am no good at games, and I refuse to make a fool of myself!"[33] Bowling proved an exception. Adolf enjoyed it so much that he had a bowling alley installed in the basement of his mountain vacation home. But he kept the hobby mostly secret, lest "the bowling associations....make me an honorary president of every club."[34] Relatability was a liability for a dictator who supposedly sacrificed his own happiness for Germany's larger ends.[35]

With intimate associates, Adolf relaxed. Before the war, he loved picnics. His valet recalled such outings as a time when a small circle got to witness Adolf as "jovial, comradely and unproblematic."[36] (Problematic Adolf was presumably an unpleasant picnic partner.) Driving in the countryside, he and his entourage would stop at a pretty spot and lay out rugs and blankets. Mirthful imbibing followed. "People ate and drank what they fancied, told anecdotes and jokes (in good taste), recounted experiences and made future plans," recalled Adolf's valet. The dictator himself "would sit or stretch out in our midst on a blanket and join in," drinking mineral water, coffee, or tea while others drank alcohol and smoked. The tyrant took it easy, laughing and joking.[37] He pissed in the woods with the other guys.[38]

His early relationships with young women were likely for show and devoid of sex.[39] In 1926, at age thirty-seven, he became involved with sixteen-year-old Maria Reiter, an innocent and beautiful blond-haired girl. Adolf, wearing high boots and carrying a whip, came on strong, giving "Mimi" rides in his Mercedes, asking her to call him Wolf, awkwardly kissing her in a forest and calling her a "woodland spirit."[40] This inappropriate relationship came to an end after Adolf refused to marry Mimi; the child subsequently tried to hang herself. Another "relationship" followed when Adolf became obsessed with his half-niece, Geli Raubal (age twenty-one), after she moved into his Munich apartment in 1929. Adolf—whom Geli called "Uncle Alf"—developed strong feelings for the young woman. He dominated her life. Refused to let her date any men.[41] Geli shot herself in the chest on September 18, 1931, prompting Adolf to leave her bedroom untouched—as a shrine.[42]

Enter Eva Braun. Adolf became involved with Eva after Raubal's suicide. Eva, barely in her twenties, did everything she could to work her way into Adolf's personal life, attempting suicide on two occasions to rebel against his indifference and gain his attention.[43] While Adolf privately embraced Eva thereafter, he hid their relationship, worried it might reflect poorly on a leader whose only focus should be his country. The young woman wasn't present at official functions, and the dictator refused her public displays of affection in even informal circumstances.[44] They had a robust sex life nonetheless—at least according to Adolf's valet.[45] When it was all over, Adolf promised to marry Eva. And he ultimately kept his pledge—just before giving her the opportunity to commit suicide with him.[46]

◆◆◆

The rapidity of German democracy's collapse after Adolf took power in 1933 remains terrifying. The NSDAP quickly ordered law enforcement to assist its party militias in attacking political opponents and German Jews.[47] A fire in the Reichstag (the German parliament) on February 27, set by a single communist, led to emergency measures to prevent further "terrorist acts." Warning of a looming communist threat, Adolf's cabinet—with President Hindenburg's approval—issued an emergency decree, suspending most civil protections under the democratic constitution.[48] After the NSDAP won 44% of the vote in March 1933 elections, it muscled through the "Law to Remove the Distress of the People and the State" to give Adolf's cabinet (under Hindenburg's authority) the power to decree laws without the Reichstag until 1937.[49] The NSDAP persuaded the Deutsche Zentrumspartei—a large, centrist Catholic party—to join them so they could meet the required two-thirds threshold to suspend the constitution.[50]

A little over fifteen months later, Adolf's party purged its political enemies, as well as members of its own militia, in the "Night of the Long Knives." His minions executed powerful militia commander Ernst Röhm, murdered former German Chancellor Kurt von Schleicher, and put Vice Chancellor von Papen under house arrest. (Adolf's actions impressed Soso in Moscow; "What a great fellow! How well he pulled this off!"—remarked the Soviet dictator with admiration.)[51] When President Hindenburg died of old age weeks later, the regime—acting the same day as his passing—had all German soldiers pledge allegiance to Adolf.[52] ("I will render unconditional obedience…"[53]) Three weeks later, the regime held a national vote combining the powers of president and chancellor. Total authority passed to Adolf.[54]

For a time, Adolf's audacity on the global stage won huge returns for Germany. He rejected the ruinous terms of the Versailles Treaty, ordered a massive rearmament campaign, and took back control of the German Rhineland in March 1936. His regime seized Austria and Czechoslovakia from 1938 to 1939 before invading Poland—the latter of which finally brought declarations of war from Britain and France. Yet stunningly, Germany defeated Poland, Belgium, Norway, Denmark, France, and Greece in brief blitzkrieg campaigns. British armies fled. By the fall of 1940 only the British Isles themselves, woozy and unbalanced, remained in the war. Adolf appeared invincible.

The decision to attack the Soviet Union in June 1941 proved his undoing. The invasion—a racial war of annihilation—resulted in horrifying crimes against humanity (as depicted in Elem Klimov's 1985 *Come and See*.)[55] German soldiers burned down villages with civilians inside and starved millions of Soviet POWs to death while roving SS squads (*Einsatzgruppen*) murdered Jewish men, women, and children. The Soviet people—with vigor and courage that surprised Adolf— fought the German invaders to the death.[56] The war cost approximately 26.6 million lives in the Soviet Union and devastated one third of the country—including the destruction of 1,710 towns and 70,000 villages.[57] The damage was akin to destroying everything of economic value in the United States from Chicago to the Atlantic seaboard.[58]

Concentration camp populations—and the use of slave labor— grew with every new invasion. Adolf's regime imprisoned Jews, Roma people, homosexuals, religious dissidents, and political opponents, among myriad other victims. It "euthanized" individuals with physical and mental disabilities alongside the sick and elderly.[59] Dachau—just a half hour's drive from Adolf's favorite Italian restaurant in Munich— became shorthand for Hell.[60]

Death camps for European Jews followed in Eastern Europe from 1942 to 1945. Survivor Primo Levi's words on Auschwitz grapple with dehumanization beyond our understanding:

> Then for the first time we become aware that our language lacks words to express this offence, the demolition of man....We had reached the bottom. It is not possible to sink lower than this; no human condition is more miserable than this, nor could it conceivably be so. Nothing belongs to us anymore; they have taken our clothes, our shoes, even our hair; if we speak, they will not listen to us, and if they listen, they will not understand. They will even take our name: and if we want to keep it, we will have to find in ourselves the strength to do so, to manage somehow so that behind the name something of us, of ours as we were, still remains.[61]

Millions of human beings murdered in gas chambers. Countless souls worked to death. Shells of sapiens returned to their most primal form. Merciless evil and total loss directed by Adolf.[62]

◆ ◆ ◆

The dictator himself disliked distressing images. He refused to see suffering, and never went near a concentration camp.[63] Even visiting wounded German soldiers was too much for him.[64] He was not, to be sure, without feelings though. He had moments of empathy, generosity, levity. He might, for instance, let a bodyguard have the night off to go out with a girl[65]; or worry about the well-being of his secretaries[66]; or pick-up hitchhikers and give away his coat[67]; or brush it off when someone accidentally called him and shouted "You're crazy!" after Adolf answered: "The Führer speaking."[68] But as a whole, he showed no compassion for misery that took place beyond his immediate person. The war was his obsession—but not the suffering of soldiers, or their victims. He had served with distinction in World War

I. He'd seen real combat in its early months and had later become a trusted runner who delivered messages to the front-lines; he experienced both a wound and a poison gas attack.[69] But none of this did very much to heighten his concern for combatants on either side—much less those his regime later murdered.

Adolf's most normal relationship was with his German shepherd—Blondi.[70] Adolf, a "dog-lover," adored his pet.[71] There was a real connection there.[72] At first glance, the canine only offered a safe bond rooted in domination.[73] But Blondi—"a very docile and clever dog," as one of the secretaries recalled—was playfully disobedient, something Adolf enjoyed talking about in lighter moments.[74] (For example: Adolf would order the dog to lie down in the corner during military briefings; Blondi would submit with audible displeasure; once the dictator looked away, the dog would creep forward to rest its snout on Adolf's knee; the master would order Blondi away.[75]) The German Shepherd performed impressive tricks (*Sing, Blondi!*), and the dictator took pleasure in playing with her.[76] As the Soviets closed in, Adolf watched a doctor feed Blondi a cyanide capsule. The secretary Traudl saw Adolf immediately afterwards—"his face looked like his own death mask"—as he retreated into his private room. He was unmoved by the horrific suffering of millions. But his dog's death shattered him.[77] (Adolf's valet: "…it was easier for him to sign a death warrant for an officer on the front than to swallow bad news about the health of his dog."[78])

Adolf loved Adolf. His secretaries and closest associates, who spent an enormous amount of time with him during tea hours and meals, heard his monologues on an endless loop—about his youth in Vienna, vegetarianism, "the years of struggle," his belief that smoking caused cancer, the history of humanity, etc.[79] "The evenings required endurance," remembered another secretary.[80] But none of this mattered in the end. As the war turned against Germany in 1943, Adolf became more somber. Some sources say the shift came after Stalingrad. Others emphasize a more gradual decline. Growing sadness. Isolation. Self-pity. A bodyguard, looking through a window at the end of 1942, once spied Adolf sitting alone—listening to a record by the Jewish singer Joseph Schmidt—"slumped....immersed in thought, the loneliest man in the world....at his saddest."[81] Back in 1936, Adolf had prophesized two possible outcomes for how everything would end: he would completely triumph, becoming one of the greatest men of all time—or end his days as one of the most deplored.[82] Eternity's enmity haunted him.[83]

Drugs—including chamomile enemas—helped him deal with it all.[84] So he became a pulsating blender of despondency spiked with boiled pig-liver slop and opiates. According to one account, by October of 1944 he was taking 120 to 150 pills per week, along with 8 to 10 injections.[85] His doctor gave him Acidol-Pepsin, Antiphlogistine, Argentum nitricum, Benerva forte, Belladonna Obstinol, Betabion, Bismogenol, Brom-Nervacit [a barbiturate for sleep[86]], Brovaloton-Bad, Cafaspin, Calcium Sandoz, Calomel, Cantan, Cardiazol [a cardiac and respiratory stimulant, which at the time was sometimes prescribed in high doses to treat schizophrenia[87]], Cardiazol-Ephedrin, Chineurin, Cocaine, Codeine, Coramin, Cortiron, Digilanid Sandoz, Enterofagos, Enzynorm, Esdesan, Eubasin, Euflat, Eukodal [oxycodone], Eupaverin, Franzbranntwein, Gallestol, glucose, Glyconomr, Gycovarin, Hammavit, Harmin, Homburg 680, Homoseran [made from menstruation blood], Intelan, Jod-Jodkali-Glycerin, Kalzan, Karlsbader Sprudelsalz, Kissinger-Pills, Köster's Anti-gas pills, Leber hamma, Leo-Pills, Lugolsche Lösung, Luizym, Luminal [a barbiturate], Mitilax, Mutaflor, Nateina, Neo-Pycocyanase, Nitroglycerine, Obstinol, Omnadin, Optalidon, Orchikrin [a supposed aphrodisiac made from bulls' testicles], Penicillin-Hamma, Pervitin [methamphetamine], Perubalsam, Progynon, Profundol, Prostakrin, Prostophanta, Pyrenol,

Quadro-Nox [a narcotic later tested in treating psychoses[88]], Relaxol, Rizinus-Oil, Sango-Stop, Scophedal [containing scopolamine, oxycodone, and ephedrine[89]], Septojod, Spasmopurin, Strophantin, Strophantose, Suprarenin [adrenaline], Sympatol, Targesin, Tempidorm-Suppositories, Testoviron [testosterone], Thrombo-Vetren, Tibatin, Tonophospan [prescribed today to cattle, horses, pigs, goats, sheep, dogs, and cats[90]], Tonsillopan, Trocken-Koli-Hamma, Tussamag, Ultraseptyl, Vitamultin, and Yatren.[91]

But then the drugs began to run out in 1945. And he fired his doctor.[92]

◆ ◆ ◆

Adolf's last trip to the front came in March 1945 in eastern Prussia. Driving over plowed fields and rural pastures to reach a command post as Russian artillery sounded in the distance, farmers and their wives crowded around him, surprised to see him near the fighting. Adolf's presence made those civilians feel like he might still save Germany.[93]

The reality was horrifyingly to the contrary. Adolf's war brought widespread pillage, rape, and murder when Soviet soldiers arrived to end it. They killed an estimated 100,000 German civilians in the eastern half of the country and raped 1.4 million females—nearly one out of five in the region—with age making little difference.[94] When women begged for mercy, Soviet soldiers often pantomimed the murder of babies by German soldiers in the USSR.[95] Entire German families killed themselves as the Russians approached.[96] The dictator delivered doom not just to his perceived enemies, but to his own people. Over seven million Germans died in the Second World War.[97]

As the Soviets reached Berlin's outskirts, Adolf hid in his bunker. On April 20, 1945—his fifty-sixth birthday—he woke at 2 PM, ate breakfast, and took cocaine eye drops. Then he spent a long time playing with one of Blondi's puppies.[98] As his citizens lived "an end with horror" (better than "horror without end," as the saying went[99]), the dictator sat with Eva and his secretaries, making clear that he would triumph in Berlin "or go under."[100] "He hadn't noticed," his secretary Traudl recalled, "that there were four young women at his table who wanted to live, who had believed in him, who had hoped for victory from him."[101]

Old men, young teenagers, and remnants of the German military fought desperately to slow the Soviet advance into the capital. Women phoned the Reich Chancellery screaming for help as Soviet soldiers sought to rape them. Meanwhile Adolf chose suicide.[102] His "destiny" left behind the smell of bitter almonds from cyanide and gunpowder from the shot that took his life—and a world forever traumatized.

His memory is our shared burden.

CHAPTER FOUR
THE MIND OF SOSO

Loneliness imprisoned Soso. His hardness—like icy metal to which wet skin sticks—kept everyone wary. He projected coldness born of pathological suspicion. 100-ton silence. On his wall the painting "Reply of the Zaporozhian Cossacks" hung alongside photos of happy children.[1] His dark brown eyes hinted at oppression.[2] His glance betrayed calculation, a sharp but damaged mind simmered in distrust—cognizant that tyranny, meant to preempt threats, always left him vulnerable to new perils. (A book from his personal library had a quote from Genghis Khan underlined—"The conqueror's peace of mind requires the death of the conquered."[3]) So his omnipresent face threatened everyone. Intimacy only brought insecurity. Forget vulnerability. This was a man responsible for the murder, incarceration, and forcible exile of twenty-six million human beings.[4]

Just the same, he once loved his daughter. Svetlana had relished his hugs and games as a little girl—at least when "little papa" was around, which wasn't much. He sent her loving letters in the mid-1930s.[5] "I give you a big hug, my little sparrow," he wrote, before mocking himself as her housekeeper—"From Setanka-Housekeeper's wretched Secretary, the poor peasant...."[6] The cheeky child sent him demands: "I order you to take me [to the theater] with you." "I submit," replied Dad.[7] Svetlana's innocence elicited kindness.

The rupture came when Svetlana grew up, increasingly resembling her dead mother. She exchanged love letters with the wrong man during the war. An ugly blow up ensued. "But I love him!" shouted the daughter. "Love!" howled the father—slapping her twice, the first time he had ever hit her. "Such a war going on and she's busy the whole time fucking."[8] *Searing words. Permanent hurt.* The relationship became distant.[9] Svetlana saw him less and less in his final years. "I'm busy," he answered when she sometimes called about visiting. *Click.*[10]

In his early seventies, Soso chased security as he always had—through oppression. Secret police savaged "suspects" on his orders. ("Beat them until they confess! Beat, beat, and then beat again. Put them in chains, grind them into powder."[11]) Yet the man who saw enemies everywhere hated being alone. He made his henchmen hang out with him in the middle of the night. He was easygoing when happy—poking Khrushchev playfully, calling him "Mikita" with a faux Ukrainian accent.[12]

But when Soso turned sour, fear paralyzed his dinner guests. They knew doom awaited if they crossed him—that the threat of physical annihilation (his most loyal bodyguard) hung in the air. So his minions sat obediently while he derided them as "blind kittens" who "...can't recognize your enemies." Soso urged everyone to *drink more* as he often imbibed only lightly. He listened, and observed. Drunk comrades, exhausted from the day, feared alcohol's candor. (*In vino veritas!*)[13] Missteps could mean not only execution, but unfathomable pain—a beastly "interrogator" pounding you in the same rainbow-colored bruise over, and over, and over. Confess and be shot—or die of blunt force trauma. Soso only had to make a call.[14]

The regime taught its citizens to worship Soso. His people's father and best friend, their leader and savior, their teacher and guide, their commander and caretaker—he was the Vozhd [leader] who had secured the Bolshevik revolution, the Generalissimo who had defeated Nazi Germany.[15] According to what people read and saw in daily life, his only concern, day and night, was the future of the socialist revolution and their well-being. Millions, of course, had no illusions about his brutality and the cruel realities of daily life in the Soviet Union. But so many good men and women—including even American intellectuals like W.E.B. Du Bois—believed in Soso for wide-ranging reasons.[16] When the dictator died, sounds of crying echoed even in the gulag (along with cheers). "I thought that our lives would collapse," recalled one prisoner on learning of Soso's death. "And how could we live?....I bawled my heart out....I never blamed him for anything."[17] The dictator's authority suffocated, but its sudden absence left many gasping.

◆◆◆

Soso was more than a ruthless thug. If a poor theorist—no match for the Party's most brilliant minds—he was an extraordinary organizer. He was also a sharp editor (trusted to run the Bolshevik newspaper *Rabochy Put* during the October 1917 revolution). He read ravenously, especially history. He prepared his own articles and speeches.[18] If his writing was reductive, *and boring*, few could render Volodia's ideas comprehensible for the masses like him.[19] Soso—a fanatical communist—created a cult of personality around Volodia. He advanced his own power through the guise of continuing what the founder had started.[20]

Soso was physically unimpressive. He was not tall (five feet six); had a peculiar gait and a bum arm.[21] He was a poor orator who spoke with a Georgian accent. Nevertheless he was politically sharp. He had a remarkable memory and excelled in reading people.[22] He could be outrageously rude—"You're a pathetic person," he once told Trotsky, "bereft of an elemental feeling of truth, a coward and bankrupt, impudent and despicable..."[23] But he was suave and personable when necessary—a "people person."[24] He remembered names—from political opponents to household help—and behaved outwardly humble even as propaganda deified him.[25] Wore haggard jackets dating back to the civil war ("...this one has another ten years in it") and battered boots (sometimes with holes). Smoked the same tobacco as ordinary workers.[26] Disliked long bureaucratic meetings.[27] A hint of relatability proved valuable for him.

◆ ◆ ◆

In March 1922, Volodia appointed Soso as general secretary of the Communist Party of the Soviet Union. Volodia wanted order—and Soso took immediate advantage, appointing his own loyalists at the national, regional, and local levels, and cementing close connections with the secret police.[28] Note, however, that Soso was not a dictator for much of the 1920s.[29] He initially had no choice but to share power after Volodia's death in January 1924. Machiavellian politicking soon took care of his rivals though. He forged alliances to defeat opponents before turning on those same allies. Long before this "outstanding mediocrity" could kill perceived enemies, he simply outmaneuvered them.[30]

Political victory tasked Soso with transforming the Soviet Union into a powerful communist state. The conspiratorial Bolshevik thought war loomed and aimed to modernize the USSR rapidly. With that objective, Soso plunged the country into mass industrialization and agricultural collectivization from 1928 onwards. (The dictator—avid student of the past that he was—used Russian history to justify the rapid campaigns. He warned: "One feature of the history of old Russia was the continual beating she suffered because of her backwardness....We are fifty or a hundred years behind the advanced countries. We must make good this distance in ten years. Either we do it, or we shall go under.")[31] The regime exiled two million "kulaks"—so-called "rich peasants"—to distant, often uninhabitable regions, while imprisoning and murdering hundreds of thousands of others.[32] It forced most everyone else in the countryside onto collective farms. Soso then sold his people's grain on the global market for capital to purchase industrial equipment. The famine that followed killed five to seven million people in 1932 and 1933, but the dictator still *exported food* to build factories in the USSR.[33] Some in Ukraine ate their own children to survive.[34]

◆ ◆ ◆

Soso suffered personal tragedy throughout these events. His thirty-one-year-old wife—Nadya—committed suicide in 1932, leaving him a second-time widower. He was a bad husband, neglectful and insensitive. But the couple's letters reflect deep emotion. Soso: "Hello, Tatka [a tender nickname]....I miss you so much...My kisses! Your Joseph." Nadya: "I ask you so much to look after yourself! I am kissing you passionately just as you kissed me when we were saying goodbye! Your Nadya."[35] Fleeting moments of pure romance.

Soso had known Nadya's revolutionary family for decades, meeting her when she was just three years old. Years later, at the height of the Russian civil war, they became romantically involved before marrying in 1919 (Soso age forty; Nadya age eighteen).[36] The new wife was young yet independent, determined to have both career and family. Two years after marrying, Nadya birthed a son, Vasily, after walking herself to the hospital. Their daughter, Svetlana, arrived in 1926. Domestic help frequently took care of the kids. Husband chose power. Wife pursued education.[37]

By the early 1930s Soso's questionable fidelity tormented Nadya; she apparently struggled with mental health issues too, and they fought a lot.[38] Nadya was not afraid of Soso, however. She yelled at him with vigor. On occasion, her scorn drove the dictator to lock himself in the bathroom, hiding, as she pounded on the door screaming: "You're an impossible person. It's impossible to live with you."[39] It was a difficult marriage.

It came to a tragic end after a nasty argument. Nadya shot herself. It wrecked Soso.[40] "He was shaken because he couldn't understand why it had happened," his daughter later reflected. "What did it mean?....He was too intelligent not to know that people always commit suicide in order to punish someone. He saw that, but he couldn't understand why."[41] The anguished husband cried beside Nadya's open casket, full of woe. "She left me like an enemy," he said despondently. "I didn't save her."[42] His son, Vasily (age eleven), ran forward at one point, "hanging onto his father, saying 'Papa, don't cry!"[43] Before the coffin closed, Soso took Nadya's head in his hands and kissed her. Mourners wailed. Tragedy.[44]

Soso's ensuing grief was self-centered. The pain was *his pain*. He perceived Nadya's suicide as a betrayal—a loved one's treason.[45]

"How could Nadya...," he ruminated at the dinner table. When a relative lamented the mother leaving her children, Soso growled: "Why the children? They forgot her within a few days [*sic*]: it's me she made a cripple of for life."[46] Yet even solipsistic Soso recognized that a mother's loss meant his kids needed him. (He reviewed and signed their homework when present at their Moscow residence thereafter.)[47] "The children," he later mourned, "grew up without a mother....Nannies, governesses...could not replace their mother. Ah Nadya, Nadya...how much I and the children needed you!"[48]

Soso was different after 1932.[49]

◆ ◆ ◆

Another stinging loss came on December 1, 1934 when a lone gunman assassinated Soso's friend and party underling, Sergei Kirov. After Nadya's loss, Soso had drawn closer to Sergei.[50] Vacationing together, the two picnicked and drank Georgian wine, mischievously encouraging bodyguards to drink with them.[51] They were "like a pair of equal brothers, teasing one another, telling dirty stories, laughing," as one family member recalled—"Big friends, brothers and they needed one another."[52] In Moscow, Sergei often slept on Soso's couch, developing an endearing relationship with Svetlana.[53] Soso and Sergei did not always get along, and had disagreements in 1934, but in many respects Kirov was his best friend.[54]

Less than forty-eight hours after the dictator bade Sergei farewell for the last time, the phone rang. *Kirov's dead.* Soso reacted immediately. He put out a short decree (127 words) on how to handle "terrorist agents"—no right to a defense attorney; no right to appeal; "the highest degree of punishment."[55] Next he called for the death of "all well-known monarchists we have in jail...hostages," ordering the immediate execution of "five or ten," lashing out in anger.[56] Then, that very evening, Soso boarded a train for Leningrad where he personally interrogated the assassin and his spouse.[57] The killer only realized Soso himself was sitting in the room when shown a portrait; he was a disaffected party member whose wife might have been sleeping with Sergei.[58]

"I am absolutely an orphan," Soso murmured to his brother-in-law the night before Sergei's funeral.[59] The next day, the dictator stood stonily beside another open casket—his face "absolutely impenetrable," as one henchman remembered.[60] Before the coffin closed, Soso bent down—similarly to his wife's funeral—and kissed his friend on the forehead to the sound of roaring cries. "Goodbye dear friend, we'll avenge you."[61]

The ensuing investigation heightened suspicions of a larger conspiracy. Authorities learned that police had previously arrested the assassin—with a pistol—near Sergei's home but had released him. Sergei's bodyguard, moreover, died in a car crash while on his way in for police questioning.[62] ("How could it happen?" Soso asked incredulously.[63]) Many observers, starting with Khrushchev, took these occurrences as obvious evidence that Soso himself had murdered Sergei and then covered it up.[64] It was absolutely possible.[65] But existing evidence and decades of investigations suggest that easy conclusion ignores the inconvenience of a random historical act. Either way, Soso soon sent history spiraling downwards.[66]

◆ ◆ ◆

Soso used Sergei's death as a pretext for widespread purges that brutalized Soviet society from 1936 to 1939. The dictator started with old rivals in the party, blaming them for Kirov's murder, before eradicating the Bolshevik old guard. The secret police tortured one group after another, forcing ridiculous confessions in show trials that preceded executions. Then Soso terrorized the whole country.[67] In 1937, his secret police sent out literal death quotas—ordering authorities in Belorussia, for instance, to uncover "kulak, criminals, and other anti-Soviet elements." *Execute 2,000. Deport 10,000.*[68] (The head of secret police—who spent 850 hours with Soso from 1937 to 1938— told security officials: "Better to arrest too far than not enough....Beat, destroy without working out....If...an extra 1,000 people will be shot, that is not such a big deal."[69]) Lower-ranking security officials—eager to prove their loyalty—overfilled quotas. Moscow approved.

A living nightmare followed. Sudden pounding on the door at 2 AM. Torture in a dungeon. A death sentence. (*No appeals.*) If you avoided the firing squad, gulag slavery in a frozen wasteland often awaited. It was a vicious cycle, all-consuming: arrests, interrogations, executions; followed by more arrests, interrogations, executions.

All roads led to Soso. He oversaw the arrest of 1.5 million "enemies" and the execution of at least 700,000.[70] The dictator— though he saved a person here and there—personally signed execution lists totaling some 39,000 people.[71] He toyed with high-level victims like former friend and ally Nikolai Bukharin, who had eulogized Nadya at her graveside in 1932.[72] In the run-up to Nikolai's arrest, Soso coincidentally called him just as police served an eviction notice to vacate his Kremlin apartment—Soso's old apartment, the very one where Nadya killed herself.[73] The dictator feigned irritation when Nikolai complained about the eviction.[74] The following month—on New Year's Eve—Soso sent Nikolai a document with accusations against him. February saw his arrest.[75]

In December 1937, following torture, Nikolai wrote Soso a deeply emotional letter. Desperate for a pardon, or at least a painless death, he invoked Nadya:

...as I write this, I am shuddering all over from disquiet and from a thousand emotions....When I was hallucinating, I saw you several times and once I saw Nadezhda [Nadya]....She approached me and said: 'What have they done with you Nikolai...? I'll tell...[Soso]...to bail you out.'....I know that Nadezhda...would never believe that I had harbored any evil thoughts against you....Oh, Lord, if only there were some device which would have made it possible for you to see my soul flayed and ripped open![76]

No response. The dictator, however, saved Nikolai's letter until the day he died.[77] One wonders what Soso thought of him invoking Nadya—whether it only heightened his determination to destroy him. He often annihilated those who knew the intimacy of his past life. "It was as though my father," remembered Svetlana, "were at the center of a black circle and anyone who ventured inside vanished or perished or was destroyed in one way or another."[78] Soso cannibalized his own humanity.

◆◆◆

Despite his fears of foreign invasion, Soso's purges weakened the Soviet Union before the Second World War.[79] His subsequent August 1939 pact with Adolf proved another devastating blunder. When German soldiers poured across Soviet borders on June 22, 1941, shock silenced Soso. "Did you hear me?" repeated Soviet General Georgy Zhukov in an early morning phone call. The dictator's quiet breathing was his reply.[80]

That day Soso was pale, stuffing his pipe, struggling to function.[81] Adolf "surely doesn't know about this," he murmured nonsensically.[82] Soviet forces fought bravely, but suffered devastating losses. German panzers plunged into Soviet territory. Moscow might fall. "Everything's lost," Soso complained miserably. "I give up....We've fucked it up."[83] He didn't go to work on June 30—actually stopped answering his phone. Peril paralyzed him. Perhaps he experienced, if only briefly, the helplessness of his own victims. Vulnerability before merciless evil.[84]

Henchmen urged Soso to get a hold of himself, and soon he did. Assuming command of a "State Defense Committee," the dictator ordered collapsing Soviet troops to fight to the death—*or else*. When German forces reached the outskirts of Moscow in October 1941, the dictator ultimately refused to evacuate. His orders: defend Moscow. The battle stopped at the capital's edge, and Soso's regime celebrated the Bolshevik Revolution's 24th anniversary on November 7. Rejecting the threat of German bombers, the regime audaciously held a military parade in Red Square.[85]

"The perfidious attack of the German brigands and the war which has been forced upon us," Soso admitted in his speech for the occasion, "have created a threat to our country." But the Soviet state, he reminded his people, had survived worse. In 1918, he recalled:

> Three-quarters of our country was at that time in the hands of foreign interventionists. The Ukraine, the Caucasus, Central Asia, the Urals, Siberia and the Far East were temporarily lost to us. We had no allies, we had no Red Army—we had only just begun to create it; there was a shortage of food, of armaments, of clothing for the Army. Fourteen states were pressing against our country.[86]

The Bolshevik regime prevailed then. They would win again—this time with more resources and allies. Soso offered his people victory amid catastrophe. "Can there be any doubt," he stated, "that we can, and are bound to, defeat the German invaders?" Monotone ferocity marked the end of Soso's anniversary address: "For the complete destruction of the German invaders! Death to the German invaders!"[87] Germany's war of extermination, the Soviet dictator made clear, would be paid back in kind.[88]

From 1941 to 1943, Soso made one military blunder after another, overruling his generals, ordering doomed offensives. He terrorized his own troops—requiring the shooting of retreating Soviet soldiers (Order 227: "Not one step back!").[89] But as the war continued, Soso did what Adolf couldn't—he shut up and listened. The desire to prevail inspired common sense. He granted his marshals and generals greater autonomy, the right to disagree with him, and ultimately allowed an orderly and professional decision-making process. Working relentlessly all the while, his regime marshalled the awesome resources of the Soviet Union, overseeing the creation of armed forces eventually totaling 11 million men and women.[90] Through relentless cruelty and determination—with the invaluable help of Western allies—Soso led the USSR to its bloody victory.[91]

◆ ◆ ◆

Oppressive norms returned at Cold War's dawn. Fear replaced postwar joy. Soso removed triumphant marshals and generals; banished liberated Soviet POWs to the gulag; deported entire populations; and purged potential enemies.[92] Atherosclerosis restricted blood flow to his aging brain. His intense paranoia and ruthlessness—traits that started in his youth—grew worse. More than ever, something was *off*.[93]

A "persecution mania," explained one of Soso's closest colleagues, grew more apparent in his final years. He "had broken down"—was "very jittery," pathologically suspicious, swinging to extremes.[94] He turned on old collaborators, threatening new purges.[95] He became convinced doctors conspired to kill him—and put his own in literal chains—as he blamed Soviet Jews for plotting against the regime, encouraging their further persecution in the shadow of the

Holocaust.[96] He also became increasingly worried about foreign spy agencies recruiting women, and frequently asked underlings how they met their wives, whom one was dating, etc. (These chilling questions, remembered Khrushchev, meant "disaster might be around the corner."[97])

Servility did not ensure salvation. When a Polish communist came across as too reverent, Soso complained: "What kind of fellow is this....He sits there all the time looking into my eyes....Why does he bring a notepad and pencil with him? Why does he write down every word I say?"[98] Reserve signaled higher loyalty than sycophancy. Even worship might bring doom. A cursed tightrope.

When among Western ambassadors and diplomats, Soso *doodled wolves*, glancing up, content with his visitors' discomfort.[99] With his own people, he talked softly, making few hand gestures. His face, not his tongue, spoke loudest. He rarely yelled. ("I was always aware," recalled a leading Soviet diplomat, "...of how expressive his face was, especially his eyes.") His relentless gaze crushed subordinates. His stare terrorized.[100]

Still, his lingering need for human contact remained a marker of shared humanity. Into old age, he continued to relieve his isolation with company and occasional parties, where guests had drinks and sometimes told racy jokes. Now and then Soso joined them in singing revolutionary or folk songs. He had a good voice.[101] His long-time housekeeper, Valechka—a buxom woman with "a snub nose and a gay, ringing laugh"—offered female companionship, though we know nothing of their love life.[102] Valechka, uneducated and apolitical, became Soso's sort of common law wife.[103] He was the best man to ever walk the earth, she insisted after his death.[104]

Soso relished his heavily protected country estate. Barbed wire, a fortified gate, a large security force with attack dogs, and bodyguards—not to mention a surrounding fifty-acre park—offered impenetrability. This inverse prison—meant to protect him from the outside world—offered security from enemies with whom he had yet to deal. Their time would come.[105] Soso largely lived and worked in a single room with a table, fireplace, and couch—on which he often slept, falling asleep while reading. He was simple like that.[106]

It was there, on March 1, 1953, that Soso collapsed on the floor from a stroke. For hours, he lay helpless in his own urine—alone, his anxious guards waiting outside, too nervous to see why he hadn't emerged. (Eventually they sent in a maid under the pretext of bringing mail; it was she who finally discovered his condition, and summoned help.)[107] In Soso's last feeble moments on March 5, his daughter, among others, rushed to his side. He looked around with "a terrible glance, insane[,] perhaps angry and full of the fear of death," recalled Svetlana. He raised his left hand "as though he were pointing to something above and bringing down a curse on us all."[108] Fighting what he could not control, the final terror was his own.[109]

CHAPTER FIVE
RENZHI REBELS AGAINST LIFE

RENZHI AND SONG BINBIN

The respirator pumped, breathing for the dying Chinese dictator. He battled Lou Gehrig's disease and had a failing heart—not to mention diseased lungs and kidneys. Yet the old man struggled to live. He rebelled against death itself. "Is there anything else you can do?"—a leading party official asked his doctor. Nothing more, came the reply. Deathbed scenes.[1]

One might have mistaken Renzhi for a corpse if his listless eyes—dulled by oblivion's approach—didn't blink on occasion. His face was no longer plump. His gray skin seemed ready to slide off his body and slither out the door. He stared listlessly, a bluish tint trespassing on his visage.[2] He lay on his bedsore-covered left side. Sucking air through an oxygen mask. A tube kept him from starving. "Ah...Ah...Ah," he wheezed, trying to talk.[3]

The frail octogenarian dwelled on the end. He had pulled together his underlings the prior June, reflecting on his legacy. Leading the Chinese Communist Party to victory—he emphasized—stood as his major triumph. He insisted further on the importance of the Cultural Revolution. *Continue the mission*, he told high ranking officials—peacefully if possible, through "shock tactics" if necessary.[4] "Only Heaven knows" how they would deal with everything to come.[5] It was time for the "superior man" to die.

◆◆◆

That Renzhi won the Chinese Civil War and established the People's Republic of China in 1949 remains stunning. For decades, he risked a brutal death at the hands of Chiang Kai-shek's nationalist regime. ("He who is not afraid of death by a thousand cuts dares to unhorse the emperor," declared the communist dictator in 1957.[6]) Once the nationalists attacked the Chinese Communist Party (CCP) in 1927, starting the Chinese Civil War, Renzhi avoided a brutal death by joining communist forces in the Jinggang mountains of southeast China. (Nationalists later nailed one of his closest friends to a wall and tortured him to death.[7]) Renzhi embraced armed struggle. "Power comes out of the barrel of a gun," he told his colleagues famously in August 1927.[8]

In the early 1930s Chiang Kai-shek's nationalist armies launched a series of "extermination campaigns" against his CCP base, among others. Renzhi argued for guerilla war.[9] In contrast, Soviet-trained leaders of the CCP ordered direct battles that nearly destroyed communist forces until they fled west in October 1934. Their epic Long March followed—6,000 miles across rivers and grasslands and mountains and swamps. 86,000 people started. Just 7,000 to 8,000 finished.[10] By October 1935, when communist forces reached the "Yan'an Soviet," a safe-haven in northwest China, Renzhi had emerged as the dominant leader.

The CCP grew thereafter by appealing to Chinese patriotism. In the wake of Japan's invasion of Manchuria—and its total war on China from 1937 onwards—the Party's emphasis on national unity inspired Chinese to flock to their ranks.[11] As a result, the CCP grew in size from some 40,000 members in 1937 to 800,000 in 1940 to between 1.2 and 2.7 million by 1945.[12] The Chinese had been "like a sheet of loose sand" until Japanese aggression unified them, noted Renzhi—employing the words of late nationalist leader Sun Yat-sen.[13]

Many of those who reached the Yan'an Soviet, however, found themselves in a prison of hardship—a preview of communism to come. When the writer Wang Shiwei, for example, criticized inequities in the communist party hierarchy, officials subjected him to sixteen days of public interrogations, castigating him as unworthy of life ("a spineless leech!").[14] A year later, Wang condemned himself in front of reporters ("I deserve to be executed. I should have been executed a thousand times."), thanking "magnanimous" Renzhi for "mercy."[15] (The Party could help almost anyone become "a good person," Renzhi later reflected.[16]) Guards eventually decapitated Wang Shiwei and tossed his corpse in a waterless well.[17]

When civil war resumed after Japan's defeat in the Second World War, Renzhi's troops outwitted the nationalists. Embracing mobility, they retreated as nationalist forces occupied major cities in Manchuria. When the strategic balance shifted, communist armies surrounded those same urban areas, starving out their enemies—and civilians.[18] In late 1948 and 1949, the communists swept southwards, victoriously. Extreme inflation, corruption, repression, and decades of war had destroyed public faith in the Nationalist regime. The Chinese people craved stability—even from the communists.[19] Renzhi proclaimed the establishment of the People's Republic of China on October 1, 1949. "The Chinese people have stood up," he yelled into the microphone in Beijing's Tiananmen Square with a thick Hunan accent. The crowd roared.[20]

◆ ◆ ◆

Renzhi stood five-foot-eleven. Balding, with a healthy belly, and an undescended testicle. He adored eating fatty pork and spicy foods.[21] Was a bad father (though the death of his oldest son, Anying, in the Korean War pained him deeply).[22] Smoked profusely. Enjoyed dancing. Loved swimming. Read constantly—especially Chinese history.[23] Wrote poetry.[24] Married (willingly) three times, ending up with former actress Jiang Qing, who worshiped her husband yet mistreated most everyone else.[25]

You might have met this man poolside, clad in a bathrobe, gregarious, eager to put you at ease. He liked to greet guests with a history book in hand to start a conversation that would diminish nerves and establish rapport.[26] Laughing and joking, he would get you to open up while only carefully revealing his own thoughts.[27] One wrong word might cause his surface kindness to disappear. A raised eyebrow could mean trouble. Renzhi forgot nothing. Was vengeful, ruthless. And he won, over and over. Longtime associates like Zhou Enlai learned always to support him—*always*.[28]

No one controlled Renzhi. He rebelled against everyone and everything—against time itself, refusing basic routines.[29] ("I graduated from the University of Outlaws," he liked to say.[30]) If he announced that he would swim in the swift currents of the Yangtze River, he demanded your support *and participation*. His revolts prevented others' control. He would not tolerate competition. Wanted to know everything, too. Those who worked for him received the same question day after day: "Any news?" All developments, significant and trivial, were of interest. Secrets were dangerous.[31]

But Renzhi, according to his personal doctor, struggled to control his own mind. Psychological neuroses plagued him, particularly during times of political strife. Insomnia, dizziness, itchiness, impotence, panic attacks.[32] Had someone poisoned his swimming pool? Was an assassin hiding in the attic of his villa waiting to kill him? He worried about these things.[33] The dictator routinely did not sleep for long stretches—sometimes up to 30 hours—and became hopelessly addicted to sleep medications like chloral hydrate and sodium seconal. These drugs, he discovered in the process, offered a good buzz if he stayed awake; he often got high on them before meetings and dance parties.[34]

In terms of manners, Renzhi enjoyed behaving like an unpolished provincial. Unapologetically, he farted and burped in front of others.[35] He spoke crudely—"farmyard language."[36] If one was about to enter his room in later years, he sometimes yelled out: "Have a good fart before you come in." If one clashed with him on a given issue, he might suggest you *go shit and then try being more reasonable*.[37] He often reproached subordinates with ribald language: "You've farted quite enough you clown!"[38] When he would write or give speeches, such "Rabelaisian" language made an appearance.[39] ("If one of our foreign masters farts," he wrote in mockery of his countrymen's lackey-like behavior before foreign imperialists, "it's a lovely perfume."[40]) Yet even as Renzhi relished the role of ill-mannered rustic, he maintained an air of superiority rooted in unwavering belief in his own intellectual abilities and self-conceived heroism—"the gnomic sage of the world revolution."[41]

Smell the fart of the farmyard narcissist.

Renzhi's sexual appetite was insatiable.[42] After taking power, he regularly treated female dancers tasked with entertaining him as concubines, justifying his sexual escapades with a Daoist belief about young women prolonging old men's lives. Not content with one sexual partner at a time, Renzhi enjoyed orgies and even had a special bed (higher on one side) to prevent him from falling out during intercourse.[43] Older and educated women sometimes declined his sexual advances, but younger women, groomed by propaganda, rejoiced.[44] ("To be brought into...[his] service," his long-time doctor recalled, "was, for the young women who were chosen, an incomparable honor, beyond their most extravagant dreams."[45]) So Renzhi took advantage—stealing innocence, cruelly using young women as sexual servants.[46] Sometimes he took an interest in male bodyguards, too—asking for "groin massages." His doctor once saw him grope a male guard and try to pull him into bed.[47]

Eventually, Renzhi caught genital herpes and became a carrier for trichomonas vaginalis, the latter of which infected his dance-troupe-concubines after he refused treatment. When urged at least to wash his genitals, he stated disgustingly: "I wash myself inside the bodies of *my women*."[48] The famed general Peng Dehuai challenged his boss's sexual practices, criticizing Renzhi for behaving like an emperor with a harem. To no avail. And Peng later met a terrible end.[49] The dictator's will was unquestionable. It defined his relationship with everyone around him. *His people* fueled the bright heroic sun that supposedly brought warmth and happiness to those about to be tossed into the fire.

◆ ◆ ◆

Modernization, Renzhi believed, had to emerge from the destruction of old China. Under his rule, hundreds of millions of peasants imbued with revolutionary ferocity would rebel against reality and destroy the traditions that had undermined China's power over the prior century.[50] Harnessing the country's enormous population (a "real iron bastion…absolutely impossible for any force on earth to smash"), everything was possible.[51] Renzhi's regime sought to build "new people." It both encouraged and demanded individuals of questionable loyalty—doctors, teachers, clerks, managers, engineers—embrace "re-education." Learning "the right answers, the right ideas, and the right slogans" of the new China was a necessity.[52] The marriage law of 1950 gave women the right to divorce and outlawed forced marriages.[53] Land reform followed. Hundreds of millions of landless peasants— roughly 88% of rural households—received plots. Party cadres urged attacks on "class enemies" during that process, leading to the deaths of up to a million people. Renzhi applauded. It was the destruction of old village modes of life.[54]

More direct terror against perceived political foes followed from 1950 to 1952. Renzhi offered his lieutenants clear guidance: identify one enemy for every thousand people.[55] His government ultimately executed 710,000 "enemies," a killing rate of 1.2 per 1,000 in the country over those two years.[56] (Another ranking figure in the regime claimed 2,000,000 executions.[57]) Millions of others faced imprisonment, surveillance, and marginalization.[58]

Still, the first years of the People's Republic of China symbolized a new era of hope for many Chinese. That great people had endured a century of humiliation and foreign imperialism; the Qing Dynasty's collapse in 1911; the subsequent break-up of China into warring fiefdoms; civil war between communists and nationalists; the Japanese invasion; and total economic misery. Renzhi's regime had finally reunified the country under one authority. It fought inflation and boosted industrial output.[59] It reduced illiteracy.[60] It asserted China's power abroad, fighting the United States and its UN allies to a standstill in Korea, ending a string of military defeats going back to the nineteenth century.[61] People hoped for a better future.

Renzhi felt the pace of change too gradual though. China, he declared in January 1958, was like an atom that the CCP could smash open, creating a nuclear chain reaction of energy—destruction for the sake of creation. Armed with the might of hundreds of millions of peasants, China could catch up with industrial powers like Britain in fifteen years.[62] Starting in April of 1958, Renzhi sought to do just that, in what became known as the "Great Leap Forward." He pushed the rapid creation of new "People's Communes" on huge state-run collective farms, compelling families to give up private property and join.[63] Communes would provide housing, healthcare, childcare, and food. These state farms—in principle—would end China's historic food insecurity and break the private market by allowing the government to monopolize grain output and earn capital for industrialization by selling excess grain abroad. Backyard steel mills— meaning a half-million rudimentary homemade mills, manned by some forty million workers—would boost steel production to boot.[64]

Renzhi's extensive travels around the country throughout 1958 left him in awe. Everywhere he went, communes showcased Potemkin façades of extraordinary progress. At the same time, party cadres swept up in the frenzied energy of the campaign promised larger and larger production targets. 150 tons of rice per acre. 300 tons of rice per acre. 500 tons of rice per acre. "The corn will grow higher the more you desire," went the saying of the time.[65] The people could "launch satellites!"—so to speak.[66] Officials, in turn, pushed poorly conceived planting strategies to make it all a reality—deep ploughing, massive fertilizer use, and close cropping, which peasants (with decades of farming experience) knew would fail.[67]

After harvests turned disastrous in many provinces, party cadres and militias seized large volumes of what grain there was and let communes go hungry. <u>At least forty-five million people died</u>.[68] Starvation, disease, and violence followed—an endless ocean of suffering, one of the worst catastrophes in human history. A survivor remembers Renzhi's famine in her village:

> On a muddy path...dozens of corpses lay unburied. In the barren fields there were others; and amongst the dead, the survivors crawled slowly on their hands and knees searching for wild grass seeds to eat. In the ponds and ditches people squatted in the mud hunting for frogs and trying to gather weeds. It was winter, and bitterly cold, but...everyone was dressed only in thin and filthy rags.... Sometimes...neighbours and relatives simply fall down as they shuffled through the village and die without a sound....The dead were left where they died because...no one had the strength to bury them....At night some...went into the fields to cut the flesh from the corpses and eat it....A woman had killed her own baby and her husband had eaten it....Human beings turned into wolves.[69]

Repeatedly, similar stories played out. Woe and agony. Insanity wrought by hunger. Some desperate families ate mud only to suffer tortuous deaths as it hardened into dirt in their stomachs and intestines, absorbing fluid and blocking bowel movements.[70] Party cadres and militias maintained control with horrifying violence throughout it all. Torture, intentional food deprivation, and suicide killed 6-8% of the Great Leap Forward's victims.[71]

Renzhi and the leadership were responsible.[72] Liu Shaoqi, Chairman of the People's Republic of China and designated successor, told Renzhi as much in July 1962. "So many people have died of hunger!" he emphasized heatedly. "History will judge you and me, even cannibalism will go into the books!"[73] With these comments, Liu challenged Renzhi's self-identity—the dictator's conviction that he was a heroic savior. That doomed Liu.[74] (Not long after in November 1964, Renzhi started ridiculing him: "Let's change over now. You be Chairman [of the Chinese Communist Party]....You should take over the role of telling people off."[75])

In May 1966, Renzhi unleashed the "Great Proletarian Cultural Revolution." Eager to destroy political opponents and renew "class struggle," he urged youths to rebel against "counterrevolutionary" authority. On June 5, 1966, the regime-run *People's Daily* printed an old quote from Renzhi: "The laws of Marxism are intricate and complex, but in the final analysis they boil down to one thing: 'To rebel is justified.'"[76] A group of self-proclaimed "Red Guards"—teenagers from Tsinghua University High School—soon wrote the dictator, telling him they had written "To rebel is justified" in a big character poster hung at school. The dictator replied on August 1: "You say it is right to rebel against reactionaries; I enthusiastically support you."[77] Red Guard groups proliferated throughout China. Frenzied adolescents dressed in military uniforms with red armbands and raged against authority. Expressing support, the dictator wrote his own big character poster: "Bombard the party headquarters."[78] Elites were fair game.

Anarchy erupted at colleges and schools. Students, quoting Renzhi, lashed out at "reactionary" teachers and administrators. Belligerency begot bloodshed. On August 5, girls at an elite Beijing school beat their vice principal to death with nail-spiked clubs.[79] A public rally on August 13 in the capital, with tens of thousands of Red Guards, saw the beating and whipping of five people—"hooligans"— who had denounced the violence. (Premier Zhou Enlai—the Red Guards' next victim, if Renzhi wished it—sat on stage, offering tacit approval.)[80] A rally in Tiananmen Square on August 18 involving more than a million Red Guards saw Renzhi, clad in military uniform, greet the rebelling students. Youths—stammering, sobbing, applauding— screamed: "Long Live Chairman Mao!", singing revolutionary songs praising him.[81] Renzhi's new successor, Lin Biao, oversaw the creation of little red books with the leader's sayings and called on students to destroy "all the old ideas, old culture, old customs, and old habits of the exploiting classes."[82] *Obliterate old China.*

Engaging with students after the rally, Renzhi met a small spectacled teenage girl, Song Binbin—a Red Guard from the school where students had tortured the vice principal to death. Binbin pinned a red armband on him. *Be martial*, the dictator told her.[83]

On August 21, 1966, the CCP's central committee forbade security officials from reining in the Red Guards.[84] Terror consumed Beijing over the next month. Students at Beijing Third Girls Middle School tortured their principal to death. The dean committed suicide. Red Guards at a different middle school in the capital poured boiling water on their principal. A middle school at Beijing Teachers' College saw students murder a biology teacher before making other teachers pummel her corpse. Students at elementary schools in the capital forced teachers to swallow nails and human waste. 1,770 murders and suicides occurred in Beijing alone by the end of September 1966.[85]

Renzhi had set the tone decades earlier.[86] Red Guards repeatedly quoted a famous passage from his 1927 report on "land reform" in Hunan province[87]:

> A revolution is not a dinner party, or writing an essay, or painting a picture, or doing embroidery; it cannot be so refined, so leisurely and gentle, so temperate, kind, courteous, restrained and magnanimous. A revolution is an insurrection, an act of violence by which one class overthrows another.[88]

Those who disagreed ("It's terrible!") were branded class enemies themselves. Indeed, the measure of revolutionary morality was one's willingness to support violent measures ("It's fine!").[89] Destruction, Renzhi had always believed, would make possible a new and better world. So Red Guards—backed by Renzhi's wife, Jiang Qing, and the regime's Cultural Revolution Group—raided the homes of leading party officials, subjecting them to violent "struggle sessions"— essentially a show trial by an angry crowd, culminating in verbal and physical abuse.[90] They destroyed precious historical artifacts from China's "feudal" past, even despoiling Confucius's hallowed tomb.[91] Nothing was sacred—*save Renzhi*. China, for a time, became the upside-down world. Once-innocent kids committed evil acts—or witnessed them complicitly—because the ideological lens of the time rendered good as bad and bad as good.[92]

And then there was Liu Shaoqi. Doomed and terrified and eager to avoid a brutal end, he asked Renzhi to let him retire to the countryside as a simple peasant.[93] Denied. After Liu's arrest in 1967, Red Guards terrorized him (and his wife) in struggle sessions before vast audiences. Kept in solitary detention and denied medical care, he eventually died in bed on November 12, 1969, covered in bed sores, tied down with gauze strips.[94] With cruel irony, Liu's death certificate listed his occupation as *unemployed*.[95]

Renzhi's Cultural Revolution ultimately resulted in the deaths of up to two million people—not to mention countless broken lives and endless trauma.[96] However, its myriad stories include not only brutality—but also the heroism of brave Chinese who stood against savagery and protected family and friends. Renzhi could not destroy the immense dignity of the Chinese people.[97]

◆ ◆ ◆

The dictator remained unpredictable into old age. In the shadow of the Cultural Revolution, Renzhi abruptly pursued better relations with the United States, culminating in Richard Nixon's stunning visit to Beijing in February 1972. Yet the eighty-year-old's end was on the horizon just two years later. His eyesight was failing. His speech had become almost indecipherable. Muscles on the right side of his body wasted away.[98] Physicians knew he would be dead within two years. No one told him.[99]

Renzhi and his staff distracted themselves with foreign movies.[100] With a projector and a large television from Hong Kong, his assistants sometimes screened two movies a day—including *The Sound of Music*—even after the dictator himself became too sick to watch. Though still politically aware (and always dangerous), Renzhi became an infant in certain respects—unable to walk, or use the bathroom independently, or speak intelligibly. He had to lie on his left side to breathe, and his hands and feet trembled.[101]

But even after a third heart attack on September 2, 1976, Renzhi still asked whether he might pull through. A man who had no interest in surrendering to death what he had relied on throughout his entire life—*the power of will*—was "fighting on," as his doctor remembered. "It's all right, Chairman," the physician replied comfortingly. "We will be able to help you." For a brief instant, the dying man looked happy, content with his life's rebellion—and then he stopped breathing. The doctor felt no sadness.[102]

CHAPTER SIX
REALITY STARES DOWN SONG-JU

"I am taking up smoking again," remarked Song-ju after his last speech on July 6, 1994. He was anxious.[1] In the Cold War's aftermath, his country was crashing. Factories stood still. People starved.[2] War loomed with the United States.[3] Allies like the Soviet Union and East Germany had ceased to exist. Unable to get by with counterfeiting money and selling drugs, the regime dared Washington to launch airstrikes over its nuclear weapons program, trusting it would ultimately offer a sweet deal instead. It was a dangerous time.[4]

The North Korean dictator admitted challenges—a testament to the situation's extremity. "We are faced with quite a few problems we need to solve in economic work," Song-ju acknowledged in his July 6 speech. "The [farming] situation in other counties is not so good" and "….the socialist market has disappeared," he lamented further.[5] By the end of the address, as his secretary observed, his face had become "grave and dark," his speech tired.[6] Chest pains tormented him as he blamed party officials for problems his own policies had created. Everyone was silent.[7]

The next evening at 10 PM, the ailing North Korean dictator supposedly phoned a Party secretary in a far northern county, inquiring about food supplies.[8] "There has been some shortage in supply....But you need not worry, sir," went the predictable answer. "You people keep telling me not to worry," replied the exasperated old man, "but how can I not worry when we can't distribute rations on time for the people?"[9] It was Song-ju's final night alive. And even he had to grapple with the fact his regime couldn't feed its own citizens.[10]

Song-ju had lived opulently in marble palaces for decades, but events in the last years of his life upended most everything he sought to achieve as leader. If he once humbly dreamed of every Korean north of the 38th parallel having plenty to eat and a good roof over their heads, his people now went hungry, becoming scarecrows, ghosts abandoned by his incompetent leadership and an unworkable economic system.[11] Even if the regime survived, the country faced prolonged misery. The most vulnerable would suffer. The only certain "success" his regime could claim was its defiance of the United States over its nuclear program. (It poured money into developing nuclear weapons while children starved.)

But for Song-ju, alone on a rainy night, none of this mattered for much longer.

◆ ◆ ◆

Korea—the nation for which Song-ju fought Japan in the 1930s—demanded independence after the Second World War. The defeat of Japan in 1945 liberated Korea from Japanese colonialism. But its people deeply resented Washington and Moscow's decision to split the peninsula into two zones along the 38th parallel.[12] The creation of a northern zone occupied by Soviet troops and a southern one occupied by Americans divided a nation with well over a thousand years of history.[13]

The foreign-sponsored creation of two antagonistic regimes thereafter—the Republic of Korea (capitalist South Korea) and the Democratic People's Republic of Korea (communist North Korea)—all but ensured civil strife. Both states claimed to represent the Korean people. Neither recognized the existence of the other. There was only Korea. (North Koreans still remind foreigners of as much. "There's no such country called 'North Korea,'" as the country's World Cup soccer coach told reporters in 2010. *"Next question."*[14])

Song-ju emerged as the leader of North Korea in the fall of 1945 only because Soso hand-picked him.[15] His first public speech underwhelmed. Koreans expected a hardened leader—not a baby-faced thirty-something. That Song-ju supposedly had "'a haircut like a Chinese waiter'" and spoke in "'a monotonous, plain, and duck-like voice,'" as history's gossip columns tell us, had not helped.[16] The American media, for its part, ridiculed him as an imposter who had never fought Japan—a "plump puppet," as a letter in *Time* put it in 1948.[17] That was a mistake. Song-ju was a serious man.[18]

As the new North Korean leader, Song-ju demanded Korean reunification through force as soon as possible.[19] South Korea's leader, elderly Syngman Rhee, wanted the same.[20] The United States prevented South Korea from attacking. But Soso heavily armed North Korea, letting Song-ju invade South Korea on June 25, 1950.[21] North Korean forces captured Seoul in just three days. South Korea faced extinction—until the United States intervened.[22]

Perceiving the North Korean invasion as part of a Soviet plot for global domination, Washington poured troops into South Korea under the banner of the United Nations, preventing a quick North Korean victory and Korean reunification.[23] The ensuing struggle erupted into a broader Cold War conflict after U.S. and South Korean troops invaded North Korea in the fall of 1950, prompting the intervention of Chinese forces that sent both reeling back down the peninsula. Bloody stalemate followed, and the cease-fire that stopped active fighting in August 1953 was not a peace treaty.[24] The standoff continues. Korea remains divided. And dangerous.

The twentieth century's "nastiest little war" decimated Korea.[25] All sides committed war crimes.[26] Around 3,000,000 Korean civilians died—along with 520,000 North Korean and 415,000 South Korean soldiers, 40,000 United Nations combatants (including 36,574 Americans), and at least 148,000 Chinese (China suffered 900,000 casualties overall).[27] The war permanently separated around 10,000,000 Koreans, mostly family members, who never saw each other again.

Song-ju's regime blamed the United States.[28] *One cannot begin to understand North Korea's extreme resentment of the U.S. without acknowledging the war's extraordinary suffering.*[29] It was a struggle born of decades of foreign involvement in Korea—not just Song-ju's invasion.[30]

◆ ◆ ◆

When the 1953 cease fire took effect, Song-ju was only forty-one years old—still a young man with a "quick flashing smile under a mop of bushy, black hair."[31] But his youth belied decades of hardship and loss. In the prior twenty years, he had fought Japanese imperialism, escaped death by fleeing to the Soviet Union, led a new communist state, waged war for reunification, and witnessed his country's devastation. He had suffered personal tragedies, too. His three-year-old son, Man-il, drowned in 1947. On the eve of the Korean War, the child's mother (Song-ju's wife)—a former guerilla named Jong-suk, who had risked her life with him in the struggle against Japan—died in childbirth. Two small children—a boy named Jong-il and a girl named Kyong-hui—remained from the marriage.[32] Not having a mom must've been hard on them.[33]

JONG-IL, SONG-JU, AND JONG-SUK IN HAPPIER TIMES

This individual—former guerilla-turned-communist dictator-turned-family man—sought to make his power unassailable after the Korean War. He was ruthless, executing potential opponents and outmaneuvering competing political factions as he paid lip service to Moscow and Beijing.[34] But he also proved himself wily and charming, acting "generous and warm" with friends.[35] Armed with a deep voice—speaking "from his belly like an opera singer"—he was good-looking (at least until a baseball-sized tumor grew on the back of his neck in the early 1970s).[36] In party meetings during the regime's first twenty years—recalled high-ranking defector Hwang Jang-yop—he came across as "conscientious, wise and dignified."[37] He listened, particularly to ordinary workers.[38] He could be humble with high-ranking officials as well, offering self-deprecating lines like "I wasn't a big part of the partisan struggle against the Japanese, but it's better than nothing" or "I never dreamed back then that I would become the leader.'"[39] Astute political skills cemented his dominance.

◆ ◆ ◆

Song-ju's regime rebuilt North Korea in the 1950s and 1960s through aid from other communist countries and the extraordinary exertion of the Korean people. Cities rose from rubble.[40] The country's economy grew rapidly until the mid-1960s, outpacing South Korea's.[41] If all major decisions had gone through Moscow before and during the Korean War—and China stationed troops in the country until 1958— Song-ju proved in the 1960s that he was no puppet.[42] His regime declared its independence—all while playing both Moscow and Beijing for maximum aid.[43]

With regard to the U.S. and South Korea, North Korea remained extraordinarily aggressive, regularly clashing with both on the peninsula.[44] Such incidents include North Korea's capture of the USS *Pueblo*, an American spy ship, in January 1968, and a failed commando raid to assassinate South Korea's president the same year. (Not to mention the 1976 Panmunjom Axe Incident, when North Korean soldiers clubbed two US soldiers to death.) Vitriolic exchanges with few rivals in diplomatic history occurred during meetings with U.S. officials at the "truce village" of Panmunjom. (A North Korean general, for instance, told an American negotiator during the *Pueblo* crisis in 1968: "'A mad dog barks at the moon'....If you want to escape from the same fate of [President John F.] Kennedy, who is now a putrid corpse, don't indulge yourself desperately in invectives at this table…"[45]) Par for the course.

North Korea—from its own perspective—was a tiny country standing up to a nuclear-armed superpower that kept its nation divided and threatened annihilation.[46] Readying for renewed war and still determined to achieve reunification, Song-ju's regime zealously fought "American imperialism"—a fundamental shift from Korea's past weakness before Japan. Someday, Song-ju promised his people, North Korea would reunify the country under the "Democratic People's Republic of Korea." North Korea even claimed Seoul as its capital until 1972![47]

Within North Korea, Song-ju turned himself into a supreme being, transforming his country into the most religious place in the world.[48] The regime hung his framed portrait in every home and office, requiring citizens to revere it.[49] (To run into a burning building to save it remains a hallowed act.)[50] North Koreans had to worship Song-ju as the most exalted leader in Korea's long history, the greatest of the greatest of the greatest. As his 1970 official biography puts it: he was "the great Leader of our forty million Korean people, peerless patriot, national hero, ever-victorious, iron-willed brilliant commander and one of the outstanding leaders of the international communist movement and working-class movement."[51]

Subjected to the regime's relentless propaganda, and largely lacking access to the outside world before the 1990s, many North Koreans believed that Song-ju's love was indeed a sacred truth on which to build their lives. ("We shall live forever in His kind care," states the North Korean opera *Song of Paradise*. "His grateful love has given us eternal life.…We shall relate His everlasting love age after age. Oh, we shall be loyal to…our Leader, our Great, Fatherly Leader."[52]) His people's resulting faith emerged, in part, from the same religious inclinations that so many of us share: the need to believe there is a higher power who protects and loves us, the hunger to rest easy in the bosom of a savior. While unknown numbers understood it as nonsense, many good men and women *believed*.[53] (We might well have, too.[54])

Either way, Song-ju's ruthless human rights abuses ensured no one would dare challenge his cult.[55] The regime subjected citizens to terrifying supervision and repression. It categorized the entire population into 51 subcategories based on perceived loyalty.[56] 70 to 75% of the populace, Song-ju noted in a 1961 speech, were suspect or "irredeemably hostile."[57] Only 5%—"the elect," if you will—were beyond reproach, with perfect working-class backgrounds, no family in South Korea, and no past connection to the Japanese or Americans.[58] (This caste-like loyalty system—*Songbun*—still defines diverse aspects of life in North Korea, determining where one can live, go to school, and work.) The capital, Pyongyang, became a showcase city for the most politically reliable. Those at the bottom of the hierarchy suffered misery in far-flung provinces. Or worse: gulag camps. The tiny fraction of souls who escaped from the latter have reported crimes against humanity that degrade human dignity in unimaginably horrific ways.

It's still going on as you read this. Hell exists.[59]

◆ ◆ ◆

Throughout his time in power, Song-ju lived a life of lavish abundance. He (and then his son, Jong-il) "enjoyed the most luxurious, abundant and cushy lifestyles that no other head of state in the world could have imagined possible," confessed high-ranking defector Hwang Jang-yop.[60] Indeed the country was full of their opulent mansions:

> All around the city of Pyongyang are several special facilities, or what can be termed 'special royal villas,' equipped with all sorts of luxuries from performing arts centers to medical facilities and even exclusive

hunting grounds. There is probably no other country in the world both in the past and present that has as many royal villas as North Korea. Any place deemed to boast the slightest scenic beauty is designated as a site for one of these royal villas. An army of escorts guard all these places, and hostesses are stationed there round the clock in readiness for a royal visit.[61]

If Song-ju was a communist, it was to the extent that he compelled his people to labor in a brutal planned economy that he believed would foster prosperity. But nothing was spared for his own comfort and security. (China's Red Guards—with rare accuracy during the Cultural Revolution—ridiculed Song-ju as "'fat'" and "'a millionaire, an aristocrat and a leading bourgeois element in Korea.'"[62]) Song-ju's regime built a vast underground tunnel system in Pyongyang for him if war resumed, and even set up a "Longevity Institute" to prolong his life.

When it came to sex, Song-ju—like Renzhi—embraced the belief that intercourse with young women would extend his years. Defector testimony has claimed that organized teams of concubines served the North Korean dictator and his son, Jong-il. Regime officials selected beautiful young women from around the country—including young teenagers—and then groomed them for sexual exploitation.[63] Defectors later claimed that illegitimate children from this abuse grew up in royal villas throughout North Korea before later serving in the regime.[64]

◆ ◆ ◆

From the 1970s onward, Jong-il emerged as Song-ju's successor, and the elder dictator "became increasingly conceited and sloppy" as his son expanded his cult of personality to new heights of hyperbole.[65] Jong-il, for his part, attracted a reputation as a "plump playboy, fond of western movies and liquor," to use the *Washington*

Post's words.[66] Grisly North Korean terrorist attacks against South Korean targets in the '80s—blamed on Jong-il—added presumed insanity to the mix; observers questioned whether the successor was mentally ill. In reality, neither Song-ju nor his son were mad. They were despots who used terror as a tool of state, governing a weak regime surrounded by adversaries, intensely afraid of threats that might undermine their power.[67]

But then everything changed. As Jong-il took greater control of North Korea in the late '80s and early '90s, the communist world melted down.[68] The People's Republic of China had embraced capitalistic reforms ("socialism with Chinese characteristics") and established diplomatic relations with South Korea. Communist regimes throughout eastern Europe collapsed. The Soviet Union dissolved. And the stunned North Korean leadership faced a new world. "Self-reliance" became a punishing reality.[69] Allies no longer delivered generous aid disguised as "trade." Newly privatized Russian companies wanted hard currency for resources needed to keep the lights on in Pyongyang. Unable to maintain oil supplies, the North Korean electrical grid broke down. Many factories stopped producing chemical fertilizers for crop production, and the government couldn't power water pumps to irrigate fields. Harvests failed. Citizens—who had received rations from the state for decades—began to go hungry.[70] *Trust the Party*, reiterated regime officials in response.[71] ("Let's Eat Two Meals a Day"—a regime campaign urged its citizens from 1991 onwards.)[72]

On top of this grave situation, North Korea engaged in an escalating crisis with the United States after Pyongyang's withdrawal from the Nuclear Nonproliferation Treaty in March 1993. The Clinton administration considered airstrikes to prevent Song-ju's regime from obtaining nuclear weapons. U.S. military officials cautioned President Clinton that renewed war would kill or wound an estimated one million Korean civilians and thirty thousand U.S. soldiers—and cause one trillion dollars in damage. North Korea gambled (correctly) that no U.S. administration would risk such a catastrophe.[73]

◆ ◆ ◆

Song-ju was near the end by this point. Heart disease threatened his life. His hearing and eyesight were going.[74] Even as he started to grasp the enormity of his regime's crises, the old man took comfort in propaganda, bragging about his country to foreigners. There were no beggars or homeless people, he earnestly told American visitors in April 1994; a Hong Kong businessman who lost his wallet with $10,000 in it—he boasted—had it returned within two hours...not a dollar missing.[75] Asked about his son, the ailing dictator responded: "I am so proud of him. As an elderly man, I cannot read easily, and every day my son dictates reports into a cassette recorder so I can listen to them later on. But he keeps me fully informed. He is truly a filial son."[76] Fantasy offered relief.

Still armed with bright eyes and a firm handshake, Song-ju appeared for his last act in June 1994 when he met former U.S. President Jimmy Carter at the height of the nuclear crisis. The North Korean leader appeared—as the president of CNN remembered from that trip—not only "remarkably healthy" for an old man, but "feisty, quick-witted, and very much in command."[77] In his meetings with Carter, the North Korean leader not only expressed openness to a nuclear deal for massive energy assistance, he agreed to a summit meeting with South Korea's president. The curtains hadn't fallen yet.

In the last month of his life, Song-ju stayed at his favorite mountain resort to prepare for the summit meeting. He fantasized about imminent Korean reunification under a confederation government (an idea reinforced by a report from Jong-il claiming that

South Koreans adored him).[78] He allegedly called for more resources to go to the devastated civilian economy, as well as aid for the hungry.

On the night of July 7-8, Song-ju reportedly got into a heated argument with Jong-il about these measures before retiring to his bedroom. By himself. His personal secretary found him face down on the floor.[79] "The Great Heart stopped beating," reported the North Korean media. The cries of Song-ju's people resounded, echoing the misery of his youth.[80]

PART TWO

ORIGINS

If I knew for a certainty that a man was coming to my house with the conscious design of doing me good, I should run for my life.

- Henry David Thoreau

CHAPTER SEVEN
MEET VOLODIA'S PARENTS—AND SASHA

The boy who would become a communist dictator grew up in a well-kept, middle-class household—with servants.[1] His parents, Ilya and Maria Alexandrovna, had six kids in all—Anna (oldest); Sasha; Volodia; Olga; Dmitri; Maria (youngest). Though the family had known tragedy—losing two infants—it was a big, loving crew.[2] Ilya and Maria had a close relationship. They were decent, thoughtful people who adored their children and made every effort to ensure they would surpass their own accomplishments.[3] Both led by example in their sobriety, hard work, and dedication to education. Mom and Dad, though not wealthy, gave the children a pleasant upbringing. Theirs was a house full of scientific works, books in German and French, and sheet music—a home that valued intellectual curiosity and study. Ilya read aloud some evenings.[4] They had a backyard garden (with a small gazebo for drinking tea); Maria harvested strawberries and other fruit with the kids. In woods and hills around town, Volodia and his siblings romped about and enjoyed sledding, ice-skating, canoeing, and swimming.[5] They had a tree at Christmas and dyed eggs at Easter.[6] It was a happy childhood.[7]

◆ ◆ ◆

Ilya and Maria came from diverse backgrounds. Ilya, a descendant of serfs, was born in a far-flung corner of his country. Ilya's father was sixty-six years old when he was born; his mother was forty-one.[8] They likely had central Asian ancestry, a point that led future commentators to describe Volodia as "the monster with Mongolian eyes" and (with even more overt racism) "the man from Simbirsk who is as Asiatic in his appearance as he is in his soul, *full of cunning*."[9] Ilya's elderly father, a tailor, died when he was a boy, and his big brother took on the responsibility of providing for his education. Ilya made good use of his older sibling's sacrifices on his behalf, earning acceptance to Imperial Kazan University with stellar grades—an impressive feat considering that college was almost wholly reserved for elites.[10]

After graduating, Volodia's father became a physics and math teacher. The central government later tasked him with establishing and overseeing primary schools in the province surrounding the town of Simbirsk. In that leading administrative position—with his civilian rank something akin to a military general—authorities awarded Ilya the status of hereditary noble. Respectful subordinates addressed him as

"Your Excellency." This was a striking climb up the social ladder, a product of Ilya's intelligence and hard work.[11]

On the maternal side, Volodia's mother, Maria, came from a diverse family. Her father was Jewish—which Volodia's future regime tried to keep out of historical records—while her mother was German and Swedish. Volodia's maternal grandfather was a smart, if eccentric, doctor. (He supposedly believed temperature extremes would make his children physiologically stronger and dressed them lightly in cold weather.)[12] To diminish anti-Semitic discrimination faced by his family, Maria's father converted to Christianity and raised Volodia's mother as such.[13] In her youth, Maria came of age on a beautiful country estate called Kokushkino, where her father—the grandfather of a future communist dictator, mind you!—owned serfs for a time.[14] After Maria's mother died young, a German aunt raised her, providing an excellent education; she became fluent in German and French and a talented pianist.[15]

Ilya and Maria married in 1863 after meeting that year. The family grew with the birth of Anna in 1864 and then Sasha in 1866. Volodia followed in 1870 along with Olga in 1871, Dmitri in 1874, and Maria in 1878.[16] As parents, Ilya and Maria believed deeply in liberal education. Faith in as much defined Ilya's career. He traveled constantly to rural areas for his job, leaving his family to set up schools with good teachers.[17] Literacy, Volodia's father believed, would liberate the poor from crushing poverty and ameliorate his country's woes; education would do greater good than guns ever could. In that vein, Ilya was a liberal conservative who rejected revolutionary tumult. His rise into the nobility apparently demonstrated that his country's political and economic system—whatever its faults—would allow others like him to follow suit. A true believer in gradual change, Ilya was loyal to the government. There is every reason to believe he would have loathed what became of Volodia—and Sasha.[18]

◆ ◆ ◆

VOLODIA, AGE 4, AND LITTLE SISTER OLGA

Volodia's mother, Maria, ran the home when Ilya was gone. She did well, scrupulously managing the family's finances and overseeing the kids' education, bringing in tutors to help educate the younger ones.[19] Maria herself was an excellent teacher who made learning fun, teaching her children, for instance, to pun in Russian, German, and French. Through Maria, Volodia and his siblings studied novels, foreign languages, music, and art from their earliest years.[20] (Volodia could read and write by age five and had an in-home tutor till nine.[21]) For a while, the kids even put together a faux-literary journal (*Saturday*) for which they wrote articles under cheeky pennames—particularly useful for little Volodia, whose intellectual life would revolve around writing and publishing.

Maria was not only a talented pedagogue, but a loving and patient mother. Her approach to parenting contrasted with Ilya's quick temper and seriousness.[22] She was a model of quiet strength for her children. She never yelled. She disciplined through persuasion.[23] ("Mama…you know, she's simply a saint," Volodia wrote in his late twenties.[24]) The kids adored her.

◆ ◆ ◆

Big brother Sasha, not Volodia, was always his family's "first hope."[25] The second-oldest of the six, he was even-tempered and disciplined, kind in every respect. Volodia, four years younger, imitated Sasha. His family found it funny. When someone asked Volodia's preference on a given circumstance, the little boy often looked to Sasha, trying to interpret his big brother's opinion before replying: "Like Sasha."[26] Then and later, Volodia undoubtedly felt pressure to emulate him. His older brother's ethical character and academic accomplishments were exemplary.[27]

The two brothers were outwardly similar. Both were reserved in public and had introspective demeanors that suggested deep thought. Neither sought close friends at school. Each preferred the pleasure of his own company (and books) to the attention of extroverts. They were both extremely intelligent, and earned the best grades.[28]

The two were different beneath the surface though. Sasha was shy—quiet even before his own father at the dinner table.[29] He rarely cried.[30] Volodia, in contrast, was rambunctious.[31] The high-strung little brother—"reddish, bulky, bouncing"—required extra attention from Ilya and Maria.[32] He often preferred to break toys than play with them.[33] The brown-eyed boy was also domineering towards his younger siblings—especially his little sister Olga. He yelled a lot. Disrupted schoolwork. Played mischievous pranks (but was quick to apologize!). Got put in time-out—the first of many exiles to come.[34]

◆ ◆ ◆

At age nine, Volodia started school at the local gymnasium where Sasha had studied since the same age. It offered eight years of education—akin to middle and high school.[35] His father's position made it possible for the brothers to attend tuition-free. (Both passed a required examination with ease.) Clad in a dark blue, military-esque uniform with brass buttons, Volodia went off to school like his big brother.[36] When it came to their studies, Ilya demanded excellence. He never had an alternative to academic success; he'd delivered as a young man. Now his sons would do the same.[37]

Such high expectations proved no issue.[38] Both boys crushed a curriculum consisting of math, science, history, geography, religion, and foreign languages (ranging from German to ancient Greek).[39] They dominated academically. Their headmaster—"by a curious freak of history"—was Fyodor Kerensky, father of the same man Volodia would overthrow in October 1917.[40]

Volodia actually did so well in school that Ilya expressed concern that his son wasn't struggling enough—that it was all coming too easily for a boy who still had to learn to work hard.[41] Day after day, big sister Anna remembered, the following scene played out at home:

> Volodia would rush up…and report hurriedly, without stopping: in Greek five [A], in German—five [A]. I can still see the scene clearly: I am sitting in father's study and I catch the contented smile which father and mother exchange as their eyes follow the bulky little figure in uniform, with the reddish hair sticking out from under the school cap…in Latin—five [A], in Algebra—five [A]….[42]

Eager to keep pace and surpass big brother Sasha's towering intellect, the young man became more inclined to intensive study in his teenage years, turning into a voracious reader and developing the self-discipline his father hoped to see.[43] In school, Volodia mostly hid his irascible temperament. He never got in trouble. He was patient with fellow students, helping them with their work.[44] The self-confident young man did not show-off his intellectual gifts. No need to flaunt the obvious.[45]

As he entered adolescence, Volodia apparently had little interest in girls, though that would come later. Translations of Cicero, not the opposite sex, inflamed his passions. Books—not breasts—absorbed him. (No word on onanism.)[46] Volodia devoured Gogol, Pushkin, Tolstoy, and Turgenev.[47] Turgenev's novels particularly fascinated him. The teenager read them over and over, becoming a sort of expert on them.[48] Volodia knew the characters of Turgenev's *Smoke* "almost by heart" and used "Voroshilov"—a condescending know-it-all character—to mock political opponents.[49] (In his 1901 work "The Agrarian Question and the Critics of Marx," he referenced *Smoke* and derided a fellow Marxist as "Voroshilov" *fifteen times*.[50]) Turgenev's works often intertwined tales of love with stories of imperial society's "feckless landed nobleman and well-meaning but ineffectual intellectuals," to borrow the apt words of one biographer.[51] If Volodia had no interest in politics yet, Turgenev's novels portrayed a version of his country he knew intimately. They would provide a lens through which the young man saw a problematic society in need of solutions.[52]

◆ ◆ ◆

When Volodia was thirteen in May 1883, big brother Sasha graduated from the gymnasium. First in his class, Sasha received the school's vaunted gold medal.[53] He gained admission to prestigious St. Petersburg University. Sasha would make a great professor of natural science if he could excel in the big city. As he left, apprehensive Ilya urged him to steer clear of politics.[54] Sasha, away in the capital, largely complied and buried himself in the lab. His older sister Anna soon gave him company when she moved to St. Petersburg to study to become a teacher.[55]

Back home in January 1886, Ilya felt poorly. As Maria and the kids ate lunch one day, the father appeared in the doorway of the dining room, gazing at his loved-ones before going to lay down. That last look was a good-bye, the desire to see those who mattered most before the end—at least that's what his kids remembered thinking.[56] Ilya began to shake violently not long after. His breath soon gave out as a brain hemorrhage took his life. He was 55. (Volodia died of the same cause at nearly the same age.) Authorities—wary of Ilya's progressive educational reforms—had only just forced him into an early retirement, much to the frustration of the loyal public servant.[57]

Ilya's funeral took place the day after his death. A big crowd of well-wishers offered the family comfort. Teachers repeated that there would never be another like Ilya.[58] The local newspaper celebrated the patriarch's contributions to improving local schools, praising him for his "sincere and warm love" and his "truly indefatigable and extraordinarily many-sided activit[ies]" on behalf of provincial education.[59] Others who benefitted from Ilya's hard work said similar things for years to come.[60]

Ilya's death shocked Sasha and Volodia. The brothers had led comfortable, placid lives until then. Their upbringings were largely devoid of the miseries that existence often inflicts on young people. But now, they suffered. The big brother, far away in St. Petersburg, did not even know of his father's death on the day his family buried him. His mother, Maria, remembered that Sasha had an organic chemistry test scheduled for the same day; she refused to send him word until afterwards.[61]

The news blindsided Sasha. Pacing back and forth in his room, he looked "like a wounded animal" as he struggled to make sense of his dad's sudden loss.[62] Yet, in the spirit of Ilya's commitment to education, Sasha gritted his teeth and studied hard. Onward and upwards to the bright future his father had wanted for him. "I have received a gold medal for my biological work on segmented worms," the undergrad wrote his mother just weeks after Ilya went in the ground.

Sasha did not, however, tell his mother about a new interest that was attracting his attention. Away from studies on worms, a place where his parents had long feared he might tread. That's where Sasha was going. Mom had no idea. Neither did Volodia.[63]

◆ ◆ ◆

The younger brother acted out after his father's death. The loss of his dad's authority had removed an impediment to misbehavior, and Volodia's pugnacious response to the ensuing power vacuum spoke to a youth coping with loss that seemed wholly unfair. He was fifteen years old, increasingly caustic towards his mother, peering into manhood while grappling with the death of the most important man in his life. His family stood witness as the young man spouted off truculently, his words a blend of hormonal combativeness and bitter grief.[64] Volodia, big sister Anna recorded, "was in that age of transition when boys are especially rude and aggressive. This became even more apparent in him—who had always been rather rough and self-confident—now that his father was no more....I remember how disturbing to me was Volodia's harshness of behavior."[65] Puberty exacerbated grief. Grief exacerbated puberty.

For the first time, Volodia became more critical of society at large. During long walks with his older sister, he began to speak negatively of his teachers and to reject the existence of God.[66] Though Ilya had required the family to attend church, in his absence Volodia derided religion as a fabrication. At sixteen, he became an atheist—like Sasha.[67] ("Religion," Volodia later wrote in his own play on Marx's words, "is a sort of spiritual booze, in which the slaves of capital drown their human image."[68]) Volodia's skepticism marked a growing rebelliousness—an inclination to reject forcefully what he saw as nonsensical—that threatened to spill over into the public realm. An internal tempest of teenage angst, critical inquiry, and personal loss drove that sea change.[69]

In the summer of 1886, Sasha and Anna returned from St. Petersburg and joined the rest of the family at Kokushkino, the country estate where Maria had grown up. It was the only family reunion after Ilya's death. Sasha buried himself in his studies, spending his days doing the usual experiments on worms—but now also consuming Marx's *Das Kapital*. Volodia, with whom Sasha shared a room at Kokushkino, often rested on a couch nearby, reading Turgenev, expressing little interest in his brother's newfound passion for political economy. Sasha made little effort to engage his brother on the subject.[70] A gulf grew between them.[71] Sasha took umbrage at Volodia's disrespectful attitude towards their mother (going so far as to refuse to play chess with his little brother unless he listened to her).[72] When big sister Anna later asked Sasha's thoughts on Volodia, he was frank: "Undoubtedly a very able person, but we don't get on."[73] The siblings were too different to invite mutual interest in one another. It would take Sasha's death for Volodia to want to *know him*.

◆ ◆ ◆

Ilya's loss marked the end of a sobering influence on both Sasha and Volodia. As the head of household, Ilya had almost never talked politics. Only in 1881, when far-left terrorists assassinated Tsar Alexander II, had the father expressed angry indignation at political radicalism. What thoughtless rogues, what stupid people could have done such a thing? Extremism, the father exclaimed before his kids, would push the country in the wrong direction. Ilya, dressed in full uniform, took his family to a memorial service for the Tsar. Volodia, ten, and Sasha, fourteen, sat in the pews not knowing they would have more in common with the assassins than with their own father.[74]

Ilya's dedication to education, the middle-class upbringing he and Maria provided, would help make his children's ensuing revolutionary "careers" possible. Volodia and Sasha—of course!—were the beneficiaries of everything they would come to despise: so-called "bourgeois education" and "class exploitation." Volodia himself recognized this paradox after becoming a communist dictator. How else could he complete a 1922 questionnaire about his social background with the terse answer: "Nobleman." Dark humor from the man sending hereditary nobles and landlords like his own father (*like himself*) to their deaths as "enemies of the people." No mercy for bloodsuckers.[75]

Thank God Ilya hadn't lived to see it.

CHAPTER EIGHT
BENITO, DAD, AND VICTOR HUGO

ALESSANDRO

"Had I had a different sort of father, I should have become a different sort of man," Benito reflected near the height of his power.[1] Dad was Alessandro. By trade, a blacksmith; in reality, a small-town revolutionary. Born in 1854 in an old village called Predappio, surrounded by hills, Alessandro grew up amid the convulsions of his country's unification. His region, Romagna, was known for its political radicalism—fertile land for the politically cantankerous. Predappio itself, as Benito later put it, was infamous for its "quarrelsome" inhabitants.[2]

Around age 10, Alessandro apprenticed as a blacksmith and attained a basic education. He—like his future son—became an avid reader. Books about the downtrodden (from Victor Hugo's *Les*

Misérables to Emile Zola's works) attracted his attention, a point of maximum significance not so much for Alessandro as Benito. The latter's politicization began with his father's bookcase. In a childhood home snuggled away in the hills of a rural town, Victor Hugo's words encouraged outrage at poverty. Interest followed in the revolutionary means through which one might improve the lives of the poor.[3]

Benito's dad worried deeply about the working poor, about the neglected masses. Radical newspapers calling for action, and the general social unrest in his region, inspired him to embrace an amorphous blend of socialism and anarchism that emerged like shadow demons from the groaning fields of the impoverished poor.[4] By his early twenties, Alessandro had led workers in the streets, organized voters, stared down police blockades, experienced jail, and endured police surveillance. He was no intellectual, but knew men and women who lived in poverty; and the socialist gospel offered redemption—his body of Christ, his GOOD NEWS![5]

Alessandro authored crude articles riddled with bread-and-butter clichés from the socialist political milieu. "It is indeed disheartening!!!"—one piece read:

> Poverty is increasing! For several weeks, throngs of workmen of all ages have been seen passing by here daily on the way to Florence in search of work. Watching these poor pariahs of society who are in a pitiful state, lean, pale, sickly, and poorly dressed, one sees stamped on their faces the distress they have been suffering....Poor humanity![6]

Such articles urged sweeping societal change and (in addition to works by Hugo, as well as Fiorentino and Manzoni) made up Benito's earliest reading materials.[7] Though respected in the region, Alessandro—the so-called "father of Predappio socialism"—never made it to the political big time. His revolutionary career peaked as a town council member and as a deputy mayor.[8]

And then there was Mamma. Mamma Rosa. Poor Rosa. Alessandro's political activism caused her endless irritation. If only her husband dropped politics and focused on his blacksmith's forge—labor that actually turned a profit. Rosa, though probably smarter than Alessandro, was simpler. She had no interest in politics. She was religious (unlike atheist Alessandro), and the providence of the infinite comforted her. Her renowned work as an elementary school teacher provided further fulfilment—and a living for her family. Stability had its perks.[9]

Rosa had met Alessandro in 1877. He was twenty-four, handsome, well-built. "A heavy man with strong, large, fleshy hands," as Benito's ghostwritten English autobiography described him.[10] Rosa, nineteen, was kind and vibrant, her smile camouflaging anxiety.[11] She knew Alessandro was more than a blacksmith. But consider how he pursued her, slipping a note into a student's notebook for her to find, and sending her love letters. Rosa embraced Alessandro in response— choosing him over a rare scholarship at a university in the provincial capital and an offer to teach at a first-rate school. She had fallen in love, and marrying Alessandro meant she would remain a village teacher. Rosa's exasperated parents balked. It took them four years to consent to a wedding. Alessandro ultimately agreed to a Catholic ceremony and pledged to stop his revolutionary activism to gain their approval. (Like many a revolutionary currency, his promises held little value.) The couple married in 1882.[12]

With Alessandro's heart tied to the socialist movement, he never adequately provided for his family. Rosa's humble teaching income barely covered their expenses. Tensions built as Alessandro went away organizing. When home, he worked lackadaisically at the blacksmith forge—and then gave away much of his earnings (like Hugo's Bishop Myriel).

ROSA

Papa even went into debt to give away money he didn't have. (By one account, he had a mistress who also got a cut.)[13] When Rosa's parents died and the couple inherited their property, Alessandro actually sold it and gave away the proceeds.[14] *BUT YOUR OWN FAMILY IS IN NEED!*—Rosa probably exclaimed in response. Dad, as Benito's autobiography put it generously, was "excessively altruistic."[15] Here was a father, Benito would emphasize, who contributed the "treasure" of moral goods—hurrah for the socialist ideal!—rather than material wealth.[16] If only political principles filled hungry bellies.

Alessandro's political activism eventually threatened Rosa's teaching job. Parents withdrew their kids from her classes to avoid associating with the family. And financial difficulties compelled her to take on extra work when she wasn't teaching—spinning flax and toiling at a weaving loom for goods to trade for food. Rosa even begged a government official (unsuccessfully) for a bonus at one point. For love of children will a mother prostrate and humble herself in such a manner.[17]

◆ ◆ ◆

Benito—Rosa and Alessandro's first child—was born on July 29, 1883. Alessandro named him after revolutionaries.[18] Benito didn't talk until past age three, prompting a doctor to tell Rosa (with what proved to be wicked irony) not to worry...he would soon have plenty to say.[19]

The family made a life in a battered three-story building, where authorities moved Rosa's school in 1884. Her classroom, along with the family's living quarters, occupied the second floor, with Benito's sometime-blacksmith shop located downstairs. An outside staircase led to the second floor, and the classroom served as an anteroom to the family's apartment. (Imagine Alessandro passing through Rosa's full classroom as he came and went.) Two rooms—a kitchen and a bedroom—accounted for the family's private space. Benito and a younger brother, Arnaldo (born in 1885), shared a bed in the kitchen, while Rosa and Alessandro shared the bedroom with a little sister, Edvige (born in 1888). Mattresses were "rough cotton shells" packed with corn leaves. Lunch often consisted of vegetable soup while radishes or chicory accounted for dinner. On Sundays, the family ate mutton, boiled into soup for maximum nutrition. Everyone ate. Circumstances could have been far worse—and were for many other families. Regardless, Benito characterized it as a rather "austere and melancholy" home.[20]

◆ ◆ ◆

During cold winters as a boy, Benito gathered with locals in a cowshed and listened to readings of Victor Hugo's *Les Misérables*.[21] Consider his innocence grappling with the profundity of that tale about what happens when the law—when society—lets a vulnerable person slip overboard. The "swell of the abyss" pulls that unfortunate soul away. Stormy waves spit in their face. "Dark depths" suck them downwards. Yet the ship sails on, unwilling to stop in stormy seas. Passengers don't take notice—or don't care—about the individual left to die in oceanic infinity, bobbing up and down, alone, an inconsequential speck, "...part of the abyss, part of the foam." They only have "salty brine" for a final drink as waves toss them around—as if the "water were so much hate." The fallen, *Les Misérables* makes clear, try to keep their head above water, but know they will drown.[22]

Consider how such stories symbolized what Benito saw around him in a time of extreme social inequality. His childhood milieu encouraged concern for those poor souls abandoned by society. And long before a fatuous modality of 140 words made children dumber, Hugo's literary masterpiece inspired kids like Benito to believe they could reject the madness; they did not have to leave the drowning man behind.[23] To master "the imperturbable tempest" that supposedly "obeys the infinite alone," that was the task about which such a child could dream.[24] The tyranny Benito subjected his people to started with revulsion at poverty learned from his father—and Victor Hugo.

◆ ◆ ◆

Childhood was not without its pleasures though. Benito relished his family's bookcase, including Alessandro's love letters to Rosa, which he read mischievously. The boy enjoyed *briscola*, playing that card game in the cowshed in winter, perhaps while listening to Hugo. He also spent lots of time tramping around outside, developing a passion for birds (especially owls). One of his favorite pastimes became hunting for eggs and catching birds to keep as pets.[25] He grew to love music as well, and he later learned to play the trumpet and violin, the latter of which would supposedly prove useful for seducing women.[26]

Young Benito also enjoyed getting into trouble. "An audacious young buccaneer," that's how his mistress's later biography described him. Benito, he himself later admitted, was a "restless brat…a very bold country thief."[27] He was a rascal who relieved rural boredom with mischief. The kid liked fighting, for one thing. He found himself "not displeased," for example, when students at a new school threw rocks at him.[28] With pompous nostalgia, his 1928 autobiography describes his allegedly fearless character amid the raining stones:

> I returned their fire. I was all alone and against many. I was often beaten, but I enjoyed it with that universality of enjoyment with which boys the world around make friendship by battle and arrive at affection through missiles.[29]

Benito's combative spirit demonstrated he was not an easy target. His refusal to back down demanded recognition—or combat.

BENITO

As he grew up, Benito took to stalking around with his younger brother, Arnaldo, and friends—eyes wide-open for trouble. In what seems a typical example, Benito once stole bird-decoys near a local river and evaded capture when the owner gave chase, escaping with his "prey" in hand.[30] When it came to discipline, Alessandro would deliver a "sharp smack over the head" but never spanked Benito in an especially harsh way. Rosa was the real disciplinarian, and her oldest son feared disappointing her.[31]

Predictably, this restive child hated church. He deplored the candles, the incense, the organ. Couldn't abide by them. Couldn't sit through Mass without escaping outside.[32] Dad didn't exactly help matters by urging priests, as he wrote in one newspaper at the time, to "throw the cassock into the purifying flames of progress and put on the honored doublet of the worker."[33] What could Rosa do when her son sought to take after Alessandro?

For sure, Benito was an audacious and edgy kid willing to take chances.[34] His early years reflect gumption, the kind that later made for sweeping political ambitions. Even as a little boy standing before his mother, he supposedly exclaimed: "I shall shake the world."[35] (He "was always arrogant," remembered a cousin frankly.[36]) Benito was a child who believed he was special. In the years that passed, he rarely tired of grandiosely pronouncing his determination to change the world. "Yes, I am obsessed by this wild desire—it consumes my whole being," he later told his mistress-cum-biographer, emphasizing, "I want to make a mark on my era with my will, like a lion with its claw! A mark like this!"....before supposedly scratching the back of a chair with his hand. Typical melodrama.[37]

No accomplishment—no amount of adulation—ever satiated Benito's endless hunger for personal affirmation. The "atmosphere of frustration and envy" in which Benito grew up encouraged as much, as one historian noted.[38] His ideological mentor Angelica Balabanoff (more on her later) described Benito aptly in this regard: "His hatred of oppression was not that impersonal hatred of a system by all revolutionaries. It sprang from his own sense of indignity and frustration, his passion to assert his own ego, and from a determination for personal revenge."[39] Such feelings—along with the early influence of his father and literature—reinforced his desire to do something big in life.

◆ ◆ ◆

Benito's education began at four when Rosa taught him the alphabet. After he learned to read the following year, he continued learning in his mother's classroom until age eight when he moved to a different school (presumably the one where kids threw rocks at him). In 1892, Rosa convinced Alessandro to send Benito to yet another—a Catholic boarding school in the town of Faenza. Monks ran it.[40] The school was expensive, eating up half of Rosa's teaching salary. But she cared deeply about Benito attaining a first-rate education and made it happen.[41]

Benito did not want to go. The night before departing, the frustrated boy got into an argument with a friend and tried to punch him, but hit a brick wall instead. Sobbing, his hand bandaged, Benito left the next morning with his father. The donkey pulling their cart on the roughly twenty-mile journey tripped and fell just as they got underway—a bad omen, observed Dad. Arriving at the boarding school six hours later, Benito cried. Alessandro hugged him and left. The gates closed.[42]

If Rosa hoped the Faenza boarding school would instill discipline in her strong-willed boy, she was mistaken. Benito's experiences there only traumatized him and inspired greater rebellion. The school was strict, reminiscent of the Petit-Picpus Convent in *Les Misérables*. Benito had gone from running loose in the countryside to the control of a monastic order—monks who didn't mess around. With little joy to be had, the religious school was an echo of the "phthisis of civilization" about which Victor Hugo had warned.[43]

◆ ◆ ◆

Strict discipline slapped Benito in the face. The monks watched the students closely from the moment they woke till bedtime. Benito quickly fell into depression, recalling mournfully: "I thought of my parents, my friends, my lost freedom."[44] The school's exacting schedule exacerbated his homesickness, its constancy serving as a reminder of his prior autonomy. Benito remembered it with acerbic humor: rise and shine at 6 AM in the winter; 5 AM in the summer; mandatory mass, forty-five minutes every day ("even before having coffee"); breakfast ("an indecent broth"); study hall from 7:30-8:30; morning classes, each of which started and ended with a prayer; recreation time: 11:30-

12:00; lunch: a main dish, soup, bread (but "no wine"). No talking during meals; only the sound of cutlery on plates and bowls filled the air, along with a designated student reading aloud the Salesian Bulletin.[45]

Meals put class inequities front-and-center. The school organized tables into three groups based on how much parents paid— in other words, the monks divided the kids by socioeconomic class. Benito was in the poorest and largest group, which received the worst food. That slighted his pride, every day.[46] It was unfair, fumed the son of a socialist activist—*for himself* most of all. Anger at class inequality fueled steam engine resentment spinning wildly in his chest, threatening to come apart and hurt those around him.

The rest of the daily schedule consisted of more classes, study hall, and recreation time before dinner at six. A prayer session marked the end of the day. As students readied themselves for bed, the monks demanded silence for another reading of the Salesian bulletin. Most days followed this schedule—except Sundays (when the kids could take a walk) and special holiday events.[47] Though Benito struggled with this new routine, he proved himself a competent student. School records, even as they noted his difficult temperament, indicated as much. He was smart.[48]

◆ ◆ ◆

The teachers tormented Benito. When, for example, his feet swelled from the cold in the winter of 1892, and he asked to use the bathroom reserved for wealthy students (presumably to get warm water to soak his feet), his dorm teacher laughed at him. After Alessandro visited and saw his son limping, he became irate and protested the neglect. The monks, in response, registered that Benito's father was a "people's leader" and heightened supervision of his boy, punishing him for his father's perceived political sins.[49] On another occasion, when Benito wandered off from a group of classmates on a Sunday walk, school officials accused him of trying to run away. (He probably was!) They revoked his recreation time for three months. While other children played in the courtyard, the monks made the boy stand in a corner, forbidden from speaking or moving.

Predictably, Benito resisted like hell, resentment brightening his flaming eyes. In one instance, a priest—a "worthy Christian educator", as Benito recalled bitingly—"violently slapped" his face and knocked him to the ground for keeping a musical beat with his hands during a prayer. Benito, bleeding from his nose and mouth, fought back.[50] The priest in question—"Master Bezzi," as was his title—demanded submission. Benito chose struggle. "Blinded by pain and anger," the young child jumped to his feet and hurled an inkwell at the teacher, narrowly missing him. That almost got him expelled. Instead the monks punished the boy by refusing him the main course at dinner and further revoking his recreation time. Imagine the nine-year-old before an empty plate as everyone ate, stomach groaning, somber fury pulsating.[51]

Bezzi, naturally, became Benito's nemesis. A triangular-face, clad in a thin gray beard, defined the priest's "abominable" visage. He had small, scrutinizing eyes, "monkey hands," and an unctuous voice, giving emphasis to syllables in his pronunciation. He had a shrieking laugh. He was short.

After the inkwell incident, Bezzi had it out for Benito. At the end of that first year, the priest calmly told Benito to come with him so he could return some confiscated books. Instead—at least according to Benito's memory—the priest took the child into a room and produced a cane. Benito screamed as the priest beat him until another adult intervened. Bezzi was a model tyrant.[52]

The trauma reverberated into summer. At home the boy told his horrified father about everything, and his family feared Benito might commit suicide. (His grandmother followed him near the river, worried he would drown himself.) But the warm summer break soon saw the boy hell-raising anew—much to "the despair of his parents, and the worry of his neighbors."[53] When autumn approached, Rosa and Alessandro—for reasons difficult to grasp, no matter how much of a delinquent this kid was—sent Benito back to the boarding school after "much discussion," as their son remembered.

Gravely, Benito went.[54]

◆ ◆ ◆

Fourth-grade hell followed. The place was tougher than ever. The monks punished Benito for God-knows-what in his first weeks back, restarting a cycle of oppression and resistance, tyranny's turbines turning in a battle of wills. The ten-year-old quickly learned to appear contrite when it served him to do so—anything to avoid giving school officials an excuse to mess with him.[55]

That second year, Benito wrestled with religious lectures on the evils of humanity. Hell started beyond the school's walls, according to the monks.[56] Unimaginable villains roamed the larger world. (The kids may have wondered how horrendous the worst of the Lord's creatures were if Bezzi represented the best.)[57] Benito, away from his family again, fell asleep crying at times. Theatrical performances about the bloody sacrifices of Christian martyrs didn't make sleeping any easier.[58]

First Communion only heightened the boy's stress. To prepare their souls to receive the body of Christ, a friar took over shepherding the kids on the path towards salvation, leading them in weeklong instruction and prayer. As the big day approached, the friar chose Christmas Eve (of all nights) to terrify the children. God, he stridently warned, would kill impure souls who received the Eucharist. Instant death! It had happened to a boy in Turin, warned the friar. The boys' only recourse was to embrace the required fasting and *confess everything*, lest the children face a fire-and-brimstone Yahweh who supposedly crushed sinful tots like cockroaches. Benito was horrified. He—*who had no shortage of sins to confess*—believed it all. And fess up he did: sins he had committed, sins he had not—everything. Why take a chance?[59] At the moment of truth, Benito's heart pounded before the Lord the monks compelled him to love out of fear—"the essence of sadomasochism, the essence of abjection, the essence of the master-slave relationship," as Christopher Hitchens once put it.[60] Yet God did not destroy him as he received the Eucharist.

The body of Christ—"now a prisoner in my bowels," recalled Benito—had little effect in quelling his rebellious spirit.[61] The boy soon led a protest with other poor students when they received bread infested with ants. Swift punishment silenced their calls for better food. A short time later, the school finally expelled Benito when he got into a fistfight with another student and stabbed him in the hand with a pocketknife.[62] The wounded student screamed, prompting a teacher to lock Benito in a room and fetch help. The boy had done something terrible. He wept in fear, begging forgiveness, knowing he was in for it. A key turned in the lock—*in walked Bezzi*, bellowing "Your conscience is as black as coal." (Benito never forgot those words.)[63] "You will sleep with the guard dogs tonight!" fumed Bezzi.[64]

Harsh punishment was appropriate. But what followed—based on Benito's own recollection at least—was extreme. Bezzi dragged the boy outside, leaving him to confront the guard dogs if he wanted to get back into the dorms. Intrepidly, and true to form, Benito tried to do just that. He stealthily crossed the courtyard, only to discover that the dorm's iron gates were locked. He shook the gate in frustration until the sound of snarling dogs proved that a terrible error. The terrified ten-year-old clambered up the gate as hounds jumped from below, getting a taste of his trousers—*but not his flesh*. He pulled himself over the top and groaned on the other side.[65] What would have happened if Benito had not made it over in time?

CHAPTER NINE
KLARA'S LOVE FOR ADOLF

ALOIS

The father of the man who would lead Nazi Germany came from complicated circumstances. Born out of wedlock to a forty-two-year-old peasant mother in 1837, Adolf's father, Alois, grew up an illegitimate child. Alois's mother married when he was five, but never revealed the identity of his true father before dying five years later. Thereafter, the brother of Alois's step-father adopted the little boy and raised him as a member of his own family. As a young teenager, Alois trained to be a cobbler in Vienna but ultimately joined the Austrian Civil Service at age eighteen. Less than ten years later, Adolf's father attained a position in the customs service—a respectable career that defined his self-esteem.[1]

And then there was Alois's love life. It was—as one historian put it with spectacular sobriety—"a private life of above average turbulence—at least for a provincial customs officer."[2] By his thirties, Alois, unmarried, had an illegitimate daughter. In 1873, Alois, age thirty-six, married a fifty-year-old sickly woman, Anna. (Town gossip: he bought her a coffin before she had a chance to die.)[3] She was the daughter of a conveniently wealthy inspector. Alois, however, cheated on Anna with the maid, Fanni. In 1880, ailing Anna had enough and left Alois, preferring to die single. Adolf's father then married the maid Fanni, who bore him a son (Alois, Jr.) in 1882 and a daughter (Angela) in 1883. Sometime afterwards, the cliché of sex with the maid struck again when Alois began an affair with a teenage domestic servant named Klara. Fanni—herself a former mistress—suspected as much, and fired Klara right away. Tuberculosis soon intervened though, and Alois brought Klara back to keep house after Fanni sought clean air in the countryside. Alois, true to lascivious form, impregnated Klara as Fanni lay dying. Just months after the latter passed away, Alois married Klara on January 7, 1885 (after receiving permission from the church, since they were technically second cousins).[4] Twenty-three years younger, Klara didn't even call Alois by his first name. She called him "Uncle."[5]

KLARA

Klara started taking care of Alois's two kids (Alois, Jr. and Angela) and having children of her own. ("She was," remembered her doctor, "a simple, modest, kindly woman....tall, had brownish hair which she kept neatly plaited and a long, oval face with beautifully expressive gray-blue eyes.")[6] After giving birth to the child she'd been carrying on her wedding day—her first son, Gustav—she bore Alois a daughter, Ida, in 1886. The next year brought another son, Otto—who died just days after birth. Death came again to the household the following winter, in the form of diphtheria; it took both Gustav and Ida, leaving Klara once again without children of her own.

Then on April 20, 1889, she gave birth to Adolf.

Of another son and daughter, Edmund and Paula, born in 1894 and 1896 respectively, Adolf's mother lost the former (her third son) to a childhood illness at age six. Only Adolf and Paula survived into adulthood.[7] Having suffered so much woe, Klara showered Adolf and his sister with the love that the deaths of their siblings prevented the poor woman from dispensing more widely.[8]

ADOLF

◆ ◆ ◆

Adolf's father, Alois, was "a curmudgeonly, taciturn old man, a smart libertine," as one acquaintance put it.[9] More to the point: Alois was an asshole.[10] Self-righteous and cold, he was to his kids what Adolf would be to an entire country: unfeeling, demanding, merciless. The father's pride about rising from backwater bastard to lower-middle-class civil servant was overbearing.[11] When he retired for health reasons in 1895, he embraced beekeeping and casual drinking. He moved his family to a small village outside of Linz in 1898.[12] His home life revealed a man who disliked retirement and who (despite having sired eight of them!) didn't care for kids.[13] Alois avoided them by hanging out at local taverns. When he returned home, a good buzz apparently did nothing to temper his demands for absolute submission. Violence crushed challenges to his authority.[14] (Adolf's half-brother, Alois, Jr., recalled beatings with a heavy leather whip.[15]) The father, half-sister Angela later stated, hit young Adolf "more than 2 to 3 times a week" when the boy didn't come home after school.[16] Simply put: Alois had no compunction about beating his children, much less the family dog, and he did so more than the "norm" for the time.[17]

Adolf's older half-brother, Alois, Jr., could take no more by age fourteen and fled (assuming Alois didn't throw him out of the house). This left seven-year-old Adolf to square off with his abusive crank of a father. And Dad, lamentably, had lots of free time. Alois, one of Adolf's schoolmates remembered, "demanded total obedience. Frequently he put two fingers in his mouth, let out a piercing whistle, and Adolf, no matter where he may have been, would quickly rush to his father." Alois, the schoolmate continued, "often berated him, and Adolf suffered greatly from his father's harshness."[18] "There were violent scenes," recalled a close friend, "which often ended in the father giving him a good hiding, as Adolf told me himself."[19] It had to have been difficult for the little boy.[20]

Parental tyranny, as it often does, only inspired rebellion, and Adolf defied Alois as he grew up. As sister Paula put it, he started to "challenge...my father to extreme harshness and...got his sound thrashing every day."[21] These words—though unfairly inferring that a child deserved as much—spoke to a struggle of wills. At one point as a boy, as Adolf himself recalled, he tried to run away from home by squeezing through a barred bedroom window. Struggling, he removed his clothes to get through but reversed course when he suddenly heard his father coming up the stairs, jumping back and covering himself with a tablecloth. Alois burst out laughing at the sight, calling for his wife to come check out their "toga boy." It was humiliating for an individual who feared ridicule. Shame reverberated.[22]

Such defeats, if we are to believe Adolf's personal account, did nothing to end his willingness to battle his father. Adolf declared years later, for example, that he eventually put an end to his father's physical abuse by refusing on one occasion to make a sound as Alois beat him. An adventure novel—lauding a refusal to show pain as bravery—supposedly inspired him. Armed with something akin to the image of the stoic Native American being tortured to death while making no sound, Adolf claimed to have "counted silently the blows of the stick which lashed my rear end." Terrified Klara watched from the doorway.[23] Never again did Alois hit him, Adolf insisted.[24] This triumphant account sounds like the memory of an aspiration—not reality. Adolf, remember, was an inveterate liar who favored accounts of the person he imagined himself to be.

Adolf later said his father's violent discipline was "necessary." Dad, he wrote, "had sown the seed for a future which neither he nor I would have grasped at that time."[25] Nor did Adolf express resentment towards Alois. To the contrary, remembered his aforementioned close friend, "Adolf spoke of his father with great respect. I never heard him say anything against him…he respected him more as time went on."[26] Adolf rationalized the actions of his father—the first model of authority in his life—as appropriate.

Adolf's relationship with his mother, Klara, was the opposite of the one he had with his father. ("How often," recalled his sister, "…did my mother caress him and try to obtain with her kindness, where the father could not succeed with harshness!")[27] Klara's doting love was an antidote to Alois's unbending severity. "I respected my father, but I loved my mother," Adolf later emphasized.[28] No doubt, Klara earned her son's admiration. She was a kind and gentle soul who cared immensely for Adolf.[29] Unlike the overbearing Alois, Klara had a calm, loving demeanor.[30] She knew what it meant to grieve—to bury children—but still had the courage to love. She drenched Adolf and Paula with affection, eager to appreciate them as treasures she could still hold. Adolf never forgot as much. Her support helped him find his own path in life.[31]

◆ ◆ ◆

Adolf started primary school (*Volksschule*) at six. He was a bright little boy, and well-behaved.[32] The material was easy for him. Outside of the classroom, he was a normal child, playing "Cowboys and Indians," "Cops and Robbers," war games, and all the classics of romping kids. He spent idyllic summers in the country village where his father was raised.[33]

As Adolf grew up, he took singing lessons and became a choir boy—and apparently had a pretty good voice. The child appreciated the splendor of church festivals. The priesthood even beckoned briefly, as it had to his father before him, and young Adolf shrouded himself in an apron and practiced "long and fervent sermons."[34] (His interest in "things priestly," writes one biographer, "ended as quickly as it began. Before long he was caught smoking."[35] He only begrudgingly became a confirmed Catholic at fifteen.[36]) Within his home, there was little to encourage intellectual curiosity. Adolf later spoke of his father's "library," but his dad never owned much more than an illustrated work on the Franco-Prussian War.[37]

In September 1900, after five years of primary school, Alois and Klara sent eleven-year-old Adolf to school (*Realschule*) in the town of Linz.[38] The transition went terribly. Adolf had to walk an hour each way (more than three miles). Though he enjoyed the time outside, the distance made it hard for him to make friends. His new school was also more challenging, and Adolf proved unwilling to work hard. The boy was immature, lazy, and stubborn. His grades plummeted.[39]

Adolf ended up doing so poorly that he was held back twice and had, on a third occasion, to take a special examination to move to the next grade. He increasingly didn't want to do his homework. His behavior worsened. Tensions mounted with dad.[40] Adolf later tried to distract from his dismal academic performance by claiming he had intentionally done poorly to spite his father. But in reality, Adolf probably didn't have the self-discipline or interest to succeed in school.[41] A French teacher recalled the "lean, pale" young man as "decidedly talented" but with "little control over himself"—a "stubborn...bossy, and quick-tempered" student, someone for whom it was "obviously difficult...to fit into the framework of a school."[42] Adolf—like many other notable historical figures, both laudable and repugnant—did not function well in a tightly constricted educational environment.[43] His willful manias were not well-received.

Adolf's grades boded poorly for him joining the Austrian customs service and following in his father's professional footsteps. He didn't mind though; he *hated* the customs service and civil servants; wanted nothing to do with Alois's profession.[44] Speaking years later, he remembered when his father took him to visit a Linz customs office in the hope of exciting the boy about his career. It didn't go well. Adolf felt "repugnance and hatred" for the office, viewing it as "a government cage" with aging men "crouching on top of one another, as close as monkeys."[45] Again, Adolf *loathed civil servants*. Bringing up the words to him as a young man—much less telling him to pursue such a career—infuriated him. (The role of civil servant, of course, necessitated bureaucratic expertise and patience he didn't have.)

For the rest of his life, Adolf spoke in blistering terms about book-learning, pooh-poohing individuals who did well in school or had higher degrees with the disgust of an anti-intellectual, uninformed and arrogant. "Some children begin their school careers as excellent book-learners," he later said in this vein. "They pass the barrage of examinations brilliantly. In their own eyes, everything is at their feet. What a surprise it is for them when they see a comrade [Adolf?] succeeding who is cleverer than they are, but whom they used to regard as a dunce!"[46]

And then there were Adolf's old teachers. He deplored them. They'd had the right to evaluate his performance and behavior, to hold him accountable and point out that he had to work hard to succeed. Such efforts, a former teacher recalled, frustrated a young man wanting nothing short of submission from his peers.[47] In later decades, Adolf remembered most of his former teachers as "absolute tyrants," with "no sympathy," who sought to transform their students "into erudite apes like themselves." He continued with more self-pity: "If any pupil showed the slightest trace of originality [again, himself?], they persecuted him relentlessly, and the only model pupils whom I ever got to know have all been failures in afterlife."[48]

One of the few teachers whom Adolf saw fit to praise in retrospect was a history teacher named Leopold Pötsch, a staunch German nationalist who gave public speeches on the subject in Linz.

Pötsch's stories of German heroism, Adolf later claimed in his "autobiography," inspired students to no end, including outright crying. As a result of Pötsch's teaching, Adolf's favorite subject became history, and the young man even drew a pencil sketch of the teacher in 1904.[49] (In June 1929, as Adolf's political "career" grew, Pötsch was surprised to find himself mentioned in the former student's book, and reached out for a signed copy.[50]) This teacher alone did not awaken feelings of German nationalism in Adolf—that is a more complex story—but his emphasis on the subject was a signpost of the early influences to which the young man was exposed.[51]

◆ ◆ ◆

All of Adolf's troubles at school diminished in importance after his father died on January 3, 1903. Alois died at 10 AM in a local tavern.[52] His death immediately relieved tensions at home, and the young man probably did not mourn his father's passing too much.[53] Adolf continued to squeak by at school thereafter, but his poor grades eventually compelled his transfer to another school in Steyr, some fifty miles away. His mother was dedicated to his education and came up with the money to board him for the 1904-1905 school year. But Adolf, away from Mom and hating school, did no better.[54]

By September 1905 he'd had enough. After passing a re-sit geometry exam that month, he claimed that he got drunk—supposedly the only time in his life—and used his report card as toilet paper.[55] (A good story, wiping his ass with others' evaluations of him, but likely a falsehood.[56]) Adolf dropped out after the exam, citing a lung ailment, and returned to his mother's embrace in Linz.[57] From then on, Adolf had nothing to do with his former schoolmates. Indeed, when one such acquaintance approached him during a stroll in Linz, sauntering up with a big smile and taking him by the arm and asking how he had been, Adolf recoiled. He made zero effort to be friendly, much less polite. On fire, Adolf replied: "What the devil is that to you?" before shoving the well-wisher aside and walking away.[58]

Free from school, Adolf lived in one of two bedrooms in Klara's apartment. She, little sister Paula, and hunchback aunt Johanna shared the other bedroom and kitchen and did all the cooking and cleaning. Essentially a high school drop-out, the unemployed teenager contributed nothing to his widowed mother's income.[59] To the contrary, he stayed up late at night and slept in as he pleased (a nocturnal habit that persisted into adulthood). He took long walks around town and in surrounding hills. He read newspapers, many of which were decidedly anti-Semitic, and discovered politics.[60] He attended the opera in his finest clothes, his ivory-handled cane along for the ride. He went to the wax museum—browsing the *"For Adults Only"* section—and even saw a risqué film at a "charity benefit" for the Red Cross (which horrified the prudish young man).[61] He took piano lessons after his mother bought him a grand piano, though that didn't last because practicing scales required discipline.[62] He drew and painted. He read Karl May adventure novels. He tried to write poetry. These experiences made up the happiest days of his life, a period "almost like a dream," he later recalled.[63] He had no responsibilities—and loved it.[64]

Klara quietly echoed her late husband's professional aspirations for Adolf, urging him to consider a stable career path, pointing at his father's pipes on display, a memorial to his iron will.[65] But the mother "lacked the strength and energy to put into effect the father's will," remembered Adolf's best friend at the time. "She, who forgave everything, was handicapped in the upbringing of her son by her boundless love for him."[66] Perhaps Adolf's mother—to the contrary—simply had no interest in subjecting her son to repression that had thus far only inspired resistance. Rather than imposing stringent discipline, Klara offered her teenage son autonomy to consider what he might do with his life. She gave him space, and joyful days followed—for a time.[67]

CHAPTER TEN
KEKE SACRIFICES FOR SOSO

BESO

The parents—Keke and Beso—had lost two sons in five years. After Keke became pregnant again, Beso and his mother-in-law traveled to a local monastery; *let this baby live*, they beseeched God, promising to offer a sacrifice in return. The possibility of losing a third child terrified them. Keke and Beso *wanted* a baby, and were eager to do anything they could to see the next one survive.[1]

That child—Soso, the so-called "man of steel"—was born sickly on December 9, 1879.[2] He lived. His earliest years gave Beso and Keke several scares regardless. When he was a toddler, for instance, he suddenly stopped speaking. His anxious parents hurried to the monastery to sacrifice a sheep and have a mass said in his name.[3] (Beso said: "Just let the child survive, and I'll crawl...[to the monastery] on my knees with the child on my shoulders."[4]) A bout of smallpox—

which nearly killed Soso at age six, leaving his face pockmarked—did nothing to alleviate their anxiety.[5] Nor did two carriage accidents in his childhood that left the boy with an odd gait and a bum arm.[6]

Soso's father, Beso, was a descendant of herders and serfs. As a young man, Beso left behind his humble origins by traveling to Tiflis (today's Tbilisi in Georgia) to work in a shoe factory. After learning the trade, he moved to the town of Gori as a cobbler. Along the way, he learned to read and became fluent in several languages (Russian, Armenian, and Azeri). Skilled in his craft, Beso would soon open his own shoe shop—a real accomplishment. This unmarried bachelor was neither dumb nor unattractive. Fresh from the city and stylishly dressed—with a killer mustache to boot—he caught the eyes of young women. He would, it seemed, make a great husband.[7]

Soso's mother, Keke, was also a descendant of serfs. She was a pretty teenager ("chestnut-haired with big eyes") when someone brought it to her attention that Beso was interested in her.[8] Soon, Keke's brother told her the cobbler wanted to marry. "I blushed, tears came to my eyes, and I hung my head in shame," remembered Keke.[9] Her smiling brother spoke highly of Beso in response. "I was not able to refuse," recalled Keke. "In the back of my mind, I was even glad, because my peers had long set their eyes on Beso and dreamed of being his fiancée."[10] The bride-to-be was seventeen.

Beso and Keke married in May 1874 in a big traditional wedding. Despite others' jealousy, the newlyweds were initially very happy. Beso, Keke remembered, was "a good family man."[11] He had a career and attended church. He even got along with his mother-in-law. Moreover, their home always had butter—a point one shouldn't trivialize in any historical period.[12] It was this household into which "very tender and thin" Soso emerged from Keke's womb.[13] He was a cute baby. He mashed beans all over his face. He liked flowers, and got excited when his uncles played instruments for him.[14] He sucked wine off Beso's finger.[15] The boy, by his mother's account, was a blessing who made his parents laugh.[16]

Then alcohol ruined everything. Beso had started drinking after the death of the couple's first son, and did not stop after Soso's birth. Even as Keke took pleasure in raising their new boy, her husband boozed with customers at his shop. (The fact that clients sometimes used wine as currency—and that Beso occasionally did business in a tavern—didn't help.[17]) Beso ignored entreaties for sobriety and became increasingly disrespectful towards Keke and his mother-in-law. Trembling hands soon interfered with his work.[18] The family drifted from home to home, and Soso ultimately lived in nine from age four to fourteen.[19]

Beso soon became violent. He got into brawls. (People called him "Crazy Beso.") He hit his wife amid rumors of infidelity.[20] He beat Soso in merciless drunken rampages. He once slammed the little boy to the floor so hard he urinated blood.[21] On another occasion, the father went to Soso's school, demanding to see him; teachers and fellow pupils concealed the boy and convinced Dad he wasn't there.[22] Beso, recalled a friend of Soso's, abused his son as if he were a dog, "beating him for nothing."[23] The child's misery extended to his concerns for his mother. "My Soso," recalled Keke, "was a very sensitive child. When he heard his father's voice and loud singing, he would immediately cling to me and tell me to hide in a neighbor's house until dad had fallen asleep…"[24]

Both Keke and Soso fought back. The wife, as Soso later told his own daughter, hit her husband when he drank too much.[25] She defended her son as well, leading Beso to strangle her on one occasion while Soso ran for help.[26] The boy once threw a knife at Beso to protect his mother. (Dad gave chase in response, sending frantic Soso fleeing in search of refuge.)[27] Such turmoil plagued Soso's childhood. Keke recalled that Soso became "very worried about his father's behavior; he became reserved and sad. He no longer went out to play with his peers."[28] After Beso and Keke later split up, the mother tried her best to shield the boy from her own misery:

> I have spent many nights crying. [But] I couldn't dare to cry in the daytime when it affected the child. He [Soso] would cling to me and stare at my eyes with a sad expression. He would tell me not to cry or else he would cry, too....I would laugh and kiss him, pretending that there was not a shadow of sorrow in my heart.[29]

Soso in these moments was both a kind child and a victim of his father's substance abuse.

Outside the home, slingshots, rowdy boys, and fistfights offered the kid refuge from such family drama. Soso quickly proved himself a natural-born leader of his own juvenile street gang. Though small, he became known as a tough fighter, particularly good at wrestling. Forged in violence at home, a blow to the nose didn't scare him, and he struggled bitterly against any who challenged him. Fighting came naturally.[30]

SOSO

Beso's behavior, by the way, never completely severed his relationship with Soso. When a storekeeper spread a lie that Beso had failed to pay a debt, eleven-year-old Soso stood up for his dad. The gutsy child convinced the man to reverse course by *threatening to burn down his store.* ("...I was not joking. That's all there was to it," he recalled years later.[31]) Soso also declined to acknowledge his father's abuse at the height of his power years later. He expressed no resentment, telling writer Emil Ludwig: "My parents were uneducated people, but they treated me not badly at all."[32] But this recollection contrasted from that of Soso's childhood friend, Josef Iremashvili. "Through him [Beso]," said Josef, "Soso learned to hate people. The young boy matured far too early to independent thought and observation. Soso hated his father most of all."[33] We can never know the extent to which Beso's behavior affected Soso. Yet one thing is certain: it did nothing to diminish his lifelong misanthropy. And no one (*no one*), the future dictator learned, can withstand interminable beatings.[34]

KEKE

All of this being said, the defining story of Soso's childhood begins and ends with Keke—not Beso. His mother dreamed the boy would make something of his life—that he would become a priest or maybe even a bishop. She beat Soso too, but dedication to her son's education was her most important contribution to his life.[35] That Beso flatly opposed educating Soso was a serious problem in a culture demanding subservience from women; her husband's insistence on the boy joining the shoe trade put her in a difficult spot. Regardless, Keke challenged Beso. The child, already age seven, *had to receive an education*, Keke argued. She would do extra work as a laundress or baker—an idea which Beso also opposed—to make it happen.[36] Having an educated son would be a disaster, warned Beso. The father—as Keke later recalled— "got very upset, saying the child belonged to him." Mom disagreed: "It was I who the child belonged to and I was going to direct his life as I wanted."[37]

After Beso erupted in anger at the news Soso was learning to read, Keke left him. She and Soso moved in with her brothers. With the help of family friends, they got Soso, approaching age nine, into school in September 1888. (It was no easy feat—the school only accepted priests' sons, so she got a friendly priest to lie that Soso was the son of a deacon.)[38] Soso excelled academically until a carriage accident (the second of his life) nearly killed him in January 1890, running over his legs and leaving him unconscious.[39] Soso recovered, but Beso soon intervened and took him to Tiflis.[40] The kid, contended Beso, should stay in the city and learn the shoe trade. Keke—in response—"shook the entire world" to get Soso back, "calling my brothers...godfather...and Soso's teachers for help."[41] She rejected suggestions that she should compromise with Beso, or even reconcile with him.[42] Beso himself ultimately sent her money and promised to quit drinking, pleading for another chance. Why not take Soso out of school to become a cobbler and reunite the family, asked her brothers?

No, said Keke. "Everybody praises him [at school]. How can a mother take such a child out of school?....He must study. As long as I live, I can't betray him. I can't commit this sin."[43] Mom prevailed, and Beso continued on his way—a "victim of wine."[44]

Keke scraped by—struggling for every kopeck—to keep the kid in school. (She even cleaned the place as a side job.)[45] Family and friends provided indispensable assistance—including, most significantly, a local wine-seller named Koba (rumored to be Soso's real dad) who helped with tuition payments. Koba also opened his family's dinner table to the boy, providing a positive male influence in his life.[46] Benefiting from such kind support—not to mention Keke's endless toil—Soso became a star student at the Gori Theological School.[47] "He was," recalled a fellow pupil, "a very capable boy, always coming first in his class....[and] first in all games and recreation."[48] Soso was hardworking and well-behaved, even once voluntarily marking himself late to class. He was personable too, capable of an easy laugh and admired by his peers (especially when he once pointed out a hated teacher's math error!). But books—rather than people—quickly emerged as his real passion. The child became a relentless reader. He was the kind of kid who reads during lunch and sits contentedly with a book during recess.[49]

Keke's determination—along with Soso's sharp intellectual abilities and hard work—eventually enabled the young man to gain acceptance to Tiflis Theological Seminary at age fifteen.[50] Though this entailed onerous expenses, the resourceful mother somehow made it work. The seminary ensured that her son would receive something approaching a college-level education—a remarkable feat considering the family's poverty and the prevailing educational standards of the time.[51] Keke wept when she saw Soso in his seminary uniform, the fruition of so much hard work. When the teenager broke down crying on the way to Tiflis—*what if Dad shows up and tries to make me become a shoemaker?*—Keke declared: "As long as your mom is alive, no one will be able to prevent you from getting an education."[52] This tough woman had ample reason to think her son would make a respectable priest. Her dreams were coming true.

◆ ◆ ◆

Soso, a quiet and shy student in the big city, initially excelled at the seminary. He would spend five years there.[53] He sent his mother weekly letters, promising to rescue her from poverty.[54] Russian priests at the strict institution, however, helped awaken Soso's appreciation for the power of unfettered tyranny. Their use of police-state-like surveillance—and a willingness to send unruly seminarians into a dark cell with little explanation—encouraged rebellion in Soso and his peers.[55] ("In protest against the outrageous regime [of the priests] and the jesuitical methods prevalent at the seminary," recalled Soso, decades later, "I was ready to become, and actually did become, a revolutionary, a believer in Marxism as a really revolutionary teaching.")[56] Illicit books only emboldened him further. They absorbed Soso's imagination as he thought about the world around him more critically. *Life of Jesus* by Renan (which challenges Jesus's divinity); Hugo's *1793*; Dostoevsky's *The Devils*; *What Is to Be Done?* by Chernyshevsky. All of these provocative works, among many others, inflamed the young man's intellect just as he also started to read Marx, Engels, and Plekhanov.[57]

Perhaps Kazbegi's *The Patricide* had the biggest impact on him. That work—about a daring Georgian rebel named Koba (the same name as his aforementioned patron)—told a wild tale about a struggle against Russian oppression. It offered Soso the opportunity to daydream about heroic narratives and a protagonist who embraced struggle over comfort.[58] The character Koba, recalled a friend from the time, became

"Soso's God and gave his life meaning. He wished to become Koba. He called himself 'Koba' and insisted we call him that. His face shone with pride and pleasure when we called him 'Koba.'"[59] Indeed Soso later adopted "Koba" as his revolutionary pseudonym, enabling him to identify with his country's traditions and culture while effectively preaching against them as a Marxist internationalist.[60]

From his third year onwards at the seminary, Soso lost his fear of God. Grew his hair out. Behaved more abrasively towards the priests. Defiance and revolutionary ideas became his pursuit.[61] Keke heard of her son's growing rebellion—"what demon," she wondered, "had inspired him to become a rebel."[62] (The idealistic pursuit of "truth"—the search for *The End of History*!) Worried for her son, Keke rushed to Tiflis to put a stop to his rebellious behavior and help him avoid a reckoning with seminary officials—if not legal authorities. But Soso, age 21 by this point, had abandoned Plato's cave. And he responded with uncharacteristic fury at Keke intervention, demanding she butt out. (He had never treated her with such disrespect before, she recalled in old age.) Keke begged Soso to change course. "Don't ruin me son," she told him, "You're my only child. How can you beat [Tsar] Nicholas [II]? Stop being a rebel. Let this be done by those who have brothers and sisters." Soso embraced the aging woman.[63] Keke pleaded with him to finish his studies. Her son responded with comforting words, wiping away her tears. "Someone has lied to you, mom. Don't you see? I am still in the seminary. I'm not a rebel and I'm not doing anything wrong. If I were a rebel, they would have me put in Metechi Prison."

"It was his first lie," Keke recalled solemnly.[64] A moment when Soso turned his back on everything his mother had worked so hard to give him. Alas, in April 1899 Soso left the seminary, neglecting to show up for examinations the following month. He had only been a year away from completing his studies, and, ironically, his grades had somehow improved over his last year.[65] "The neighbors' whispers [of Soso's rebellion] turned out to be true," Keke remembered.[66]

When Soso soon found himself in Metechi Prison, Keke rushed to try and save him anew. But whom should she run into on the streets of Tiflis? Beso. "He wants to turn the world upside down....It's all your fault," her ex-husband drunkenly raged at her, his fists tightening ominously. "If you hadn't insisted on his education, he would have become an excellent foreman by now."[67]

How those words must have stung, after all she had done.[68] Keke had to have wondered if her son's life would have gone differently under his father's tutelage in a shoe factory.[69] In the midst of her evening prayers, did Keke ever wonder how it could be that Beso— Beso!—had been right all along?

Soso expressed great respect for his mother in the decades that followed. He always said he loved her, but he seldom saw her.[70] Rarely visited. And Keke refused to move to Moscow. She chose, instead, to live like a pauper in a closet-like room in a Tiflis palace, which she only moved into at the insistence of local authorities.

In their last meeting in 1935, Keke asked her son: "Who exactly are you now?" His explanation: "Remember the tsar? Well, I'm like a tsar." "You'd have done better to have become a priest, " replied Keke. Soso enjoyed that reply, found it amusing for years to come. He was, as his daughter recalled, "delighted by her scorn for what he'd accomplished, for the acclaim and the worldly glory."[71]

Keke was one of the first people Soso truly betrayed.

CHAPTER ELEVEN
RENZHI IS A MADDENING CHILD

YICHANG

Renzhi *hated* his father. As the leader of the People's Republic of China years later, he openly said as much. If the old man were still alive, Renzhi (age seventy-five) declared in 1968, he would have him "jet-planed," his head shoved down and his arms pulled back painfully behind him....like arrows about to shoot off in the distance.[1]

The irony behind such animosity is that Renzhi and his father were so similar in temperament. Renzhi's dad—Yichang—was exceedingly demanding of himself and others. He was a hard individual, driven and pugnacious. Renzhi brought him up randomly in later years, recalling beatings at his father's hands. He could, for instance, go from discussing the strength of Maotai cocktails (sixty-five proof) to blurting out that his father was harsh and unkind. (He literally did this in 1971 before the Prime Minister of Japan.)[2] Renzhi's feelings about his father were an iceberg; something larger always remained beneath the surface, obscured from view.[3]

Yichang may have been a bad father, but his life was a small success story. He was born into a debt-ridden family and married by age fifteen to Renzhi's mother Qimei, who was just twelve years old. As a result of his own father's debts, Yichang, a tall and robust man, had to join the army. Not only did he avoid doing any fighting during that time, he also saved enough money to pay back his dad's debts. Following his military service, Renzhi's father worked hard and repurchased his family's land through one successful capitalist venture after another. Then the master of his own crops, Yichang's labor and dedication—and his wife's hard work—allowed him to accumulate capital and purchase more land, eventually raising the family's class status to that of "rich peasants," as Renzhi later admitted. In addition to having a farm capable of producing large quantities of rice, Yichang grew his profits by transporting it—as well as the rice of poor peasants—to city markets where he could mark up the price. His efforts led to a prosperous farm with a large home (including six rooms), part of which Yichang, true to his frugal nature, rented out. Renzhi's father didn't mess around about money any more than he did his facial hair, which he kept tidy. Not a light-hearted man, Yichang.[4]

QIMEI

Renzhi revered his mother, Qimei. She was a medium-sized woman, with sensitive eyes and an empathetic personality, who never raised her voice to Renzhi. On the farm, she took on wide-ranging duties—caring for children, cooking, collecting firewood, spinning thread, and mending clothes.[5] Though Qimei was illiterate, she did not lack self-confidence and actively participated in family exchanges, often quietly engaging her son about the best way to deal with Yichang. Her keen analytical mind caught Renzhi's attention from a young age.[6] "I worshipped my mother," the son remembered fondly. "Wherever my mother went, I would follow."[7] Renzhi loved her.

When it came to understanding the world, Qimei took comfort in Buddhism and urged her son (and husband) to embrace the faith. Those efforts did not leave Renzhi with any lasting respect for religion, but they "clearly imparted...a distinctive ethical stance" rooted in "a desire to correct the problems of the world through action," as one scholar has observed.[8] When a teacher later lectured Renzhi about the need for superior individuals to tackle the world's problems, his mother's Buddhist teachings had already heightened his interest in discussions about one's ethical obligations to others.[9] Renzhi would eventually begin to view the two as interconnected—one could not serve his fellow man if unwilling to pursue personal accomplishment *for the sake of others.*

When Renzhi's mother died at age fifty-three, in 1919, the oldest son wrote a moving oration for her funeral. "The noblest aspect of mother's character"—the grieving young man (twenty-six years old) recorded—"was her impartial love that extended to all, far and near, related or unrelated." She hated injustice and believed in being an ethical person above all else. "The heartrending details of her sufferings," Renzhi continued in sorrow over what she could not achieve during her lifetime, "are too numerous for me to write down," stating further:

> ....She left the world without fulfilling her wishes and completing what she wanted to do. This was her greatest mental anguish....During her illness, she used to hold our hands, heartbroken. She kept calling on us to do good....The radiance of her abundant virtues was so sincere that its effect will last forever. As for her unaccomplished wishes, we pledge to fulfill them....My heart is set and determined.[10]

Qimei's legacy encouraged her son to make something of his life—to be the "superior man" for his people, for her. Renzhi's future, his mother had no way of knowing, would lead to the death of all her other children.[11]

◆ ◆ ◆

Qimei had given birth to Renzhi in 1893, the Year of the Snake. He was a large infant, and the young mother—who had already lost two sons shortly after birth—was initially terrified her breasts would not provide enough milk. Renzhi spent his earliest years with his mother's family in a nearby village. His grandmother and other maternal relatives took a special liking to him.[12] At age eight, he started school, studying with other kids in the home of a local tutor. His father, Yichang, agreed to pay for these studies so his son could help him with accounting and Confucian teachings in the legal system—though he insisted the boy still do manual labor on the farm. Renzhi, as a result, worked on his father's farm early in the morning until school started; in the afternoons, he returned and helped in the fields until dark.[13]

In school, Renzhi proved poor in math but excellent in memorizing Confucian teachings. (He had a sharp memory.) He also fell in love with reading.[14] As the sun went down on his family farm, Renzhi curled up with a book in bed, reading late into the night next to a bean-sized flame from a vegetable oil lamp. He covered his window with a blue cloth so his father, who could not fathom reading for pleasure, did not catch him.[15]

◆ ◆ ◆

Renzhi's determination to rebel against authority began early. On one steamy school day, for instance, Renzhi convinced his classmates to ditch and go swimming. When his fellow students hesitated at a nearby pond's edge, perhaps rethinking their decision, Renzhi dove-in, leading everyone else to join. The boy's galling nerve inspired others (for years to come). When his irate teacher tracked the students down and fumed waterside, Renzhi dismissively told him that Confucius approved of swimming in cold water. This kid was obstreperous and precocious and daring. Not easy to deal with at any age.[16]

Renzhi rebelled against his teachers' use of corporal punishment, running away from school at age ten in protest. Maybe realizing that a whipping would be in store at home, he wandered around for three days, walking in a big circle around his village. When his family—probably freaking out—found him safe, the boy was surprised that his dad did not beat him. To the contrary, Yichang took his son's concerns about school more seriously. Even Renzhi's teacher eased up on him. It was, he remembered years later, "a successful 'strike'"—one of his earliest triumphs. Audacity, the boy learned, was more often rewarded than not. Mettle outweighed restraint. Boldness paid.[17]

Teachers, however, deplored Renzhi's obstinacy. He went through four instructors by age thirteen. Yichang was angry about his son's impudence, but remained focused on (literally) capitalizing on his education, putting the boy to work with account books and an abacus. Renzhi resisted. He resented his father's authoritarian control and frequently hid with a book. Yichang derided him as lazy, asking how he could waste time reading when there was so much to be done on the farm.[18] When the father began to denounce Renzhi as unfilial, the latter used his education as a weapon. Young people, the son declared (in line with Confucian tradition), only had to remain obedient to elders who treated them fairly. Yichang, Renzhi argued, was three times older and should do more farm work than him. Imagine his father's consternation![19]

Tensions came to a head when Yichang denounced his eldest son before guests. Renzhi criticized his father in response, running out of the house and humiliating the head of family in front of visitors. Qimei went after her son, urging him to return, as Dad gave chase too, assuredly threatening swift justice. Renzhi came upon a deep body of water. He threatened to drown himself if his father approached. Tense negotiations ensued. If Renzhi would return and kowtow, Yichang promised, they could forget the incident. Renzhi countered: he would give a one-knee kowtow—but only if his father would not beat him. Good enough. "Thus the war ended," Renzhi remembered, "and from it I learned that when I defended my rights by open rebellion my father relented, but when I remained meek and submissive he only cursed and beat me more."[20] Lessons reaffirmed—weakness brought disaster; struggle created opportunity.[21]

Amid these squabbles with Yichang, Renzhi took lessons to heart from classic Chinese novels like *Water Margin, The Romance of the Three Kingdoms*, and *Journey to the West*. Their stories of heroism captivated him, and he read them repeatedly.[22] *Water Margin*'s emphasis on Robin Hood-esque rebels who holed themselves up in a mountain fortress, willing to fight and die rather than submit, inspired him for years to come (including in the Jinggang Mountains and during the Long March).[23] The book's protagonist, Song Jiang, was not the outlaw authorities considered him; as the book states, he "always assisted those in distress and raised those who had been crushed down by life." In that vein, Song Jiang embodied characteristics that Renzhi's propagandists later imparted to him. Song was "The Welcome Rain" whose "influence was like the falling of rain on parched soil," and Renzhi was "the very red sun that shines most brilliantly in our hearts."[24] *Water Margin* encouraged Renzhi to admire rebels who compelled cruel leaders to change their ways.[25] When he later listened to debates among his friends about what could be done to save their country, Renzhi exclaimed "Imitate the [*Water Margin*] heroes of Liangshanbo!"[26] He fixated on rebels whose personal triumphs became indistinguishable from society's. The hero captivated him.[27]

◆ ◆ ◆

RENZHI

Though Renzhi stopped attending school in his home village at age thirteen, he continued his education on the farm, reading deep into the night and irritating his father.[28] Yichang, demanding his son grow up and embrace responsibility, arranged for him to marry an eighteen-year-old girl the following year. Teenage Renzhi wanted no part of it, but he (and the poor young woman) had no choice. They met on their wedding day. After a traditional ceremony, they were expected to retire to the bedroom to consummate the union. Qimei, as the mother-in-law, would have been tasked with checking the sheets for blood to confirm the new wife's prior virginity. Apparently, however, young Renzhi refused to sleep with his "comely" new wife.[29]

And Renzhi detested arranged marriages from then on. (In his twenties he wrote an article denouncing them as "indirect rape." Parents, he lamented, "indirectly rape their sons and daughters" by forcing them into such unions.[30] This was rich, considering Renzhi's later practice of compelling others to submit to his sexual whims.)

Following Renzhi's wedding in 1907, he fled home to avoid his new wife. Took refuge in the house of a law student for six months.[31] He hid away, reading old novels about heroic rebellions.[32] Amazingly, despite Renzhi's flight and humiliation of his father, Yichang accepted the marriage's failure and eventually agreed to send his son to a new school (Dongshan Higher Primary School) fifteen and a half miles away. The teenager departed—*Water Margin* in tow—for the promises of further education. It was to be an awkward transition.[33]

The gangly kid, clad in a plain jacket and country trousers, speaking in a rural dialect, stood out. Many of his new peers came from affluent families and dressed in fancy uniforms and leather shoes.[34] Renzhi was also up to six years older, and much taller than some of the students. (Several actually mistook him for an intruder—a "savage young bandit"—when he first showed up.)[35] Outside of classes, Renzhi hung around a fish pond, uncomfortable and devoid of friends.[36] Looked down upon for his provinciality, Renzhi "felt spiritually very depressed," as he recalled.[37]

Books offered comfort, and Renzhi read extensively.[38] *Great Heroes of the World* particularly absorbed him. In its pages, he learned about Napoleon, Catherine the Great, George Washington, Jean-Jacques Rousseau, and Abraham Lincoln. Renzhi borrowed the book from a peer (who would regret having lent it to him since it was returned full of pen markings). Reflecting on the plight of his country before the threat of foreign imperialism, Renzhi opened *Great Heroes of the World* and directed the lender to a page noting that George Washington had led his country through eight years of bitter fighting before winning independence. Their nation's struggle might require many more years than that.[39] As Renzhi wrestled with as much, books calling for the reform and modernization of China suggested that his people badly needed a new hero.[40] Who would be its George Washington?[41]

◆ ◆ ◆

Though Renzhi excelled academically and earned the praise of his teachers, the young man lasted less than a year at Dongshan. In the spring of 1911, he left for the much larger city of Changsha to try another school.[42] The provincial, now eighteen-years-old, relished modernity's delights on arrival, standing in awe of paved streets, shops with foreign goods, electric lights, trains, and more. Renzhi had every reason to be thrilled. He remained free of his father's farm and got to continue his education in a modern city.

Revolution intervened in October 1911. Tumult gripped his country as its centuries-old dynasty collapsed. The promise of a new national future gripped almost everyone, including Renzhi. Swept up in the excitement, the young man wrote his first political essay—contradictory and crude—calling for a new government. He then cut off his long braid, which the old regime had required all men to wear, and joined a friend in forcibly removing the braids of others. (Those who proved hesitant, Renzhi proudly stated, were "assaulted...in secret....A total of more than ten falling victim to our shears.")[43] Physicality put to work for aggressive political ends—and not for the last time.

Enthusiasm about the changing political environment soon prompted Renzhi to close his books and join the army.[44] The teenager loved it. He ended up not having to do any fighting and was well-paid, enabling him to buy newspapers, food, and even water from peddlers. (Apparently he couldn't stomach the indignity of toting his own water.) Yet, as always, books won out, and he left the army to resume his education after half a year.[45]

But what type of school would Renzhi now attend? Grappling with as much, he considered diverse career paths. He thought about becoming a police officer, a lawyer, a businessman, a soap-maker, etc.[46] (Maybe in an alternative universe he became a soap-making connoisseur along with Volodia the lawyer, Adolf the artist, Soso the priest, and Benito the elementary school teacher.) It wasn't that simple though. The choice before Renzhi wasn't really about a career. It was about his unceasing drive towards greater self-actualization—about how he could realize, and bring to fruition, the heroic persona that throbbed inside him. No, Renzhi would not have lasted long as a soap-maker. That wasn't who he imagined himself to be.

Renzhi ended up spending a wholly unnecessary amount of money on registration fees for different institutions and studying at a local high school for another half year before deciding to study on his own.[47] (Dad, who generously supplied money for Renzhi to apply to at least five schools, was not pleased.) The young man eventually hit the stacks of Hunan Provincial Library, his self-education becoming all-consuming. Like an ox galloping into the vegetable garden to devour everything (as Renzhi later put it), he gulped it all down.[48]

The library was on the first floor of a building on a high hill in Changsha and had wide-ranging offerings, including translated books from abroad. Every morning, Renzhi—tall, dressed simply—stood outside, in good weather and bad, waiting for the library to open. He was free to lose himself in books about charismatic leaders and glorious exploits. How did Renzhi make sense of such works in the context of his own time and place and hopes and dreams and fears? Was it study as self-internalization? The "great man of history" myth as a self-fulfilling-prophecy?[49]

Yet Renzhi's self-study consisted of far more than reading about Napoleon and the like. His time in the library was about *The Wealth of Nations*; *The Origin of Species*; *Evolution and Ethics*; *System of Logic*; *The Study of Sociology*; *The Spirit of the Laws*. He supposedly drew up categories for systematic study—classics, history, philosophy, *belles-lettres*, you name it. Ancient Greece and Rome were in the house. So were works of poetry and romance. He conquered the essential books of his country's remarkable culture while trying to read as many translated works from abroad as possible. In the process, Renzhi pored over a world map on the wall, geographically placing the diverse historical events about which he read.[50] At lunch, he would break to consume a couple rice cakes before going back and reading until closing time. The teenager did nothing else for six months.[51]

Not all was perfect. Amid these library exploits, Renzhi lived in a guild house with outspoken students and crusty veterans. Arguments escalated between the two until, one night, they erupted into outright violence. The ex-soldiers mercilessly attacked their book-bearing counterparts. Renzhi hid in the bathroom to avoid getting hurt.[52] Picture the future dictator trembling with fear, asking himself if this was how it was going to end—*in the shitter?*

Renzhi's father was not happy about any of this. Yichang had been giving his ungrateful son money to live in the big city and study, but he was done. No further funds were forthcoming. Time to find a career. Renzhi understood, and soon came across an advertisement for a teacher training school—the First Normal School. It stated: "Tuition and Board Free. Educational Work After Graduation. Education Lays the Foundation of a Country."[53] Emi Xiao, a friend whom Renzhi met at Dongshan Primary School (and the younger brother of later close friend Xiaoyu), encouraged him to apply.[54] Renzhi did so successfully. Starting in the spring of 1913, he attended First Normal School for five years. The twenty-year-old had finally found a tolerable career path.[55]

Unlike his earlier experience in Dongshan, his new school peers largely accepted him. He was well-liked. He did poorly in subjects for which he did not care, but intensively studied what he found interesting and continued his habit of reading late into the night. He began to obsess over his country's history and philosophy, taking extensive notes and filling the margins of books with reflections.[56] He also improved his writing after a teacher mocked his flat style. Nicknamed "Yuan The Big Beard," that instructor taught him how to write a formal essay in the traditional style. ("I can still turn out a passable Classical essay if required," Renzhi reflected with pride years later.[57])

There were other impressive teachers. One named Xu Teli had participated in the 1911 Revolution and pushed for a new constitution, cutting off his own finger and writing a petition in blood demanding as much. Renzhi all but kowtowed to him on a daily basis. Such teachers were a model of sincerity. They encouraged sobriety and seriousness in students like Renzhi, especially when it came to discussing the challenges endangering their nation. From such instructors, Renzhi learned how to write and think in a disciplined manner—indispensable skills for the struggle to come.[58]

CHAPTER TWELVE
SONG-JU'S CHRISTIAN CLAN

HYONG-JIK

Born on April 15, 1912—the day the *Titanic* sank—Song-ju was a "dragon from an ordinary well."[1] Two years before his birth, Korea had lost its independence to Japan, and he grew up a child of a colony. "The waves of modern history that spelled the ruin of Korea," his ghost-writers state, "swept mercilessly into our house."[2] Like so many millions suffering the ravages of colonialism, Song-ju's family struggled in poverty. They resisted foreign oppression when they could, while also trying not to starve. Times were tough.

Kim's father, Hyong-jik, was born in 1894 to a family of farmers and grave-keepers. They lived in a beautiful spot near the Taedong River called Mangyongdae, where they tended to ancestral burial sites.[3] Song-ju spent his first years there, just outside Pyongyang. (Today his "childhood home" serves as a shrine—bright with fresh paint—where immaculately dressed, precious kids "spontaneously" materialize and sing songs for tourists.[4]) Hyong-jik was born with little social mobility, but married well, at age fifteen, and managed to climb the social ladder slightly. His bride was seventeen-year-old Pan-sok, the daughter of a leading member of a Christian church.[5] The bride's family was not exactly pleased about the union (with a family of grave-keepers!), but the groom, Hyong-jik, was at least Christian.[6]

The marriage enabled Song-ju's father to attend a five-year secondary school in Pyongyang called Sungsil Academy, an institution founded by American Protestant missionaries to train teachers and spread the Christian faith. Pan-sok's family likely helped him gain admission. Hyong-jik received a Western-style education at the school.[7] While Song-ju's scribblers later claimed his dad and other students at the institution "strenuously fought against the American missionary gangs," no records indicate that he and his peers were anything but normal students.[8] Another focus for Hyong-jik at Sungsil Academy—we are supposed to believe—was struggling against the Japanese.[9] He allegedly started a reading group at the school to promote patriotism before traveling to nearby provinces to organize against the Japanese occupation. That seems like a stretch, but a peer from the school—who went on to become a leading member of the Korean Presbyterian Church—did remember Hyong-jik as "zealous for the liberation and revival of the nation."[10] Unquestionably, Song-ju's dad deplored Japanese colonialism.

In that regard, Hyong-jik became involved in 1917 with a nationalist anti-Japanese organization (after leaving Sungsil Academy in 1913, without graduating).[11] The group recruited Hyong-jik, an elementary school teacher at the time, while drawing on the Christian community for support.[12] A Japanese police report corroborates his participation and records that—in a classic display of cool-and-tough revolutionary zeal—Hyong-jik joined peers in writing pro-independence posters with their own blood.[13] Japanese police intervened before long, arresting the group's twenty-odd members in early 1918. Hyong-jik, with three young boys and a wife at home, was in serious trouble.[14] Local Christians, Song-ju's memoirs claim, gathered at Hyong-jik's school each morning to pray for his release. He supposedly served an unpleasant stint in prison.[15]

◆ ◆ ◆

PAN-SOK

A word on Pan-sok (Song-ju's mom) and Christianity. For starters: she was born into a fervently Presbyterian family. (Her father's cousin was a church minister who, despite his religious faith, later became a leading member of Song-ju's communist regime.[16]) She was a passionate Christian. Her name actually derived from "rock" in Matthew 16:18, as in "on this rock I will build my church."[17] Pan-sok, as a future reverend remembered her, attended daybreak church services and participated in Bible study gatherings and revivals. Her family's life was intertwined with the church.[18]

Even Song-ju's memoirs admit (begrudgingly) that his parents attended church services. Yet his mother—we are to believe—only did so to catch a break from domestic drudgeries. The son supposedly shook her awake at the end of church services.[19] ("Mother, do you go to church because you believe in God," Song-ju allegedly asked. Pan-sok: "I do not go to church out of some belief [*sic*]. What is the use of going to 'Heaven' after death? Frankly, I go to church to relax [*sic*]."[20]) But such fabrications aren't the point here. It's that Song-ju's mother was so devout that her son—a communist dictator—admitted her involvement in church. His regime would lie about the most nonsensical of things, but Song-ju acknowledged a fleeting glimpse of reality when it came to his mother's Christian faith.

Song-ju's father (the son's memoirs tell us) was an atheist who had participated in church services only as a cover for revolutionary activities. "There is nothing in church," he supposedly told his son. "You must believe in your own country and in your own people, rather than in Jesus Christ."[21] (Conceding his father's involvement in church, again, hints that there was probably more to the story.) Hyong-jik, when he attended services, apparently taught churchgoers to sing the gospel of revolution and encouraged resistance to Japan. Dad jammed on the organ during services and taught Song-ju to do the same.[22] (Decades later, when U.S. forces captured Song-ju's bunker in Pyongyang, they found an organ—along with "gaudy rugs" and busts of himself and Stalin. As horrific air-raids leveled the city, did Hyong-jik's son take pleasure playing the instrument, reveling in memories of his childhood?[23])

Song-ju, for his part, didn't admit to embracing Christianity in his youth beyond a brief flirtation. "At first," Song-ju's memoirs concede in this regard:

I, too was interested in the church and sometimes went...with my friends. But I became tired of the tedious religious ceremony and the monotonous preaching of the minister, so I seldom went to church....Some miserable people thought they would go to 'Heaven' after death if they believed in Jesus Christ.[24]

Those "miserable people" were, of course, his own family—folks in pursuit of providential relief from the harsh difficulties of poverty and imperialism. Song-ju's parents raised him Christian. (At the height of his power in 1981, by the way, he actually asked a foreign guest from his early days to say grace at lunch. Then the dictator himself said *amen*. Delicious irony.[25])

Despite efforts to play down his religious upbringing, Song-ju's memoirs remember the Christian community of his youth fondly. "I received a great deal of humanitarian assistance from Christians....I do not think the spirit of Christianity that preaches universal peace and harmony contradicts my idea advocating an independent life for man."[26] From Song-ju's perspective, however, that faith had a major flaw: it might make believers soft. How could Christians "turn the other cheek"?[27] Song-ju's struggle for national liberation against merciless enemies would not countenance as much.

On the other hand, zealous Christianity provided Song-ju an excellent example of how to run a totalitarian state. His regime's cult of personality would reflect striking parallels to fanatical religious sects, relentlessly indoctrinating people in his image, demanding they embrace his absolute truth...or be struck down. Song-ju, following the lead of ex-seminary student Soso, would become a jealous god who understood the power of faith-based dogma over devoted followers. He would compel his people to study his works like bible verses, fostering cultish loyalty by deadening minds with propaganda. He would punish heretics with fire-and-brimstone consequences.[28] What wonders this would work in maintaining power as his people screamed fanatical praise with *conviction*, loving him—the faith real for many—*believing* he held up five fingers when there were clearly only four. "Working for the church while your family dies. Singing Hallelujah with the fear in your heart"—that's how it would be for his people.[29]

◆ ◆ ◆

After Hyong-jik's release from prison, police kept close tabs on his family. Eager to avoid prying eyes and desperate for opportunity, Song-ju's clan soon packed for Manchuria. Through the mountains, to the wildlands of the north, rugged in more ways than one, they went. The despot-to-be was nine. Across the border, his dad gave up teaching and sought to make a living as a doctor of natural medicine. Kindness, rather than skills or qualifications, made him popular among his countrymen.[30] Although Hyong-jik supposedly remained involved in the movement to resist Japan, the only significant thing he did along those lines was inadvertent: he sent Song-ju to a Chinese school. There, the son learned to speak Mandarin, which proved extremely important in years to come—far more significant for his country's fate than any anti-Japanese organizing his dad ever did.[31]

After two years abroad, Hyong-jik decided to send Song-ju home to live with his maternal grandparents—to get to know his own country and witness the misery of his people under foreign rule, as Song-ju's memoirs put it.[32] According to the official mythology, his parents sent their eleven-year-old on the 250-mile journey *alone*. The boy went back across the Yalu River and down the northern half of the peninsula, traversing mountains and braving snowstorms, all by his lonesome (or at least that's what Song-ju's memoirs want us to believe). His father set safeguards of course—plotting the journey for the boy, telling him where to stop, sending word to friends of his impending arrival, and asking for updates via telegraph.[33]

If this journey actually happened, it was surely a difficult but rewarding adventure. The eleven-year-old, his memoirs explain, crossed mountains, rode a train, and met friendly farmers, one of whom provided a lift on an ox-pulled sleigh and gave him toffee.[34] And in March 1923, the story continues, Song-ju arrived at Mangyongdae before flabbergasted grandparents, his grandmother remarking that Hyong-jik was "more hard-hearted than a tiger" for sending him alone.[35]

◆◆◆

The boy found hard times in the motherland. His grandparents' food consisted of various types of gruel. The Japanese had recently arrested his maternal uncle—who would die in prison—and authorities still watched the family closely.[36] Song-ju's country quivered under foreign rule. Poverty reigned.[37] Not only small villages like Mangyongdae suffered privation, but Pyongyang as well, with many living in slums with straw-mat doors and boards for roofs. Song-ju blamed his country's colonial overlords. Animosity towards imperialism took hold as he supposedly started to envision a better future for his people. Song-ju studied in Pyongyang for over two years before returning to his family in Manchuria.[38]

In the spring of 1926, Hyong-jik became ill. The end was suddenly nigh for dad. Song-ju's ghost-writers describe his coming loss eloquently: "Spring was bringing a rich lifeblood to everything alive on Earth and everything was singing of the new season. But alas, this could not restore my father's health."[39] Hyong-jik died on June 5, 1926, leaving Song-ju, now age fourteen, without a father—or a country. Song-ju's memoirs say he wept by a river and stared in the distance towards his homeland.[40]

◆◆◆

SONG-JU

After completing elementary school, Song-ju's education continued in the Manchurian towns of Huadian and Jilin. By January 1927, his memoirs insist, he became involved in revolutionary politics for the first time, a primer on socialism and a biography of Lenin piquing his interest.[41] The seventeen-year-old supposedly began to read voraciously at a local library, the currency of ideas providing sustenance.[42] We are to believe he absorbed Marx, Gorky, Lu Xun, and diverse Chinese classics.[43] (Who knows whether all of this is true—if, for instance, needed translations of *Das Kapital* were even available, or whether a teenager without a high-school education could have digested such texts.[44]) But perhaps Song-ju embraced the library and engaged in self-study. Books would have distracted from the hardships of life, offering him answers about the world.[45] (We know he enjoyed reading Chinese classics in old age.[46]) The path to revolution began in the library for so many others.

Song-ju then attended Yuwen Middle School in Jilin. His family remained poor, unable to buy him shoes. But his "infirm" mother worked around the clock for his school fees and dressed him in a "neat and tidy school uniform."[47] Class differences in the community, Song-ju's memoirs claim, led him to resent social inequality. The teenager supposedly started to wonder why haves and have-nots exist; why some ride in rickshaws and others pull them; why few reside in huge houses while so many exist on the streets.[48] His young father freshly buried, his family struggling to pay his tuition—the shoeless teenager had reason to feel bitter about as much. Adolescents the world-over have brooded about less.

Song-ju's experiences at the middle school in Jilin helped push him towards revolutionary action.[49] Beginning in 1928, a literature teacher named Shang Yue, a supporter of the Chinese Communist Party and later a prominent historian, particularly influenced the young man.[50] Shang, as the teacher himself recalled in 1955, "used the classroom to talk about the problems of imperialist aggression," inspiring students like Song-ju with exemplary stories about revolutionary heroes.[51] "The examples that most interested those heroic young children," the teacher wrote:

> were the snippets I knew about Lenin and Gorky's difficult, revolutionary struggles. For instance, [when I told the students about] how Lenin in prison wrote with milk to direct the comrades outside to struggle against the Tsar, and the great events where Lenin struggled to build a prosperous society of Socialism and Communism, those teenage children, especially [Song-ju], expressed insuppressible happiness from their hearts. Some said, 'We need to learn from Lenin.' Some said, 'Let's go to the Soviet Union.' But [Song-ju] was silent. I asked him, 'Don't you like [the idea of] going to the Soviet Union?' his answer was, 'I really want to go to study in the Soviet Union, but we can't build a socialist society here unless we drive off the Japanese devils' imperialism. The most important thing today is to drive off the Japanese devils.[52]

In this classroom, Song-ju's desire to fight Japan intersected with his budding enthusiasm for Marxist ends.

Song-ju became one of Shang Yue's favorite pupils.[53] The teacher offered him (and his students in general) long feedback on papers, pushing progressive ideas and criticizing "incorrect thoughts."[54] Song-ju, the teacher recalled, wrote essays condemning the oppression of his people and extolling heroes of his country's past.[55] Shang Yue supposedly allowed the future dictator to borrow *Dream of the Red Chamber* as well as Gorky's *Mother*, and suggested he become a proletarian writer.[56] Though some "reactionary" Chinese teachers gave the teenager a hard time, Shang Yue remembered that Song-ju got along well with political and non-political students alike, from both his homeland and China, demonstrating an early talent for "uniting the masses."[57] Shang Yue only wished he had helped the young man more.[58] The passionate teacher made a lasting impression on Song-ju.[59] Decades later, as a dictator, he still inquired about his teacher's well-being.[60]

Song-ju's grandfather, however, was supposedly appalled when Shang Yue invited his grandson, along with other favored students, to visit his home.[61] A teacher—the grandfather informed the teenager—"must give his pupils the firm belief that their teacher neither eats nor urinates; only then can he maintain his authority at school...a teacher should set up a screen and live behind it." If students caught sight of their teacher's private life, the old man warned, they would inevitably lose their awe of him.[62]

This anecdote provides insights into Song-ju's future rule. As the supreme leader of his country, he would not allow his people to believe he was ordinary in anyway; he would have to appear omnipotent and all-knowing—godlike. Many, as a result, could not imagine their brilliant, iron-willed commander pissing or shitting; including his name in the same sentence as those crude words could result in the direst consequences. "He was our father's father and our mother's father," a defector later reflected. "He was an invincible warrior....He could travel for days without resting. He could appear simultaneously in the east and in the west. In his presence flowers bloomed and snow melted."[63] Later in life, when Song-ju developed a baseball-size tumor on the back of his neck, photographers would not include it in photos; the broader public could not know of such personal defects; evidence of physical mortality didn't jibe with Song-ju's superhuman mythology. Too close of interactions with one's "pupils"—obviously!—could only undermine their faith. Better to live lavishly behind the Oz-like screen. Yes, Song-ju ultimately agreed with his grandfather.

◆ ◆ ◆

The teacher Shang Yue proved too radical for Yuwen Middle School, and officials fired him after six months. Song-ju himself did not last much longer once revolutionary politics opened his eyes and ears. He began attending lectures—actively considering ongoing ideological debates—and became close to the family of Methodist minister Rev. Sohn Jong-do, a fellow expatriate who had known his father. The Sohn family provided Song-ju with money for school expenses and a boarding room in their church. The young man also found a seat at their dinner table on holidays, where he ate bean curd and rabbit stew gratefully. Before long Song-ju took part in political and social events at their church, his early religious faith becoming more intertwined with radical nationalist feelings.[64] Armed with a quick grin, he started to have a lot to say. He stood out.[65]

Yuwen Middle School expelled Song-ju in May 1929 after he joined an organization of nationalists and communists. The intense vigilance of local police, emphatically opposed to communism, uncovered the group after only two meetings.[66] Song-ju ended up in jail. Authorities, he later claimed, abused him with "finger-breaking torture"—which seems almost benign compared to what his future regime would do to repatriated defectors (including newborn babies of women who had returned pregnant).[67] Song-ju spent several winter months in an unheated cell; he remembered it in old age as "unbearably musty." (A thought that makes one wonder what he, as a young man, would have had to say about North Korea's Yodok Concentration Camp.[68]) Fortunately for him, Song-ju's jailers did not repatriate him to Japanese authorities, who would have imprisoned him further or killed him. (If only North Korean defectors arrested in China today could be so lucky.)

Song-ju served seven and a half months in prison while Rev. Sohn's family did what they could to help him.[69] The teenager supposedly spent that time thinking about what to do when released, how he might work in a more aggressive manner against the Japanese—planning "the future of the...revolution," as his memoirs recall bombastically.

In reality, Song-ju was a nobody emboldened by his own insignificance, increasingly determined to *do something*. So much had already been taken from him as the offspring of "an unfortunate, ruined nation"—a fatherless son without a country, primed by poverty and imperialism to take action against a larger enemy. He was an ideal candidate to pick up a gun.[70]

PART THREE

STRUGGLE

"It is one of the mysteries of our nature that a man, all unprepared, can receive a thunderstroke like that and live. There is but one reasonable explanation of it. The intellect is stunned by the shock and but gropingly gathers the meaning of the words. The power to realize their full import is mercifully wanting. The mind has a dumb sense of vast loss—that is all…"

- Samuel L. Clemens

CHAPTER THIRTEEN
TRAGEDY STRIKES VOLODIA'S FAMILY

SASHA

While kids have long gone off to college and returned Marxists, few become terrorists. Sasha was an exception. It was not easy for Volodia's older brother to come to believe that bloodshed was the answer to his country's problems. But once he "entered on this road"—as one writer put it—he "travel[ed]...it with conviction, honestly, directly, and to the end, knowing full well that it would lead to the gallows."[1] The striking pace of Sasha's radicalization remains a testament to the power of newfound ideological convictions to transform one's worldview and compel them to take previously unthinkable actions.

It probably started before college. It's impossible to know what the older brother thought when he sat in a church pew at age fourteen watching the memorial service for slain Tsar Alexander II. But he stood witness that day to a revolutionary rejection of everything his father represented. There were citizens in his country, he learned, who pursued radical change through violence.[2] In the two years that followed, Sasha and big sister Anna read taboo works by social critic Dmitry Pisarev.[3] In doing so, they came across Pisarev's article "The Thinking Proletariat" about Nikolai Chernyshevsky's *What Is to Be Done?*[4] That article said "new people" would lead the way to a better world. Scientific notions of progress would drive such individuals, and there would be no contradiction between their thoughts and actions. "New men don't sin and don't repent," Pisarev wrote of this champion for a better society. Such individuals reflect deeply on the greater good's needs, and then take decisive action.[5] The article spoke glowingly of a revolutionary character from *What Is to Be Done?* called Rakhmetov. That character, Sasha learned, was disciplined and unyielding in advancing his cause. He ate raw beef ("to build physical strength") and slept on a bed of nails to toughen himself up for arrest and torture.[6]

Volodia's older brother went on to read *What Is to Be Done?*— an important step for him towards the scaffold. Chernyshevsky's coded language encouraged the conviction that "new people" [revolutionaries] would scientifically transform the world [through socialism]; gender equality would reign; men and women would live in perfect harmony, working together communally to create paradise.[7] At some point, Sasha began to ponder if he had a moral obligation to be one of these "new people," if he could be like Rakhmetov and dedicate himself completely to the cause of humanity's betterment. Perhaps he even started to wonder whether his father was wrong about politics. *Was silence complicity? Was a lack of action guilt?*

◆ ◆ ◆

Months before Ilya passed away, Sasha began to devour books by Marx and Plekhanov in St. Petersburg.[8] He also started participating in university study groups that provided a setting for students to exchange ideas beyond their formal studies. One of these groups brought Sasha into contact with a student named Petr, who—unbeknownst to Sasha—hoped to carry on the activities of a terrorist organization ("the People's Will") that had assassinated Tsar Alexander II in 1881. Petr sought comrades for murder.[9]

Sasha increased his participation in these study groups after Ilya's death. Most notably, he joined an economics group, studying political economy with the same rigor he brought to his work on worms. Marx's systematic analysis of social and economic contradictions—his emphasis on "scientific outcomes"—appealed to him.[10] Sasha walked his subsequent path to conspiracy as a focused autodidact, not as a wild-eyed zealot. Remember, this was an intelligent young man.[11]

Sasha's shift to outright radicalism came after a student demonstration in St. Petersburg in November 1886. He, and up to a thousand other students, gathered in the heart of the capital to commemorate the death of a sharp critic of the country's political system, Nikolay Dobrolyubov. On a cloudy, rainy, chilly day, the students tried to hold a ceremony at the writer's grave. Police blocked the cemetery's entrance: Disperse, they commanded. Hundreds of students, Sasha and Anna included, refused. They roared instead. Held hands in solidarity. Fired political slogans at police like artillery shells. Sasha fumed when a police chief confronted the students and a mounted officer hit one of his friends with a rifle butt. The authorities' aggressiveness stunned him. His countrymen, he realized, could not even hold a demonstration without risking harsh punishment.[12]

Nor could they use the written word to express their discontent. Sasha discovered as much when he and a small circle of students drafted a declaration denouncing the police and then sent it to potential sympathizers around the capital. The students naively used mailboxes near their university, which wide-eyed government censors often monitored. Police intercepted the offending letters, of course, and Sasha's options in the struggle for a new future suddenly seemed like submission to tyranny—or extreme action. Then his friend Petr brought up a new plan: Why not use terror?[13]

Petr told Volodia's older brother and a fellow student named Orest about a conspiracy to overthrow the government—and kill Tsar Alexander III. Sasha was uncomfortable. He opposed violence. Besides, the socialist transformation they sought to foster required greater study before taking action. Petr disagreed. So did Orest. No more studying, no more theory. Oppression compelled decisive action. Time to act.

So Ilya and Maria's son made a fateful choice. The son decided to bring on a transformation through terror that was bold and daring and would perhaps force even his father to admit from beyond the grave that circumstances had demanded rebellion after all. *Sasha was in.*

But did he consider what his actions might mean for Volodia?[14]

◆ ◆ ◆

In January 1887, Sasha joined Petr, Orest, and some twelve other conspirators, most of them students, in planning the assassination. They would kill Alexander III on March 1, 1887—the sixth anniversary of his father's assassination. The group fancied themselves a "terrorist faction." But they were amateurs, throwing away their lives for a conspiracy that, even if successful, was hardly going to lead to the government's collapse. The prior murder of Alexander II had accomplished nothing—except inviting greater repression. Ill-conceived ideological convictions drove Petr, Orest, and Sasha towards terror. That their planned attack—throwing bombs loaded with strychnine-laced shrapnel in a busy square—would murder innocents did not deter them.[15]

But Sasha's co-conspirators were careless. Petr brought too many people into the plot, undermining its secrecy, even as Sasha urged greater caution. Yet Sasha did not walk away. He deepened his involvement. He wrote the group's manifesto. He even pawned his gold medal from the university—literally selling out his father's dreams—for cash to buy nitric acid and guns. Sasha then used his scientific know-how, born in the makeshift labs of his childhood, to help build bombs.[16]

Reality intervened. In February, police censors stumbled upon a letter written by one of the conspirators. It read: "What's possible is the most merciless terror, and I firmly believe that it will actually happen in the near future."[17] That was worth investigating. Police arrested the addressee, who gave up the sender's identity and address. Surveillance of the conspirators followed. On March 1—the very day of the planned assassination!—police took a number of the conspirators into custody without realizing they were armed with pistols and bombs. *They had been on their way to kill Alexander III.* Authorities found out when one of the assassins tried (unsuccessfully) to detonate a bomb disguised as a book in the police station. The plot unraveled.[18]

Police quickly arrested Sasha. Big sister Anna was apprehended too. (Sasha had hidden the plot from her; she had no idea what was going on.[19]) Petr and Orest were nowhere to be found. They had fled before the big day. Authorities ultimately caught Petr hundreds of miles away—though Orest escaped abroad. In custody, Sasha took complete responsibility. "The idea of forming a terrorist group belongs to me," he stated. "I took part most actively in its organization…getting money, recruiting people, finding apartments, etc.…I did everything possible insofar as my abilities and strength and knowledge and convictions permitted." ("This sincerity is actually touching…," Tsar Alexander III said sarcastically after reading the case file.)[20] Sasha showed no contrition. He was eager to prove the courage of his convictions.

Ready for the noose.

◆ ◆ ◆

"This is serious," remarked sixteen-year-old Volodia upon reading the letter announcing his big brother's arrest. "It may end badly for Sasha."[21] Horror seized his mother, Maria, when she heard. She immediately tried to depart for St. Petersburg—to save her children—but discovered her family name had become toxic overnight. No one in town would accompany her on the hundred-mile sleigh trip to the nearest railroad station. She was no longer the mom of a star student. *Her boy was a terrorist.* And everyone knew it. Volodia never forgot how quickly friends and neighbors turned on his family.[22] The younger brother realized how much he did not understand about the vortex of societal tensions that swept them up. He never viewed the world in the same light again. Innocence ended. Adulthood started.[23]

After Maria reached St. Petersburg, she spent a month going to police headquarters, pleading to see her kids.[24] Authorities allowed her to see Anna—but not Sasha. Desperate, she appealed to the Tsar and begged for her children's lives. Mull Maria's misery:

> The grief and despair of a mother give me the boldness to turn to Your Majesty as my only defense and help. I ask for mercy, Your Majesty: mercy and charity for my children. My oldest son, Alexander [Sasha], who was graduated from the gymnasium with the gold medal, also received a gold medal at the university. My daughter, Anna, studied successfully as a student in the Courses of Higher Education for Women in St. Petersburg. And now...I all of a sudden no longer have an older son and daughter. Both of them are imprisoned, standing accused of involvement in the villainous affair of March 1. There are no words to describe the full horror of my situation. I have seen my daughter and talked with her. I know my children too well, and as a result of my personal meetings with my daughter I have become convinced of her complete innocence...

> About my son I do not know anything....Authorities have refused me permission to see him and have told me that I must consider him as forever lost to me. Oh, Your Majesty! If I could even for one moment imagine that my son is a villain, I would have courage enough to renounce him [sic], and my reverence and respect for Your Majesty would not allow me to intercede for him. But everything I know about my son precludes the possibility of imagining him as a villain. My son was always a convinced and sincere hater of terrorism [sic] in whatever form. He was always religious [sic], deeply devoted to the interests of the family, and he wrote to me often....Comparing the fact of his accusation of an exceedingly grave state crime with the facts regarding my son's views in the recent past, with his dedication to science, with his dedication to the interests of the family, I see an irreconcilable contradiction—a contradiction which presents itself as something totally incomprehensible to me. He was always too religious, humane and honest to—being in his right mind—become involved in a villainous affair....He was too dedicated to his family to stain its name with disgrace and shame. He had too high a regard for his noble origin to stigmatize it.

Oh, Your Majesty! I implore you, spare my children! Return my children to me. If my son's mind and sense by chance have become obscured, if criminal designs have crept into his soul, Your Majesty, I will reform him….Mercy, Your Majesty. I beg for mercy.[25]

This plea makes painfully clear that Maria had no idea the transformation her son had gone through. It speaks to the suffering of a mother grappling with the reality that everything she and her late husband had feared for their children was coming true. It was no longer a nebulous catastrophe threatening a loving family—something they could tell themselves was an illusion. It was real, and all-consuming.

◆ ◆ ◆

The Tsar actually read Maria's appeal. (The ruler followed the case of his would-be-assassins closely.) *Let the woman see her son*, he ordered police. It was no act of mercy though. It was punishment of a different kind. "It seems to me," the Tsar wrote in his order, "that it is desirable to give her permission to see her son, so that she can convince herself what sort of a person her dear little son is, and to show her his testimony, so that she can see what kinds of convictions he has."[26] The ruler wanted the mother to realize what her boy had become.

Their reunion was breathtakingly emotional. Upon seeing his mother enter the prison cell, Sasha sobbed. He threw himself at her knees. He apologized for what he was doing to her and the family. But he could not take any of it back. Sasha explained: he was her son, but also a citizen of an oppressed country; he had no option other than to resist tyranny.[27] Maria—her face surely bewildered, tear-stained— responded: "Yes, but these means are so terrible."[28] There was no alternative, emphasized Sasha. *Prepare for what was to come*. Authorities would hang him. He would die. She would have to look to Volodia and the other kids for solace. Mom refused to accept this. She briefly returned home with delusional news that Sasha would likely receive life imprisonment in Siberia. The family would move with him, Maria insisted.[29]

◆ ◆ ◆

The trial began April 15, three days after Sasha turned twenty-one. Ringleader Petr denied everything. He blamed Orest for the plot.[30] Sasha did the opposite. The "small and thin" young man, "with a mass of dark hair piled above his tall, pale forehead," lacking any facial hair, spoke powerfully before the court in a calm manner.[31] He took full responsibility—even whispering to a co-conspirator to blame him for everything. To questions on why he had not tried to escape abroad, Sasha stated that he preferred to die a martyr. This defendant, the prosecution came to realize, claimed guilt for things they knew he had not done.[32]

The purpose of his testimony, Sasha made clear, was to explain the group's motivations. The court allowed him to speak at length (a right Volodia's future regime never would have granted). And his mother was there in the small audience, listening, along with the judge and the prosecutors, as he explained himself:

> I can trace to my early youth the vague feeling of dissatisfaction with the social system[,] which penetrating more and more into my consciousness, brought me to the convictions which inspired me in the present case. But only after studying the social and economic sciences did this conviction of the abnormality of this existing system become fully confirmed to me, and the vague dreams of freedom, equality, and brotherhood took shape for me in the strictly scientific forms of socialism....Given the government's attitude to intellectual life, not only socialist propaganda, but even general-cultural propaganda is impossible; even the scientific examination of

questions is seriously impeded. The government is so powerful, the intelligentsia so weak and so concentrated in a few cities, that the government can deprive it of...the last vestiges of freedom of speech....Our intelligentsia is so weak, physically, and so unorganized, that at the present time it cannot enter upon an open struggle, and it is only through terror that it can defend its right to thought and to intellectual participation in the life of society. Terror is the form of struggle....the only form of defense available to the minority[,] which is only strong spiritually and in the conviction of its righteousness against the majority's...physical power....[33]

Sasha's words moved his mother. ("How well Sasha spoke: so convincingly, so eloquently.") Until the drama proved too much, and she left the courtroom in tears.[34]

Authorities gave Sasha what he wanted. They sentenced him, along with Petr and three other conspirators, to hang.[35] *Beg for mercy*, Maria urged her son in response. The Tsar might commute his sentence to life imprisonment. *No*, said Sasha—"I cannot do this after everything I have admitted at the trial....That would be insincere." Even a prosecutor present in the room, eyes welling up, chimed-in: "He is right! He is right!"[36] Maria's oldest son had little interest in begging forgiveness so he could wither away in a prison cell for decades to come. (But would he have made it to 1905—or even 1917?)[37]

Regardless, Maria and a defense attorney eventually convinced Sasha to submit something to the Tsar. His request did not admit guilt, or ask forgiveness from the man he would have murdered, but sought "mercy...[to] restore my mother's health...and deliver me from the agonizing knowledge that I will be the cause of my mother's death and bring misfortune to my entire family."[38]

Rejected.

Maria's last words to her son were not good-bye. "Take heart, take courage," she shouted to him through iron-bars.[39]

♦ ♦ ♦

Then it was time to die. The guards came to get Sasha early in the morning on May 8, 1887. He was taken into the courtyard of his island prison, walking to the gallows just as the sun rose on a beautiful spring morning, dawn offering one last pleasure. The priest put a cross before Sasha. He kissed it. Co-conspirator Petr shoved it away. Up the stairs and across the scaffold went the men. Brusque brevity marked the executions' execution. Bodies swung.[40]

Maria was on her way to visit Anna when she bought a newspaper. The printed word, blunt as ever, reported Sasha's death. Devastation.[41]

A thousand miles away, Volodia was finishing high school. Three days before Sasha's execution, he wrote a paper on a play by Pushkin. On the day in question, he aced a geometry final.[42] Soon newspapers reported Sasha's hanging. Local authorities put up posters publicizing it. Still, Volodia continued his finals, conquering trigonometry, then breezing unflappably through translations of Thucydides.[43]

VOLODIA

But the execution was on his mind. The night before one such test, a fellow pupil—who had not yet heard about Sasha—found Volodia sitting on a bench outside. Are you OK? the classmate asked. Why aren't you studying? Silence. Sighs. Volodia tried to speak, but nothing came out. The sympathetic student remarked on the nourishing warmth and stillness of the May evening. *They hanged my brother*, said Volodia. The peer had no response. And the two sat quietly for a long time, before walking and parting with a handshake.[44]

Volodia graduated number one in his class, giving the school no choice but to award him the valedictorian gold medal. Yet they denied him the honor of having his name inscribed on a plaque with prior award winners. His name would have gone next to Sasha's.[45]

Maria soon returned from St. Petersburg. Trauma had frozen her hair white—though at least she returned with Anna, whom authorities released under strict conditions. Maria proceeded to sell the family's house and possessions. They were moving.[46]

◆ ◆ ◆

Volodia had not seen any of it coming. True, his brother's interest in politics had grown markedly over the prior year. But the little brother had never felt concerned, had never dreamed of his big brother becoming a terrorist. "A revolutionary cannot devote so much time to the study of worms," Volodia remembered thinking as Sasha worked tirelessly on his thesis.[47] The *why* of it all eluded the younger sibling—he did not comprehend how his brother could have become radicalized so quickly. Volodia could not understand until he grasped the same ideas that had inspired Sasha.[48]

He started with the conviction that Sasha must have felt he was doing the right thing—"that he had to act like this," that "he couldn't act in any other way."[49] If such thinking offered solace by preserving his brother's integrity, it did not hold back Volodia's immense curiosity. The determination to understand pushed him to investigate further. When a friend (who had shared an apartment with Sasha) visited, seventeen-year-old Volodia peppered him with questions. What were Sasha's last months like? What had the police asked? What was his trial like? What did Sasha's face look like during his testimony? What were his brother's political views exactly? He needed *to know*.[50]

Something changed in Volodia that summer. He read books that had absorbed Sasha—starting with Chernyshevsky's *What Is to Be Done?*. He had read it at fourteen and not thought much of it. But now he read the novel from the perspective of a sibling hanged for crimes against the Tsar—from the vantage point of trying to understand how it might encourage one to become a revolutionary.[51] Picture Volodia's face as he read about the character of Rakhmetov, whose transformation resembled his own brother's:

> At the age of sixteen he'd come to Petersburg a nice, ordinary lad [raised by an 'intelligent, well-educated, ultraconservative father'] having just completed his course of study at the gymnasium; he was a kind, honest young man....But soon he began to hear that among his comrades were some very clever minds whose way of thinking differed from that of others. He found out the names of five or six of these students....to seek the acquaintances of some of them. He happened to become friendly with [a main character named] Kirsanov; that initiated the process of his rebirth into an extraordinary man....The first evening he listened to Kirsanov avidly[,] he wept and interrupted Kirsanov's words with exclamations that cursed the things that must perish and blessed those that must survive [coded language for the overthrow of imperial society and revolution]. He asked, 'What books should I read first?' He acquired what he needed and then read for more than three days and nights in a row....He'd...adopted a set of original principles to govern his material, moral, and spiritual life....He said to himself, 'I

shall not drink one drop of wine. I shall not touch any women'….He adopted a very austere way of life….He dressed very modestly….He maintained a Spartan way of life….Rakhmetov managed to accomplish a great deal because in apportioning his time….not a quarter of an hour a month was wasted on recreation; he needed no rest….During the first months of his rebirth he spent almost all his time reading. But this phase lasted only a little more than half a year. When he realized that he'd acquired a systematic way of thinking according to those principles he considered correct, he said to himself at once:…'I'm now ready for life…'[52]

"Ready for life" meant the pursuit of revolution; it meant the willingness to die for it.

What Is to Be Done? used its feminist protagonist Vera Pavlovna to describe what the post-revolutionary future would look like—what Sasha had dreamed about; what Volodia now started to envision. Vera, the story explained, turned her seamstress workshop into what was clearly a microcosm for a future socialist society. There were no profits or wages in the traditional sense. Instead, all employees owned the shop equally; all worked energetically for mutual benefit according to rules collectively agreed upon; all received an equal share of profits; all reinvested a portion of the profits back into the shop, using accumulating capital for collective benefit—to buy materials in bulk, hire new workers, offer loans to employees, purchase a communal living space, buy food for everyone, and open new shops, further expanding the enterprise.[53] This "seamstress shop" modeled an economy without exploitation, one that would lead to a paradise that Vera saw in her literal dreams, a society in which men and women lived in "eternal spring and summer and joy everlasting."[54] These verses had helped stir Sasha to action; now they inspired Volodia. It was not *The Communist Manifesto* or *Das Kapital* that started the brothers on the road to revolution. It was their favorite novel: *What Is to Be Done?*[55]

Volodia devoured it in July 1887. He now *felt* its narrative, engaging with it on a personal level in a time of immense tragedy. He left no doubt about its importance for his life. Years later when someone questioned its value, he replied furiously: "Chernyshevsky's novel fascinated and captivated my brother....It captivated me. It *ploughed me over*....It is a work which gives one a charge for a whole life."[56] The book not only transformed Volodia's worldview—it helped him understand his brother's loss.

◆ ◆ ◆

In the fall of 1887, Volodia went to college. The government would not allow him to attend St. Petersburg University despite his stellar academic standing.[57] He was the sibling of a terrorist—a legacy to live down, rather than live up to.[58] Fortunately for the younger brother, a glowing letter of support from good-hearted Headmaster Kerensky (again, the father of the man Volodia would overthrow in 1917) offered crucial assistance. Volodia's mother, said the letter, would keep her "extremely talented" son under close supervision at university. Authorities acquiesced, allowing the younger brother to attend Imperial Kazan University, his father's alma mater. His family followed to watch over him.[59]

Volodia didn't last a year. Participation in a student protest in December 1887 was enough to warrant his expulsion and arrest.[60] When a policeman took him into custody, reproaching him for the futility of his actions, Volodia paraphrased one of his brother's favorite authors (Pisarev), and retorted sharply: "The wall is rotten. One good shove and it will collapse."[61] This was no longer Volodia talking—this was Vladimir Lenin.

For that budding revolutionary, there was now no purpose to life other than achieving the total transformation of society into a socialist utopia.[62] The aim of creating that new world for "new people," of bettering the lives of men and women everywhere, was all that mattered. There was no morality outside the realization of those ends. "And what is a good person?" Lenin asked ruefully in exile before wincing at the "nonsense of the intelligentsia about moral consciousness.'"[63] Any action—regardless of how extreme one might consider it—was acceptable if it helped put an end to class oppression. The stakes were a new world for mankind. No rules in the pursuit of paradise.[64] No room for bourgeois "morality."[65] It was with this attitude that the future dictator rejected his sister Anna's efforts to help feed the poor during a famine in 1892. *Let them die!* he argued—let the deaths of the poor hasten the collapse of capitalism and the arrival of the revolution! "The worse, the better!"[66] This man emerged out of Sasha's death.[67]

If you could go back and challenge him on any of this, Lenin might laugh and openly concede contradictions in his background—that he was "to some extent a scion of the landed gentry....a landlord's child."[68] But he might reject your questions and take an interest in *you*. Staring you in the eye, six inches from your face: "Yes, Comrade, but what are you doing for *this* revolution?"[69] "You are for whom? For the Revolution or against it? *If against it, to the wall!*"[70]

This person might have materialized even if Sasha had become a professor specializing in worms, but his brother's hanging unquestionably helped radicalize him. His supreme self-confidence burned even brighter once it was fueled by the remnants of Sasha's failed ambitions.

Could Volodia succeed where his big brother had failed?[71]

CHAPTER FOURTEEN
BENITO TAKES THE STAGE

After Benito stabbed a kid at his boarding school—and guard-dogs tried to eat him—the monks made clear he was not welcome back in the fall. (They also sued his parents for back tuition.)[1] Alessandro and Rosa found a new boarding school for their son in Forlimpopoli, a little over twenty miles away from home. In the fall of 1894, they sent the irascible boy there after he passed special examinations and earned a scholarship. The school, as Benito later reflected, was a paradise compared to his old one; it healed his wounded dignity and quieted his difficult temperament. The boy spent six years in its halls, beginning with the fifth grade, where he ultimately studied to become a teacher—like his mom.[2]

Everything was better. The school was secular. The food was edible. The dorms were nice. The teachers were solid. And his grades were good overall. The resulting breathing space enabled the eleven-year-old to feel comfortable enough to engage others and seek out a mentor of sorts in a grandfatherly teacher named Alessandro Massi, whom the young man sought to please. With peers, Benito was reserved and stern, but largely left alone. He spent most of his time with books, carrying piles of them to a roof where he found a happy refuge from the world.[3]

The boy's temper still caused problems though. He remained "unruly" and "sometimes indiscreet" before youth's "passing restlessness and follies," as Benito later put it.[4] Fortunately the school's authorities were "understanding and on the whole generous" when it came to his behavior.[5] Consider their response when—in the second stabbing of the little boy's academic career!—he knifed a student in the ass who smudged a page on which he was working. ("The fact, if not the wound, was serious," Benito recalled wryly.[6]) Rather than leave the boy to the dogs, school authorities sent Benito home for the year and required him to live off campus the following fall; they later let him return to the dorms regardless.[7] Tolerant indeed, the school went to great lengths to provide for the child's unique "learning profile" and demonstrated that discipline did not require terror. Benito appreciated as much—even if the latter lesson never stuck.

◆ ◆ ◆

Benito's love life took shape during his teenage years. By age sixteen, several young women infatuated him, and he found himself writing love letters, sending violets, experiencing awkward crushes, waiting in alleys for secret meetings, and making out with girls. The loss of his virginity was decidedly less innocent, however. It occurred after a friend dragged Benito to a local brothel, and a prostitute, old and overweight, took the horny, blushing teenager on her knees and began to kiss him, readying him for the act to follow. Cheap sex ensued before the young man fled in post-orgasm shame, drunk on guilt, feeling like a criminal.[8]

This sexual encounter inflamed Benito's libido nonetheless. Lubricious daydreams haunted his mind, his thoughts occupied by the mysteries of what lay beneath young women's clothes. He delighted in attending dances where, as he later wrote, the "music, the rhythm of the movements, the contact with the girls with perfumed hair and with skin that secretes an acrid sweat to smell" made his body throb.[9] Brothels relieved the pressure, but he struggled with the sexual passions of youth just the same. He also caught the clap.[10]

◆◆◆

During his last years in school, Benito's fertile mind began to produce a prodigious intellectual output—the start of what would ultimately amount to over forty-four volumes of writing, totaling thousands of pages. He wrote in the 1900-1901 school year, for example, a thoughtful essay on pedagogy—calling for greater consideration of the ways in which class inequities influence the academic performance of lower socioeconomic students.[11] He also intensified his personal studies, re-reading Dante's *Divine Comedy* (which led him to walk around at night, belting out lines from *Inferno* and *Purgatorio*) while digging into Le Bon's *The Crowd: A Study of the Popular Mind*—the latter pertinent to his future political ambitions.[12]

Around this time, Benito grew increasingly interested in public speaking, practicing for hours on end, and started to express socialist convictions, a belief system encouraged by his upbringing and the trending political convictions of the time. Seeds of political consciousness sprouted.[13] In January 1901, school authorities requested Benito deliver a memorial address for the composer and supposed nationalist hero Giuseppe Verdi. Benito made the most of the opportunity. Only eighteen, he took the stage in the city theatre, his first moment in the spotlight. His speech—like so many to come—had little to do with the designated topic. Instead, Benito delivered a wider political diatribe, showering sparks on his receptive audience. National unification—Benito exclaimed—had led to a bourgeois state at the expense of the masses! The potential of the country's national consciousness remained unfulfilled! Sweeping revolutionary change was in order! The serious young man (likely dressed in his normal apparel of black) found his place on stage. Applause gratified his simmering pride.[14]

The speech was a hit, making the papers, the first time Benito's name appeared in print. The nationally-read socialist newspaper *Avanti!*—of which Benito would later be the editor—reported the speech on its front page, and Bologna's *Resto del Carlino* printed news of the "much applauded" oration.[15] Alessandro—who may have seen the news in *Avanti!*—surely felt immense pride. His son was following in his footsteps, the promise of socialist activism taking hold in a new generation. (One wonders what Rosa thought.) Though no one necessarily saw the young man as destined for big things, the speech signified his growing self-confidence.[16] His appearance on stage affirmed that his voice, along with well-timed demagoguery, could influence the world around him and earn an audience's rapture. The power of a perceptive person's lungs was an important tool, Benito learned.[17]

BENITO

The end of his studies came in July 1901 when he graduated with honors from the boarding school in Forlimpopoli with a teaching degree and returned home to Predappio. For much of that summer and early fall, Benito studied to pass required teaching examinations, and applied for jobs. He now had in his possession, as he later recalled, "the shred of paper that enables something, the diploma by which bread can be won."[18] But rejection letters poured in. When he took the necessary exams, he found himself competing with numerous teachers, some gray with age, looking for work.[19] With no job, Benito's frustrations mounted, and the proud graduate—to use his own words—"aspired to a less ignoble youth."[20]

As the job-hunt played out, the feisty young man made locals uncomfortable. (Some called him "the Mad One," a moniker perhaps encouraged by his searing eyes.[21]) The frustrated eighteen-year-old—now a self-proclaimed socialist-anarchist—had no idea what to do with his life. So he mainly read, wrote, drank, and smoked. Sometimes he walked ten miles to Forli, something to read in-hand, to hit up the town library or take violin lessons.[22]

Such free time gave greater license to Benito's craven physical desires.[23] His sexuality became criminal. Women, like most everything to him, became objects to dominate for personal fulfillment, control offering pleasure and false security. "One fine day"—Benito openly admitted in a future memoir—he raped a young woman named Virginia behind a stairway door.[24] The victim, sobbing after the crime, rose courageously and condemned him for "stealing her honor." That might be the case, Benito replied cruelly, but he wasn't sure of what honor she could be speaking. The young man either took sadistic delight in sexually assaulting—and then taunting—his victim, or simply did not grasp the trauma he had just caused. Benito's callous bragging about the event over ten years later seems to support both possibilities. Unlike his consensual encounter with the prostitute, he felt no shame about his actions. He claimed they had sex regularly thereafter.[25]

◆ ◆ ◆

By February 1902, Benito found work as a substitute elementary school teacher in a provincial town—a position he attained, over older and more qualified candidates, only through political connections. He was a spectacular failure. Proved himself all but incapable of controlling children, his laissez-faire attitude towards discipline going poorly.

His behavior outside of school was outrageous. In just five months, he engaged in a scandalous, violent affair. Boozed. Played cards. Raided village dances with ruffians, seizing pretty girls while getting into fights, using fists and chairs as weapons. He gave a fiery impromptu political speech in May—allegedly appalling the mayor, but thrilling locals. All in a small town!

Authorities showed little interest in keeping Benito on for the following year. *Contract not renewed.*[26] By June, Benito himself wanted to move. He had liked his students overall, yes, but the daily grind was tedious. The position had paid too little. And he owed money to his landlady and the cobbler. Insult to injury: he'd nearly drowned in the local river.[27]

However, his (aforementioned) affair overshadowed his departure. The young woman was Giulia—"a beautiful twenty-year-old bride" of a soldier away on duty. At some point during Benito's posting in the provincial village, the two started sleeping together, rumors of which quickly spread. When the husband heard, he had his parents kick out the young woman—along with their infant child. Benito and Giulia continued seeing each other anyway, essentially moving into their rendezvous apartment and having sex in the meadow by the river. (One wonders: *Who was taking care of the baby?*)[28]

It was an abusive relationship—"a violent and jealous" love. Benito made Giulia do whatever he wanted. "Little by little," Benito admitted, "I accustomed her to my exclusive and tyrannical love."[29] He even reportedly stabbed her in the arm after discovering her walking alone in the street.[30] According to Benito, Giulia wept when it came time for him to leave. He abandoned her regardless, leaving her marriage and reputation in ruins.[31] The future beckoned. He would follow its call abroad to see where his domineering will might take him. With daydreams of opportunity, "his effrontery knew no limit," as one biographer put it.[32]

Challenges stood in the way. Benito couldn't simply hop on a train. He needed money (had to ask Rosa for it). He also had to seek the help of his home mayor to get a passport. The young man made clear to his mother and father that he would not go abroad destitute—he had a job lined up and a place to stay. Lies, of course, meant to yield cash and help his parents sleep at night.[33] Benito had no real plans. He sought the uncertainty of what was around the bend. "To go out into the world and try my fortune."[34]

◆ ◆ ◆

The young man departed for Switzerland on the morning of July 9, 1902, enduring a hot train ride that left his throat painfully dry. A newspaper informed him during the journey that local authorities had arrested his dad on trumped-up political charges—a development about which Benito could only stew.[35] Yet on the final train ride (twelve hours long with a third-class ticket) he managed a tranquil moment. As his countrymen slept around him, Benito stared out the train, wide-eyed, upon a beautiful moonlit evening, admiring a shimmering lake reflecting the sky and the mountainous landscape. That night, he remembered, marked a new phase in his life. He had experienced a feeling difficult to describe, this young man on the verge of adulthood, pondering what would become of himself. It was the type of feeling an individual grapples with when they recognize that the canvas of their life has been largely devoid of color or substance, but the future remains wide open. Benito craved a destiny. [36]

Dazed, the young man completed his journey after thirty-six hours of travel. To his seeming good fortune, he had met a companion who promised him a job. But that came to naught; so he ended up wandering to another town, finding work in manual labor before promptly proving himself "psychologically incapable" of it. [37] Benito did not hold back in describing his misery:

> ...On Monday morning, the 14th, I began. Eleven hours' work a day, thirty-two centimes an hour. I made one hundred and twenty-one trips with a hand-barrow full of stones up to the second floor of a building in process of construction. In the evening, the muscles of my arms were swollen. I ate some potatoes baked in ashes and with all of my clothes on, I threw myself on my bed: a pile of straw. At 5 AM on Tuesday, I woke up and went back to work. I chafed with the terrible rage of the powerless. The boss was making me angry....I should have liked to rebel and crack the skull of that upstart who was accusing me of laziness while the stones were making my bones ache, to shout in his face: 'Coward, Coward!' [38]

Benito did not attack. ("Right is on the side of the man who pays you," he corrected himself. [39]) But physical labor remained hell for him. His hands swelled and blistered. Like Vito Spatafore doing real work for the first time, he wondered if the hour hands ever moved. [40] Benito quit before the end of the week. His boss threw his wages at him: "Here is your pay and it is stolen." The sore teenager nearly resorted to combat again. But reality sobered him anew. "I was hungry and had no shoes," he recognized of his pitiful plight. [41] All he could do was grip the Karl Marx medallion in his pocket. [42]

The harsh realities of independence confronted Benito. In those first weeks, he confessed, he had almost no money—neither bed nor bread. He slept in a box under a bridge. Took refuge in a public bathroom to avoid the cold wind. Begged in the streets. Failed to recognize his haggard reflection in store windows.[43] This taste of tribulation tested Benito's willingness to endure. "Hunger is a good teacher," he later reminisced.[44]

And then there was jail. Police soon arrested Benito for vagrancy—the first of many arrests to come. His possessions: a passport, a license to teach, some change, the Marx medallion. His first stint behind bars was brief, but the experience (like others to follow) taught him lessons.[45] Incarceration demanded patience. "Prison is like a sea voyage," he later emphasized, compelling forbearance to complete the journey.[46] Benito's time behind bars ultimately made him claustrophobic, yet no less willing to cage others in later years. Better to be the jailer than the inmate.[47]

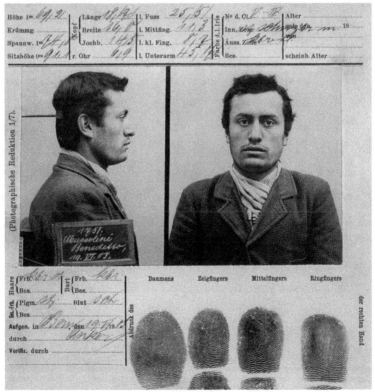

BENITO IN POLICE CUSTODY, 1903

After that first stint behind bars, Benito found an attic to sleep in. He worked odd jobs—Benito the bar waiter!—before becoming a secretary for a local trade union and recording the minutes of the organization's meetings. The job enabled him to eat and drink for free during meetings and to rent his own room. With shelter and bread, Benito became politically active, publishing articles in the socialist weekly *L'Avvenire del Lavoratore* and giving political speeches. Connections followed—along with the ability to mostly avoid physical labor.[48]

Benito met socialist intellectual Angelica Balabanoff some nine months later. She was speaking at a meeting of socialists when she noticed Benito in the audience, clutching a black hat, looking filthy and morose.[49] She approached him afterwards. Benito stared down. Replied to her questions in an "almost hysterical" tone, declaring that he was sick and couldn't work. "Nothing can be done for me."[50] "I had never seen a more wretched-looking human being," Angelica later remembered. "In spite of his large jaw, the bitterness and restlessness in his black eyes," she added, "he gave the impression of extreme timidity." Benito—if "extremely dirty"—was desperate for respect, wrought "with his own inner turmoil."[51]

Something therein led Angelica to engage him further.[52] She felt pulled to Benito. If she did not take him too seriously, she saw revolutionary potential, and wanted him to aspire to significance despite his off-putting personality. Benito, in turn, embraced Angelica as an ideological patron, as a mentor of sorts. He began to overcome his burning insecurity by opening up to her, revealing himself like a person disrobing, fostering intimacy through vulnerability. They might have been lovers, too.[53]

Benito was bombastic with nearly everyone else. He had only read *The Communist Manifesto* but challenged those who had studied Marxism for years. At times he showed bullet-proof confidence, extreme bravado obscuring inner anxieties and bottomless self-pity. But the reality was that Benito badly needed training in the socialist tenets he espoused. Angelica provided that instruction, helping the nobody-activist mature into a more effective revolutionary. She was careful of his fragile ego. Like all good pedagogues, she instilled the belief that they were learning together, preserving Benito's pride.[54]

Benito remembered Angelica's mentoring as essential for his revolutionary "career." He privately told a writer at the height of his power that, without Angelica, "I would have remained a small party activist, a Sunday revolutionary."[55] She had sharpened his blunt zealotry and disciplined his ideological thinking, if not the ultimate offspring of his ideas.[56] In the years to come, Benito publicly despised her, but remained quietly grateful for her past help.[57] She was there for him at a difficult time in his life—when he had been a moody, insufferable zero, insecure yet ravenously hungry for someone to invest in his burning eyes.

If Angelica saw something in Benito when few others did, she also thought his "egotism, his glorification of strength and physical courage, were the compensation for his own weakness, his longing for personal recognition and prestige."[58] Insecurity, she recognized, drove his audaciousness. "During all of our association," Angelica reflected later in life, "I was drawn to him by the knowledge that I was the only human being with whom he was completely himself, with whom he was relieved from the strain of bluffing."[59] But Angelica did not consider whether Benito's vulnerability was part of his bluff. Indeed, her efforts to help him speak to the future dictator's ability to pull others into his orbit even as they found him disconcerting. His insecurity, like his bravado, could seduce, and Angelica, transfixed, was never able to look away—even after she detested him. She once believed she could help Benito become a positive force in the socialist movement—that she could harness him for political ends. For Benito, it was clearly the other way around.

Anyone who had known Benito in his youth, as he himself admitted as a Fascist dictator, "could already have recognized when I was sixteen what I now am, with all the light and shade."[60] But Angelica, despite her keen intuition and erudition, never understood her peculiar friend in those early years. "Once he was well in mind and body," she remembered thinking:

> ...Once he really felt himself the equal—rather than the inferior—of other men, once his personal bitterness was allayed by human understanding and sympathy[,] his assertiveness, his childish will-to-power and his intellectual confusion would pass away.[61]

Greater study, she had really believed, would change Benito for the better. She did not grasp until it was too late that study only further emboldened his craving for personal affirmation. She did not realize that utopian notions of "human understanding and sympathy" did not apply to such a crass opportunist. Angelica failed, most of all, to see that Benito's commitment to any political ideology, even if he truly believed in it, depended on where it would take him—on its ability to further his own perceptions of personal greatness. Nothing was going to extinguish his belief that he would live up to his personal visions of grandeur when the right circumstances presented themselves. "Political activity became for [Benito]," as one scholar summarized of his years in Switzerland, "...a profession that offered the valorization of his intellectual abilities and the guarantee of a certain social prestige."[62] Angelica helped give Benito Mussolini that start—*and would regret it deeply*.[63]

In the following decades, his distorted subjectivity made him believe that his time as a Fascist leader was not only about national glory, but also the salvation of the drowning man. As an undisputed captain—a true tyrant—he embarked with his people on a fanatical voyage, ignoring the jagged shores even as he steered towards them. He pushed dissenters into the frothing waters, and ignored those who fell in of their own accord. He became determined to chart an irrationally bold course; it was the only thing that made him feel like he was living up to the person he imagined himself to be. Then his ship collided with the rocks, the deafening crack of wooden planks reverberating.

CHAPTER FIFTEEN
ADOLF AND GUSTL

One evening in the fall of 1905, Adolf met an ordinary seventeen-year-old named Gustl.

Gustl had worked a long day as his father's upholstery apprentice before rushing to the theater in Linz. Opera performances provided him a refuge, a place he could go after repairing old mattresses (some still stained with the bodily fluids of prior, deceased owners) to enjoy an evening's performance and dream of a career in music. Gustl's meager wages meant he could only buy tickets for the theatre's standing section, and so he arrived in haste on the night in question to wrangle for the best view of the stage. An unwelcome competitor, however, had taken his favorite spot.[1] "Half-annoyed, half-surprised," Gustl observed that his rival was "a remarkably pale, skinny youth, about my own age, who was following the performance with glistening eyes….He was…dressed with meticulous care and was very reserved."[2] It was Adolf.

That young man, observed Gustl, was of average height, lean and lanky. He had dark hair, a straight nose, and a high forehead, which he often covered by brushing his hair straight down. His blue eyes stood out, a defiant glare burning. (He "spoke with his eyes," remembered Gustl.) Adolescent Adolf went to great pains to look the dandy. He often wore a nice overcoat, a formal hat of some type, and carried an ivory-handled black cane.[3] (This desire to look impeccable endured into adulthood; he became pathologically paranoid of looking ridiculous in photographs.[4]) Fashion aside, Adolf often looked sickly, coughing a lot in the winter. He did not play sports, but swam on occasion and enjoyed long walks. Art was his passion.[5] He talked frequently about "relations between the sexes"—even if intercourse terrified him. The teenager was surely still a virgin, and even (allegedly) abstained from masturbation.[6] He did have a normal penis though—two good balls to boot—rumors to the contrary notwithstanding.[7]

It was this young man who returned Gustl's gaze at the opera. The two silently acknowledged each other before striking up a conversation at intermission—an exchange rooted in their mutual dissatisfaction with the casting of a certain character. Gustl was modest, lacking in strong convictions. But from the beginning, he admired the "quick, sure grasp" of Adolf, whom he recognized as "my superior" in everything except music. They bonded over opera, and Adolf found an apostle who fell silent at his beckoning, and listened. On whatever topic Adolf chose to pontificate, his manner of speaking and air of unquestionable authority captured Gustl's attention.[8]

Adolf and Gustl were soon close friends, taking long walks together in the narrow, paved streets of Linz. Horse-drawn carriages made their way beside them. Prominent citizens strolled while other local teenagers pretended to be university students. If Gustl was late for any meeting, Adolf immediately went to his upholstery shop, demanding an explanation for his lack of punctuality. *Due to a job!* (Adolf viewed his friend's employment as "nothing but a tiresome hindrance to our personal relationship," recalled Gustl.)[9]

Adolf, for his part, had far too much time on his hands. And naturally, no job. When Gustl once worked up the nerve to ask him if he was employed anywhere, Adolf replied: "Of course not." He could not countenance a "bread-and-butter job." The comment shocked Gustl, going against "every principle which had so far governed my life." What about school, Gustl queried next. Surely Adolf must be a student. That question elicited rage. Adolf ranted angrily about idiotic teachers and the uselessness of school. His former instructors, he emphasized, would receive no greeting from him should they cross paths on the street! Adolf—Gustl learned—did not like explaining himself on uncomfortable questions. Opera and art, and whatever subject he might broach—*this was the talk of the day*. These were the terms of their friendship.[10]

It was an odd bond. They were opposites. Gustl was an affable and open-minded cloud-dweller. In his own words: "a quiet, somewhat dreamy youth, very sensitive and adaptable...always willing to yield." Adolf—Gustl remembered in contrast—was "exceedingly violent [in language] and highly strung....A few thoughtless words could produce in him outbursts of temper." Cocksure Adolf had strong opinions about almost everything.[11] He even declined to call his only friend by his real name (August). Still, Adolf made a genuine effort to get along. He appreciated that Gustl indulged his diatribes.[12] Gustl, in turn, felt valued by Adolf's desire to spend time together and thus listened dutifully when his friend babbled about topics ranging from the excise duty at the Danube bridge to a collection in the streets for a charity lottery. Under shady trees, the two took comfort in each other's company.

Adolf, Gustl recalled, committed himself to enthralling him on every occasion. "I was often startled," he later wrote, "when he would make a speech to me, accompanied by vivid gestures for my benefit alone....Such rapture I had only witnessed so far in the theatre....I could only stand gaping and passive, forgetting to applaud."[13] It was dramatic, except for the fact that the speaker was never putting on an act. Searing self-conviction informed teenage Adolf's delivery, and his arrogance lent an air of magnetism (at least from Gustl's perspective), even at that young age. His tirades provided a release, verbal ejaculation from a pulsating mind. Adolf went into the woods with Gustl time after time, achieving verbal climax ("a volcano erupting....bursting out of him") while Gustl played the submissive. "The tension...was relieved," stated Gustl (with seeming obliviousness to the homoerotic innuendo of it all.)[14]

There is no evidence that the boys ever hooked up. And (despite arguments that Adolf was a closeted homosexual) no certain proof that Adolf ever had sex with men.[15] In contrast, Gustl—though possibly dissembling—characterized young Adolf as an ardent homophobe. He described his outrage when a (presumably gay) man took them to a lavish dinner in Vienna and covertly slipped Adolf an invitation to join him in his hotel room.[16]

Whatever his sexuality, Adolf didn't want Gustl to have other friends. He was possessive. Total fidelity was the unnegotiable price of his companionship. To obey Adolf's "beck and call," that's what Gustl remembered him wanting.[17] Yet Adolf—as his friend emphasized—"…was also prepared to do everything for me….He, too, had no other friend besides me."[18]

They needed each other.

◆ ◆ ◆

But what of girls? Teenage Adolf was indifferent to them. Women, then and in the future, found him good-looking. But female flirtation did nothing to excite him to action.[19] Once, when a young milkmaid—alone with Adolf in a barn—stopped milking a cow and tried to hook up with him, he ran. The flustered kid knocked over a full milk pail on his way out. Supposedly he "suddenly thought of the eventual consequences and ran away." But copulating probably petrified him more than getting the milkmaid pregnant.[20]

Only one young woman in his hometown, Stefanie, ever captured his imagination at an early age.[21] Adolf first saw her in the spring of 1906—a slim, blonde young woman, her "abundant hair still worn in the Gretel fashion," as Gustl recalled.[22] Stefanie was two years older than Adolf, from a respected family. Adolf first brought her up to Gustl by asking his friend's opinion about her, and then promptly announcing he loved her. But note—and this is the most important part of the story about Adolf and Stefanie—*she never knew he existed.* Adolf never spoke to her. Not once. If he had tried to court Stefanie, the secret admirer understood, her family would've asked about his education and career plans. And Adolf, dressed so smartly, would have been humiliated. His "relationship" with Stefanie consisted of staring at her from a distance.[23]

If from time-to-time Stefanie seemed to return his glance—or there was any type of smile—Adolf went nuts. When Stefanie "ignored" him, Adolf was "crushed and ready to destroy himself and the whole world," observed Gustl.[24] Yet as so often happened with Adolf, his delusions provided endless hours of fantastical conversation. The young man, Gustl recounted in this vein, imagined his future home with Stefanie, planning out what it would be like, and how they would do the garden—an inclination to fantasize that endured into his years in power.[25] Adolf told Gustl that the second they were introduced, they wouldn't even have to speak. Talking would be unnecessary. They would instantly understand each other.[26]

Adolf, Gustl claimed in retrospect, went on to devise a years-long plan to attain Stefanie's hand in marriage. The in-love teenager also made Gustl his spy. The resulting revelation that Stefanie danced with other men shook Adolf—as did the suggestion he learn to dance to woo her. The young woman, Adolf supposedly responded, only danced because of societal expectations. His beloved would give up such filth upon marrying him. (Demands of the heart, suspected his friend, still led him to try out a few dance steps with little sister Paula.)

Adolf's tempestuous feelings mounted in the months that followed, and Gustl claimed that Adolf actually suggested kidnapping Stefanie at one point. Common sense questions (fortunately for her sake) killed that plan in its infancy.[27] The one-sided love affair reached peak irrationality after Stefanie "ignored" Adolf one day. He considered killing himself. Only a perceived smile from Stefanie and a flower tossed from her carriage put an end to such talk. The young woman, delusional Adolf announced with relief, was in love with him after all.[28] Even after moving to Vienna in the fall of 1907, Adolf implored Gustl to provide updates on Stefanie.[29]

Though scholars have questioned the extent to which Gustl exaggerated this story, Stefanie was indeed real. The Austrian writer Franz Jetzinger tracked her down after World War II and asked about Adolf. She couldn't recall him at all. What she did remember, however, was receiving a very odd letter from an admirer; it had no name, or none was signed. The author said he would be attending the Academy of Fine Arts in Vienna and declared that Stefanie would wait for him.[30] For years, Adolf continued to talk about her. Even as late as 1913—when Adolf lived in Munich on the eve of the First World War—he bought an advertisement in his hometown newspaper offering best wishes to his "girlfriend." Stefanie, he did not know, had already wed another.[31]

Adolf's penchant for embracing fantasies with the conviction they would come true showed up in simpler aspects of daily life. For instance, Gustl recalled when he and Adolf bought a lottery ticket together. Though Adolf calculated their scant odds of winning—was capable of doing the math—he became convinced they had the golden ticket and would triumph. He wasted no time in considering how to manage their forthcoming winnings, gabbing about architectural projects they could undertake. After the boys didn't win, Adolf became furious. He blamed the *defeat* on some deeper injustice.[32] Gustl remembered the aftermath as follows:

> The day of the [lottery] draw arrived. Adolf came rushing wildly round to the workshop with the list of results. I have rarely heard him rage so madly as then. First he fumed over the state lottery, this officially organized exploitation of human credulity, this open fraud at the expense of docile citizens. Then his fury turned against the state itself....*Never did it occur to Adolf to reproach himself for having taken it for granted that the first prize belonged to him by right.*[33]

Adolf always remained committed to self-fulfilling prophecies. He never recognized reality could defy his obstinate will.

◆ ◆ ◆

No job. Not in school. What exactly was teenage Adolf doing with his life, other than hanging with Gustl and staring at Stefanie? He had an answer for that. He was going to be a great artist! A magnificent artist! No doubt about it![34] (Klara, recorded the family's doctor, "encouraged his boyish efforts to become an artist....Despite their poverty, she permitted him to reject a job which was offered in the post office, so that he could continue his painting.")[35] Amid long walks and hours-long tirades about one flight of fancy or another, Adolf convinced himself that he was one, and spent much of his time drawing in his mother's home. His bedroom became a universe of sketches, a world of artistic ability unto itself. He had some talent, to be sure, but rarely finished anything. Gustl recalled that Adolf frequently carried a pencil and paper and readily took them out in the street to sketch buildings (his favorite subject). When Adolf was not drawing, he indulged his passion for water-color painting.[36]

Teenage Adolf *was an artist*, to an extent. He drew and painted for creation's sake. But he was also an "artist" in that his claim to the title—as one biographer put it—was "a rationalization of his incapacity for any kind of disciplined effort."[37] (Haven't we all known someone who fits that description perfectly?) By declaring himself an artist, he parried unwelcome questions about a life devoid of responsibility, making it less painful to explain his lack of education and employment. Claiming he was an artist gave him a path, even if it led nowhere for the moment.

In addition to drawing and painting—and a fervent passion for music (Wagner!)—young Adolf was an odd sort of bibliophile. He read for hours on end, adoring Karl May's adventure stories about the American Wild West, and frequently carried around a volume of *Die Deutschen Heldensage* [*The Sagas of the German Heroes*].[38] "I could not imagine Adolf without books," recalled Gustl of these years in Linz and then Vienna. "He stacked them in piles around him. He had to have with him at his side the book he was currently working through.... Whenever he went out, there would usually be a book under his arm."[39] Works by Nietzsche, Goethe, Gustave Le Bon, Heinrich von Treitschke, Martin Luther, James Fenimore Cooper, William McDougall, and Friedrich Schiller caught his eye.[40]

Yet Adolf's reading rarely consisted of a cover-to-cover effort. The same lack of sustained focus that sabotaged his performance elsewhere undermined his auto-didacticism. A close henchman from his later time in power remembered that Adolf never actually *read* a book, per se. He did not have the patience. He just skipped to the final chapter, recognizing that the most important points would be reiterated there.[41] This was a person who felt he already understood much of what books could teach him. What he did not know, he could assuredly master with a cursory reading. He largely read to affirm and reinforce what he already believed—not to challenge himself with new ideas.[42] This young man, then, had a limited knowledge of his printed loves. His impatience made him intellectually shallow. Substance was superfluous.

Adolf was not stupid though. He had an incisive, penetrating mind. His superb memory stood out to those around him.[43] As an adult, he could explain the essence of a text or topic with cogency—could grasp basics very quickly, and communicate them articulately. This skill often gave the false impression of mastery on wide-ranging issues.[44]

Architecture was an area of genuine talent for Adolf. He knew a great deal about it. A more natural predisposition towards the field, we might assume, encouraged his boundless enthusiasm for it.[45] Young Adolf endlessly walked the streets of Linz, and later Vienna, his face staring up and down at minute details in buildings. He admired. He scowled. He sketched. Spent innumerable hours dreaming of how to improve those structures. Gustl's words speak to the intensity of his friend's fantasies:

> [Adolf] gave his whole self to his imaginary buildings and was completely carried away by them. Once he had conceived an idea he was like one possessed. Nothing else existed for him – he was oblivious to time, sleep and hunger....There he stood...analyzing the style, criticizing or praising the work, disapproving of the material – all this with such thoroughness and such expert knowledge as though he were the builder....Then he would get out his drawing pad and the pencil would fly over the paper. This way, and no other way, was the manner of solving this problem, he would say....He could give full vent to his mania for changing everything....Usually he carried around in his head...half a dozen different building projects.[46]

Sketches in Adolf's bedroom bore witness to such sweeping architectural visions. They were a testament to the egocentric teenager's belief that he could almost always improve on others' designs.[47] Such thinking reverberated into his political "career," leading him to pursue ambitions from which even Otto von Bismarck shied away. "Genius" inspired greater audacity—and, with time, increasingly extreme actions. "I've always gone for broke," Adolf admitted in August 1939.[48]

♦ ♦ ♦

At some point during this time in Linz, Adolf seriously considered what he was going to do with his life. Could he actually become a great artist? A two-week trip to Vienna (some 120 miles away) in the spring of 1906 gave the teenager a lot to think about. Thrilled by the artistic treasures of that bustling metropolis, Adolf decided to return in the fall of 1907 and apply to the Vienna Academy of Fine Arts. Any entrance exam would be a formality, he believed. The academy would gladly have him. Adolf could then begin his studies and make his artistic fantasies a reality. His mother, Klara, was happy. Her son would finally pursue a concrete path beyond the streets of Linz.[49]

Yet tragedy loomed. In January 1907, Klara saw family doctor Eduard Bloch—a kind and respected Jewish physician—complaining of intense chest pain.[50] ("She spoke in a quiet, hushed voice; almost a whisper," recalled Dr. Bloch.)[51] She had initially ignored the discomfort, but the pain only became worse, keeping her up at night. An examination by Dr. Bloch revealed the worst, though he did not tell Klara right away. Instead, the doctor asked Adolf (age seventeen) and Paula (eleven) to come to his office the next day without their mother. There, Dr. Bloch informed them that Klara had advanced breast cancer and would die without an immediate mastectomy. Even then, full recovery was doubtful.[52] The family, the physician told the children, should deliver the news and support Klara in deciding what to do. Dr. Bloch recalled Adolf's response:

> Adolf['s]...reaction to this news was touching. His long, sallow face was contorted. Tears flowed from his eyes. Did his mother, he asked,

have no chance? Only then did I realize the magnitude of the attachment that existed between mother and son. I explained that she did have a chance; but a small one. Even this shred of hope gave him some comfort.[53]

Adolf's mom had surgery four days later and—after twenty days in the hospital—recuperated in the spring and summer of 1907.[54] (Dr. Bloch visited Adolf and Paula after Klara's procedure. "Does my mother suffer?" Adolf asked the physician, his voice breaking.)[55] Mom grappled with the likelihood of death and her children's future without her. What would become of her eleven-year-old little girl? What would Adolf— just entering manhood, unemployed, without parents—do with his life? "'Adolf is still so young,'" Klara told Dr. Bloch over and over, almost speaking to herself.[56] Set against his dying mother's anxieties about his future, Adolf's decision to attend art school, his sudden willingness to commit, suggests he wanted to ease her worries.

A WATERCOLOR BY ADOLF

But the Vienna Academy of Fine Arts still had to accept Adolf. He traveled to Vienna in September to inquire about the entrance exam, "armed with a bulky packet of sketches," never doubting the institution would have him.[57] Though those drawings earned him the opportunity to take the six-hour entrance exam, his work underwhelmed. "Test drawing unsatisfactory. Few heads"—read his evaluation.[58] Rejected. Adolf did not understand. "The news…struck me like a bolt from the skies," he recalled years later.[59] Dismayed, Adolf asked the academy's rector for further explanation. His work, the rector replied, demonstrated that he was better suited for architecture. The problem with that career-path was Adolf hadn't graduated from secondary school (realschule), a prerequisite for studying architecture.[60] Adolf ignored the rector's counsel by reapplying the next year.[61]

This rejection belied everything Adolf believed about himself. He had revealed his artistic abilities to the world, only to have them judged inadequate. It was crushing. And Adolf couldn't bear to tell the truth to his dying mother, the one person (other than Gustl) who believed in him. So he lied. He told his family he aced the entrance exam. Inventing realities was always his strong suit.[62]

◆ ◆ ◆

As Adolf "began classes" that fall of 1907, Klara's situation worsened back home. Her deterioration stunned Gustl when he visited her in November. "How wilted and worn was her kind, gentle face. She was lying in bed and stretched out her pale, thin hand to me," remembered the friend. Adolf—Klara told Gustl—had sent optimistic letters from Vienna; she didn't want him to come home and neglect his studies at the academy. Gustl, concerned that Adolf didn't understand the gravity of his mother's situation, offered to write on her behalf. But Klara demurred. She promised to contact him herself.[63]

The next month, Adolf burst into Gustl's upholstery shop with the pained expression of a child whose mother was dying. "His face was so pale as to be almost transparent," recalled the friend. "His eyes were dull and his voice hoarse. I felt that a storm of suffering must be hidden behind his icy demeanor. He gave me the impression that he was fighting for life against a hostile fate."[64] "Incurable, the doctor says," repeated Adolf to himself, heartbreak spilling out through the seams of his rage.

Adolf devoted himself to Klara in her last days. He behaved selflessly, lovingly tending to her. He treated his mother with the respect and dignity she had always deserved but rarely received. Gustl recalled coming to their apartment and finding Adolf in a blue apron, scrubbing the kitchen floor. He had moved his mother's bed into the kitchen so she could be in a heated room day and night, and had put the couch next to her bed—exchanging it for the cupboard—so he could sleep next to her. Adolf did all of the cooking, discussing meals with his mom each morning and making her favorite dishes. (Younger sister Paula and Dr. Bloch corroborated Gustl's account of this adoring care.) Adolf "spoiled my mother during this last time of her life with overflowing tenderness," recalled Paula. "He was indefatigable in his care for her."[65] Such devotion brought joy to Klara's heart until she passed away on December 21, 1907 at 2 AM. She was just forty-seven years old.[66] Her eighteen-year-old son, unable to sleep, sat beside her body with a picture he had drawn of her—"to preserve a last impression," as the family doctor recalled.[67] She died under the Christmas tree, Adolf would recall mournfully.[68]

Klara's funeral took place on December 23. Adolf walked around aimlessly afterwards, alone, without parents, until the early hours of Christmas Eve morning.[69] The holiday symbolized misery for him thereafter. (Even in the mid-1930s, he would refuse to have a

Christmas tree in his residence and would stay in his room from December 24th to the 26th.)[70]

Extreme grief consumed the young man. Dr. Bloch, no stranger to deathbed sorrow, recalled that he had never witnessed "anyone so prostrate with grief as Adolf."[71] Days later, the young man and his sisters visited the doctor to thank him for helping Klara. Shaking the physician's hand and looking him in the eye, Adolf said: "I shall be grateful to you forever" and then bowed. (Later allowed to depart Nazi-occupied Austria for the United States, Dr. Bloch noted in 1941 that "Favors were granted me which I feel sure were accorded no other Jew in all Germany or Austria."[72])

Yet Adolf's intense pain did little to inspire empathy for his fellow man. Countless innocents later died incomprehensibly cruel deaths on his orders, but Adolf never grasped the grief he caused, nor did he associate it with the searing pain he once felt over his mother's loss. There would be no lasting connection between his personal grief and grief as a human condition writ large. He did not interpret mourning as a phenomenon that should inspire a shared understanding of what it means to suffer and foster empathy for the human condition. "I would prefer not to see anyone suffer, not to do harm to anyone," Adolf stated in September 1941, honestly or disingenuously. "But when I realize that the species [sic] is in danger [sic], then in my case sentiment gives way to the coldest reason."[73] These were the words of a fanatic, someone so convinced of the righteousness of an evil ideology that one could do nothing but oppose and destroy him. But on Christmas Eve 1907, Adolf was not yet that monstrous tyrant.

◆ ◆ ◆

On New Year's Day, Gustl accompanied Adolf to his parents' graves. They stared silently at the fresh snow-covered mound where

Klara had gone into the ground. Adolf "looked hard and severe, and there were no tears in his eyes...," observed Gustl. "I stood by his side and prayed."[74] On the way home, Adolf told his only friend he would spend January in Linz and then return to Vienna. He had no interest in an offer to apprentice as a baker. Nor would he join his little sister Paula in living with half-sister Angela and her husband (whom he despised). He had enough money from his mother's estate—in addition to an orphan's pension that he and his little sister would receive—to get by in the big city for a year or so.[75] He eventually cut ties with his family altogether. And Paula wouldn't hear from him for thirteen years.[76]

Before leaving town, Adolf convinced Gustl's conservative father to let his son explore a career in music in Vienna. Adolf, Gustl recalled gratefully, engaged his father as if the "...whole matter [w]as of no great importance and, in particular implied that the decision rested with my father alone....I should go to Vienna for a trial period only to look around for a while..."[77] When Gustl subsequently arrived (with his father's consent), he found Adolf waiting at the train station, looking the part of the cosmopolitan urbanite. His friend wasted no time in dragging Gustl to the Vienna opera, leaving the latter awestruck by the splendor of it all.

The two decided to share a room in a dingy neighborhood, managing to squeeze in a rented grand piano for Gustl. As Adolf stayed up all night and slept late, Gustl had little time for dillydallying. He (easily!) gained admission to the Vienna Conservatory of Music. ("I had no idea I had such a clever friend," Adolf remarked bitterly at the news.) Adolf—having been denied admission to art school—stewed in his own failure as Gustl traded the upholstery shop for music school.[78]

The young men made a humble life in Vienna, living simply. Adolf in particular subsisted largely on milk, bread, butter, and the like.[79]

◆ ◆ ◆

Fantasies offered Adolf sustenance, and Gustl indulged his cockamamie ideas anew. Adolf would write a great play! Adolf would solve overcrowding in Vienna's housing! Adolf would craft an opera! Adolf would create a mobile orchestra to bring the joy of Wagner to the peasants![80] Such free-flowing schemes, ruminations of an unproductive tramp, took up a lot of Gustl's time. But rather than moving out to focus on his studies, Gustl became a sounding board, raising critical questions and even doing homework on Adolf's behalf—consulting the Musician's Union, for instance, on how much it would cost to hire musicians for a mobile orchestra.[81] "How much time and energy did I lose in these nocturnal activities with my friend?" reflected Gustl years later. "Why...did I not go?" It wasn't only homesickness—it "was an incredible earnestness in him, a thoroughness, a true passionate interest in everything that happened and, most important, an unfailing devotion to the beauty, majesty, and grandeur of art."[82] Adolf's obsessions transfixed his friend. They would do the same to others, for years to come.

Of course Adolf still wanted Gustl to have no other companions. (He erupted when Gustl once brought home a young woman for a music lesson.[83]) And he still had no interest in sexual relationships with women, even as they pursued him more directly.[84] When he and Gustl once looked at an apartment, for example, the lady of the house—"not so young, but very elegant," dressed in a silk robe and fur slippers—expressed particular interest in Adolf moving in. Then her robe slipped open for an instant, exposing panties and presumably a glimpse of breasts. ("Oh, excuse me, gentlemen.") Adolf "turned as red as a peony" and fled, Gustl in tow.[85]

◆ ◆ ◆

This time in Vienna increasingly frustrated Adolf. He became "unbalanced," from Gustl's perspective. He lashed out angrily over trifling things, misanthropic sentiments ringing out of him.[86] Yet Adolf's life was not devoid of opportunity altogether. The owner of the house in Linz where his family had lived recommended him to a renowned opera stage designer in early 1908, offering (what would seem) a fantastic opportunity to work in both opera and art. But the stubborn teenager declined, perhaps afraid—as scholars have mused— to subject his "artistic genius" to further scrutiny.[87]

Adolf and Gustl's friendship came to a sudden end in July 1908. Gustl had just finished his first semester at the conservatory and headed home for the summer, arranging to keep his apartment with Adolf and see him again in the fall. Upon Gustl's return, however, he found a new tenant in their old room. Adolf had moved out. Left no forwarding address. What Gustl did not know was that the Vienna Academy of Fine Arts had just rejected Adolf, again; they didn't even let him take the entrance exam the second time around.[88] This second rejection likely encouraged the abrupt break. Continuing to live with Gustl would have compelled Adolf to confront ever-mounting insecurity vis-à-vis his only friend. Gustl was succeeding as a music student. Adolf was going nowhere—and he couldn't handle feelings of inferiority.

◆◆◆

Gustl had no communication with Adolf until after he became Chancellor of Germany in January 1933. Learning that news, Gustl— then a humble civil servant!—remembered a late evening back in 1905. The two had attended Wagner's opera *Rienzi, der letzte der Tribunen.* Adolf was intensely excited about the show, but left it quiet and subdued. When Gustl tried to ask his thoughts, Adolf snapped at him with a "strange, almost hostile glance" to shut his mouth.[89] Unwilling to engage, Adolf strode briskly through the streets wearing a black overcoat, collar turned upward, a dark hat shielding his eyes. The teenager appeared pale and unfriendly; Gustl scampered behind, uncertain of their destination, pulled along in the damp darkness.

Adolf led the way to Freinberg, the mountain overlooking Linz. At the top, he supposedly took Gustl's hands in his own, squeezing firmly. And then he began to speak with intensity. "It was," Gustl recorded, "as if a second ego spoke from within him, and moved him." A verbal deluge poured forth. Gustl, the reliable audience-of-one, listened attentively as the mounting fury of Adolf's words considered new ambitions. Eyes burning, Adolf Hitler declared that one day *he* might receive a mandate to lead a people to freedom. "It was a young man whose name then meant nothing who spoke to me in that strange hour," remembered Gustl. "He spoke of a special mission which one day would be entrusted to him and I, his only listener could hardly understand what he meant."[90]

CHAPTER SIXTEEN
LOVE AND LOSS FOR SOSO

Soso the revolutionary exuded grisly determination in the
years after he left the seminary.[1] Authorities had exiled him to

Siberia in the dead of winter in 1903; but soon he escaped back to Tiflis. *A wanted man.*

He was, according to police records, "ordinary...of average height and build," neither tall nor especially short.[2] His left arm, as a mug shot demonstrates, was shorter than his right. He had two webbed toes on his left foot (a sign of Satanic influence, according to period superstitions).[3] His face was attractive, pockmarks doing nothing to deter female admirers.[4] But Soso was more ideological gangster than Lothario.[5] And he defied, then as always, simplistic summation. "Very severe" but "a deeply feeling person."[6] A "jokester" who hated laziness among his peers.[7] A young poet who chose Marx.[8] Thoughtful and educated but ruthless.[9] Call him Koba.[10] Intimates still referred to him as Soso.

◆ ◆ ◆

In the revolutionary year of 1905, Soso, shabbily dressed and olive-skinned, met his wife-to-be, Kato, in an apartment used as a hideout. Her brother, Alyosha, had invited him. It was just behind the South Caucasus military headquarters in Tiflis. (The darkest place in the room, as the saying goes, is beneath the candle.) Kato and her sisters worked as seamstresses in the building, making dresses for the wives of high-ranking military officials as revolutionaries schemed nearby.[11] Soso hung out there, sitting in a corner, smoking and writing. It was an exciting time. ("Life...is seething," Soso wrote of that year's uprisings. "The ship of the revolution has hoisted sail and is speeding towards freedom....Let the thunder roar still louder, let the storm rage more fiercely."[12])

Unlike his peers, Soso was not looking for a "stern, emancipated" female revolutionary—a woman "who chain-smoked and practiced free love...and understood that morality had no part to play in the brave new world."[13] But Kato, devoutly religious (like his mother), attracted him.[14] She even shared his mom's name: Ekaterina. Kato was "ravishingly pretty," with dark brown hair, and buxom.[15] In the company of others, she was reserved, not as outspoken as Keke. She did not care much for politics but revered Soso's intellect. His ideas— and presumably his ability to explain complex ideological principles simply—spellbound her. Kato idolized him. Yet she wasn't naïve. She knew what Soso and his band of Bolsheviks were up to. She was an educated woman (for the time) and thought for herself.[16] Her choices mattered—more than she ever could have known.[17]

KATO

♦♦♦

Sometime in late spring of 1906, Soso and Kato started having sex in the back room of the seamstress shop. Mannequins, stuffed with secret papers, stood witness—*hearts and minds at stake*.[18] (The arrival of police inspectors sent Soso scurrying out a back window on one occasion.) Kato was pregnant by summer. The lovers decided to get married. Soso even agreed to a religious ceremony—a decision that surely thrilled his fiancé.[19] His mother, if also pleased, worried about what kind of life Kato could expect from Soso. ("Soso got married," Keke told a niece. "She's a little woman, but what kind of family is she supposed to conduct, I wonder?"[20])

Soso and Kato initially had trouble finding someone to marry them. The groom was an outlaw, remember! But a priest Soso had known from the seminary eventually agreed to conduct the ceremony—so long as it happened late at night. The couple agreed, and a full orthodox wedding took place at Zion Cathedral at 2 AM on July 16, 1906. A handful of guests, including militant atheists and seminary drop-outs, attended. A joyful reception followed in the early morning hours, at which one of Soso's minions (Kamo) joked: "Where are the stupid police now? We are all here. Let them come and arrest us like sheep."[21]

The couple initially enjoyed a post-wedding glow at odds with Keke's perceptive doubts. Soso was better to Kato than anyone else in his life. He spoke gently to her, with affection, his yellow-tinted brown eyes sparkling. This woman, Soso told his only daughter years later, "was very sweet and beautiful: she melted my heart."[22] ("How much he loved her," a later witness agreed.[23]) "I was amazed," observed the husband of Kato's sister, "how Soso, who was so severe in his work and to his comrades, could be so tender, affectionate and attentive to his wife."[24] No other person rivaled Kato's importance to Soso—save Keke.

But the marriage soon left no doubt that Kato—with child on the way—couldn't compete with the revolutionary epoch. Her husband's rabid pursuit of a new era for humanity did not allow for a long honeymoon period. Soso carried on with the revolution like a mistress while his pregnant wife waited at home. He eluded capture as authorities hunted him, making his way from safe house to safe house, raising funds for the Party, writing works like "Anarchism or Socialism."[25] He surfaced at home like a crocodile comes up for air.[26]

Kato looked to the Almighty for help. She prayed for her husband to find a new path. A friend recalled years later that Kato:

> looked after [her] husband's welfare with all her heart, spending her nights in frequent prayer while waiting for her Soso, who was busy at his meetings, praying that he might turn away from ideas that were displeasing to God and revert to a quiet home life of labour and contentment. So this restless man alone found love in his own impoverished home where only his wife, child, and mother were free from the scorn he poured out upon everyone else.[27]

Kato knew the perils of loving him. The lifestyle of a revolutionary was no surprise to her. Her brother, Alyosha, was a Bolshevik, and she had observed how Soso lived before they married.[28] But she selflessly loved him just the same.

Authorities raided Kato's apartment in November 1906. They arrested her, five months pregnant, and demanded to know Soso's whereabouts. Kato gave them nothing. Her sister, Sashiko, quickly attained her release by convincing the wife of a police colonel—for whom she had once made a dress—to advocate for her sister's freedom. After further petitioning, authorities let Soso's wife avoid a prolonged jail stay and remain in the custody of a local police chief's wife. That kind woman, as it would happen, had once worked as a seamstress alongside Kato and her sister. Triumph for the bonds of fashion.[29]

Soso was miserable upon hearing of his wife's arrest. He hurried home, and even succeeded in visiting Kato *at the home of the police chief*. He (incredibly!) claimed to be a "village cousin." The policeman's spouse—knowingly or not—allowed husband to see pregnant wife. Kato (if not Soso) made a good impression, because she was soon given two hours of freedom each day with her "cousin" until police eventually dropped any charges against her.[30]

One wonders what pregnant Kato thought in those weeks. Did her choices burden her—the budding consequences of a life she had chosen for herself *and her unborn baby?*

◆◆◆

In March 1907, Kato gave birth to a boy named Yakov (the formal name of Soso's stand-in father, Koba, growing up). The couple had the baby christened. Soso was ecstatic. Called the infant Laddie.[31] The baby's tears made writing more difficult—to Soso's revolutionary chagrin—but the new dad hugged and kissed Yakov just the same. The man's "love for wife and child became ten times more," recalled one of his friends.[32]

But domestic pleasures were short-lived.

Soso's work kept him busy. And distant. In late April, he traveled to London for a Party congress before visiting Paris.[33] Then he returned home in early June and assisted in planning a daring heist.[34] Aforementioned Kamo—an indefatigable Bolshevik throat-slitter—played the lead role. It took place in Yerevan Square in Tiflis on June 13, 1907. Kamo (disguised as a calvary officer) led some twelve gangsters in attacking two coaches carrying cash to the State Bank in the Georgian capital. Kamo's bandits threw homemade grenades—

"apples"—at the coach guards and horses. Blood and gore splattered. Premature deaths and grieving mothers followed. In the midst of the carnage, Kamo's thieves snagged the money as he maniacally fired his gun in the air to distract onlookers.[35] Soso did not participate. Far too dangerous. But one can imagine him quipping "How r-r-revolutionary" upon hearing the robbery netted 250,000 rubles—the equivalent of more than $3.4 million.[36] Kamo, disguised as a prince traveling with a new wife (a female participant from the day's butchery), fled abroad to deliver the money to Volodia.

They did not realize the bills were marked.[37]

◆ ◆ ◆

Kato, holding baby Yakov, felt explosions from the robbery as she sat nearby on a balcony with her sister. ("We rushed inside, absolutely terrified," recalled Sashiko.[38]) When Soso arrived home later that night, he announced the robbery's success, and informed Kato that they would be moving. To Baku. 360 miles away. Thirteen hours by train. Kato's family protested (and continued to do so into the 1930s.)[39] The move was a terrible idea. It would leave Kato and Yakov isolated in a polluted city, knowing no one, waiting in some hut, lonely and apprehensive in the sweltering heat, as Soso continued his never-ending revolutionary struggle.[40]

Unmoved, Soso arrived in Baku with Kato and Yakov in mid-July.[41] They moved into a small shack next to the Caspian Sea. The dwelling's exterior was depressing, but Kato kept the inside perfectly clean. She and Yakov played on a wooden bed. Newly made curtains adorned the windows. And a sewing machine, a faithful friend that couldn't leave her, was in the corner.

Soso was gone much of the time. When he came home, he would return in the dark morning before departing with the dawn. He often disappeared into the criminal chaos of Baku, a cesspool of danger. Kato waited on the bed with Yakov. Hot and lonely.[42]

Soso's revolutionary activities mounted. Support for the Party grew among the workers. His dedication was boundless. He labored ceaselessly as Volodia peddled radicalism and misanthropy from abroad. His messianic faith in the future—"overthrow of the tsarist regime...war against the treacherous liberal bourgeoisie"—pushed him to work ever harder. If the "task of the proletariat"—argued Soso—"is consciously to take this path and worthily to play the part of leader of the revolution," he would be at their forefront.[43] Visions of a socialist utopia eclipsing the bourgeois sun moved him, and the altar of his Bolshevik worldview demanded human sacrifices. So he let Kato and Yakov rot—and these were people he loved.[44]

Kato went on waiting each day still, eating bad food, her stress mounting as she ached for home, the baby crying in the oppressive heat. She, like Soso's mother, feared the outcome of his revolutionary pursuits. Anxiety devoured her mundane days. If authorities arrested her husband, they would send him back to Siberia—if they didn't hang him.[45] And there was always the possibility that Soso might never come home. Just gone forever one day without explanation, an infinite wait spreading out before her. What awesome relief she must have felt whenever Soso returned home; that is, until he promptly left again, abandoning her anew, the cycle repeating. Kato's sister seemed to foresee catastrophe on the horizon. She wrote Kato, imploring her to return home to Tiflis. Kato's response ("How can I leave Soso?") reflected the same unshakable loyalty that Soso's mother, Keke, had showed him as a boy ("How can I pull him out of school?"). Unrequited fidelity.

Soso recognized his wife and child's miserable situation and made no secret of it in conversations with friends, signifying his own disquiet with what he had brought to pass. He cursed himself for having married Kato, for having put her and the baby in such an awful position. But these insights did nothing to break his dependence on the revolution.[46] ("Soso loved her very much," explained a friend at the time, "but if you didn't know Soso's character well, you would not understand his love. Wife, child, friend, were good for him only if they were not hindering him in his work…"[47]) Soso, then, carried on like an addict who knows their actions are destroying what they hold dear. Yet he continued, seemingly unable to change, onwards towards the muffled rumble of funeral drums. It was self-destruction as self-realization.

◆ ◆ ◆

Kato became thin and sickly. She begged Soso to go home to Tiflis. But her husband took no action until October when he finally recognized the seriousness of his wife's situation. To the train station they went, bound for home. A long, stifling ride followed—a difficult journey for a young baby, much less a sick mother. Searching for relief from the heat, Kato apparently drank foul water at a station along the way. Not good.

What a sad sight they must have been upon arrival in Tiflis. Soso wasted no time in depositing Kato with her family and returning to Baku. He could not ignore the cause. Not even for his ailing wife. Two weeks passed before word came to return. Time was short. *Soso blinked*.[48]

He found Kato dying. He hugged her withered body, a newfound commitment that meant little, save providing her comfort. Her bloody diarrhea wouldn't stop. Her fever refused to subside. And an ever-darkening red rash grew on her body, blackening, spreading like a poisonous vine.[49] Soso stared into her weak eyes, her feeble face, with the understanding he could have protected her. He could have prevented this moment.

Kato's inexorable demise was a consequence of his own egotism, his obsession with putting the revolution first. *The fucking revolution.* The inevitable ideological triumph he believed in more than ever. Soso finally saw the irreversible consequences of his own decision-making, the reality of his actions, the beginning of a heavy, irreparable loss—a dark chasm opening within him in which his soul would free-fall endlessly. He knew (of course!) it was all his fault. The magnitude of culpability weighed on him with awe-striking, sublime terror.[50]

From then on, Soso knew that Dostoevsky got it wrong.[51] "The most terrible agony," states *The Idiot*, "may not be in the wounds themselves but in knowing for certain that within an hour, then within ten minutes, then within half a minute, now at this very instant—your soul will leave your body and you will no longer be a person, and that is certain; the worst thing is that it is certain."[52] But Soso realized it's not our own death that strikes the deepest terror, not the end of our own individuality and ambitions—it's the realization that our loved ones inevitably perish. He lived that epiphany before Kato's deathbed. *The devil was as terrible as he was painted.* And Kato's misery bore into him.[53] That woman had supported him, and now she would die for it. On November 22, 1907, Kato passed away in his arms. He shut her eyes.

◆ ◆ ◆

Soso's mourning was all consuming. His guilt was the kind that deepens grief with misery born of self-loathing. Soso crumbled to the floor after a photo was taken next to her open casket. Bawling. Pain boiling over. Friends took away his gun, fearful he'd turn it on himself.[54]

During the priest-led funeral procession on the morning of November 25, the widower walked behind his wife's coffin, arm in arm with a childhood buddy-turned-political opponent.[55] When the funeral procession reached the burial grounds, Soso took his old friend's hand and pointed at Kato's coffin: "This creature softened my heart of stone; she died, and with her died my last warm feelings for all human beings." Then, placing his right hand over his heart, assuredly struggling to hold it together, he stated: "It's all so desolate here inside, so inexpressibly desolate."[56] ("This hard man's pale face," even Trotsky later wrote of this moment, "reflected the heart-felt anguish caused by the death of his faithful life's companion. His emotional distress...must have been very deep-seated and enduring, for he was incapable of hiding it any longer from outsiders."[57]) "I realized," Soso later reflected, "how many things in my life I hadn't appreciated. While my wife was alive, there were many times I didn't return home at night. I told her when I left not to worry about me but when I got home, she'd be sitting there. She'd wait up all night."[58] Self-pity mingled with accountability. A mea culpa of sorts. No reprieve in the offing.

Kato's burial brought no catharsis. Soso watched as an Orthodox Church service laid her to rest. (Could he himself, in a different life, have been the priest?) He cried violently, jumping into the grave, compelling friends to pull him off her coffin. Convulsing, screaming, and weeping before her anguished family—who no doubt blamed him for her death. Once Soso returned from her grave—a sort of pathological rebirth—he actually fled his own wife's funeral. The arrival of police spelled arrest, and Soso prioritized the struggle over Kato's burial. He absconded over a fence, like a fleeing burglar, abandoning his wife anew. Emotions—even at their most intense— were not supposed to interfere with the larger ideological mission at hand. So much remained unfinished.[59]

Yet Kato's death ultimately paralyzed Soso for a time. He retreated home, a bewildered son in his mom's arms again. Efforts to console him were for naught. For once, the revolution had to wait.[60] He spent the next eight weeks sobbing, until he came to the conclusion that the revolution (not his infant son) was the only thing that could still give his life meaning. "My personal life is shattered. Nothing attaches me to life except socialism. I'm going to dedicate my existence to that," he told a friend.[61] If he had effectively sacrificed Kato for the revolution, he could not possibly turn his back on it without making his wife's death in vain. He wasted no time in abandoning eight-month-old Yakov, leaving him with Kato's family. (He would have nothing to do with the boy for decades—and even then, he would be an emotionally abusive, reprehensible father.)[62] Nothing mattered but the cause. Which, ironically, became a sort of monument to Kato when Soso used her name as a revolutionary moniker— "K. Kato"—for a time.[63]

Kato's loss drove Soso towards an ever-darker, crueler future.[64] His childhood friend recalled the shift that followed:

> From the day he buried his wife, he indeed lost the last vestiges of human feeling. His heart filled with the unalterably malicious hatred which his cruel father had begun to engender in him while he was still a child. Ruthless with himself, he became [that much more] ruthless to everyone else.[65]

Empathy—though even he was capable of it at times—would only undermine his pursuit of power. No sacrifice (save the loss of his own life) was too much in advancing his ideological ends.

Joseph Stalin became a terrifying synthesis of dogmatism, self-pity, and bitterness. Someone more sinister than before, damaged by the loss of Kato but also a worldview of his own making, one born of good fortune and education as well as trauma. The years to come would see these traits manifested in horrifying fashion. "I was witness to the spiritual deterioration of my own father," his daughter would later recall, "watching day after day how everything human left him and how gradually he turned into a grim monument to his own self."[66]

CHAPTER SEVENTEEN
RENZHI BECOMES THE HERO

In 1913, Renzhi's hunger for intellectual growth at the First Normal School in Changsha led him to become friends with a fellow student named Xiaoyu. At first, twenty-year-old Renzhi would simply pass by nineteen-year-old Xiaoyu in the halls. Both knew of the other, but Renzhi was in a lower grade and hesitated to strike up a conversation until teachers showcased their essays together. Looking over each other's work—one sly fox admiring another—the two developed a mutual respect, and Xiaoyu began to take note of Renzhi's intense work ethic. ("Every morning I used to hear him," Xiaoyu remembered, "reading aloud from the old classics...he studied hard."[1]) Months passed until Renzhi finally asked Xiaoyu if he might borrow some of his essays.[2]

They developed a quick friendship, taking long walks in the hills around school and engaging in wide-ranging conversations about history, literature, and philosophy. Both from Hunan Province, their shared heritage brought them together as "sons of the land of heroes and brigands," as Xiaoyu would later put it. Roving bands of criminals had long sought refuge in their home province's mountains, but its people were renowned for their obstinacy and fearlessness. A widespread love for the province's intense peppercorns, the friend speculated, encouraged such feistiness. Renzhi and Xiaoyu, for their part, found no peppercorn too much.[3]

◆ ◆ ◆

Renzhi was average in many ways, remembered Xiaoyu. He was "quite an ordinary, normal-looking person" with "eyes [that] were neither large nor penetrating." He spoke slowly, and was by no means a talented orator. (His gait, as Xiaoyu recalled, sometimes "reminded one of a duck waddling."[4]) The two young men differed dramatically in appearance. Xiaoyu went to great pains to bathe regularly and look presentable while Renzhi was often disheveled. He was a slob. But not in the sense of not knowing that one should take care of their appearance. Renzhi *knew* he looked like hell. He just didn't care about the fact he was supposed to worry about it. Appearances were too far down on his priority list.

Bathing—one might guess then—was not Renzhi's strong suit. He smelled. Wore his stink as a badge of peasant pride! He even teased Xiaoyu over his good hygiene, asking why he washed and brushed his teeth so often. Renzhi never brushed his teeth. Like country peasants, he only rinsed his mouth with tea water, inviting "heavy greenish film" and pus that eventually conquered his smile.[5] ("A tiger never brushes his teeth. Why are a tiger's teeth so sharp?")[6] Only "the son of a rich father!"—Renzhi scolded Xiaoyu—cared about such things.[7]

Predictably, the two also differed when it came to cleaning their rooms. Xiaoyu's was a carefully swept masterpiece, his desk the model of a tidy life. But Renzhi's was as much of a wreck as his appearance. How could "a great hero"—Xiaoyu needled Renzhi—clean up the universe if he couldn't manage his own room? Renzhi's riposte: "A great hero who thinks about cleaning up the universe has no time to think about sweeping rooms!" Discussions about topics like Bismarck's legacy—rather than bathing, cleaning, or laundry—took up Renzhi's time. If Xiaoyu never understood why "belonging to the proletariat...compelled one to be dirty," he was happy to engage his friend in debates about anything and everything. Intellectual intimacy united them, for a time.[8]

◆ ◆ ◆

One thing that both young men steadfastly agreed on was their admiration for the teacher Yang Changji.[9] Yang, who had studied in Japan and Europe, taught philosophy, ethics, and education. His expansive knowledge of Confucian classics led his adoring students to nickname him Confucius, and view him as a sort of reincarnation of that revered philosopher.[10] Yang was a disciplined, austere man who stressed the importance of will and perseverance to his students. "Every day one must do something difficult to strengthen one's own will," Xiaoyu remembered him emphasizing. That meant, for Yang, refusing to eat breakfast, and taking icy baths each morning (even in winter). "Cold water not only strengthens the will; it is good for the health!" declared the teacher. It remains unclear whether such icy baths eventually led to his untimely demise at age forty-eight—on a winter morning.[11]

YANG CHANGJI

Renzhi and Xiaoyu adored Yang because he taught them the value of their agency—that they could attempt to compel fate to obey their wishes. As foreign imperialism humiliated their people, Yang's criticism of feudal customs prompted Renzhi and other students to envision a new path for their people. They emulated the teacher. They gave up breakfast for nearly two years and strived to embrace his strict methods whenever they could.[12] His teachings particularly encouraged young Renzhi's belief that intense physical activity was indispensable for strengthening will and endurance.[13] "To wash our feet in ice water makes us acquire courage and dauntlessness, as well as audacity," Renzhi told fellow students in a clear echo of Yang.[14] Renzhi and his friends, following this mode of thought, became "ardent physical culturists," sleeping out in the open during frosts and tramping around outside during winter, cold be damned.[15] They saw Yang as a trustworthy mentor because he empowered them. He suggested they could bend reality like a thin piece of metal in their hands.[16]

There was no greater goal for an individual—Yang stressed—than to be just, moral, and virtuous.[17] To achieve any such status, one had to aim high, work hard, and serve the greater good through individual struggle.[18] The teacher defined virtuous behavior as self-cultivation for society's sake. Renzhi made clear his desire to embrace these teachings in a July 1915 letter to Xiaoyu, in which he reflected on the need to improve one's own abilities to strengthen the country. "When I think of the greatness of Professor Yang," Renzhi lamented at the same time, "I feel I will never be his equal."[19]

Yang called it "the Way." Establish an ironclad will! Refuse to let time or hardship diminish your commitment to the greater good! ("Faith in rebirth through heroic effort"—as one writer characterized it.[20]) A "person with a strong will," Yang explained to his students, "can suppress his evil desires…can withstand the oppression of the

246

powerful" and "succeed…in casting great influence upon the world." Since the beginning of civilization, the teacher emphasized, "those who have died for the Way had rather die than see their will violated."[21] When Xiaoyu wrote to Renzhi on the same topic the following month, the latter replied excitedly, but with even more anxiety than before: "I am frightened morning and night and [am] ashamed to face up to [the ideal of] the superior man."[22] Unyielding belief in inevitable triumph was still to come for Renzhi, his steely confidence in utero.

Yang's regular declaration to his students that one must "Destroy the 'habitual self,' [and] realize the 'ideal self'" especially influenced Renzhi's emerging conviction that his country's suffocating traditions—like an individual's bad habits—would have to be obliterated for national renewal.[23] To achieve a dramatic rebirth, Renzhi came to believe, his country would have to be destroyed and rebuilt. As he saw it, this principle—destruction for transformative progress—applied not only to individuals and nations, but even the universe. "From the demise of the old universe," he would reflect, "will come a new universe, and will it not be better than the old universe!"[24] If you want to understand Renzhi's later assertion that "without destruction there can be no construction," return to Yang Changji's classroom.[25]

RENZHI

The teacher adored Renzhi and Xiaoyu. Of Renzhi in particular, he wrote after one conversation in April 1915, "it was truly difficult to find someone so intelligent." Yang encouraged Renzhi to be ambitious, noting that many people with "unusual talents" had risen to power from rural beginnings. Renzhi, the teacher wrote in a letter, would almost certainly "have a great future."[26] He was the type of young man who couldn't be ignored.

Frequently, Yang invited Renzhi and his fellow students over to his house to continue lessons and speak about the world. The teacher—one such student remembered—urged the young men to "advance toward our ideal life." He also engaged them in discussions about the "virtuous person" and their ability to influence the world.[27] Xiaoyu, however, remembered these gatherings a little differently. He mostly recalled Yang's daughter, Kaihui. The teacher, Xiaoyu claimed, wanted him to marry her—until he learned Xiaoyu already had a wife.[28]

KAIHUI

It was Renzhi—not his close friend—who fell in love with Yang's daughter. After the teacher's sudden death in 1920, Renzhi and Kaihui started an intense relationship. Boisterous love-making in school dorms provoked complaints. Their ensuing marriage was doomed to failure, though it produced several sons. Renzhi was unfaithful. His own desires always came first.[29]

Still, there was no doubting the sincerity of feeling between the two. Years later, when Renzhi's enemies arrested Kaihui, she refused to denounce him; chose execution by firing squad instead. As a result, on a cloudy morning, armed men stripped Yang Changji's daughter to a thin blouse and marched her out of town, tied up like a criminal. They shot her outside the city gates. She didn't initially die. She lay suffering. Writhing on the ground. Fingers digging into the dirt. Determination sustaining her weakening heart. Her executioners went to lunch. And then murdered her again.

If he died a hundred times, Renzhi would mourn, it would not be enough to compensate for Kaihui's loss. Even into old age, he would describe her as the greatest love of his life.[30] A poem written by Renzhi—for a widow in 1957—speaks to these sentiments:

> I lost my proud Poplar and you your Willow,
> Poplar and Willow soar to the Ninth Heaven.
> Wu Gang, asked what he can give,
> Serves them a laurel wine.
>
> The lonely moon goddess spreads her ample sleeves
> To dance for these loyal souls in infinite space.
> Earth suddenly reports the tiger subdued,
> Tears of joy pour forth falling as mighty rain.[31]

The majesty of these words reflect the sublimity of loss, what the immensity of the end can mean for lovers. When Renzhi spoke of Kaihui—the child of the man who opened his eyes to the power of his will—what was it he so mourned? Was it only self-pity, or was it genuine sorrow? When do those two become the same thing?

◆ ◆ ◆

Such self-awareness was, perhaps, far in the future as Xiaoyu and Renzhi grew closer over the summer of 1917. They spent those months exploring Hunan on foot, clad as beggars.[32] In Thoreau-like fashion, they took no money. The goodness of strangers fed them. "The attraction of the beggar's life for me," Xiaoyu recalled, "was the ability to overcome physical and psychological difficulties inherent in living outside the accepted pale of society."[33] Off they went. Wandering across five counties on foot, more than three hundred miles, "without using a single copper," that's how Renzhi remembered it.[34]

At one point—or so the story would go—they came across a young woman who refused to believe they were actually beggars. She looked closely at Xiaoyu and Renzhi—both twenty-somethings—before announcing: "I can see that both of you are great men!" But what exactly makes a man great, Xiaoyu queried? The young woman brushed aside the question. A fortune teller of sorts, she could tell by their faces, which piqued Renzhi's interest. "If you know how to read faces, please will you read ours?" he asked. She hesitated: What if her words made them angry? Don't worry, exclaimed Renzhi. No one would get offended.

Renzhi, the young fortune-teller stated, would either become a powerful political official or a kind of gangster. One way or another, immense ambition and ruthlessness would take him far. "You," she told him, "have no sentiment at all! You could kill ten thousand or even a hundred thousand people without turning a single hair!" Of course, she warned, Renzhi's enemies might kill him first, though he would be safe if he made it to age fifty.

Xiaoyu jumped in. What about his fortune? Xiaoyu, the fortune teller declared, was almost the opposite of Renzhi. He was deeply sentimental, a wandering spirt who would travel far yet never settle down. His essence, she concluded, was like "pure, clear water" to the "very strong brandy" of Renzhi's. As they parted, the two friends thanked the young woman, and Xiaoyu ventured that someday his friend might invite her to be his adviser after he became a powerful leader, or a famous bandit. She laughed hard: No way! Not possible. A man with so little feeling would never remember her.

This "exchange with the fortune teller"—be it exaggerated or invented by Xiaoyu—reflected his later conviction that Renzhi was cold, calculating, driven.[35]

◆ ◆ ◆

As the two continued their journey, they clashed on what defines a heroic leader. This proved particularly true during an exchange about Chinese Emperor Liu Bang, who established the Han dynasty around 202 BCE. Renzhi emphasized that Liu Bang "should be considered a great hero!" He was, after all, the first man in their country's history to start life as a peasant and end his days as emperor. Xiaoyu pushed back: Liu Bang was a tyrant who "got rid of one despot only to become another himself." "I suppose," Renzhi argued (according to his friend's recollection years later):

> that you think that after his revolutionary forces had gained control of the country, he should have established a democratic republic. Two thousand years ago democratic republics had never been thought of! People had never heard of such a form of government! It was impossible for him to visualize a democratic system in those days.[36]

Xiaoyu balked: "But even if he couldn't visualize a democratic republic, he could at least have avoided being a cruel despot!" Renzhi: "You can't really call him cruel, if you take into account the age in which he lived and compare him with other Emperors of the time." But what about the fact—Xiaoyu fired back—that he turned on, and butchered, many of the same friends who fought for him, that he went so far as to have some of their families murdered? "He bore a knife in his breast in the place where his heart should have been!" Renzhi, unflustered, responded that those same friends might have overthrown him. Liu Bang would not have remained emperor long if unwilling to act in such a manner. "So in order to be successful in politics, one must kill one's friends?" asked Xiaoyu heatedly. "We both knew," Xiaoyu remembered of the tension, "that he [Renzhi] was identifying himself with Liu Bang in his ambition."[37]

Renzhi—maybe then, certainly later—yearned to be like that emperor, to be a country boy who rose to power through iron resolve. Heroes, Renzhi would believe, had to engage in isolated acts of evil for greater ends. The "truly great person," he later wrote, casts aside "restraints and restrictions" at the decisive moment, his will like "a powerful wind" akin to the force driving an "irresistible sexual desire for one's lover."[38] "Conscience," he declared, "is only there to restrain, not oppose"—to help one more effectively achieve their impulses.[39] The "superior man" *had* to make hard, disturbing choices.

In that same vein, Renzhi sent a letter to Xiaoyu towards the end of his time in school, lamenting the overthrow of a hated military governor in Hunan. Yes, he wrote, that governor had killed more than ten thousand people—but had he not restored order in the process? Bloodshed, Renzhi's message made clear, would be the "inescapable outcome of policy" ensuring stability and the people's welfare.[40] For his part, Xiaoyu could not see how the ends so often justified the means in his friend's logic.

Such disagreements did not prevent the two young men from forming a new political organization the following year. In a nighttime talk in the hills overlooking Changsha, they decided to found the "New People's Study Association" to cultivate the good character of their people and encourage societal reforms.[41]

They started by recruiting small numbers of their classmates. Renzhi then wrote an open letter to nearby schools, denouncing the untrustworthiness of governmental officials and calling for anyone interested in saving their nation to join them. (Afraid of mockery rather than repression, Renzhi signed his appeal "twenty-eight-strokes"—the number of pen strokes it took to write his formal name.) The organization that then took shape represented one seed (of many) that would germinate and sprout into the future political party that Renzhi came to dominate. It wasn't important so much for what it did, as for the relationships it forged.[42] (Many of its members later died gruesome deaths at the hands of Renzhi's political enemies.[43])

Xiaoyu and Renzhi's friendship deteriorated in the years that followed. The latter grew increasingly interested in communism—and took inspiration from Emperor Liu Bang.[44]

◆ ◆ ◆

Renzhi's thinking about morality, and one's obligations to others in particular, evolved from 1917 to 1918 as he studied Friedrich Paulsen's *System of Ethics*.[45] Paulsen's arguments about the relativistic nature of ethics encouraged the twenty-four-year-old to believe that one's time and place define what is ethical—that morality's boundaries are amorphous and constantly shifting. Renzhi recorded some twelve thousand words in the margins of *System of Ethics*, leaving a clear sense of his thinking about Paulsen's arguments. "In the broad sense, there is no universal human morality," Renzhi wrote next to Paulsen's statement that "The Englishman and the African each has his own ways and virtues, and that since the circumstances of their lives are different[,] they subsequently have different moralities." Reflecting on the inclination of people in the present to denounce the immorality of the past, *System of Ethics* stated the following before Renzhi's eyes:

The average person tends to feel that if what those in the past did is incompatible with today's morality then it must be rejected as wrong. When we read the history of the Middle Ages, and see that Christians hated those of other beliefs and often arrested and tortured heretics and witches, and even killed and burned them, we strongly condemn them. Such brutality was truly barbarous. But the use of barbarous punishments in a barbarous age was not impermissible. And perhaps it was inevitable that such means were employed in the process of advancing from barbarism toward civilization. If the brutal punishments of the past had not existed, perhaps the cities of the Middle Ages would not have been able to move toward the complex social life of today...

Renzhi lapped this up. He had drawn on similar logic in his debate about Liu Bang with Xiaoyu. "Morality is different in different societies, and with different persons," he wrote in the margins.[46]

But what are the guiding principles of each person's decision-making towards others if a universal code of morality does not exist? The simple answer, Paulsen made clear, is that people prioritize their own self-interests. "The human will," Paulsen stated in this regard, "seeks the welfare of the individual and of others as its goal, and the relationship between how much something benefits oneself and how it benefits others may be highly complex and variable." Renzhi was not satisfied with this, writing in the margin: "I really find that this explanation is incomplete." He took Paulsen's arguments further, writing: "Self-interest is primary for all persons...[and] this serves the interest of others," before adding: "...the self cannot but benefit others" and "the starting point of altruism is the self." This logic suggested not only that serving one's fellow man would serve oneself but that *serving oneself would serve one's fellow man*. This latter generalization seemingly implies that self-interested decision-making serves the greater good because contrary actions would be to one's own detriment and thus would be avoided. "If I open my eyes wide," Renzhi continued, "and say that mankind is the greater self, and say that all living things are the greater self, and then say that the universe is the greater self, does this negate self-interest? *Why should self-interest be unworthy?*"[47] In other words: why shy away from openly pursuing one's own self-interest if it is synonymous with the public good?

But here comes the rub. Individualism—Renzhi wrote of his conclusions on Paulsen's text—represents one of two essential principles for ethical behavior: "Every act in life is for the purpose of fulfilling the individual, and all morality serves to fulfill the individual."[48] According to this perspective, we do not, then, express sympathy and work towards the well-being of others for them per se— but for ourselves, for our own egoism and selfish interests (a very Nietzsche-like point). The second principle Renzhi emphasized is "realism," the reality of one's immediate present—the need for each person to recognize the demands of the current day for their own life. "I am responsible only for my own subjective and objective reality," Renzhi wrote, before adding further:

> The past that I have not known, and the future that I do not know, are irrelevant to my individual present reality. Nor do I believe the saying that historical human beings are responsible for continuing the past and leading the way to the future. I develop only myself so that internally my thoughts and externally my actions achieve their ultimate ends. After I die, I place myself in history where later people may see that I had indeed fulfilled myself....Later generations may speak well of me, but I derive no pleasure from this because it belongs to the future and not to my present reality.[49]

Why should a person—the inverse of this thinking suggests— worry about the judgments of future men and women who might condemn one's actions rather than praise them? If future conceptions of morality will differ from our own; if only the here-and-now matters for each person; if individualism and self-interests are actually the foundations of ethical behavior and a better world; if we are only responsible to ourselves in the immediate moment, why should one not take decisive actions rooted in our own will *for the greater good*? The two supposedly reinforce each other. If one has the steely determination to live this way—to better the world around them for the sake of themselves and everyone else—what could they not achieve if their will was unbending?

Alas, the path of the "superior man" spilled out in the distance before Renzhi. An expansive landscape! A speeding train of heroism bursting forth in his self-centered consciousness towards greener pastures and blue skies![50] He had embraced an "ethical" code that justified everything he could—or would—ever do. *Forget your flawed notions of presentism and ignorant idealism about selfless morality.*

The young "hero" began his struggle.

◆◆◆

"Tell me, what do you really think of this fellow, Mao Tse-tung?" a friend asked Xiaoyu in 1926. "Has he any real ability, knowledge, natural endowment, or talent?"

Xiaoyu replied vaguely, asking contemplatively: "What is talent? Who is a genius?" What could be said, admitted Xiaoyu, was that his school friend was an extraordinarily capable person who, like few others, could craft and work towards long-term goals. He could calculate his odds of success in a given situation and win over others through force of argument. "If you say he has talent, that he's a genius," Xiaoyu added, it could be said in the sense of bandit brilliance, the cold and wily calculations of an individual who triumphs in a *Battle Royale*-like-world. Such a person [like Emperor Liu Bang] might gain ultimate power—or become a fearsome criminal. Who could know? "From ancient times," Xiaoyu concluded, "it has been said that heroes all like to interfere with other people's business. The hero is one of the world's madmen. He is always a source of trouble."[51]

The true hero would disagree.

But all of this was in the future when Mao attended school with Xiaoyu. The future dictator was still finding his way, sorting out his ideas. His emerging ambitions were not nefarious so much as idealistic and, from his perspective, noble. His eyes glimpsed a brutal Hobbesian landscape. His nation screamed for a savior to take decisive action against oppressive odds. Prosperity and glory would only appear on the horizon after struggle and inevitable destruction. Then the altruism of the "superior man" began with him, and so too did the misery he inflicted on countless innocents for their supposed benefit.

CHAPTER EIGHTEEN
COURAGE, TERROR, AND SONG-JU

By age 18, Song-ju was a radical nationalist with communist inclinations. Fresh out of prison in the city of Jilin, he decided to move to a small Manchurian town. His budding desire to struggle on behalf of his imprisoned nation and take action against the Japanese nudged him towards bolder efforts. Nationalistic fervor framed his worldview more than ever. Before leaving Jilin, he stopped by the home of Rev. Sohn's family, pledging to remember their aforementioned help. He kept that promise decades later by welcoming the reverend's aging son into one of his palaces, calling his father "the savior of my life."[1]

After Japan invaded Manchuria in September 1931, Song-ju wanted to join the resistance. The absence of a Korean communist party led him to look to the Chinese for direction.[2] Song-ju, his memoirs admit, "began to have relations with the Chinese Communist Party [CCP] for the first time" in the winter of 1931.[3] He became a formal member the following year. The relationship made sense. The young man, like his Chinese comrades, hated the Japanese. Both sought national liberation. Communist teachings against imperialism resonated.[4]

If Song-ju's countrymen were mostly ambivalent—if not uninformed—about Marxist doctrine itself, many sympathized with communist insurgents battling Japanese forces in Manchuria. Their struggle seemed to represent the fight of "the exploited against the exploiter" in a war for national independence.[5] Koreans like Song-ju often joined the CCP to fight for national self-determination, embracing communism in the process. The latter ideology promised rapid economic modernization once colonialism collapsed.[6]

When just that came to pass in 1945, and Song-ju returned to a liberated homeland, millions of his people retained a sympathetic view of communism because they viewed it in the nationalistic context of the anti-Japanese struggle. The *New York Times* was on to something as early as February 1931 when it declared Manchuria a "danger zone" driving "tens of thousands" of Koreans to join the communist insurgency against Japan. National liberation and communism went hand-in-hand.[7]

◆ ◆ ◆

By some accounts, Song-ju began to use his famed *nom d'guerre*—Il-sung—as early as 1931.[8] Its symbolism had less to do with its literal meaning ("one star") than the fact that a number of known guerillas had gone by that name.[9] As recently as March of 1930, a communist publication in Manchuria had printed news of an Il-sung who perished for the movement.[10] Adopting that moniker was a brilliant P.R. move for Song-ju; the broader public would associate him with the heroic exploits of earlier fighters. He bought credibility with martyrs' blood. Then his own courageous actions strengthened the meaning of "Il-sung" in his people's imagination. Song-ju was a pretender who became the real deal. That fact confused critics for decades.[11]

According to the official story, Song-ju joined the communist guerilla movement in the spring of 1932.[12] Surviving peers, however, did not remember him with a weapon before 1933, and reliable records do not corroborate his participation in combat before 1935.[13] The future dictator—his propagandists claim in one of many stirring anecdotes—joined the struggle after his mother dug up two pistols that had been buried with his father, and gave them to him to form a new partisan group.[14] They claim he fought a hundred thousand battles over the next decade! Song-ju's more serious propagandists claim that he participated in 112 to 160 major battles against the Japanese from 1932 to 1941, while also "supervising" dozens of strategy sessions—another untrustworthy claim.[15] Such exaggerations insult the actual history of Song-ju's time as a guerilla and ignore a more compelling story about how the insurgency shaped him as a person.[16]

Song-ju took orders from seasoned Chinese communists. Fluency in Mandarin benefitted him immensely in that respect.[17] Indeed, friendships he forged in the CCP helped save his life after Chinese communists arrested him, along with other Koreans, as potential Japanese spies in late 1933 and early 1934. That wave of repression (the "Minsaengdan incident") eventually killed some 500 to 2,000 Koreans associated with the Chinese Communist Party. But Song-ju's allies protected him.[18] He was, as one historian put it, "one of the few Koreans the Chinese had trusted because of his facility in the Chinese language and his Chinese educational background."[19] Both were gifts from his parents.

Saved from an early death—and benefitting from a sudden lack of experienced Korean guerillas—Song-ju quickly emerged as a capable young leader.[20] He inspired loyalty and confidence among peers, and his schooling stood out. As a result, Song-ju rose through the ranks, and soon found himself in command of a "division," consisting of dozens to hundreds of guerillas at a time.[21] The young commander gained intensely loyal followers in the winter of 1935 when he took in Koreans tainted by the earlier Chinese purge, burning evidence against them and inviting them to join his division. "I believe your resolution to fight along the road to revolution more than the stacked files of statements protocols, and confessions," Song-ju told his grateful countrymen.[22] He also promised in February 1936 (to the irritation of his Chinese commanders) that his division would "embrace even former Japanese spies or running dogs without questioning their past if they repented their own deeds and swore to devote themselves into the anti-Japanese struggle."[23] It was a courageous decision.[24]

In 1936, newspapers in Song-ju's homeland began to print news of his guerilla exploits.[25] His career peaked on June 4 of the following year when he led a raid on Poch'onbo, a small border town in Korea.[26] After six months of consulting with an anti-Japanese organization of his own countrymen, Song-ju and some two hundred guerillas crossed into the homeland and seized Poch'onbo, destroying a Japanese police outpost. After raising hell and bagging ¥4,000, Song-ju and his men retreated towards the Yalu River for the safety of rural Manchuria, bringing almost ninety new recruits with them. When Japanese forces gave pursuit, Song-ju set an ambush and killed seven pursuers, including a Japanese police chief. Days later, Song-ju's band joined with another partisan group and launched a coordinated raid against a Japanese timber camp in Manchuria, killing ten Japanese soldiers and taking nine hostages, along with supplies.[27]

These actions cemented Song-ju's reputation as a serious insurgent leader, and reinforced the legend of *Il-sung*. Though militarily insignificant, the Poch'onbo raid gave his people a hero in whom to believe. Song-ju had led his men back into the homeland and brought the war to the Japanese, a move most guerilla units didn't risk. It was a symbolic triumph, a message to his own people that the struggle against foreign occupation continued. Elementary primers in Song-ju's future kingdom never let little ones grow up without celebrating it. Along with learning the words for gun, book, and grenade, they learn that all roads lead to Poch'onbo![28]

◆ ◆ ◆

Of course, uncritical generalizations of Song-ju as a freedom fighter are problematic. His men showed gallantry in battle, but were brutal to those who did not support them. When seeking new recruits, his unit drafted the hesitant at gunpoint. They threatened and terrorized villagers—especially wealthy farmers—who wanted no part in the struggle.[29] "We have returned," read one note turned over to Japanese police in April 1936:

> We and our compatriots must unite and destroy the Japanese devils....Contribute guns if you have guns, people if you have people, money if you have money and materials if you have materials. Especially we are advising the heads of tithings in your village to contribute fifty feet of satin, ten feet of yellow thin silk, fifty feet of cotton fabrics, ten balls of white thread, one copy of the Wenho [Mosquito Creek] map, and two sheets of copying paper. These must be submitted within five days as an expression of your loyalty to the anti-Japanese struggle. In case of non-compliance to this request, the people in your tithings are considered by our army as pro-Japanese...when our army comes to your village in full force to destroy the Japanese devils there will be numerous ways to take care of the people in your village. This is a special message and we do not wish any further words concerning this matter.[30]

Subsequent letters from guerilla groups like Song-ju's would be no less ominous. "Five days ago this army kidnapped members of your family but this is not to kill them," one states in demanding 150 pairs of underwear. The note continues:

> If you do not bring them by tomorrow noon, we will cut off ears of one of the kidnapped and will return them to your families, and if you do not comply within three days, we will cut off heads of all of the kidnapped and return them to you. In short, if you love your money and goods you lose your men.[31]

Song-ju's men made clear that they would allow no middle ground, no neutrals in their struggle for unquestionable ends.[32] Their adversaries were rabid Japanese dogs, frothing at the mouth, ready to gobble them up—to take off their heads. In response, they demanded unquestioning loyalty; life-and-death circumstances necessitated terror from their perspective.[33] For years, they had struggled in the wilderness—launching hit-and-run attacks and hiding in snowy mountains—all without having adequate food, clothing, and supplies. The near-impossibility of obtaining basic staples like salt, to name one example, had caused agonizing deaths.[34] It baffled Song-ju's men that there were villages unwilling to support them amid such hardship.[35]

In response, Song-ju and his men chose tyranny like a drowning man reaching for a demon's hand. They allowed their brutal survival instincts and ideological fervor to dictate who deserved empathy, and who didn't. Such mercilessness had its own kind of logic; it was an antidote to their suffering, a way to survive and continue the struggle. So they bludgeoned reality with brutality's dull blade, leaving it a bloody mess. Terror murdered decency.

◆ ◆ ◆

As the guerilla struggle raged, Song-ju, still just twenty-three-years-old, became close with Chinese commander Wei Zhengmin. Zhengmin proved an important mentor. He offered Song-ju crucial support after his young underling controversially destroyed evidence implicating Koreans in the aforementioned purge. Their mutual respect and cooperation in the years that followed encouraged renewed cooperation between Korean and Chinese communists.[36]

Zhengmin, as Song-ju's memoirs recall, didn't look like a seasoned guerilla commander. To the contrary, he appeared like a college professor or a civil servant.[37] (Had it not been for the struggle, he "might have devoted all his life to scientific research or authorship."[38]) Despite—and perhaps because of—his total devotion to expelling the Japanese invader, Zhengmin was often sick, and supposedly suffered a heart attack while leading his men in the field at one point. Wrecking oneself physically was nothing to worry about, he allegedly told Song-ju. Losing faith in the cause was far worse.[39] (Song-ju's future regime encouraged exactly that kind of thinking. Individual lives did not matter in comparison to the larger struggle.) The cause gave meaning to life and death.[40]

Zhengmin kept himself in the thick of the fight, riding a white horse while issuing orders to Song-ju and his other loyal commanders, steadfast in his refusal to submit to Japanese imperialism.[41] The threat of an early death strengthened his bond with Song-ju in particular. The latter's memoirs would praise the Chinese commander. In his final years, Song-ju remembered him warmly. The old mentor was a ghost from another world.[42]

◆ ◆ ◆

Song-ju's guerilla band included women and children. In addition to carrying arms, they served as cooks, seamstresses, and entertainers. In late 1935, Song-ju took in some twenty kids orphaned either by Japanese forces or the Chinese communists. Despite opposition—including from Wei Zhengmin—Song-ju incorporated the children into one of his units. A sixteen-year-old girl looking after them, Jong-suk, would later become Song-ju's wife.[43] The insurgency, to be sure, was a co-ed affair with male and female fighters falling in love. Both "loved the other sex while they worked for the revolution," making "…our homes in the rain of fire," as the dictator's memoirs put it.[44]

Before becoming involved with Jong-suk, Song-ju likely had a first wife named Hye-sun. His memoirs—though they do not call her his wife—relate an entertaining anecdote in which he supposedly galloped to her rescue before the enemy on an extraordinary white horse. The Japanese ultimately captured Hye-sun, wounded, in April 1940 after her guerilla band left her behind with several others. She told her captors that she was Song-ju's wife, and they sought to use her as bait to capture him. It didn't work—and she surely met an unfortunate end.[45] If Hye-sun had lived, Song-ju's memoirs note, the two would have recalled his white horse together in old age.[46]

Regardless, at some point during these events, Song-ju fell for Jong-suk. The young woman was both gorgeous and loyal—and supposedly saved Song-ju's life in 1939.[47] A female comrade who later spent time with the couple in 1942 remembered Jong-suk as "quite a beauty," a woman darkened by the Manchurian wild. "Her eyebrows were black and her eyelashes were long, making her truly attractive. Her build was even more attractive."[48] Jong-suk was provincial, skillful in defeathering chickens, but also sharp, caring, and joyful. She liked to dance.[49]

◆ ◆ ◆

The end was nigh for the guerillas by the fall of 1940. The invaders hunted them with growing success. Comrades betrayed one another. Battle and illness took lives. White horses died. The Japanese squeezed like a vise, tighter and tighter.

Song-ju's mentor, Zhengmin, was himself on the verge of death by this point. Song-ju procured his commander traditional medicines and food—"artificial terrapin blood," whatever that is—to help keep him alive.[50] Zhengmin, in return, made sure that Song-ju enjoyed liquor and cold buckwheat noodles (*Naengmyeon*) when the junior officer visited his camp. The considerate ingenuity of hungry insurgents made such things possible.[51]

Song-ju visited Zhengmin for the last time in early 1941. The Chinese commander was sickly and pasty, complaining of what felt like a stone in his chest—a description Song-ju remembered his own mother speaking of before she passed.[52] The two men discussed strategy, with Song-ju confirming that his men, in line with Zhengmin's prior instructions, were avoiding big engagements. The subject of the Soviet Union came up. Was it time to go there? Live to fight another day? Or perish in Manchuria? Song-ju's memoirs state that he urged his Chinese commander to escape and recuperate. In reality, it was likely Song-ju himself who asked to flee to the Soviet border. Zhengmin refused permission—but soon his death rendered the matter moot. And Song-ju fled to the USSR with six comrades in March 1941.[53]

Later that spring, Song-ju and Jong-suk made love in the Far East. Their mutual struggle against the Japanese had brought them closer than a normal couple; they had fought side-by-side at moments when death seemed certain, and thus knew each other in a way that few husbands and wives can. This battle-hardened intimacy led to the birth of Kim Jong-il nine months later.[54]

With a beloved son to carry on the struggle, Kim Il-sung looked towards an unknowable future, one in which his unrelenting determination to endure—to realize his vision for national independence—would prevail at any cost. Somewhere in the horror that was to come, that young man, whose heroism was once real, lost himself. He began to view himself as indispensable, the necessary means to idealized ends. That remains his people's enduring tragedy.

SONG-JU

CONCLUSION

Heroes and Villains
Just see what you've done

Heroes and Villains
Just see what you've done

-        B. Wilson & Van Dyke Parks

THE END HAS NO END

Though early challenges and trauma influenced the lives of Lenin, Mussolini, Hitler, Stalin, Mao, and Kim to varying degrees, positive trends in their youths had more direct implications for their political "careers." The presence of at least one parent who valued their education and created opportunity in their lives helped make possible each dictator's later ideological radicalization. Emotional struggles shaped who these men would become in intangible ways. But parents, books, and teachers—alongside general auto-didacticism—provided solid intellectual foundations from which to pursue noxious ideas in later years. Childhood education opened their eyes to the world, and literate despots-to-be emerged. From a young age, they relished absorbing stories that fired their imaginations and stoked a passion for myth-making.

Lenin's mother and father created a learning-centered home—one in which that future dictator found his way to Turgenev's novels about an ailing Russian society. Chernyshevsky's *What Is to Be Done?* helped the apolitical teen make sense of his big brother's radicalization and execution thereafter. Victor Hugo's *Les Misérables* stirred Mussolini's early antipathy towards poverty, perhaps his own most of all, as his father encouraged revolutionary feeling in him and his mother sacrificed for his education. Hitler was lucky to have Klara who—far from terrorizing him with demands that he become a civil servant or a baker—gave him autonomy to find his own way. Her beloved son's decision to pursue art school in Vienna delighted her. ("She admired his water colors and his sketches of the countryside," recalled Dr. Bloch. "Whether this was honest admiration or whether it was merely an effort to encourage his talent I do not know.")[1] There, he relished his own intellectual and artistic pursuits as a vagabond, continuing on a path that eventually intersected with extreme anti-Semitism and German nationalism.[2] Stalin's mother devoted her entire life to her boy, somehow triumphing over an abusive husband in deeply patriarchal Georgia. Largely because of Keke did Stalin find himself in the seminary daydreaming about the warrior Koba from Kazbegi's *The Patricide* rather than making shoes with Beso (and we didn't even get to the Soviet dictator's later infatuation with Ivan the Terrible and Napoleon.)[3] Teenage Mao, though he hated his father, owed him a debt of gratitude for making his education possible—even if dad despised his son's reading of books like *Water Margin* for pleasure. If only the teacher Yang Changji had known the effect he had on that young man, a student in whom he saw so much promise.[4] Kim Il-sung had his parents to thank for his fluency in Mandarin—and perhaps his survival of the guerilla struggle. Their insistence on education made possible teacher Shang Yue's encouragement and his recommendation of books like Gorky's *Mother*. (Go read about the indomitable Pavel Vlasov for yourself!) In short, parental love and engaging education made possible paths that led to rebellion and power. Mass murder followed.

The other most significant parallel in these dictators' youths remains their shared belief that they could play an important role in changing society—even before they could fully define what their idealized world would be. By the dawn of adulthood, burgeoning conviction in their own abilities made them individuals with whom to grapple, figures whose searing personas gave them a certain magnetic quality even when they were failing and pathetic. They came to envision a landscape in which their self-interests would be synonymous with larger ideological ends—in which their personal intervention could have a decisive impact. Such self-belief cannot be understood only through political ideologies and socio-economic factors. Each man's road to power started with subjective constructions of themselves—the origins of self-fulfilling prophecies that would become real for millions. Lenin as Chernyshevsky's Rakhmetov; Hitler as adored creative genius; Mussolini as radical revolutionary; Stalin as man of steel; Mao as people's hero; Kim as guerilla warrior. There was no teleology of evil. But their personal agency suggested that action, if not obstinate defiance, could overcome trying realities and achieve soaring objectives. Dismissing them as only fanatics, crass opportunists, or lunatics remains a grave mistake.

◆◆◆

If these patterns heighten our understanding of the domestic milieus from which these despots came, they tell us little about how to prevent the rise of such tyrannical dictators in the future. We can't possibly know whether a child—grappling with early traumas, but also enjoying the support of a devoted mother and caring teachers—will become a repugnant demagogue, a pioneering scientist, or an utterly average person. (Odds are the latter). Parents try to shield children from undue adversity, but what father or mother, honestly, can conclude that the take-away from the youths of these despots is to discourage a love of learning for fear that Victor Hugo will lead your son or daughter astray? Many certainly envision a future in which their kids, armed with an excellent education, leave home with great self-confidence, determined to "make the world a better place" and "help their neighbors." (How many among us envisioned ourselves as the hero at some point growing up, as individuals emboldened by our agency to do good?) But we don't always consider all the ways that can go terribly wrong—*and has in the past.*

What historical significance, then, do we derive from these narratives of youth? More broadly—it's worth asking again and again—

what is there to learn from history? The past—Hegel's *Philosophy of History* warns us—"teach[es] that peoples and governments never have learned anything from history, or acted on principles deduced from it."[5] Hegel wasn't being sarcastic—or denying that multitudes have labored over the ages to try to learn from the mistakes of the past to avoid repeating them. Participants in the French Revolution, he observed, cried out in vain for guidance from the history of ancient Greece and Rome, but eventually had to face reality: each moment of human history "is involved in such peculiar circumstances" and "exhibits a condition of things so strictly idiosyncratic" that generalizations about sweeping circumstances, and solutions for dealing with them, are problematic.[6] Human beings don't only repeat past errors. They make new ones. ("We will not make the same old mistakes"—Henry Kissinger said knowingly of the Nixon administration in 1969—"We will make our own.")

The infinitude of variables in time, so beyond our intellectual faculties, often overwhelm our ability to grapple with the demands of history and the immediate present. Historical change is not—as Yuval Noah Harari suggests—often a consequence of coincidence. It's a product of innumerable, compounding historical factors of sweeping complexity that define causality.[7] The data is so vast, so to speak, that it's impossible to record, much less process—yet.[8] Human experience compels our awe before as much and alerts us to a future that will frequently bend, if not break, the past's patterns with spectacular originality. Like an endlessly evolving algorithm, reality consists of identifiable trends, but also sea-change events on a macro-level that erupt furiously—like Mount Vesuvius hurling lava at innocent villagers, who, if fortunate enough to survive, explain that "random" event with made-up stories. The core point? There is no certain equation within reach of our intellectual limits for definitively understanding history—much less how we can avoid heinous dictators in the future.

But onwards we labor, aspiring to probe intersubjective realities and better understand the past with the belief that the resulting insights matter—that reading Hugo is a worthwhile step towards becoming an educated person capable of *both* good and evil. Yet what often befalls us in the process, especially when studying murderous tyrants and their crimes, is what Hegel described as "a picture of most fearful aspect," which "excites emotions of the profoundest and most hopeless sadness, counterbalanced by no consolatory result."[9] It is the "slaughtering block" of history—narratives of misery in humanity's story that make one want to "retreat into the selfishness that stands on the quiet shore, from whence we in safety enjoy the distant spectacle of 'wrecks confusedly hurled.'"[10] Gaze with macabre fascination. But don't engage on a personal level. It's too unpleasant and uncomfortable.

The humanizing narratives of *Before Evil* have been a reaction against as much. The chapters have asked you to swim out to ships heading for rocks in the distance. They aspired to make you ponder the innate dignity of the men and women on board, even the most abhorrent, on the path to the past's perdition. Reflection, I hope, has led you to consider the lives of these men in a different context—that of young people, with stories fascinating and repugnant (compelling both sympathy and condemnation), who could have gone on to different futures.

We learn nothing. We learn everything.

◆ ◆ ◆

To return to how we started, there *is* one definitive take-away worth reiterating. It's that mankind's immense capacity for inhumanity is not unique to mass murderers. It's ours. Connecting with the humanity of these men reinforces the recognition that each one of us—

under given conditions—is capable of committing terrible acts, big and small, with the conviction that to do so is acceptable, that larger ideological ambitions necessitate as much.

Each individual brings a unique psychological profile to the countless moments of history. Everyone isn't necessarily capable of the same cruelty, much less the evil of totalitarian dictators. But the struggle of each person to make sense of their lives—beginning with the events of youth—offers a richer story than psychopathology alone can provide. More broadly, historians often analyze economic, political, and social conditions that transcend any one individual. But in doing so, they should not stray too far from the most consequential element at the core of tyranny: our own humanity. The study of personal subjectivity and agency—and the power of ideas—brings despots into greater focus as individuals who tangled themselves up in Clifford Geertz's "webs of significance."

The "lesson" we derive from the youths of these awful men is recognizing that we ourselves can become the monsters we deplore. As we make hard decisions in pursuit of what we believe is right, grappling with infinite complexities amid personal challenges, we can guard against that reality by embracing empathy. This guiding value can shield us from the blinding light we often run towards in pursuit of far-reaching ends that may seemingly compel us to undertake cold means. Reject the tuneful dogmatism of sirens who pull us towards disaster by ignoring, or denying, the humanity of others—including the heinous. Encourage new generations to think of their actions through the lens of suffering we cause or diminish for others. Distinguish yourself by striving to interpret the meaning of human experience, past and present, with compassion—even if it is often lacking before the "slaughtering block" of history. Courageous opposition is needed to confront tyranny over the ages. But so, too, is love and mercy.

The onus is on us.

ON PRIMARY SOURCES

This work pays close attention to scholarly scrutiny of first-hand accounts, such as August Kubizek's *The Young Hitler I Knew*; Kim Il-sung's autobiographical *With the Century*; and Xiao Zisheng's *Mao Tse-Tung and I were Beggars*.

With Kubizek's book, for instance, I have benefitted from Ian Kershaw and Peter Longerich's careful example of what should and should not be drawn upon from that work; it was originally commissioned when Hitler was still in power and contains some errors and fabrications, especially with regard to claims of his early anti-Semitism. (See Kershaw's introduction to the 2006 Greenhill Books edition and Longerich's critiques in *Hitler: A Biography*, 17). That being said, I agree with Kershaw that Kubizek's memories remain valuable for understanding young Hitler's personality and his interest in art and music; I recognize Longerich's use of those same recollections in that regard. Concerning first-hand accounts of Hitler in power by Albert Speer, Heinz Linge, Rochus Misch, Traudl Junge, and Christa Schroeder, I embrace the guidance of Heike B. Görtemaker to reject claims of ignorance about the Nazi persecution of European Jews and the Holocaust.

I am well aware that Kim Il-sung's ghostwritten autobiography—*With the Century*—contains myriad fabrications and inaccuracies; however, the personal details they provide, especially with facts that can be corroborated, remain a fascinating source for understanding how Kim Il-sung remembered his childhood, and how he wanted the outside world to remember it. I am grateful to the counsel of Balázs Szalontai, who has long offered me warnings about the falsehoods of *With the Century* while emphasizing its value in acknowledging Kim's Christian background. When using *With the Century*, I frequently use qualifying language in the text to cue the reader to unverifiable claims.

With works like Xiao Zisheng's *Mao Tse-Tung and I were Beggars*, I acknowledge that Xiao's later bitterness towards Mao in power surely informed his recollections. However, Xiao's memories remain a rare source on Mao's evolving character in his early twenties that resonate strongly with Mao's own writings from the time. One can dispute the accuracy of its direct quotes (recalled decades after the fact), but they should not ignore its core message about the Chinese dictator's evolving worldview.

Finally, I have benefitted from the advice of Oleg Khlevniuk and Ronald G. Suny on sources relating to Stalin's personal life—especially with regard to the memories of bodyguard A.T. Rybin. As a historian, it remains fascinating to see how leading scholars (from Suny to Khlevniuk to Simon Sebag Montefiore to Stephen Kotkin) utilize or ignore works like Keke Jughashvili's memories of Stalin's childhood.

Though the debate over primary sources will (appropriately) continue, Ralph Waldo Emerson's words offer sage guidance on how we should analyze such texts: "Use what language you will, you can never say anything but what you are. What I am, and what I think, is conveyed to you, in spite of my efforts to hold it back. What I am has been secretly conveyed from me to another, whilst I was vainly making up my mind to tell him it. He has heard from me what I never spoke." (See idem., *Select Writings of Ralph Waldo Emerson* (London: Walter Scott, 1888), 219).

NOTES

Introduction

[1] Ideological fanaticism and ruthless personal opportunism often go hand-in-hand. The former often justifies the latter as individuals begin to see themselves as indispensable for bringing about a larger ideological vision. Stalin, as Stephen Kotkin notes in this vein, was "at once a militant Communist and an unprincipled intriguer, an ideologue and an opportunist..." See, idem., *Stalin: Waiting for Hitler* (New York: Penguin, 2017), 302.

[2] Hannah Arendt, *The Origins of Totalitarianism* (New York: Harcourt, Inc., 1948, 1976), 185, 192.

[3] On the latter point, a *New Yorker* article (on appropriations of Nietzsche's philosophy) states: "Hans Stark, the head of the admissions detail at Auschwitz, had a sign over his desk reading 'Mitleid ist Schwäche' ('Compassion Is Weakness')." See Alex Ross, "Nietzsche's Eternal Return," *The New Yorker*, October 14, 2019: https://web.archive.org/web/20211006104229/https://www.newyorker.com/magazine/2019/10/14/nietzsches-eternal-return
Accessed December 5, 2021.

[4] Psychologist James Garbarino's research on violent adolescents has similarly emphasized the need to avoid dehumanization. Garbarino writes: "Working in the 1950s to understand the blatantly crazy behavior of schizophrenics, psychologist Harry Stack Sullivan realized that *human behavior is more simply human than otherwise* [emphasis in original]. Nothing is more basic to understanding youth violence than remembering this point. We dehumanize adolescents...who appear in the newspapers and in the courtrooms of our nation by calling them 'super predators,' 'monsters,' or 'crazies'....Our goal should be to find the human sense in senseless youth violence, to translate Sullivan's principle into practice." See idem., *Lost Boys: Why Our Sons Turn Violent and How We Can Save Them* (New York: The Free Press, 1999), 94.

[5] As historian Roger Moorhouse has noted: "...we are kidding ourselves if we imagine that Hitler was some one-dimensional monster - all rolling eyes and rabid ranting. He was not....The Hitler that we know - the man who had millions murdered and started the most costly and destructive war in history - also had a human side: he could be affable to his staff, kiss his secretaries' hands and be kind to his dog. If this apparent humanity offends our preconceptions, then perhaps our

preconceptions need altering." See idem., "Introduction" in Heinz Linge, *With Hitler To The End: The Memoirs of Hitler's Valet* (Yorkshire, UK: Frontline Books, 2009), 15.

[6] A *New York Times* article on the film *Max* about Hitler's life after World War I makes this point clearly: "Yet no one who sees this film is very likely to risk feeling twinges of sympathy for Hitler. Indeed, in making Hitler more human, 'Max' accomplishes the considerable feat of making him more culpable as well." See Jamie Malanowski, "Human, Yes, But No Less A Monster," *New York Times*, December 22, 2002, Section 2, Page 1:
https://web.archive.org/web/20210126214557/https://www.nytimes.com/2002/12/22/movies/human-yes-but-no-less-a-monster.html
Accessed July 27, 2021.

[7] Kotkin, *Stalin: Waiting for Hitler*, 1.

[8] Alan Bullock, *Hitler: A Study in Tyranny* (London: Odhams Press, 1952); Joachim C. Fest, *Hitler*, trans. Richard and Clara Winston (New York: Harcourt Brace, 1974); Ian Kershaw, *Hitler: 1889-1936 Hubris* (New York: W.W. Norton & Co., 2000); idem., *Hitler: 1936-1945 Nemesis* (New York: W.W. Norton & Co., 2001); John Toland, *Adolf Hitler*, Vol. 1-2 (Garden City: Doubleday & Co., Inc., 1976); Peter Longerich, *Hitler: A Biography* (New York: Oxford University Press, 2019); Stephen Kotkin, *Stalin: Paradoxes of Power, 1878-1928* (New York: Penguin, 2015); idem., *Stalin: Waiting for Hitler* (New York: Penguin, 2017); Simon Sebag Montefiore, *Stalin: Court of the Red Tsar* (New York: Knopf, 2003); idem., *Young Stalin* (New York: Knopf, 2007); Ronald Grigor Suny, *Stalin: Passage to Revolution* (Princeton, N.J.: Princeton University Press, 2020); Robert Service, *Lenin: A Biography* (Cambridge, MA: Harvard University Press, 2000); R.J.B. Bosworth, *Mussolini* (New York: Oxford University Press, 2002); idem., *Claretta: Mussolini's Last Lover* (New Haven, CT: Yale University Press, 2017); Denis Mack Smith, *Mussolini: A Biography* (New York: Vintage Books, 1983); Philip Short, *Mao: A Life* (New York: Henry Holt and Company, 1999); Alexander V. Pantsov and Steven I. Levine, *Mao: The Real Story* (New York: Simon & Schuster, 2012); Frank Dikötter, *Mao's Great Famine: The History of China's Most Devastating Catastrophe, 1958-1962* (New York: Bloomsbury, 2010); idem., *The Tragedy of Liberation: A History of the Chinese Revolution, 1945-1957* (New York: Bloomsbury, 2015); idem., *The Cultural Revolution: A People's History, 1962-1976* (New York: Bloomsbury, 2016); idem., *How to Be a Dictator: The Cult of Personality in the Twentieth Century* (New York: Bloomsbury, 2019); Dae-Sook Suh, *The Korean Communist Movement,*

1918-1948 (Princeton, N.J.: Princeton University Press, 1967); idem., *Kim Il Sung: The North Korean Leader* (New York: Columbia University Press, 1988).

[9] Peter Longerich, *Hitler: A Biography* (New York: Oxford University Press, 2019).

[10] See G. M. Gilbert, "The mentality of SS murderous robots," *Yad Vashem Studies* Vol. 5 (1963): 35-41. "It is ordinary individuals, like you and me, who commit extraordinary evil…," notes James Waller in *Becoming Evil* (Oxford: Oxford University Press, 2002), 106.

[11] Jean-Jacques Rousseau, *Discourse on Inequality* (1754) in *Great Books of the Western World: Montesquieu, Rousseau*, Robert Maynard Hutchens, ed. (Chicago: William Benton, 1952), 338.

[12] As one overview of David Hume's views on this topic state: "..for an agent to be other than indifferent is for her to be concerned with, or engaged by, the matter in question and that is itself for her to have (in Hume's broad sense) a passion, to which it is related. Remove all such passions and the discovery of truths or the uncovering of falsehoods will influence the agent's actions not at all. In every case, Hume claims, reason's impact turns upon the presence of an appropriate passion. Beliefs cause action only if the agent also cares about what the beliefs are about. Reason alone, Hume concludes, is inert…" Quoted from Geoffrey Sayre-McCord, "Hume on Practical Morality and Inert Reason," in *Oxford Studies in Metaethics*, Vol. 3, ed. Russ Shafer-Landau (New York: Oxford University Press, 2008), 302; see David Hume, *A Treatise of Human Nature*, "Book II Of the Passions" (New York: E.P. Dutton & Co. Inc., 1936).

[13] Deborah Weiss argues that Wollstonecraft used her book *Letters Written During a Short Residence in Sweden, Norway, and Denmark* (1796) to challenge the prevailing perspective that feeling and suffering women were to be pitied, and that it was the height of civilization for men to save such a helpless female. Weiss states specifically: "…in Wollstonecraft's reconstructed sentimental narrative, woman's pain becomes a source of intellectual accomplishment; and women who both feel and think are transformed into agents of progress." See idem., "Suffering, Sentiment, and Civilization: Pain and Politics in Mary Wollstonecraft's 'Short Residence,'" *Studies in Romanticism* Vol. 45, No. 2 (Summer 2006): 199-221.

[14] Heike B. Görtemaker, *Eva Braun: Life with Hitler*, trans. Damion Searls (New York: Vintage Books, 2011), 5.

[15] Suny, *Stalin: Passage to Revolution*, 63.

16 Daniel Kalder makes a similar point about education in *The Infernal Library: On Dictators, the Books They Wrote, and Other Catastrophes of Literacy* (New York: Henry Holt and Company, 2018), xiv-xv.

17 For example, Hitler's rise to power became a self-fulfilling prophecy in that he would seek to achieve power through unremitting persistence—first through the failed Beer Hall Putsch of 1923 and then through obstinate political negotiations to become chancellor in 1933, a rise to power (of course) made possible by World War I, the Versailles Treaty, severe economic problems in Germany, among numerous other factors. Understanding the origins of the Holocaust, however, cannot be reduced to Hitler's ambitions for power in that it took shape as a result of both the Nazi party's ideological intentions from the start (intentionalism) and as a function of their ideology in power (functionalism); the ultimate mass murder of six million European Jews evolved as a result of both Hitler's determination to "deal" ruthlessly with the Jews of Germany and Europe, but also the Nazi party's search for implementable "solutions" to guide Nazi policy from 1933-1945 that culminated in the creation of death camps during the height of World War II for the express purpose of committing mass murder. See Christopher R. Browning, *The Path to Genocide: Essays on Launching the Final Solution*, "Chapter 5: Beyond 'Intentionalism' and 'Functionalism': The Decision for the Final Solution Reconsidered," (Cambridge: Cambridge University Press, 1992); Longerich, *Hitler*, 763-776, 806-809.

18 Library of Congress, "Revelations from the Russian Archives: Hanging Order, p. 1-2":

https://web.archive.org/web/20200122201840/http://www.loc.gov/exhibits/archives/coll.html

Accessed December 5, 2021; quoted in Service, *Lenin*, 365.

19 Idem., "The Human Hitler." *Guardian.com*, September 17, 2004:

https://web.archive.org/web/20210610070124/https://www.theguardian.com/film/2004/sep/17/germany

Accessed December 5, 2021.

20 For a recent example, see Dean A. Haycock, *Tyrannical Minds: Psychological Profiling, Narcissism, and Dictatorship* (New York: Pegasus, 2019).

21 See Kevin Dutton, *The Wisdom of Psychopaths: What Saints, Spies, and Serial Killers Can Teach Us About Success* (New York: Scientific American/Farrar, Straus and Giroux, 2012).

[22] Lloyd deMause's argument that "the history of childhood is a nightmare from which we have just begun to awaken" is not an inspiration for this book. Quoted in David E. Stannard, *Shrinking History: On Freud and the Failure of Psychohistory* (Oxford: Oxford University Press, 1980), 151.

[23] Li Zhisui, *The Private Life of Chairman Mao*, trans. Tai Hung-Chao (New York: Random House, 1994), 150.

[24] For the Spotify playlist, please go here: https://tinyurl.com/m9ff55n5 (Additional link included below). Albums by these artists—which I encourage the reader to purchase on vinyl if possible—include: **Jonny Greenwood**: "Phantom Thread (Original Motion Picture Soundtrack)"; "You Were Never Really Here (Original Motion Picture Soundtrack)"; "The Master (Original Motion Picture Soundtrack)"; "There Will Be Blood (Original Motion Picture Soundtrack)." **Steve Hauschildt**: "S/H"; "Tragedy & Geometry"; "Sequitur." **Jonas Reinhardt**: "Conclave Surge"; "Ganymede"; "Mask of the Maker"; "The Encyclopedia of Civilizations Vol. 1 Egypt"; **Loscil**: "Submers"; "Endless Falls"; "Clara"; "Plume." **Trent Reznor and Atticus Ross**: "The Social Network (Original Motion Picture Soundtrack)"; "Gone Girl (Original Motion Picture Soundtrack)"; **Atticus Ross, Leopold Ross, Claudia Sarne**: Dispatches from Elsewhere (Music from the Elsewhere Society)"; Dispatches from Elsewhere (Music from the Jejune Institute)"; **Deaf Center**: "Owl Splinters"; "Pale Ravine." **Disasterpeace**: "Hyper Light Drifter." **Oneohtrix Point Never**: "Replica,"; "Rifts"; "The Fall into Time." Full link to playlist: https://open.spotify.com/playlist/3fZdeUwPTPMOeI1Bsdtnmk?si=86ce97e6b4c9435f&nd=1

[25] Jonathan Spence, "Portrait of a Monster," in *Was Mao Really A Monster?: The Academic Response to Chang and Halliday's Mao: The Unknown Story*, Gregor Benton and Lin Chun, eds. (New York: Routledge, 2009), 39.

[26] Emphasis added. Ibid.

[27] Dean A. Haycock offers the opposite view of this same quote by Spence in *Tyrannical Minds*, Chapter Six.

Chapter 1 (Lenin)

[1] St. Augustine, *The Confessions*, trans. Edward B. Pusey (New York: Pocket Books, Inc., 1954), 4.

[2] V.P. Osipov, one of Lenin's doctors, notes that Lenin's understanding of the severity of his disease was an extraordinary challenge; the Bolshevik dictator, notes the

doctor, endured it all with "amazing calmness, with amazing patience." See idem.,
"Bolezn' i smert' Vladimira Il'icha Ul'ianova-Lenina" ["Illness and death of Vladimir
Ilyich Ulyanov-Lenin"]:
https://web.archive.org/web/20210303181033/https://leninism.su/memory
/910-bolezn-i-smert-vladimira-ilicha-ulyanova-lenina.html
Accessed July 27, 2021.

[3] Lenin's younger sister, Maria, noted that his return to Russia both energized and
deeply exhausted the Bolshevik leader in M. I. Ul'ianova, "O Vladimire Il'iche
poslednie gody zhizni," *Izvestiia TSK KPSS*, No. 2 (1991), 125.

[4] N.N. Sukhanov, *The Russian Revolution 1917: Eyewitness Account, Volume I*, trans. Joel
Carmichael (New York: Harper & Brothers, 1962), 269-272; see also Edmund
Wilson, *To the Finland Station: A Study in the Writing and Acting of History* (New York:
Farrar, Straus, Giroux, 1940, 1987), 547-554.

[5] Ibid.

[6] Sukhanov, *The Russian Revolution 1917*, 273.

[7] Quoted in Wilson, *To the Finland Station*, 551.

[8] Lenin: "We of the older generation may not live to see the decisive battles of this
coming revolution." See "Lecture on the 1905 Revolution," January 9 (22), 1917,
V.I. Lenin Archive, "Works by Decade":
https://web.archive.org/web/20210523173501/https://www.marxists.org/ar
chive/lenin/works/1917/jan/09.htm
Accessed July 27, 2021; see also *Lenin: Collected Works*, Volume 23 (Moscow:
Progress Publishers, 1964), 236-253.

[9] For a cogent overview, see Oleg Khlevniuk, *Stalin: New Biography of a Dictator*,
trans. Seligman Favorov (New Haven, CT: Yale University Press, 2015), 44-45.

[10] After Menshevik Irakli Tsereteli made these comments, Lenin took the podium
the following day and replied to Tsereteli as follows: "He said that that no political
party exists in Russia that would express a readiness to take power wholly upon
itself. My answer is: 'There is! No single party can refuse this, and our party
doesn't refuse this: at any moment it is ready to take power in its entirety."
Quoted in Service, *Lenin*, 281. Service had previously recorded that Lenin shouted
"There is!" from the floor in response to Tsereteli, see idem., *A History of Twentieth-
Century Russia* (Cambridge, MA: Harvard University Press, 1998), 49.

[11] "The Bolsheviks Must Assume Power," September 12-14, 1917, in *Lenin: Collected
Works*, Volume 2 (Moscow: Progress Publishers, 1975), 329.

[12] Robert V. Daniels, "The Leader Decides," in *The Russian Revolution and Bolshevik Victory*, eds., Ronald G. Suny and Arthur Adams (Lexington: D.C. Heath & Company, 1990), 391.

[13] Emphasis in original. "Can The Bolsheviks Retain State Power," October 1 1917, in *Lenin: Collected Works*, Volume 2, 375.

[14] "Letter to the Bolshevik Comrades Attending the Congress of Soviets of The Northern Region," October 8, 1917, in *Lenin: Collected Works*, Volume 2, 395, 400; quoted in Daniels, "The Leader Decides," 392.

[15] Lenin wrote: "Victory is certain....To wait would be a crime to the revolution." See "Letter to the Central Committee...," October 1, 1917, in *Lenin: Collected Works*, Volume 2, 392.

[16] He won a second vote by a larger margin days later. See "Meeting of the Central Committee of the R.S.D.L.P(B.)," October 10, 1917, in *Lenin: Collected Works*, Volume 2, 401-402; Service, *Lenin*, 304; Daniels, "The Leader Decides," 397; Khlevniuk, *Stalin*, 50-51.

[17] "Letter to the Central Committee Members," October 24, 1917, in *Lenin: Collected Works*, Volume 2, 416; Service's version in *Lenin*, 305.

[18] Service, *Lenin*, 305.

[19] Ibid., 306.

[20] "TO THE CITIZENS OF RUSSIA! The Provisional Government has been deposed. State power has passed into the hands of the organ of the Petrograd Soviet..." October 25, 1917, in *Lenin: Collected Works*, Volume 2, 417.

[21] Emphasis mine. John Reed, *Ten Days That Shook The World* (New York: Modern Library, 1935), 125.

[22] Oleg Khlevniuk summarizes it well: "Lenin's stubbornness was decisive. Most historians agree that without Lenin the October Revolution would probably never have happened." See idem., *Stalin: New Biography of a Dictator*, 51.

[23] Leon Trotsky's words as spoken to the Mensheviks following the Bolshevik seizure of power—"To those who have left and to those who tell us to do this we must say: you are miserable bankrupts, your role is played out; go where you ought to be: into the dustbin of history!" Quoted in N.N. Sukhanov, *The Russian Revolution 1917: Eyewitness Account, Volume II*, trans. Joel Carmichael (New York: Harper & Brothers, 1962), 640.

[24] Khlevniuk, *Stalin: New Biography of a Dictator*, 54; Khlevniuk cites: R.W. Davis, Mark Harrison, and S.G. Wheatcroft, eds., *The Economic Transformation of the Soviet Union, 1913-1945* (New York: Cambridge University Press, 1994), 62-64.

[25] Lenin stated in 1920 that "Communism is Soviet power plus the electrification of the whole country." See "Our Foreign and Domestic Position and Party Tasks: Speech Delivered To The Moscow Gubernia Conference Of The R.C.P.(B.), November 21, 1920," V.I. Lenin Archive, "Works by Decade": https://web.archive.org/web/20210610004832/http://www.marxists.org/archive/lenin/works/1920/nov/21.htm

Accessed July 27, 2021; see also *Lenin: Collected Works*, Volume 31 (Moscow: Progress Publishers, 1965), 408-426.

[26] My perverse favorite of Marx's dense works remain his equations seeking to prove his theory of dialectical materialism in mathematical terms. One mathematician charitably described Marx's equations to the writer Edmund Wilson as "the work of an intelligent (yet somewhat befuddled) beginner, who is just starting to understand the meaning of differentiation," adding further: "….There is nothing new….the mathematics itself is all cock-eyed. It is a pity to build an elaborate philosophical system on a series of gross mathematical errors." Quoted in idem., *To the Finland Station*, Appendix B, 563-565. Behold a sample of Marx's dialectical math—part of the larger theory Lenin sought to translate to reality: 1) Let $f(x)$ or $y = uz$ be a function to be differentiated; u and z are both functions dependent on the independent variable x. They are independent variables with respect to the function y, which depends on them, and thus on x. $y1 = u1z1$, $y_1 - y = u_1z_1 - uz = z_1(u_1 - u) + u(z_1 - z)$, $(y_1 - y)/(x_1 - x)$ or $\Delta y/\Delta x = z_1 \cdot (u_1 - u)/(x_1 - x) + u \cdot (z_1 - z)/(x_1 - x) = (z_1 \cdot \Delta u)/(\Delta x) + (u \cdot \Delta z)/(\Delta x)$. Now on the right-hand side let $x1 = x$, so that $x1 - x = 0$, likewise $u1 - u = 0$, $z1 - z = 0$; so that the factor z1 in $z1 \cdot (u1 - u)/(x1 - x)$ also goes to z; finally on the left-hand side $y1 - y = 0$. Therefore: A) $dy/dx = z \cdot du/dx + u \cdot dz/dx$. Which equation, when all its terms are multiplied by the common denominator dx, becomes B) dy or $d(uz) = z \cdot du + u \cdot dz$…." See "Marx's Mathematical Manuscripts 1881: On the Differential": https://web.archive.org/web/20210616101220/https://www.marxists.org/archive/marx/works/1881/mathematical-manuscripts/

Accessed July 27, 2021.

[27] Lenin had argued for as much going back to the 1905 Revolution when he called for the use of any and all violence. In "…a state of heightened excitement," historian Dmitri Volkogonov writes, "he urged the revolutionaries to adopt tactics which most people would regard as abnormal and terrible…he urged the use of knives, knuckledusters, sticks, paraffin-soaked rags, nails, slabs of gun-cotton,

boiling water, stones and acid 'to throw over the police....The range of savage tactics is so broad and carefully thought out that it is hard to believe it emanated from an educated man, a writer and journalist....At such times his powerful mind became simply possessed by revolutionary remorselessness." See idem., *Lenin: A New Biography*, trans. Harold Shukman (New York: The Free Press, 1994), 411.

[28] In rejecting the abolition of the death penalty in Bolshevik-led Russia, Lenin responded: "'Nonsense....How can one make a revolution without firing squads? Do you think you will be able to deal with all your enemies by laying down your arms? What other means of repression do you have? Imprisonment?" For this particular translation, see Leon Trotsky, *On Lenin: Notes Towards a Biography* (London: George G. Harrap & Co Ltd, 1971), "Business of Government"; for an alternative translation from the same work online: Leon Trotsky, "Forming the Government":

https://web.archive.org/web/20210216013350/https://www.marxists.org/archive/trotsky/1925/lenin/06.htm

Accessed July 27, 2021.

[29] Ibid.

[30] "Speech At A Meeting At The Former Michelson Works, August 30, 1918." https://web.archive.org/web/20211101005656/https://www.marxists.org/archive/lenin/works/1918/aug/30a.htm

Accessed December 9, 2021; Quoted in Volkogonov, *Lenin*, 220.

[31] Ibid.

[32] Khlevniuk, *Stalin: New Biography of a Dictator*, 54; Khlevniuk cites R.W. Davis et al., *The Economic Transformation of the Soviet Union, 1913*-1945, 62-64. For a disturbing photograph showing cannibalism and children, see Eric Baschet, *The Revolutionary Years: Russia 1904-1924* (Zug: Swan, 1989), 243.

[33] Quoted in Brian Moynahan, *Rasputin: The Saint Who Sinned* (New York: Da Capo Press, 1997, 1999), 201; different translation quoted in Simon Sebag Montefiore, *The Romanovs: 1613-1918* (New York: Knopf, 2016), 570.

[34] Quoted in Montefiore, *The Romanovs*, 634.

[35] Montefiore's description of their execution is particularly jarring; see Ibid., 640-646.

[36] "The State and Revolution," in *Lenin: Collected Works*, Volume 2, 253.

[37] Service, *Lenin*, 421, 434.

[38] V.P. Osipov, "Bolezn' I smert' Vladimira Il'icha Ul'iãnova-Lenina; Service, *Lenin*, 379-380. Medical textbooks, to which Lenin looked for answers, suggested heart trouble.

[39] The Bolsheviks maintained state control over the economy's "commanding heights." Ibid., 421-423, 430-431; Khlevniuk, *Stalin*, 64.

[40] The floor of his Kremlin apartment, Lenin told remodelers in July 1921, had to be made "absolutely free of squeaks"—the man who coldly sent so many to their deaths could no longer handle squeaky floors. See Kotkin, *Stalin: Paradoxes of Power*, 411.

[41] Service, *Lenin*, 438-439.

[42] Doctors told his wife and sister to find hobbies to distract him from the gloom of it all, and Lenin did for a time, developing a greater interest in agriculture— raising rabbits and cultivating mushrooms, etc. See M. I. Ul'ianova, "O Vladimire Il'iche poslednie gody zhizni," *Izvestiia TSK KPSS*, No. 2 (1991),131-132; idem., "O Vladimire Il'iche poslednie gody zhizni," *Izvestiia TSK KPSS*, No. 4 (1991),177- 178. His wife, N.K. Krupskaya, notes that he did not like being entertained but rather took an interest in topics that enlivened others—"So it was with mushrooms, with cinema, with a stereoscope." See N.K. Krupskaya, "Poslednie polgoda zhizni Vladimira Il'icha" ["The last six months of the life of Vladimir Ilyich"]:
https://web.archive.org/web/20210303184903/https://leninism.su/memory /1401-poslednie-polgoda-zhizni-vladimira-ilicha.html
Accessed July 27, 2021.

[43] Lenin knew as much even before his May 1922 stroke, records his sister—"his song was sung." See M. I. Ul'ianova, "O Vladimire Il'iche poslednie gody zhizni," *Izvestiia TSK KPSS*, No. 2 (1991),132; idem., "O Vladimire Il'iche poslednie gody zhizni," *Izvestiia TSK KPSS*, No. 3 (1991),185; Kotkin, *Stalin: Paradoxes of Power*, 414.

[44] M. I. Ul'ianova, "O Vladimire Il'iche poslednie gody zhizni," *Izvestiia TSK KPSS*, No. 3 (1991),185; Kotkin, *Stalin: Paradoxes of Power*, 414.

[45] Khlevniuk, *Stalin*, 65-66; Kotkin, *Stalin: Paradoxes of Power*, 411.

[46] Cerebral arteriosclerosis in today's terms. M. I. Ul'ianova, "O Vladimire Il'iche poslednie gody zhizni," *Izvestiia TSK KPSS*, No. 3 (1991), 185; Kotkin, *Stalin: Paradoxes of Power*, 413; Khlevniuk, *Stalin*, 65; Volkogonov, *Lenin*, 411. Volkogonov raises the issue of whether these brain issues might have influenced Volodia's radically cruel decision-making during the civil war.

[47] One of Lenin's doctor observed after the May 1922 stroke: "He is unable to perform the simplest arithmetical functions, and he has lost the ability to recall even a few short phrase, while retaining his intellect in full." Quoted in Volkogonov, *Lenin*, 412; see also M. I. Ul'ianova, "O Vladimire I''iche poslednie gody zhizni," *Izvestiia TSK KPSS*, No. 4 (1991), 180.

[48] Volkogonov, *Lenin*, 412; Ul'ianova, "O Vladimire Il'iche poslednie gody zhizni," *Izvestiia TSK KPSS*, No. 2 (1991).

[49] V.P. Osipov, "Bolezn' i smert' Vladimira Il'icha Ul'ianova-Lenina"; Ul'ianova, "O Vladimire Il'iche poslednie gody zhizni," *Izvestiia TSK KPSS*, No. 4 (1991),180-183.

[50] V.P. Osipov, "Bolezn' i smert' Vladimira Il'icha Ul'ianova-Lenina."

[51] Ibid.; Krupskaya, "Poslednie polgoda zhizni Vladimira I'icha."

[52] V.P. Osipov, "Bolezn' i smert' Vladimira Il'icha Ul'ianova-Lenina"; Volkogonov, *Lenin*, 415-416; Kotkin, *Stalin: Paradoxes of Power*, 418.

[53] Kotkin makes a strong case that Lenin's wife, Krupskaya, was the driving force behind his "testament," writing: "One thing is indisputable: the miraculous dictation could not have emerged from Lenin's innermost sanctum without the involvement of Krupskaya." See "Miraculous Dictation," in idem., *Stalin: Paradoxes of Power*, 498-501.

[54] V.I. Lenin, "Letter to the Congress [Lenin's Testament] in V.I. Lenin Archive, "Works by Decade":
https://web.archive.org/web/20210603205703/https://www.marxists.org/archive/lenin/works/1922/dec/testamnt/congress.htm
Accessed July 27, 2021.

[55] "Better Fewer, But Better," *Lenin: Collected Works*, Volume 3 (Moscow: Progress Publishers, 1975), 725.

[56] Lenin did, however, concede that the "triumph of socialism" would require many years. He allegedly told his personal secretaries in late 1923: "Of course we have failed. We thought we could create a new communist society at the wave of a magic wand. But this will take decades, generations." See V. Sirotkin, "Lessons of the New Economic Policy; Thinking Aloud by the CPSU CC Plenum," *Izvestia*, March 10, 1989, 3.

[57] N.K. Krupskaya, "Poslednie polgoda zhizni Vladimira Il'icha":
https://web.archive.org/web/20210303184903/https://leninism.su/memory/1401-poslednie-polgoda-zhizni-vladimira-ilicha.html
Accessed July 31, 2021; Volkogonov, *Lenin*, 428.

[58] Krupskaya, "Poslednie polgoda zhizni Vladimira Il'icha." On "communists don't cry," see Lenin's secretary V.D. Bonch-Bruevich's comments upon hearing of Lenin's death in idem., *Smert' i pokhorony Vladimira Il'icha* ["Death and funeral of Vladimir Ilyich"]:
https://web.archive.org/web/20210117170321/https://leninism.su/memory/913-smert-i-poxorony-vladimira-ilicha.html
Accessed July 27, 2021.

[59] Kotkin, *Stalin: Paradoxes of Power*, 493; Volkogonov, *Lenin*, 426.

[60] V.P. Osipov, "Bolezn' i smert' Vladimira Il'icha Ul'iãnova-Lenina"; Volkogonov, *Lenin*, 431.

[61] Lenin's doctor notes that the Bolshevik leader and his wife Krupskaya were both loving and attentive to one another. Krupskaya spent a great deal of time helping him as his personal speech teacher, preparing lessons. See V.P. Osipov, "Bolezn' i smert' Vladimira Il'icha Ul'iãnova-Lenina."

[62] Krupskaya as quoted in Volkogonov, *Lenin*, 434. Krupskaya notes that she, Lenin's sister, Maria, and aides could increasingly understand what Lenin wanted just through his tone and facial expression. See Krupskaya, "Poslednie polgoda zhizni Vladimira Il'icha."

[63] Geoffrey Chaucer, *The Poetical Works of Geoffrey Chaucer* (London: Routledge, 1868), 109.

[64] Krupskaya, "Poslednie polgoda zhizni Vladimira Il'icha."

[65] Service, *Lenin*, 476.

[66] Ibid.

[67] V.P. Osipov, "Bolezn' i smert' Vladimira Il'icha Ul'iãnova-Lenina"; Krupskaya notes coffee (he "drank greedily") in "Poslednie polgoda zhizni Vladimira Il'icha."

Chapter 2 (Mussolini)

[1] R.J.B. Bosworth, *Mussolini*, 31-32. Philip Morgan states that Mussolini was also wearing spectacles in *The Fall of Mussolini* (New York: Oxford University Press, 2007), 224.

[2] Romano Mussolini recalled his father using this line. See idem., *My Father, Il Duce: A Memoir By Mussolini's Son*, trans. Ana Stojanovic (Carlsbad, CA: Kales Press, 2006), 26.

[3] Sergio Luzzatto contrasts Mussolini's end with Adolf Hitler's, stating: Mussolini "…dressing up in a German overcoat and helmet….was a comical show, very different from the Wagnerian pomp of Hitler's demise. By committing suicide in

his bunker before the Russians arrived, Hitler seemed to control his destiny right to the end." See idem., *The Body of Il Duce: Mussolini's Corpse and the Fortunes of Italy*, trans. Frederika Randall (New York: Picador, 2006), 49.

[4] Bosworth, *Mussolini*, 32.

[5] Ibid.; Morgan translates the captor's announcement in dialect as "Here's fatso!" See idem., *The Fall of Mussolini*, 224.

[6] Paolo Monelli, *Mussolini: an Intimate Life*, trans. Brigid Maxwell of *Mussolini: Piccolo Borghese* (London: Thames and Hudson, 1953), 258-259.

[7] Paul O'Brien, *Mussolini in the First World War: The Journalist, the Soldier, the Fascist* (New York: Bloomsbury, 2005), 187.

[8] Quoted in Bosworth, *Mussolini*, 31.

[9] Monelli, *Mussolini: an Intimate Life*, 163-164; Romano Mussolini describes moments when his father behaved with touching affection towards him; the dictator, his oldest son records, "seemed to live more for others than for himself. He wanted all of us to be happy." See idem., *My Father, Il Duce*, 94. In contrast, Bosworth notes that "Mussolini remained a distant father, remembered as one who preferred stroking the family cat to cuddling his own offspring." See idem., *Mussolini*, 209.

[10] Monelli, *Mussolini*, 194.

[11] "Mussolini"—the dictator wrote of himself in 1944—"has proven to have as many lives as a cat." See idem., "History of a Year" in *My Rise and Fall* (New York: De Capo, 1998), 141-143.

[12] O'Brien, *Mussolini in the First World War*, 120-121.

[13] See United Press, "Il Duce's Duelist Dies in Argentina," *Spartanburg Herald*, September 15, 1937, 2:

https://news.google.com/newspapers?id=3kUsAAAAIBAJ&sjid=z8oEAAAAIBAJ&dq=duel%20swords&pg=3684%2C1474948

Accessed July 27, 2021. On Mussolini and dueling, see Bosworth, *Mussolini*, 109, 125.

[14] Mussolini, "History of a Year" in *My Rise and Fall*, 141.

[15] Bosworth, *Mussolini*, 219.

[16] Arturo Rossato's words quoted in ibid., 123 from A. Rossato, *Mussolini: colloquio intimo* (Milan: Modernissima Casa Editrice Italiana, 1923). On bullet-proof and injections, see Mussolini, "History of a Year" in *My Rise and Fall*, 14; Edda Mussolini Ciano as told to Albert Zarca, *My Truth*, trans. Eileen Finletter (New York: William Morrow and Company, Inc., 1977), 71. As Mussolini's oldest daughter, Edda, recalled: "He who had suffered the worst tortures when he had

been riddled with shrapnel during the First World War, who had crashed in his plane, who had one day been thrown from his car, and who had fought so many duels, became stiff with terror when he had to have an injection—in fact, one time he stiffened so much that the needle broke."

[17] R.J.B. Bosworth, "Introduction to the new edition (2010)," *Mussolini* (New York: Bloomsbury, 2010), 2; "Introductory essay by Alexander Stille" in Romano Mussolini, *My Father, Il Duce*, xxi.

[18] Thucydides, *History of the Peloponnesian War*, Book III, "Civil War in Corcyra."

[19] O'Brien, *Mussolini in the First World War*, 187.

[20] Smith, *Mussolini: A Biography*, 35.

[21] Ibid., 100, 150-151, 173-174; Romano Mussolini, *My Father, Il Duce*, xxi.

[22] Benito Mussolini, *My Autobiography* (New York: Charles Scribner's Sons, 1928), 66.

[23] Quoted in ibid; Smith, *Mussolini*, 39-40.

[24] Benito Mussolini, *Opera omnia* [Hereafter BMOO], eds. Edoardo and Duilio Susmel (Florence: La Fenice-Firenze, 1954), Vol. XIV, 44; cited in Bosworth, *Mussolini*, 136.

[25] See examples from the province of Ferrara—the heart of fascism—in Alessandro Saluppo, "Violence And Terror: Imaginaries And Practices Of Squadrismo In The Province Of Ferrara, 1914-1922," Ph.D. diss., (Fordham University, 2016), 155-156, 166, 184.

[26] Smith, *Mussolini: A Biography*, 49-50, 55.

[27] Ibid., 52-56; Bosworth, *Mussolini*, 167-169.

[28] Quoted in Monelli, *Mussolini: an Intimate Life*, 95.

[29] On the willingness of the Italian parliament to grant significant authority to Mussolini (despite the Fascist party only having a small number of representatives in the lower house and *none in the senate*), see Smith, *Mussolini*, 58.

[30] Bosworth, *Mussolini*, 197-203.

[31] Mussolini, *My Autobiography*, 231.

[32] Emphasis added. Ibid., 233.

[33] Bosworth, *Mussolini*, 219. On Mussolini's cult of personality, see Ruth Ben-Ghiat, *Strongmen: Mussolini to the Present* (New York: W. W. Norton & Company, 2020), 100.

[34] Smith, *Mussolini*, 145.

[35] Bosworth, *Mussolini*, 203.

[36] Ibid.; "Dictator's Birthday," *Time*, August 9, 1926, Vol. 8, Issue 6; "One Man Majority," *Time*, December 31, 1928, Vol. 12, Issue 27.

[37] Smith, *Mussolini*, 101-103, 124-130.

[38] R.J.B. Bosworth, *Mussolini's Italy: Life Under the Fascist Dictatorship, 1915-1945* (New York: Penguin, 2006), 236; Benjamin G. Martin, *The Nazi-Fascist New Order for European Culture* (Cambridge, MA: Harvard University Press, 2016), 110.

[39] Marilisa Merolla, "Jazz and Fascism: Contradictions and Ambivalences in the Diffusion of Jazz Music under the Italian Fascist Dictatorship (1925-1925)," in *Transnational Studies in Jazz: Jazz and Totalitarianism*, ed. Bruce Johnson (New York: Routledge, 2017), Chapter One.

[40] Monelli, *Mussolini*, 143.

[41] Smith, *Mussolini*, 160, 81.

[42] Ibid., 81.

[43] Regime publications took time to praise a toy machine gun that primed kids for combat, stating: "...a 'really interesting, machine gun destined to delight....The perfect replica of the real version." See Bosworth, *Mussolini's Italy*, 291-292.

[44] "Experience of politics," Smith recorded, "had taught him early in life that you could usually get away with 'ninety-seven cents-worth of mere public clamour and three cents of solid achievement." See idem., *Mussolini,* 148.

[45] Ernest Hemingway, "Mussolini, Europe's Prize Bluffer," *The Toronto Daily Star*, January 27, 1923. On Mussolini telling Hemingway he couldn't live in Italy again, see "[Letter] to Ezra Pound, 23 January [1923]": https://web.archive.org/web/20151018152114/http://assets.cambridge.org/97805218/97341/excerpt/9780521897341_excerpt.pdf Accessed July 27, 2021.

[46] From 1927 to 1943—Bosworth notes—Mussolini's regime executed 31 people (9 during peacetime and 22 during World War II) for "political crimes." The regime's "Special Tribunal prosecuted 13,547 cases and imposed 27,742 years of gaol"—a number not including "tens of thousands who were to *confino*, restricted to their homes or otherwise put under surveillance." See idem. *Mussolini*, 222-223; idem., *Claretta: Mussolini's Last Lover*, 244.

[47] BMOO, eds. Edoardo and Duilio Susmel (Florence: La Fenice-Firenze, 1958), Vol. XXIV, 145.

[48] On invoking "philosophy of the superman," see ibid.; cited by Smith, *Mussolini*, 150. On Mussolini as Trotsky's "best student," Maxim Gorky quoted Trotsky as supposedly saying: "Mussolini has made a revolution; he is our best student."

Quoted in Bernice Glatzer Rosenthal, *New Myth, New World From Nietzsche to Stalinism* (University Park, PA: the Pennsylvania State University Press, 2010), 373; Simonetta Falasca-Zamponi, *Fascist Spectacle* (Berkeley and Los Angeles: University of California Press, 1997), 51.

[49] Emil Ludwig, *Talks With Mussolini*, trans. Eden and Cedar Paul (Boston: Little, Brown, and Company, 1933), 62.

[50] Smith, *Mussolini*, 113.

[51] Bosworth, drawing on a June 1919 police report about Mussolini, states: "In every circumstance as a speaker he sparkled. His 'emotionality' and 'impulsiveness' rendered his words spellbinding, even though he lacked the gravitas of a real orator. He was, the report stated, 'at base a sentimentalist and his quality in that regard draws him much sympathy and many friends.'" See idem., *Mussolini*, 125.

[52] Smith, *Mussolini*, 113.

[53] Ludwig, *Talks With Mussolini*, 12.

[54] Smith, *Mussolini*, 125-126.

[55] Romano Mussolini describes his father telling him about how to gain the psychological advantage through eye contact in idem., *My Father, Il Duce*, 145.

[56] Human machine is Bosworth's phrase in *Mussolini*, 244. See also Alessandra Antola Swan, *Photographing Mussolini: The Making of a Political Icon* (London: Palgrave Macmillan, 2020).

[57] Bosworth, *Mussolini*, 211; Smith, *Mussolini*, 113.

[58] Monelli notes that the animal eventually showed its teeth and tried to scratch the dictator and was, as a result, exiled to the zoo; Mussolini visited it on occasion. See idem., *Mussolini: an Intimate Life*, 99; Nicholas Farrell, *Mussolini: A New Life* (London: Phoenix, 2003), 13.

[59] Quoted in Bosworth, *Mussolini*, 184.

[60] On Mussolini's lack of interest in money, see his wife's comments in: Rachele Mussolini as told to Albert Zarca, *Mussolini: An Intimate Biography by His Widow* (New York: William Morrow & Company, Inc., 1974), 84-92. Monelli records that his disinterest in money—and "astonishingly small" personal expenses—went hand-in-hand with a willingness to spend government money without thinking and a general lack of appreciation of the value of money. See idem., *Mussolini*, 120-121.

[61] Suffering from an ulcer influenced his food choices; see Bosworth, *Mussolini*, 207; Monelli, *Mussolini*, 99.

[62] See Alessandra Antola Swan, "The iconic body: Mussolini unclothed," *Modern Italy*, Vol. 21, No. 4 (2016): 361-381; Ben-Ghiat, *Strongmen: Mussolini to the Present*, 98.

[63] Monelli, *Mussolini*, 233, 247; Bosworth, *Mussolini*, 406.

[64] Ernest Hemingway, "Mussolini, Europe's Prize Bluffer," *The Toronto Daily Star*, January 27, 1923. Bosworth describes his intellectual ambitions as "painful intellectual aspirations" in idem., *Claretta: Mussolini's Last Lover*, 42.

[65] Bosworth, *Claretta: Mussolini's Last Lover*, 41.

[66] Monelli, *Mussolini*, 226, 234.

[67] Bosworth, *Claretta: Mussolini's Last Lover*, 82; Monelli, *Mussolini*, 157. "He always fell for the attraction of so-called intellectual women," writes Monelli in *Mussolini*, 150. In contrast to his views about women in society at large, his oldest daughter, Edda, notes how he raised her to be independent and "nourished great ambitions" for her. See Edda Mussolini Ciano, *My Truth*, 34-37.

[68] Quoted in Bosworth, *Claretta: Mussolini's Last Lover*, 40.

[69] Antonio Scurati powerfully depicts how the death of Sarfatti's oldest son, Roberto, in the First World War further tied her to Mussolini and the Fascist movement. See idem., *M: Son of the Century*, trans. Anne Milano Appel (London: 4th Estate, 2021), 292-295.

[70] Sarfatti, with Benito's cooperation, wrote his first major biography in 1925—a work that proved an international hit. This lover was a confident intellectual who had things to teach Benito. The same was true of an earlier intellectual partner Angelica Balabanoff (discussed in Chapter Fourteen), a Russian-Jew turned Italian communist, with whom Benito may or may not have been sexually involved. Belying this entire discussion is the fact that Benito's wife Rachele Mussolini—who was the daughter of his dad's lover, coincidentally—had zero interest in books.

[71] Monelli, *Mussolini*, 147; Ben-Ghiat, *Strongmen: Mussolini to the Present*, 126-129.

[72] Monelli cites, for example, the account of one anonymous woman who claimed that Mussolini "...squeezed her breasts" in his office and then "...threw himself violently on her." She was, the author continues, "horrified and disgusted...taking refuge in a corner of the room, [she] begged him to leave her alone." The woman—feeling the pressure of Mussolini's status as leader—ultimately returned to his office thereafter, stating: "You can't refuse a man of that importance." Idem., *Mussolini*, 153.

[73] Farrell, *Mussolini: A New Life*, 20.

[74] Carlo Emilio Gadda's words in *Eros e Priapo (da furore a cenere)* (Milan: Garzanti, 1967), 13, 42; cited and quoted by Bosworth, *Claretta: Mussolini's Last Lover*, 30, 34, 236.

[75] Bosworth, *Claretta: Mussolini's Last Lover*, 72, 236.

[76] "I am a country woman," Romano Mussolini remembers his mother saying regularly; idem., *My Father, Il Duce*, 67.

[77] Romano Mussolini, *My Father, Il Duce*, 116; Rachele Mussolini, *Mussolini: An Intimate Biography by His Widow*, 72. "Even so," his wife wrote, "there were three women who hurt me: Ida Dalser, Margherita Sarfatti, and Clara Petacci. I summoned all my strength to fight each one of them."

[78] Edda Mussolini Ciano, *My Truth*, 50. Edda wrote jocularly: "My father launched himself into political life so as to have an excuse to be absent from home...and thus be spared my mother's jealous scenes, to which he preferred the beatings of the police and his adversaries."

[79] Monelli, *Mussolini*, 243.

[80] Rachele Mussolini, *Mussolini*, 82-83; Romano Mussolini, *My Father, Il Duce*, 57-58.

[81] Smith, *Mussolini*, 173.

[82] Quoted in "Introductory essay by Alexander Stille" in Romano Mussolini, *My Father, Il Duce*, xxi; Mussolini stated on another occasion: "I'll get the Italians to gallop....in military order and uniform from morning till night; they need beating, beating, beating." Quoted in Monelli, *Mussolini*, 185.

[83] See Steven Morewood, *The British Defence of Egypt, 1935-1940 Conflict and Crisis in the Eastern Mediterranean* (London: Frank Cass, 2005), 77-78; "Introductory essay by Alexander Stille" in Romano Mussolini, *My Father, Il Duce*, xxi; on the consequences of Italian colonialism in Libya, see Ben-Ghiat, *Strongmen: Mussolini to the Present*, 38-40.

[84] On fascism and anti-Semitism before World War II, see Bosworth, *Mussolini*, 334-345; Bosworth, *Claretta: Mussolini's Last Lover*, 133.

[85] Quoted in Monelli, *Mussolini*, 187; on Italy's lack of preparation, see Bosworth, *Mussolini*, 367.

[86] Count Galeazzo Ciano, *The Ciano Diaries, 1939-1943* (New York: Doubleday & Company, 1945), 220.

[87] Quoted in Monelli, *Mussolini*, 187; Bosworth, *Mussolini*, 367-369.

[88] Bosworth, *Claretta: Mussolini's Last Lover*, 141.

[89] Mussolini's words as quoted in Monelli, *Mussolini*, 136. 7,500 Italian Jews—many of whom were arrested by Italian authorities—were sent to German

concentration camps in eastern Europe; only 610 survived. See Bosworth, *Mussolini*, 407.

[90] Quoted in Bosworth, *Claretta: Mussolini's Last Lover*, 167.

[91] On the impact of Allied air raids—the damage of which Italian citizens often blamed on the regime's lack of defensive preparations—see Morgan, *The Fall of Mussolini*, 72-84.

[92] On declining public support for the fascist regime as a result of bombing raids, see ibid; Stephen Harvey, "The Italian War Effort and the Strategic Bombing of Italy," *History* Vol. 70, No. 228 (1985): 44-45; cited by Claudia Baldoli and Marco Fincardi, "Italian Society Under Anglo-American Bombs: Propaganda, Experience, And Legend, 1940-1," *The Historical Journal*, Vol. 52, No. 4 (December 2009): 1019.

[93] Morgan, *The Fall of Mussolini*, 13-17.

[94] Ibid., 17.

[95] Ibid.

[96] Quoted in Monelli, *Mussolini*, 216.

[97] Quoted in Luzzatto, *The Body of Il Duce*, 35.

[98] Quoted in Ibid., 39.

[99] See Mussolini's description of his "rescue" in idem., "History of a Year" in *My Rise and Fall*, 137-141.

[100] Luzzatto, *The Body of Il Duce*, 39; Smith, *Mussolini*, 300; Bosworth, *Mussolini*, 403.

[101] On Edda Mussolini Ciano's description of her husband's execution and her efforts to save him, see idem., *My Truth*, 181-249.

[102] Fabrizio Ciano, *Quando il nonno fece fucilare papà* (ed. Dino Cimagalli) (Milan: Mondadori, 1991); cited by Bosworth, *Claretta: Mussolini's Last Lover*, 11.

[103] Smith, *Mussolini*, 308-309.

[104] Quoted in Monelli, *Mussolini*, 246.

[105] He was, Bosworth states in summary, "a puppet dictator" in idem., *Mussolini*, 409.

[106] Cardinal Ildefonso Schuster, "My Last Meeting with Mussolini," in *The Mussolini Memoirs 1942-1943: with Documents Relating to the Period*, ed. Raymond Klibanksy, trans. Frances Lobb (London: Phoenix Press, 1949, 2000), 254.

[107] Quoted in Ibid., 256.

[108] Monelli, *Mussolini*, 263.

[109] Bosworth, *Claretta: Mussolini's Last Lover*, 227.

[110] Luzzatto, *The Body of Il Duce*, 48-49.

[111] Cardinal Ildefonso Schuster, *Saint Benedict and His Times*, trans. Gregory J. Roettger (St. Louis: B. Herder Book Co., 1951), 359.

[112] The words of an anti-fascist journalist quoted in Luzzatto, *The Body of Il Duce*, 45.

[113] Bosworth, *Mussolini*, 411.

[114] "I have come to the last phase of my life, to the last page of my book…," wrote Mussolini in his final letter to his wife. Quoted in Monelli, *Mussolini*, 253.

Chapter 3 (Hitler)

[1] Norman Ohler, *Blitzed: Drugs in the Third Reich*, trans. Shaun Whiteside (Boston: Houghton Mifflin Harcourt, 2017), 112-186.

[2] Heinz Linge, *With Hitler to the End: The Memoirs of Adolf Hitler's Valet*, trans. Geoffrey Brooks (London: Frontline Books, 2009), 1, 185.

[3] Ibid., 185-186.

[4] Hitler quoted in Ibid., 183.

[5] Ohler, *Blitzed*, 185.

[6] Linge, *With Hitler to the End*, 178-179, 182-183. Linge, recalling these conversations, leaves out any mention of the dictator's irrational decision to declare war on the United States in December 1941. See also Dr. National Eck, "Hitler's Political Testament," *Yad Vashem*, 12-19:
https://web.archive.org/web/20210107222521/https://www.yadvashem.org/yv/pdf-drupal/en/eichmann-trial/hitlers_political_testament.pdf
Accessed July 28, 2021.

[7] Ibid., 183. Hitler reiterated his extreme anti-Semitism in the last words of his "political testament," stating: "But before everything else I call upon the leadership of the nation and those who follow it to observe the racial laws most carefully, to fight mercilessly against the poisoners of all the peoples of the world, international Jewry." See "My Political Testament," Jewish Virtual Library:
https://web.archive.org/web/20210418035432/https://www.jewishvirtuallibrary.org/hitler-s-political-testament-april-1945
Accessed July 28, 2021.

[8] Ohler, *Blitzed*, 185.

[9] Kershaw, *Hitler: 1889-1936 Hubris*, 361.

[10] Crowds sometimes proved lackluster as well. See Ian Kershaw, *The "Hitler Myth": Image and Reality in the Third Reich* (Oxford: Oxford University Press, 1987, 2010), 40-41.

[11] Ibid.

[12] Quoted in Kershaw, *Hitler: 1889-1936 Hubris*, 364.

[13] The party's original platform stated: "None but members of the nation may be citizens of the state. None but those of German blood, whatever their creed may be. No Jew, therefore, may be a member of the nation." See "Nazi Party Platform," United States Holocaust Museum:
https://web.archive.org/web/20210328101123/https://www.ushmm.org/learn/timeline-of-events/before-1933/nazi-party-platform
Accessed July 28, 2021.

[14] Thomas Childers, *The Third Reich: A History of Nazi Germany* (New York: Simon & Schuster, 2017), 166; Dick Geary, "Who Voted for the Nazis?" *History Today*, October 19, 1998:
https://web.archive.org/web/20201126050338/https://www.historytoday.com/archive/who-voted-nazis
Accessed July 28, 2021; see also Thomas Childers, *The Nazi Voter* (Chapel Hill, N.C.: University of North Carolina Press, 1983); idem., ed., *The Formation of the Nazi Constituency* (Chapel Hill, N.C.: University of North Carolina Press, 1986).

[15] Kershaw, *Hitler: 1889-1936 Hubris*, 404; idem., *The "Hitler Myth,"* 44.

[16] Ibid., *Hubris*, 404.

[17] Ibid., 410; Childers, *The Third Reich*, 168-170; Saul Friedlander, *Nazi Germany and the Jews: Volume 1: The Years of Persecution 1933-1939* (New York: Harper Perennial, 1998).

[18] Quoted in Kershaw, *Hitler: 1889-1936 Hubris*, 395.

[19] Fran von Papen offers his overview of what happened in his self-justifying memoir: idem., *Memoirs*, trans. Brian Connell (London: Andrew Deutsch, 1952), 225-245.

[20] Kershaw, *Hitler: 1889-1936 Hubris*, 420; von Papen notes that Hindenburg asked him to take on this role, stating: "I wish to emphasize that I had at no time made any such suggestions myself. It seemed a natural precaution for him [Hindenburg] to take, once he had finally made up his mind to take the dreaded plunge of appointing Hitler as Chancellor, see idem., *Memoirs*, 241.

[21] Theodor Duesterberg made this comment to new Reich Minister Alfred Hugenberg. See Kershaw, Ibid., 421.

[22] Von Papen remembered of his rationale: "The Nazis had 195 Reichstag seats, and remained a major political factor....It still seemed to me far better that the whole Nazi Party should be saddled with the responsibility of Government in coalition....Hitler...insisted again and again that the only circumstances in which the Nazis would co-operate would be under his Chancellorship....[President

Hindenburg] considered the unpleasant duty of calling on Hitler. I made what suggestions I could for keeping the Nazis within bounds....The President then asked me, as *homo regius*, to sound out the possibilities of forming a Cabinet under Hitler...." See idem., *Memoirs*, 226, 235, 238-239.

[23] Condemning the country's so-called "Jewish Press" (i.e. any newspaper critical of the NSDAP), Joseph Goebbels, finger pointed in the air, threatened: "....they shouldn't keep lying....One day our patience will reach its end and we'll just shut these Jews' insolent, lying mouths!" If the new regime's decision to commit mass genocide remained years away, such rhetoric gave German citizens—and especially German Jews—every reason to fear what the new regime would do in power. See United States Holocaust Memorial, "Goebbels speaks at Sportpalast": https://web.archive.org/web/20200327064431/https://collections.ushmm.o rg/search/catalog/irn1001951
Accessed July 28, 2021.

[24] See United States Holocaust Memorial, "Hitler's Aufruf an das deutsche Volk" ["Hitler's call to the German People"/Hitler's first speech as Chancellor, Berlin Sportpalast]:
https://web.archive.org/web/20210523012934/https://collections.ushmm.o rg/search/catalog/irn1001952
Accessed July 28, 2021.

[25] Longerich notes that "Hitler's staging of his public persona as the 'Führer' who was above it all extended to every aspect of life..." See idem., *Hitler*, 160. To avoid Hitler's private life, as noted in the introduction, risks dehumanizing him and reinforcing an "artificial" image of a leader above ordinary mortals. See Görtemaker, *Eva Braun: Life with Hitler*, 4-6, 45.

[26] Linge, *With Hitler to the End*, Chapter 2. "Before the war I often had the impression of being in the household of a busy architect and building tycoon rather than the Führer and Reich Chancellor. Sketches of buildings, outline plans, calculations, designs of all kinds, draughtsmen's implements, coloured pencils and architectural utensils were always on his table, and Hitler worked there endlessly, changing and correcting designs, consulting technical books and making comparisons."

[27] "Hitler's weakness for movies is legendary," writes Lothar Machtan. See idem., *The Hidden Hitler*, trans. John Brownjohn (New York: Basic Books, 2001), 177; Kershaw, *Hitler: 1889-1936 Hubris*, 485.

28 Speer, *Inside the Third Reich*, 91; Christa Schroeder, *He Was My Chief: The Memoirs of Adolf Hitler's Secretary*, trans. Geoffrey Brooks (London: Frontline, 2009, 2012), 105.

29 Speer, ibid., 39-40.

30 Linge's words in *With Hitler to the End*, 111. Kubizek also emphasized his sweet tooth as a young man, in *The Young Hitler I Knew: The Memoirs of Hitler's Childhood Friend* (London: Greenhill Books, 2006), 155-156.

31 Though, Linge notes he kept an expander under his bed. Ibid., 24.

32 Görtemaker, *Eva Braun: Life with Hitler*, 177.

33 Quoted in Gerhard L. Weinberg, ed. *Hitler's Table Talk, 1941-1944: His Private Conversations*, trans. by Norman Cameron and R.H. Stevens (New York, Enigma Books, 2008), 489.

34 Quoted in Linge, *With Hitler to the End*, 24.

35 Görtemaker, *Eva Braun: Life with Hitler*, 45.

36 Linge, *With Hitler to the End*, 59.

37 Ibid., 59, 69.

38 Ibid.

39 "In his estimation," Longerich writes of Hitler's own thinking, "the combination of the mature, busy, famous man and the unspoilt 'girl' ensured that his image as 'Führer' was enhanced by his also being seen as 'successful with women'…" Hitler—who Longerich argues was probably asexual—"showered these young women with compliments, gazed at them romantically, and possibly exchanged affectionate words with them, but that seems to be as far as these relationships went." See idem., *Hitler*, 161-163. On Hitler as a closeted homosexual in these encounters with young women, see Machtan, *The Hidden Hitler*, 155-158.

40 Machtan, *The Hidden Hitler*, 155-156; Kershaw, *Hitler: 1889-1936 Hubris*, 284-285; a paraphrased article of Steiner's recollections from *Der Stern* can be found in "Uneven Romance," *Time*, June 29, 1959, Vol. 73, Issue 26. Adolf had a peculiar obsession with wolves—using it as a pseudonym and naming two of his later bunkers the Wolf's Lair and Werwolf.

41 Longerich states that "we can be fairly confident that…'Uncle Adolf,' as Geli called him, did not engage in any sexual intimacy. What mattered to him was to have a companion and audience close to hand, someone who admired him….He liked to appear as the generous uncle dispensing treats….He evidently watched over her as though she were his personal possession." See idem., *Hitler*, 161-162.

42 Longerich, *Hitler*, 223; Kershaw, *Hitler: 1889-1936 Hubris*, 351-354.

[43] Görtemaker, *Eva Braun: Life with Hitler*, 48-51.

[44] Linge, *With Hitler to the End*, 48-49. He also spoke in misogynistic terms about women, warning of the "destructive influence of women on great men." See Görtemaker, *Eva Braun: Life with Hitler*, 41, 45. On Hitler's determination to hide their relationship more broadly, see "Rise to Power at Hitler's Side" in *Eva Braun: Life with Hitler*, 41-60.

[45] Linge, *With Hitler to the End*, 59-60. "My observations led me to believe that the sexual relationship [between Hitler and Braun]...had been especially active on occasion."

[46] Eva insisted on coming to Berlin to be with Hitler at the end of the war even though the dictator ordered her to stay away. See Görtemaker, *Eva Braun: Life with Hitler*, 3.

[47] See Kershaw, *Hitler: 1889-1936 Hubris*, 455.

[48] Childers, *The Third Reich*, 243-244; "Decree of the Reich President for the Protection of the People and State," German History in Documents and Images: https://web.archive.org/web/20210703110729/https://ghdi.ghi-dc.org/sub_document.cfm?document_id=2325 Accessed July 28, 2021. The decree allowed the government to impose restrictions on personal liberty and free expression—including freedom of the press, the right of assembly, and the right of association—as well as conduct warrantless house searches and confiscate property as it pleased.

[49] Longerich, *Hitler*, 292-300.

[50] Kershaw, *Hitler: 1889-1936 Hubris*, 435.

[51] Richard J. Evans, *The Third Reich in Power* (New York: Penguin, 2005), 30; Stalin quoted in Service, *Stalin*, 340.

[52] Evans, *The Third Reich in Power*, 42. Hindenburg believed he was talking to the Kaiser—"Majesty"—in his last conversation with Hitler.

[53] Quoted in Ibid.

[54] The official vote tally had 89.9% of the population in agreement. This number actually disappointed the Nazi regime—who did everything it could to boost the yes vote. Large numbers of Germans, regardless, were eager to see what Hitler—now a powerful dictator—might achieve. Kershaw, *Hitler: 1889-1936 Hubris*, 526.

[55] Elem Klimov, *Come and See* [*Idi i smotri*] (Moscow: Sovexportfilm, 1985). This film is based, in part, on Ales Adamovich's *Khatyn* (London: Glagoslav Publications, 2012), a novel about Nazi crimes against humanity in Belarus; Adamovich—a

former messenger and guerilla in Belarus during the Nazi occupation—wrote the screenplay for *Come and See.*

[56] Speer, for example, states: "At the beginning of the war in the east, Hitler, captive to his theory that the Slavs were subhuman, had called the war against them child's play. But the longer the war lasted, the more the Russians gained his respect. He was impressed by the stoicism with which they had accepted their early defeats. He spoke admiringly of Stalin...." See idem., *Inside the Third Reich*, 301.

[57] Christian Hartmann, *Operation Barbarossa: Nazi Germany's War in the East, 1941–1945* (Oxford: Oxford University Press, 2013), 160.

[58] U.S. President John F. Kennedy reminded the American people of this in his speech at American University on June 10, 1963. See "Commencement Address at American University, Washington, D.C., June 10, 1963," John F. Kennedy Presidential Library and Museum:

https://web.archive.org/web/20210716100551/https://www.jfklibrary.org/archives/other-resources/john-f-kennedy-speeches/american-university-19630610

Accessed July 28, 2021.

[59] The permanent museum at KZ Gedenkstätte Dachau on the experiences of that camp's prisoners offers chilling stories from individual files, speaking to the breadth of Nazi persecution against diverse victims. On euthanasia, see Michael Burleigh, *Death and Deliverance: "Euthanasia" in Germany c. 1900-1945* (Cambridge: Cambridge University Press, 1994); Götz Aly, Peter Chroust, and Christian Pross, *Cleansing the Fatherland: Nazi Medicine and Racial Hygiene* (Baltimore, MD: Johns Hopkins University Press, 1994).

[60] Speer, *Inside the Third Reich*, 40, 49.

[61] Primo Levi, *If This Is a Man* [*Survival in Auschwitz*], trans. Stuart Woolf (New York: Orion Press, 1959), 21.

[62] See Saul Friedlander, *Nazi Germany and the Jews, 1939-1945: The Years of Extermination* (New York: Harper Perennial, 2007).

[63] Rochus Misch, one of Hitler's bodyguards, stated (reliably or not) that he had no knowledge of Hitler ever visiting a concentration camp. See idem., with Michael Stehle, Ralph Giordano, and Sandra Zarrinbal, *Hitler's Last Witness The Memoirs of Hitler's Bodyguard* (London: Scribe, 2014), 92-93. Note: in old age, Misch questioned the events of the Holocaust as seen in Yael Katz Ben Shalom's *The Last Witness* (Alma Films); on this same topic, see Roger Moorhouse's introduction in *Hitler's Last Witness*, xv-xvi.

[64] Ian Kershaw, *Hitler: 1936-1945 Nemesis* (New York, W.W. Norton & Company, 2001), 500; see also Misch, *The Memoirs of Hitler's Bodyguard.*

[65] One of Hitler's bodyguards recalled an instance when Hitler was in an exhibition and "....I passed the time in conversation with the female cloakroom attendant. She mentioned that she would like to meet me after duty for a glass of wine, but I had to decline regretfully, because I would still be on duty and have to accompany the Führer when he left that evening. Finally, Hitler reappeared and, just as he was passing her, to my horror she said: 'I would like to go out with him this evening.' Here, she pointed at me: 'But he says he will be on duty.' Hitler looked around for our commander: 'Gesche, Gesche – Misch has the evening free.' See Misch, *Hitler's Last Witness The Memoirs of Hitler's Bodyguard*, 113-114.

[66] Traudl Junge, for example, notes that when she started working as one of Hitler's personal secretaries at age 22, Hitler urged her to let him know if any male soldiers bothered her, telling her: "...if I had any complaints of anyone pestering me, never mind who it was, I was to come and tell him about it, any time....I was grateful for his protection." Even in the decades that followed, as Junge wrestled with the evils of Hitler's regime and her complicity, she described Hitler as a "kindly paternal figure" who "...gave me a feeling of security, solicitude for me, safety....[A] 'father figure.'" See idem., *Hitler's Last Secretary,* ed. Melissa Müller, trans. Anthea Bell (New York: Arcade Publishing, 2002, 2011), 37, 218.

[67] Hitler's valet recalled the following anecdote: "...Hitler could act unpredictably...Schreck was driving Hitler...On a main highway they passed two RAD [Reichsarbeitsdienst—Reich Labour Service] youths walking to the next town. They thumbed a lift, not realizing who was in the Mercedes. Hitler told Schreck to stop and called the two youths over....Hitler invited them to climb in and chatted with them as they drove. When dropping the pair off Hitler mentioned that it looked like rain, they should keep their capes handy. One replied that he had been unemployed so long he had not been able to afford one. At once Hitler put his own trench-coat over the boy's shoulders and drove on. For those present it was an effective propaganda event shortly after the seizure of power...." See Linge, *With Hitler to the End,* 21.

[68] "A member of the SS bodyguard," remembered Heinz Linge, "had to ring the squad paymaster. At the same time Hitler wanted to phone [Albert] Speer. The SS man was to take his call in a cabin at the officers' mess. Hitler waited for his connection to Speer in the barrack hut for situation conferences. The two incoming calls arrived at the same time, and the telephonist connected them to the wrong callers.

The adjutant handed Hitler the receiver, believing that Speer was on the line. When Hitler announced himself, 'The Führer speaking,' there was a bellow of laughter from the other end. This was the paymaster who, still laughing, shouted into the receiver: 'You're crazy!' I feared an outburst of rage with serious consequences, but Hitler merely returned the receiver with the observation. 'Just someone who thinks I'm mad.' No outward annoyance and no negative consequences followed, which I found surprising since this episode occurred after the 20 July 1944 bomb plot." See Linge, *With Hitler to the End*, 144-145.

[69] Longerich, *Hitler*, 34-44.

[70] Speer notes the dog could elicit "a flicker of human feeling," see idem., *Inside the Third Reich*, 302.

[71] Linge's phrase in *With Hitler to the End*, 13.

[72] Junge, *Hitler's Last Secretary*, 92.

[73] Kershaw makes a similar point about Hitler's dog during World War I and Blondi during World War II. See idem., *Hitler: 1889-1936 Hubris*, 93.

[74] Schroeder, *He Was My Chief*, 105-106.

[75] Speer, *Inside the Third Reich*, 301.

[76] Junge, *Hitler's Last Secretary*, 38; Linge, *With Hitler to the End*, 188.

[77] Junge, ibid., 181. Blondi's puppies were taken outside and shot.

[78] Quoted in Introduction by Roger Moorhouse in Linge, *With Hitler to the End*, 2.

[79] Schroeder, *He Was My Chief*, 105, 116-117; Speer, *Inside the Third Reich*, 94-100.

[80] Schroeder, ibid.

[81] Misch, *Hitler's Last Witness*, 95-96.

[82] Speer, *Inside the Third Reich*, 101.

[83] Misch, *Hitler's Last Witness*, Chapter 8.

[84] Linge, *With Hitler to the End*, 171.

[85] Ohler, *Blitzed*, 172; Junge, *Hitler's Last Secretary*, 140.

[86] S. Nassir Ghaemi, *A First-Rate Madness: Uncovering the Links Between Leadership and Mental Illness* (New York: Penguin, 2012), 198.

[87] Also known as Pentylenetetrazol. See, for example: L.C. Cook, "Cardiazol Convulsion Therapy in Schizophrenia," in *Proceedings of the Royal Society of Medicine*, Vol. XXXI, January 11, 1938, 567-577; Kathryn Cooper and Max Fink, "The chemical induction of seizures in psychiatric therapy: were flurothyl (indoklon) and pentylenetetrazol (metrazol) abandoned prematurely?" *Journal of Clinical Psychopharmacology*, Vol. 34, No. 5 (October 2014): 602-607.

[88] W. Zick, "[Experiments in therapy of mental diseases (psychoses) with the narcotic Quadro-nox]," *Therapie der Gegenwart* Vol 93, No. 11 (1954): 432-433. https://pubmed.ncbi.nlm.nih.gov/13226303/
Accessed July 28, 2021.

[89] Ray J. Defalque and Amos J. Wright, "Scophedal (SEE) was it a fad or a miracle drug?" *Bulletin of Anesthesia History*, Vol. 21, No. 4 (2003): 12-14.

[90] See MSD Animal Health:
https://web.archive.org/web/20210121075956/https://www.msd-animal-health.co.in/products/tonophosphan-vet/
Accessed July 28, 2021.

[91] Ohler, *Blitzed*, 115.

[92] Ibid. For more on Hitler's doctor, Theo Morell, see Ottmar Katz, *Prof. Dr. Med. Theo Morell, Hitler's Leibarzt* (Bayreuth: Hestia, 1982).

[93] Linge, *With Hitler to the End*, 175.

[94] Ian Kershaw, *The End: The Defiance and Destruction of Hitler's Germany, 1944-1945* (New York: Penguin, 2011), 181.

[95] Richard J. Evans, *The Third Reich at War* (New York: Penguin, 2009), 710.

[96] Kershaw, *The End*, 357-358.

[97] See Hartmann, *Operation Barbarossa: Nazi Germany's War in the East, 1941-1945*, 157-159.

[98] Linge, *With Hitler to the End*, 188.

[99] Kershaw, *The End*, 188, 345.

[100] Junge, *Hitler's Last Secretary*, 160. Speer encouraged this, telling Hitler: "It seems better to me, if it must be, that you end your life here in the capital as the Fuehrer rather than in your weekend house." See idem., *Inside the Third Reich,* 479.

[101] Junge, *Hitler's Last Secretary*, 160. Eva Braun, however, was the exception; she was fully committed to dying with Hitler. See above endnote 46.

[102] See Misch, *Hitler's Last Witness*, 159.

Chapter 4 (Stalin)

[1] It was a reproduction of "Reply of the Zaporozhe Cossacks"; the wall also had photos of writers like Gorky. See Svetlana Alliluyeva, *Twenty Letters to a Friend: A Memoir* (New York: Harper & Row, 1967), 22, 208; V. M. Molotov with Felix Chuev, *Molotov Remembers: Inside Kremlin Politics* (Chicago: Ivan R. Dee, Inc., 1993, 2007), 164.

[2] Molotov described Stalin's eyes as "beautiful....dark brown." Idem., *Molotov Remembers: Inside Kremlin Politics*, 164.

[3] Oleg Khlevniuk, *Stalin: New Biography of a Dictator*, trans. Seligman Favorov (New Haven, CT: Yale University Press, 2015), 138.

[4] Ibid., 38.

[5] Alliluyeva, *Twenty Letters to a Friend*, 149-153. Dmitri Volkogonov, "Stalin: Man and Communist" in *The Stalin Revolution: Foundations of the Totalitarian Era*, Robert V. Daniels, ed. (Lexington: D.C. Heath & Company, 1997), 25; idem., *Stalin: Triumph and Tragedy* (New York: Grove Weidenfeld, 1991), 153.

[6] Alliluyeva, *Twenty Letters to a Friend*, 151.

[7] Ibid.; quoted in Oleg, *Stalin: New Biography of a Dictator*, 256; Rosemary Sullivan, *Stalin's Daughter: The Extraordinary and Tumultuous Life of Svetlana Alliluyeva* (New York: Harper, 2015), 61.

[8] Quoted in Alliluyeva, *Twenty Letters to a Friend*, 180; Simon Sebag Montefiore includes the curse word in *Stalin: Court of the Red Tsar*, 450.

[9] Alliluyeva, *Twenty Letters to a Friend*, 153.

[10] Ibid., 208.

[11] Quoted in Montefiore, *Stalin: Court of the Red Tsar*, 629.

[12] Joshua Rubenstein, *The Last Days of Stalin* (New Haven: Yale University Press, 2016), 10.

[13] Quoted in Montefiore, *Stalin: Court of the Red Tsar*, 631; Molotov, *Molotov Remembers*, 177.

[14] If not all NKVD interrogators were sadistic torturers, interrogations could get very, very, very bad. See the example from Kotkin, *Stalin: Waiting for Hitler*, 548.

[15] See, for example, "Our teacher, our leader, and beloved friend. Greetings to our beloved....Thank you for our happy childhood. There is no brighter one in the world!" See 0:44-1:46 in "Stalin and the pioneers of the Bolshoi Theater": https://www.youtube.com/watch?v=ioegwSXzPqI
Accessed July 28, 2021.

[16] W. E. B. Du Bois viewed Stalin and Soviet Union, in part, through the lenses of a global struggle for racial justice. See idem., "Stalin and American Negroes," Unpublished article for *Pravda* discussing race relations after Stalin's death, March 1953:
https://credo.library.umass.edu/view/full/mums312-b214-i052
Accessed December 9, 2021.

Accessed July 28, 2021. Du Bois eulogized Stalin after his death, writing: "Joseph Stalin was a great man....His judgment of men was profound. He early saw through the flamboyance and exhibitionism of Trotsky, who fooled the world....Such was the man who lies dead, still the butt of noisy jackals and of the ill-bred men of some parts of the distempered West." See idem., "On Stalin," *National Guardian*, March 16, 1953:

https://web.archive.org/web/20210712041942/https://www.marxists.org/reference/archive/stalin/biographies/1953/03/16.htm

Accessed December 9, 2021. See also David Levering Lewis, *W. E. B. Du Bois, 1919-1963: The Fight for Equality and the American Century* (New York: Henry Holt and Company, 2000), 556-557.

[17] Quoted in Steven A. Barnes, *Death and Redemption: The Gulag and the Shaping of Soviet Society* (Princeton, N.J.: Princeton University Press, 2011), 204.

[18] Khlevniuk, *Stalin: New Biography of a Dictator*, 94-95; Volkogonov, "Stalin: Man and Communist" in *The Stalin Revolution*, 21. On Stalin's revolutionary career as an organizer, see Suny, *Stalin: Passage to Power*.

[19] Volkogonov, "Stalin: Man and Communist" in *The Stalin Revolution*, 18; Stephen Kotkin, *Stalin: Paradoxes of Power*, 419.

[20] Khlevniuk, *Stalin: New Biography of a Dictator*, 95; Kotkin, *Stalin: Paradoxes of Power*, 419.

[21] Kotkin, *Stalin: Paradoxes of Power*, 76, 427.

[22] Describing the 1943 Tehran summit with Roosevelt and Churchill, Andrei Gromyko recalled: "I cannot remember a single occasion at the conference when Stalin misheard or misunderstood a major statement from either of his two partners. His memory worked like a computer and missed nothing....I came to realize just what extraordinary qualities this man possessed." See idem., *Memoirs* (New York: Doubleday, 1989), 85.

[23] Quoted in Kotkin, *Stalin: Paradoxes of Power*, 642.

[24] Kotkin's words in ibid., 425; see also Volkogonov, "Stalin: Man and Communist" in *The Stalin Revolution*, 15.

[25] Ibid.

[26] Service, *Stalin: A Biography*, 438; Khlevniuk, *Stalin: New Biography of a Dictator*, 215-216.

[27] Service, *Stalin*, 190.

[28] Kotkin, *Stalin: Paradoxes of Power*, 424; Service, *Stalin*, 190.

[29] Kotkin, ibid., 425-426. The position of general secretary had so many valuable levers, Kotkin notes, that Soso, "would have had to show uncommon restraint, deference, and lack of ambition not to build a personal dictatorship within the dictatorship."

[30] Trotsky's much quoted words; translated as "eminent mediocrity" in *Stalin: A Critical Survey of Bolshevism* (New York: Alliance Book Corp. Longman, Green and Co., 1939), Chapter IX. THE INHERITOR:
https://web.archive.org/web/20180715215506/https:/www.marxists.org/history/etol/writers/souvar/works/stalin/ch09.htm
Accessed July 28, 2021.

[31] Stalin used Russian history to justify the rapid plunge into the five-year plan. See Joseph Stalin, *Works 13* July 1930-January 1934 (Moscow: Foreign Languages Publishing House, 1952), 40-41.

[32] Khlevniuk, *Stalin: New Biography of a Dictator*, 116.

[33] Ibid., 38, 116-122.

[34] On examples of cannibalism and parents, see Anne Applebaum, *Red Famine: Stalin's War on Ukraine* (New York: Penguin Random House, 2017), 306.

[35] Letters between Stalin and Nadya in the Russian State Archive of Socio-Political History quoted by Montefiore, *Stalin: Court of the Red Tsar*, 7-8.

[36] "To a young woman from a revolutionary family," Khlevniuk writes of Nadya Alliluyeva, "he must have seemed like the ideal man: a tried-and-true revolutionary, brave and mysterious but also personable." Idem., *Stalin: New Biography of a Dictator*, 252. Stalin—Nadya surely did not know—had previously impregnated a fourteen-year old girl named Lidia Pereprygin in exile in Siberia. See Suny, *Stalin: Passage to Revolution*, 560; Montefiore, *Young Stalin*, 282-286.

[37] Khlevniuk, ibid; Montefiore, *Stalin: Court of the Red Tsar*, 34. For a discussion of Nadezhda Alliluyeva at the Industrial Academy, see William Taubman, *Khrushchev: The Man and His Era* (New York: W.W. Norton & Company, 2003), 85.

[38] Service, *Stalin*, 234. Molotov describes Nadya as a particularly jealous wife in *Molotov Remembers*, 173.

[39] Nikita Khrushchev, *Memoirs of Nikita Khrushchev: Volume 1: Commissar, 1918–1945*, ed. Sergei Khrushchev (State College, PA: Penn State University Press, 2013), 45.

[40] Nadya Alliluyeva's loss brought suggestions that Stalin himself might have killed her. See, for example, Khrushchev, *Memoirs of Nikita Khrushchev: Volume 1*, 45; Volkogonov, *Stalin: Triumph and Tragedy*, 154.

[41] Alliluyeva, *Twenty Letters to a Friend*, 122.

[42] Molotov, *Molotov Remembers*, 174; Montefiore, *Stalin: Court of the Red Tsar*, 108. Roy A. Medvedev and Volkogonov recorded different recollections—which Montefiore challenges—that Stalin did not attend the civil funeral and burial. See Medvedev, *Let History Judge: The Origins and Consequences of Stalinism* (New York: Columbia University Press, 1989), 303; Volkogonov, *Stalin: Triumph and Tragedy*, 154.

[43] Montefiore, *Stalin: Court of the Red Tsar*, 108.

[44] Ibid.

[45] In the last years of Stalin's life, Nadya Alliluyeva's portrait hung in his dacha's dining room and study as well as in his Kremlin apartment—a reminder of what he lost. See Volkogonov, *Stalin: Triumph and Tragedy*, 155.

[46] Quoted in Service, *Stalin*, 294. On the kids struggling with the loss of their mother, see Montefiore, *Stalin: Court of the Red Tsar*, 107.

[47] Montefiore, *Stalin: Court of the Red Tsar*, 116.

[48] Service, *Stalin*, 294.

[49] His daughter Svetlana Alliluyev stated that Nadya's death "was…devastating for my father" in Thames TV Production, "Stalin":
https://youtu.be/TZw3sN4XeNo?t=596
Accessed July 31, 2021. Lazar Kaganovich: "After 1932, Stalin changed," quoted in Montefiore, *Stalin: Court of the Red Tsar*, 110.

[50] Montefiore, *Stalin: Court of the Red Tsar*, 112.

[51] Aranovich, *I Served in Stalin's Guard: an Experiment in Documentary Mythology* [*I was Stalin's Bodyguard: Interviews with A.T. Rybin*] (Moscow: 1989), 10:52-11:00:
https://youtu.be/GRNl2jBrx2A?t=652
Accessed July 31, 2021.

[52] Quoted in Montefiore, *Stalin: Court of the Red Tsar*, 113.

[53] Ibid., 114.

[54] Molotov described Kirov as "Stalin's favorite," in idem., *Molotov Remembers*, 221. On tensions in 1934, see Matthew E. Lenoe, *The Kirov Murder and Soviet History* (New Haven: Yale University Press, 2010), 673-674.

[55] For the text of the Dec. 1 law, see "Central Executive Committee, On the Amendment of the Criminal Procedural Codes of the Union Republics. December 1, 1934": http://soviethistory.msu.edu/1934-2/the-kirov-affair/the-kirov-affair-texts/decree-following-kirovs-murder/

Accessed July 28, 2021. See also J. Arch Getty and Oleg V. Naumov, *The Road to Terror: Stalin and the Self-Destruction of the Bolsheviks, 1932-1939* (New Haven: Yale University Press, 2010), 140-147; Lenoe, *The Kirov Murder and Soviet History*, 251-256.

[56] Quoted in Lenoe, *The Kirov Murder and Soviet History*, 253.

[57] Ibid., 263-268; Molotov, *Molotov Remembers*, 220.

[58] On portrait, see Lenoe, *The Kirov Murder and Soviet History*, 265; on potential affair see ibid., 175-176, 670-672.

[59] What irony considering his own mother was still alive. Quoted in Montefiore, *Stalin: The Court of the Red Tsar*, 154.

[60] Khrushchev, *Memoirs of Nikita Khrushchev*: Volume 1, 85.

[61] Quoted in Montefiore, *Stalin: Court of the Red Tsar*, 155.

[62] Lenoe argues Borisov died in an actual car accident, see idem., *The Kirov Murder and Soviet History*, 673, 264.

[63] Quoted in Montefiore, *Stalin: Court of the Red Tsar*, 153.

[64] Khrushchev most of all believed this; see idem., *Memoirs of Nikita Khrushchev: Volume 1*, 86-90.

[65] Lenoe outlines how it could have happened (while offering critical doubts) in *The Kirov Murder and Soviet History*, 673-676.

[66] Lenoe, *The Kirov Murder and Soviet History*, 673-692; Khlevniuk, *Stalin: New Biography of a Dictato*r, 133.

[67] Khrushchev's de-Stalinization speech later emphasized that Stalin eradicated the ranks of the old Bolshevik party in the process, murdering 98 of 139 central committee members (70%!) from the 1934 Party Congress and arresting 1,108 of 1,966 of its delegates. See Nikita S. Khrushchev, "Cult of Personality," in *The Stalin Revolution: Foundations of the Totalitarian Era*, 201.

[68] Getty and Naumov, *The Road to Terror*, 474.

[69] Montefiore, *Stalin: Court of the Red Tsar*, 229-230.

[70] Ibid., 229.

[71] Ibid.

[72] Kotkin, *Stalin: Waiting for Hitler*, 112.

[73] After Nadya's death, Bukharin offered to swap apartments as a gesture of sympathy. See Montefiore, *Stalin: Court of the Red Tsar*, 115.

[74] Kotkin, *Stalin: Waiting for Hitler*, 349.

[75] Ibid., 368

[76] Getty and Naumov, *The Road to Terror*, 560.

[77] It was one of three found in his desk. Montefiore, *Stalin: Court of the Red Tsar*, 647 note.

[78] Alliluyeva, *Twenty Letters to a Friend*, 222.

[79] Eradicating his own army's officer corps—including three of five ranking marshals—was a particularly poor decision that, in part, left his army woefully unprepared to fight even Finland in the 1939-1940 Winter War.

[80] Georgy Zhukov, *Marshal of Victory: The Autobiography of General Georgy Zhukov* (1974; South Yorkshire: Pen & Sword Books, 2013), 428.

[81] Ibid., 429

[82] Khlevniuk, *Stalin: New Biography of a Dictator*, 199. The German dictator, Stalin had believed, would not be so foolish as to wage a two-front war.

[83] Quoted in Montefiore, *Stalin: Court of the Red Tsar*, 374.

[84] Khlevniuk, *Stalin: New Biography of a Dictator*, 205; Molotov, *Molotov Remembers*, 239.

[85] Khlevniuk, *Stalin: New Biography of a Dictator*, 218.

[86] J. V. Stalin, "Speech at the Red Army Parade on the Red Square, Moscow November 7, 1941," J.V. Stalin Archive, Works by Decade:
https://web.archive.org/web/20210419231336/https://www.marxists.org/reference/archive/stalin/works/1941/11/07.htm
Accessed July 28, 2021.

[87] Ibid.

[88] Stalin on November 6, 1941: "The German invaders want a war of extermination with the peoples of the U.S.S.R. Well, if the Germans want to have a war of extermination, they will get it. (Loud and prolonged applause.) See "Speech at Celebration Meeting of the Moscow Soviet of Working People's Deputies and Moscow Party and Public Organizations, November 6, 1941":
https://web.archive.org/web/20210420044555/https://www.marxists.org/reference/archive/stalin/works/1941/11/06.htm
Accessed July 28, 2021.

[89] Khlevniuk, *Stalin: New Biography of a Dictator*, 223-224.

[90] Ibid., 231.

[91] For a revisionist history of the Second World War that emphasizes the extent to which Stalin's regime depended on U.S. assistance, see Sean McMeekin, *Stalin's War: A New History of World War II* (New York: Basic Books, 2021).

[92] See, for example, Stalin's mass deportation of Chechens from Chechnya.

[93] Khlevniuk, *Stalin: New Biography of a Dictator*, 197; Rubenstein, *The Last Days of Stalin*, 49-50.

[94] Molotov, *Molotov Remembers*, 324, 212.

[95] Stalin, for instance, fired long-time personal secretary Alexander Poskrebyshev while turning on Molotov and Mikoyan in the halls of power. Molotov put it bluntly: "I might not have remained in one piece had he lived on…" See idem., *Molotov Remembers*, 327.

[96] See "Chapter Three: Stalin's Paranoia and the Jews" in Rubenstein, *The Last Days of Stalin*, 56-95.

[97] Edward Crankshaw, Strobe Talbott, eds., *Khrushchev Remembers* (New York: Little, Brown, 1970), 177.

[98] Ibid., 178.

[99] See John Lewis Gaddis, *George F. Kennan: An American Life* (New York: Penguin, 2011), 264.

[100] Gromyko, *Memoirs*, 99.

[101] Khlevniuk, *Stalin: New Biography of a Dictator*, 5-6.

[102] Alliluyeva, *Twenty Letters to a Friend*, 125; Montefiore, *Stalin: Court of the Red Tsar*, 294.

[103] Montefiore, *Stalin: Court of the Red Tsar*, 291-294.

[104] Ibid., 650.

[105] Rubenstein, *The Last Days of Stalin*, 13.

[106] Khlevniuk, *Stalin: New Biography of a Dictator*, 4.

[107] Rubenstein, *The Last Days of Stalin*, 10-11.

[108] Alliluyeva, *Twenty Letters to a Friend*, 10.

[109] Gromyko recalled Molotov's words soon after Stalin's death—he described the dictator's last moments differently from Svetlana Alliluyeva's: "'At one moment…he suddenly came to himself, and half opened his eyes….He then pointed slowly at the wall….On the wall there was a photograph with a simple subject: a little girl feeding a lamb with milk….With the same slow movement of his finger, Stalin then pointed to himself….The dying man was comparing himself with a lamb.'" See idem., *Memoirs*, 103.

Chapter 5 (Mao)

[1] Dr. Li Zhisui, *The Private Life of Chairman: The Memoirs of Mao's Personal Physician*, trans. Tai Hung-chao (New York: Random House, 1994), 5.

[2] Ibid., 6-7.

[3] Ibid., 3, 587; Pantsov and Levine, *Mao: The Real Story*, 570-571.

[4] Pantsov and Levine, *Mao: The Real Story*, 571.

[5] Ibid.

[6] The original Chinese text ("舍得一身剐，敢把皇帝拉下马") may also be translated as "to be willing to be flayed, to dare to unseat an emperor." See "Speech At The Chinese Communist Party's National Conference On Propaganda Work, March 12, 1957," *Selected Works of Mao Tse-tung*: https://web.archive.org/web/20210611061607/http://www.marxists.org/reference/archive/mao/selected-works/volume-5/mswv5_59.htm Accessed July 28, 2021; Dikötter, *Mao's Great Famine*, 23. Red Guards would later cite this quote during the Cultural Revolution as justification for attacking Liu Shaoqi and Deng Xiaoping. See Roderick MacFarquhar and Michael Schoenhals, *Mao's Last Revolution* (Cambridge: Belknap Press of Harvard University Press, 2006), 146.

[7] On Cai Hesen's death, see Liyan Liu, *Red Genesis The Hunan First Normal School and the Creation of Chinese Communism, 1903-1921* (Albany, NY: SUNY Press, 2012), 208, EN 55. For further details, Liyan Liu cites Cai Chang, "Huiyi Xinmin xuehui de huodong" [Reflections of the activities of the New Citizen Association] *in Xinmin xuehui ziliao* [Documents Collection And Memories of the New Citizens' Study Society], ed. by *Zhongguo geming bowuguan and Hunan sheng bowuguan* [The Editorial Committee of the Archives of Chinese Revolution and Hunan Provincial Archives] (Beijing: Renmin chubanshe, 1980), 574.

[8] Stuart R. Schram and Timothy Cheek, *Mao's Road to Power Revolutionary Writings*, Volume VIII (New York: Routledge, 2015), xxv.

[9] The future dictator: "When guerrillas engage a stronger enemy, they withdraw when he advances. Harass him when he stops; strike him when he is weary; pursue him when he withdraws." See Mao Zedong, *On Guerilla Warfare* (1937) at Mao Tse-tung Reference Archive: https://web.archive.org/web/20210420094413/https://www.marxists.org/reference/archive/mao/works/1937/guerrilla-warfare/ch01.htm Accessed July 28, 2021.

[10] Jonathan Spence, *Mao Zedong* (New York: Viking, 1999), 83-86; Stuart Schram, *Mao Tse-Tung* (Middlesex, UK: Penguin Books, 1966), 188.

[11] Nationalist leader Chiang Kai-shek, in contrast, rejected working with the communists. The Japanese, he argued, were an external "skin disease" while the communists threatened China's heart—an existential threat. See S. C. M. Paine,

The Wars for Asia, 1911–1949 (Cambridge: Cambridge University Press, 2012), 227.

[12] Paine, *The Wars for Asia, 1911–1949*, 224.

[13] The Chinese expression translated literally is "a plate of loose sand." Quoted in Hans van de Ven, *China at War: Triumph and Tragedy in the Emergence of the New China* (Cambridge, MA: Harvard University Press, 2018), 134, 153.

[14] Quoted in Julia Lowell, *Maoism: A Global History* (New York: Knopf, 2019), 41.

[15] Quoted in Lovell, *Maoism: A Global History*, 41-44; Jung Chang and Jon Halliday, *Mao: The Unknown Story* (New York: Random House, Inc., 2006), 241-243.

[16] Li, *The Private Life of Chairman*, 204.

[17] The guards did this on their own initiative; Mao had told them: "Neither release nor execute Wang Shiwei." See Dao Qing, *Wang Shiwei and Wild Lilies Rectification and Purges in the Chinese Communist Party 1942-1944*, trans. Nancy Liu and Lawrence R. Sullivan (Armonk, NY: M.E. Sharpe, 1994; New York: Routledge, 2015), 66-67; Short, *Mao: A Life*, 389. See also Lovell, *Maoism: A Global History*, 41; Chang and Halliday, *Mao: The Unknown Story*, 241.

[18] 160,000 starved to death in Changchun, for instance. See Dikötter, *The Tragedy of Liberation*, 3, 19. See also Harold M. Tanner, *Where Chiang Kai-shek Lost China: The Liao-Shen Campaign, 1948* (Bloomington, IN: Indiana University Press, 2015).

[19] Dikötter, *The Tragedy of Liberation*, 27.

[20] Li, *The Private Life of Chairman Mao*, 88.

[21] See ibid., 81-83, 100.

[22] Pantsov and Levine, *Mao: The Real Story*, 388; Pantsov and Levine cite Li Min, *Moi otets Mao Tszedun* [*My Father Mao Zedong*] (Beijing: Izdatel'stvo literatury na inostrannykh iazykakh, 2004),145-146.

[23] Li, *The Private Life of Chairman*, 67-68, 93, 122.

[24] See "Mao Zedong Poems," Marxist Internet Archive: Mao Zedong: https://www.marxists.org/reference/archive/mao/selected-works/poems/index.htm
Accessed June 29, 2021.

[25] See Ross Terrill, *Madame Mao: The White Boned Demon* (Stanford, CA: Stanford University Press, 1999).

[26] Li, *The Private Life of Chairman*, 100.

[27] Renzhi's indirect style, Henry Kissinger recorded, was "laconic" with "rich use of analogy, symbolism, allusion, and earthy humor"; he engaged "…his agenda in a seemingly casual, even haphazard manner. See Gerald R. Ford Presidential

Library, National Security Adviser Trip Briefing Books and Cables for President Ford, 1974-1976 (Box 19), "Mao Book, December 1975," 3: https://web.archive.org/web/20210413033128/https://www.fordlibrarymus eum.gov/library/document/0358/035800388.pdf

Accessed July 28, 2021; see also Dean A. Haycock, *Tyrannical Minds*, Chapter 6.

[28] Li, *The Private Life of Chairman Mao*, 127.

[29] Ibid., 121.

[30] Ibid., 120.

[31] Ibid., 81, 120.

[32] Ibid., 110. Li states: "Mao's neurasthenia was rooted in his continuing fear that other ranking leaders were not loyal to him and that there were few within the party whom he could genuinely trust. The symptoms became much more severe at the beginning of a major political struggle."

[33] Ibid., 233-234, 478.

[34] Ibid., 113.

[35] Rebecca Karl, *Mao Zedong and China in the Twentieth-Century World* (Durham, NC: Duke University Press, 2010), 8. He refused to use sit-down toilets after he had access to them—which, along with passing gas and burping—also related to prevailing cultural norms to an extent.

[36] Clare Hollingworth's words in *Mao and the Men Against Him* (New York: Jonathan Cape, 1985), 29-31. On his "earthiness" in language, see Lovell, *Maoism: A Global History*, 34-35.

[37] Hollingworth, *Mao and the Men Against Him*, 30.

[38] Quoted in Pantsov and Levine, *Mao: The Real Story*, 495. "To fart" (as Mao is using the phrase here colloquially in Mandarin) carries a similar meaning in English as "to speak bullshit" or "to be full of shit."

[39] Schram's words in *Mao Tse-Tung*, 73; idem., *The Political Thought of Mao Tse-Tung* (Cambridge: Cambridge University Press, 1989), 143.

[40] Quoted in Schram, *Mao Tse-Tung*, 73.

[41] Julia Lowell's words in *Maoism: A Global History* (New York: Knopf, 2019), 35.

[42] Dikötter, *The Cultural Revolution*, 39.

[43] Li, *The Private Life of Chairman Mao*, 80, 93-94, 358. On the traditional Daoist belief that an older man's longevity is strengthened by absorbing the bodily fluids of a young woman in sexual intercourse, Li Zhi-Sui cites: Douglas Wile, *Art of the Bed Chamber: The Chinese Sexual Yoga Classics Including Women's Solo Meditation Texts* (Albany, N.Y.: SUNY Press, 1992).

[44] Li, *The Private Life of Chairman Mao*, 356.

[45] Ibid.

[46] Ibid., 362-363.

[47] Ibid., 358. Ravenous lust—opposed to same-sex attraction—likely drove this behavior, at least according to Li Zhi-Sui.

[48] Emphasis added. Ibid., 363-363, 490-491.

[49] Ibid., 94; Chang and Halliday, *Mao: The Unknown Story*, 333, 536. During the Cultural Revolution in January 1967, Red Guards brought Peng to Beijing in chains; he was ruthlessly abused in repeated struggle sessions until he died in 1974. See Jürgen Domes, *P'eng Te-huai: The Man and the Image* (Stanford, CA: Stanford University Press, 1985), 217-224.

[50] "The thought, culture and customs which brought China to where we found her," Mao added a decade later, "must disappear." See "Interview With Andre Malraux," *Selected Works of Mao Tse-tung*:
https://web.archive.org/web/20210514140437/https://www.marxists
org/reference/archive/mao/selected-works/volume-9/mswv9_50.htm
Accessed July 28, 2021.

[51] See Chapter 8: People's War in *Quotations from Mao Tse Tung*.
https://web.archive.org/web/20210419164804/https://www.marxists.org/r
eference/archive/mao/works/red-book/ch08.htm
Accessed June 18, 2021.

[52] No one, of course, would have said *right* ideas, answers, and slogans in Mandarin. Dikötter, *The Tragedy of Liberation*, 49.

[53] Felix Wemheuer, *A Social History of Maoist China: Conflict and Change, 1949-1976* (Cambridge: Cambridge University Press, 2019), 71-73.

[54] Dikötter, *The Tragedy of Liberation*, 74, 76, 81-82; Lovell, *Maoism: A Global History*, 99; Jonathan Spence, *The Search for Modern China* (New York: W.W. Norton & Company, 1990), 106; R. Keith Schoppa, *The Columbia Guide to Modern Chinese History* (New York: Columbia University Press, 2000), 106.

[55] Dikötter, *The Tragedy of Liberation*, 87.

[56] Ibid.

[57] Ibid., 100.

[58] Ibid.

[59] Pantsov notes that this helped inspire support—or at least a disclination to oppose—more far-reaching campaigns like the Great Leap Forward. See idem. and Levine, *Mao: The Real Story*, 453.

[60] Schoppa, *The Columbia Guide to Modern Chinese History*, 109-110.

[61] For a discussion of how anti-colonial resentment influenced Chinese public opinion and foreign policy in these years, see Masuda Hajimu, *Cold War Crucible: The Korean Conflict and the Postwar World* (Cambridge: Harvard University Press, 2015).

[62] "Speech At The Supreme State Conference 28 January, 1958," *Selected Works of Mao Tse-tung.*
https://web.archive.org/web/20210619063524/https://www.marxists.org/reference/archive/mao/selected-works/volume-8/mswv8_03.htm
Accessed July 28, 2021.

[63] Schoppa, *The Columbia Guide to Modern Chinese History*, 112.

[64] Dikötter, *Mao's Great Famine*, 59.

[65] See Zhang Langlang's comments in the documentary: Sue Williams, dir., *China: A Century of Revolution* (Ambrica Productions, Inc. and WGBH Educational Foundation, 1994), 43:40-44:00:
https://www.youtube.com/watch?v=PJyoX_vrlns
Accessed July 28, 2021.

[66] Dikötter, *Mao's Great Famine*, 37.

[67] On close-cropping, for example, see Ibid., 39-40.

[68] Dikötter, *Mao's Great Famine*, 333.

[69] Jasper Becker, *Hungry Ghosts: Mao's Secret Famine* (New York: Henry Holt and Company, 1996), 4.

[70] Dikötter, *Mao's Great Famine*, 284

[71] Ibid., 298.

[72] The regime, regardless, tried to blame natural disasters. See "Summary of the Conversation between Comrade Peng Zhen and Romanian Ambassador in China Barbu Zaharescu," March 28, 1961, History and Public Policy Program Digital Archive at the Woodrow Wilson International Center for Scholars, PRC FMA 109-03792-03, 6-13. Translated by Lu Sun:
https://web.archive.org/web/20210214164827/https://digitalarchive.wilsoncenter.org/document/120005
Accessed July 28, 2021.

[73] Dikötter, *Mao's Great Famine*, 337.

[74] This did not stop Liu Shaoqi from leading a ruthless campaign of repression on Mao's behalf in the "Socialist Education Campaign" from 1963 to 1964, which resulted in the persecution of 5 million party members and the deaths of 77,000. See Ibid., 21-26.

[75] Quoted in Dikötter, *The Cultural Revolution*, 25.

[76] Pantsov and Levine, *Mao: The Real Story*, 516.

[77] Quoted in Ibid., 516; Dikötter, *The Cultural Revolution*, 71; MacFarquhar and Schoenhals, *Mao's Last Revolution*, 87.

[78] Pantsov and Levine, *Mao: The Real Story*, 508.

[79] Dikötter, *The Cultural Revolution*, 73.

[80] Ibid., 74.

[81] Pantsov and Levine, *Mao: The Real Story*, 509. Of course—as Dikötter noted in a 2016 interview—much of the praise and slogan-shouting was not necessarily sincere. See New Economic Thinking, "Understanding China's Cultural Revolution":
https://youtu.be/N9iVDCzGyiE?t=360
Accessed July 28, 2021.

[82] Quoted in Dikötter, *The Cultural Revolution*, 75.

[83] Emphasis added. MacFarquhar and Schoenhals, *Mao's Last Revolution*, 108; Pantsov and Levine, *Mao: The Real Story*, 510; Dikötter, *The Cultural Revolution*, 75.

[84] Pantsov and Levine, *Mao: The Real Story*, 511

[85] Dikötter, *The Cultural Revolution*, 75, 79.

[86] MacFarquhar and Schoenhals, *Mao's Last Revolution*, 74.

[87] See Zhu Danian's comments in Carma Hinton's documentary *Morning Sun* (2003) about the cultural revolution:
https://youtu.be/gaz8sVaK8s4?t=305
Accessed July 28, 2021.

[88] Emphasis added. See "Report On An Investigation Of The Peasant Movement In Hunan, March 1927," *Selected Works of Mao Tse-tung*:
https://web.archive.org/web/20210607155939/https://www.marxists.org/reference/archive/mao/selected-works/volume-1/mswv1_2.htm
Accessed July 28, 2021.

[89] Ibid.

[89] For an overview of this, see Hinton, *Morning Sun* (2003):
https://youtu.be/gaz8sVaK8s4?t=356
Accessed June 18, 2021.

[90] The Cultural Revolution Group included Mao's wife—Jiang Qing—as well as Chen Boda, Kang Sheng, Zhang Chunqiao, and Yao Wenyuan, among others. (The Gang of Four emerged from it in the struggle to succeed Mao.) On its formation, see Dikötter, *The Cultural Revolution*, 56-57.

[91] See Michael Schuman, *Confucius: And the World He Created* (New York: Basic Books, 2015), 95-96.

[92] See, for instance, Jung Chang's story about herself as a teenage girl who opposed the violence of the Red Guards but could do nothing to stop it; in idem., *Wild Swans: Three Daughters of China* (New York: Simon & Schuster, 1991, 2003), 276-446.

[93] Macfarquhar and Schoenhals, *Mao's Last Revolution*, 147; cited by Pantsov and Levine, *Mao: The Real Story*, 518.

[94] Dikötter, *The Cultural Revolution*, 235.

[95] Pantsov and Levine, *Mao: The Real Story*, 519.

[96] Dikötter, *The Cultural Revolution*, xviii.

[97] Wang Rongfen remains a powerful example. A college student in September 1966, Wang wrote Mao four letters challenging the cruelty of the Cultural Revolution. ("As a member of the Communist Party, please think about what you are doing," she wrote.) Wang then went to the Soviet Embassy, where she chugged a bottle of insecticide to commit suicide and avoid the extreme retribution that would follow. She woke up in a police hospital. After years in jail, she was sentenced to life imprisonment in 1976 and sent to a labor camp. There, she nearly died after her steel handcuffs—which grew tighter when she moved—became fused into her wrists, cutting more and more deeply. Wang describes her experiences in those handcuffs as follows: "When we ate, we were on the floor like beasts, and they didn't have toilets. When my period came it just went into my trousers....They treated livestock better than they treated us." She was released from prison in 1979. See Interview with Wang Rongfen: "Dear Chairman Mao, Please Think About What You Are Doing,'" Radio Free Asia, May 16, 2016: https://web.archive.org/web/20210409045914/https://www.rfa.org/english/news/china/china-cultrev-05162016173649.html
Accessed July 28, 2021.

[98] Li, *The Private Life of Chairman*, 580.

[99] Ibid., 580-582.

[100] Ibid., 617.

[101] Ibid., 617, 622-623, 589, 3, 569.

[102] Ibid., 9.

Chapter 6 (Kim)

[1] Quoted in John H. Cha and K.J. Sohn, *Exit Emperor Kim Jong Il: Notes From His Former Mentor* (Bloomington, IN: Abbott Press, 2012), 70.

[2] For an overview of this period, see Adrian Buzo, *Politics and Leadership in North Korea: The Guerilla Dynasty*, second edition (New York: Routledge, 2018), 117-150.

[3] On U.S. perceptions of North Korea during this period, see Brandon K. Gauthier, "The Other Korea: Ideological Constructions of North Korea in The American Imagination, 1948-2000," Ph.D. diss., (Fordham University, 2016), 303-316. Available online:

https://independent.academia.edu/BrandonKGauthierPhD

[4] See Andrei Lankov, *The Real North Korea: Life and Politics in the Failed Stalinist Utopia* (New York: Oxford University Press, 2013), 21, 150-153; Buzo, *Politics and Leadership in North Korea*, 117-118.

[5] Kim Il-sung, "On Effecting a New Revolutionary Turn in Socialist Economic Construction, Concluding Speech at a Consultive Meeting of the Senior Officials in the Economic Sector," *Works*, Vol. 44 December 1992-July 1994 (Pyongyang: Foreign Languages Publishing House, 1999), 418-433:

https://web.archive.org/web/20210418154223/https://www.marxists.org/archive/kim-il-sung/cw/44.pdf

Accessed July 28, 2021.

[6] Quoted in Cha and Sohn, *Exit Emperor Kim Jong Il*, 70.

[7] Ibid.

[8] Ibid. "Beginning in the early 1990s, the North Korean government began reducing rations for the northeastern part of the DPRK before finally cutting off food shipments to that region (including the second largest-city in the DPRK) altogether. This policy—called a "triage" by Andrew Natsios—effectively left millions to starve in the northeast so Kim Jong Il's regime could ensure its own survival by prioritizing food rations for Pyongyang and areas of the country considered most loyal to the regime." Quoted from Gauthier, "The Other Korea: Ideological Constructions of North Korea in The American Imagination, 1948-2000," 336, FN 135; see also Andrew Natsios, *The Great North Korean Famine: Famine, Politics, and Foreign Policy* (Washington, D.C.: United States Institute of Peace, 2001), 106-109.

[9] Quoted in Cha and Sohn, *Exit Emperor Kim Jong Il*, 70-71.

[10] Ordinary North Koreans like Yo Man Chul and his family of five, as *Time* reported that same year, had already chosen to risk fleeing to China because the only alternative was death. "I thought there was no difference," Yo explained, "between dying while fleeing or dying by starvation." Quoted in Edward W. Desmond, "The Hard Way Out," *Time*, November 7, 1994, 53; cited in Gauthier, "The Other Korea," 337, FN 136.

[11] As Kim Il-sung stated in a 1957 speech: "Our people in the near future will live on rice and meat soup, dressed in silk clothes, and in the tile-roofed houses. This is not a daydream but the reality of tomorrow. Under the system of exploitation it would only be a dream, but under our system it is a reality within reach. We can visualize tile-roofed houses, herds of pigs and fruit-laden orchards." See idem., "Speech at the Conference of Activists from the Agricultural Cooperatives in North Hwanghae Province," December 20, 1957," in *Works*, Vol. 11 (Pyongyang: Foreign Languages Publishing House, 1982), 412.

[12] See Bruce Cumings, *Origins of the Korean War: Liberation and the Emergence of Separate Regimes, 1945-1947*, Vol. 1 (Princeton, NJ: Princeton University Press, 1981).

[13] On Korea's rich history, see Lee Ki-baik, trans. Edward W. Wagner and Edward J. Shultz. *A New History of Korea* (Seoul: Ilchokak Publishers, 1984).

[14] "YOU SAY POTATO, I SAY DPR KOREA," *Tampa Bay Times*, June 15, 2010: https://www.tampabay.com/archive/2010/06/15/you-say-potato-i-say-dpr-korea/#
Accessed July 28, 2021; see also Gauthier, "The Other Korea," 6-7.

[15] See Andrei Lankov, *From Stalin to Kim Il Sung: The Formation of North Korea, 1945-1960* (New Brunswick, NJ: Rutgers University Press, 2002), "Chapter 1: North Korea in 1945-8: the Soviet Occupation and the Birth of the State," 1-48.

[16] See Robert Scalapino and Chong-Sik Lee, *Communism in Korea*, Vol. 1 (Berkeley, CA: University of California Press, 1972), 324-325, 338; Cumings, *Origins of the Korean War*, Vol. 1, 397-403; Bradley K. Martin, *Under the Loving Care of the Fatherly Leader: North Korea and the Kim Dynasty* (New York: St. Martin's Press, 2006), 52. O Yong-jin's "An Eye Witness Report"—cited by Scalapino & Lee, Cumings, and Martin—states that Kim had "'a haircut like a Chinese waiter'" and spoke in "'a monotonous, plain, and duck-like voice.'" Bruce Cumings mocked that "anticommunist account," stating: "I heard similar accounts from Koreans in the south who claimed to have attended the same meeting; there is no way to verify such impressions....These things belong in gossip columns." See *Origins of*

the Korean War, Vol. 1, 557, EN 62; cited in Brandon K. Gauthier, "This Day in History: When Kim Il Sung Took Power," *NKnews.org*, October 9, 2012. https://web.archive.org/web/20130208021124/https://www.nknews.org/2012/10/this-day-in-history-when-kim-il-sung-took-power/ Accessed July 28, 2021.

[17] See "Right Way to the Left," *New York Times*, March 3, 1946, 32; Richard J .H. Johnston, "Communist Issue Growing in Korea," *New York Times*, April 27, 1946; "Letters: Plump Puppet," *Time*, May 31, 1948, 8; cited in Gauthier, "Other Korea," 34.

[18] One headline for a 1946 Associated Press article, however, described the new leader as a rough and tumble "Asiatic Paul Bunyan"—"a newly arrived character as colorful and controversial as ever figured in a mystery drama." Kim Il-sung, the news wire story stated, was a "shadowy figure" viewed by conservatives in Korea as a fake imitating the role of a famed guerilla who fought the Japanese. "Real or imposter, general or politician, this man may someday become a powerful figure in Korea," the article concluded presciently. See AP, "Asiatic Paul Bunyan: 'Legendary' Hero Returns to Korea Leading Army," *Salt Lake Tribune* (Salt Lake, UT), January 27, 1946, 6.

[19] Though Stalin refused Kim Il-sung's initial requests in August and September 1949 to support a North Korean invasion, Kim continued to work actively to change the minds of Soviet and Chinese officials. "Kim," states a Soviet document about a January 1950 party, "excitedly told [Soviet] counselors…that now that China was completely liberated, the liberation of the Korean people in the south of the country is next in line….'I can't sleep at night recently thinking about how to resolve the question of the unification of the whole country. If liberation…is postponed, I will lose the confidence of the Korean people.'….Kim Il-sung [the document explains]…spoke in an excited fashion, but it was not accidental….He obviously thought the issues through and his objective was to explain his attitude and sound out our responses." See Wada, Haruki, *The Korean War: An International History*, trans. Frank Baldwin (Lanham, MD: Rowman & Littlefield, 2014), 52-53; cited in Gauthier, "The Other Korea," 50, FN 21.

[20] Syngman Rhee planned to invade North Korea and reunify Korea as soon as possible; days before the Korean War, he admitted to a U.S. visitor that he planned to use force to reunite the peninsula within a year, adding that it would not amount to "aggression"—the reason being that Korea was one country. See

Masuda Hajimu, *Cold War Crucible*, 77; cited in Gauthier, "Other Korea," 36, FN 101.

[21] On Kim Il-sung's efforts to convince Stalin and Mao to allow the North Korean invasion, see Wada, *The Korean War: An International History*, 45-74. See also: Kathryn Weathersby, "'Should We Fear This?' Stalin and the Danger of War in Korea," Cold War International History Project Working Paper No. 39 (July 2002); and "Korean War Origins, 1945-1950," The Woodrow Wilson International Center for Scholars:

https://web.archive.org/web/20210423121437/https://digitalarchive.wilson center.org/collection/134/korean-war-origins-1945-1950

Accessed July 28, 2021; cited in Gauthier, "Other Korea," 48, FN 18.

[22] For a succinct overview, see Brandon K. Gauthier, "The day South Korea faced the merciless reality of extinction," NKnews.org, June 25, 2013:

https://web.archive.org/web/20130704071746/https://www.nknews.org/2 013/06/the-day-south-korea-faced-the-merciless-reality-of-extinction/

Accessed July 28, 2021.

[23] The North Korean invasion—on the verge of quickly occupying all of South Korea—finally stalled at the ROK and UN's Pusan Perimeter in southeast Korea in August 1950. As North Korean forces raced south over the prior month, U.S. forces carried out desperate airstrikes to stop the North Korean advance, killing numerous civilians in the process. As one 1952 history of the conflict, written by USN Captain Walter Karig, admitted: "So, we killed civilians, friendly civilians, and bombed their homes; fired whole villages with the occupants—women and children and 10 times as many hidden Communist soldiers—under showers of napalm, and the pilots came back to their ships stinking of the vomit twisted from their vitals by the shock of what they had to do....The objective here was to halt and destroy an enemy whose savagery towards the people he professed to be succoring was more callous than the Nazis' campaign of terror in Poland and the Ukraine, an enemy who murdered wire-fettered prisoners of war, an enemy allowed to take his chances with death as a soldier in combat would most certainly buy a hero's niche in the heaven of his barbaric choice by taking the life of at least one American soldier." See Karig et al., *Battle Report*, vol. VI, *The War in Korea* (New York: Rhinehart and Company, 1952), 111.

[24] See Brandon K. Gauthier, "What It Was Like to Negotiate With North Koreans 60 Years Ago," TheAtlantic.com, July 26, 2013.

https://web.archive.org/web/20211209044439/https://www.theatlantic.co
m/international/archive/2013/07/what-it-was-like-to-negotiate-with-north-
koreans-60-years-ago/278130/

Accessed December 28, 2021.

[25] S.L.A. Marshall's words quoted in Gauthier, "Other Korea," 43; Max Hastings, *The Korean War* (New York: Simon & Schuster, 1987), 329; David Halberstam, *The Coldest Winter: America and the Korean War* (New York: Hachette Books, 2007), 1.

[26] On killings by North Korean forces, see Gauthier, "The Other Korea," 118-119; Sheila Miyoshi Jager, *Brothers At War: The Unending Conflict in Korea* (New York: W. W. Norton & Company, 2013), 94-97; William C. Latham, *Cold Days in Hell: American POWs in Korea* (College Station, TX: Texas A&M University Press, 2012), 39-41. On U.S. and ROK atrocities, see Bruce Cumings, *North Korea: Another Country* (New York: The New Press, 2004), 1-41; idem., *The Korean War: A History* (New York: Modern Library, 2010), chapter seven. For an overview of the American bombing of irrigation dams in North Korea, see Brandon K. Gauthier, "This Day in the History of the DPRK: June 18, Juche 41 (1953)," NKnews.org, June 17, 2012:

https://web.archive.org/web/20140222234939/https://www.nknews.org/2
012/06/this-day-in-the-history-of-the-dprk-june-18-juche-41-1953/

Accessed July 28, 2021. More broadly on the U.S. bombing campaign against North Korea—which destroyed every town in the country and caused immense suffering—see Robert A. Pape, *Bombing to Win: Air Power and Coercion in War* (Ithaca, N.Y.: Cornell University Press, 1996), 137-173.

[27] Other U.N. casualties came from the United Kingdom, Canada, Australia, France, Turkey, Thailand, the Netherlands, Greece, Colombia, Belgium, Ethiopia, the Philippines, South Africa, and Norway. See the next endnote for sources on casualties.

[28] The Department of Veterans Affairs lists the number of Americans killed in Korea ("in theater") as 36,574; but 17,672 "non-theater" deaths occurred during these years as well, thus bringing the total American death total to 54,246. On casualties, see Department of Veterans Affairs, "America's Wars," Nov. 2020; Michael H. Hunt and Steven I. Levine, *Art of Empire: America's Wars in Asia from the Philippines to Vietnam* (Chapel Hill, N.C.: University of North Carolina, 2012), 172; Max Hastings, *The Korean War*, 329; cited by Pantsov and Levine, *Mao: The Real Story*, 387; see also Jodi Kim, *Ends of Empire: Asian American Critique and the*

Cold War (Minneapolis, MN: University of Minnesota Press, 2010), 275 EN 19; Ramsay Liem, "History, Trauma, and Identity: The Legacy of the Korean War for Korean Americans," *Ameriasia Journal* 29, no. 3 (2003-4): 114.

[29] The North Korean regime, of course, has done as much as possible to heighten its people's hatred of the United States. For a brief example, see AFP News Agency, "Lessons in loathing at North Korea's museum to 'US atrocity,'" June 7, 2018: https://www.youtube.com/watch?v=AQsR-e7fD7E
Accessed July 28, 2021.

[30] The Korean War was both a civil war and a cold war conflict. For an overview of Korean history in the century before its outbreak, see Bruce Cumings, *Korea's Place in the Sun: A Modern History* (New York: W.W. Norton & Company, 1997), 1-260. On Cold War events surrounding the conflict as a whole, see Masuda, *Cold War Crucible*.

[31] Anna Louise Strong's words in *Inside North Korea: An Eye-Witness Report* (Montrose, CA: Soviet Russia Today, 1949), 18.

[32] Lankov, *The Real North Korea*, 54; Bradley K. Martin, *Under the Loving Care of the Fatherly Leader*, 207-208; Brandon K. Gauthier, "The Day Kim Jong-il Was Born," February 15, 2013:
https://web.archive.org/web/20130220055933/https://www.nknews.org/2013/02/the-day-kim-jong-il-was-born/
Accessed July 28, 2021.

[33] A North Korean "biography" of Kim Jong-il describes the loss of his mother as follows: "The little boy spent that day unaware of his mother's death, staring out the window excitedly. When a car pulled up, he rushed outside, bewildered to see a family member rush into the house, grab clothes for his mother, and then leave abruptly. His confusion turned into pain by the next morning. Attending his mother's funeral, Jong Il hugged her dead body, bawling. When female soldiers tried to pull him away, Kim Il-sung responded: "Leave him alone. Tomorrow he will have no mother any more in whose embrace to cry.'" See Choe In Su, *Kim Jong Il: The People's Leader*, Vol. 1 (Pyongyang: Foreign Languages Publishing House, 1983), 48-54; quoted in Gauthier, ibid.

[34] On factions within the North Korean leadership and challenges to Kim's authority, see Lankov, *From Stalin to Kim Il Sung*.

[35] Martin, *Under the Loving Care of the Fatherly Leader*, 188; Hwang Jang-yop (Former International-Secretary of KWP), "The Problem of Human Rights in North Korea (2), trans. Network for North Korea Rights and Democracy:

https://web.archive.org/web/20030202184515/www.nknet.org/en/keys/las tkeys/2002/8/04.php

Accessed July 28, 2021. For more on Hwang's experiences, See Hwang Jang-yop, *Naneun Yeoksaui Jillireul Boatda* [*I Saw the Truth of History*] (Seoul: Sidaejeongsin, 2010).

[36] A defector's words in Martin, *Under the Loving Care of the Fatherly Leader*, 188. On the tumor, google "Kim Il-sung tumor."

[37] Hwang Jang-yop, "The Problem of Human Rights in North Korea (2).

[38] Ibid.

[39] Hwang Jang-yop (Former International-Secretary of KWP), "The Problem of Human Rights in North Korea (1), trans. Network for North Korea Rights and Democracy:

https://web.archive.org/web/20030626015154/http://www.nknet.org/en/keys/lastkeys/2002/7/03.php

Accessed July 28, 2021.

[40] See Cheehyung Harrison Kim, *Heroes and Toilers: Work as Life in Postwar North Korea* (New York: Columbia University Press, 2018); Brandon K. Gauthier, "Book Review: Cheehyung Harrison Kim, *Heroes and Toilers*," *Journal of American-East Asian Relations*, Vol. 26 (2019), 325-328.

[41] Lankov, *The Real North Korea*, 70-72.

[42] Kim Il-sung and PRC Premier Zhou Enlai announced the withdrawal of Chinese forces in February 1958.

[43] North Korea, for instance, directly emphasized its right to pursue communism in its own way while distinguishing itself from both the Soviet Union and China. In Korean, see: "Chajusongul Onghohaja," *Rodong Sinmun*, August 12, 1966; for an English language translation of the same article, see: "Supplement to the Pyongyang Times: Let Us Defend Independency: Article of the *Rodong Sinmun*, August 12, 1966," *The Pyongyang Times*, 68, no. 68, August 18, 1966; see also Gauthier, "The Other Korea," 164.

[44] On clashes in the mid and late 1950s, for instance, see Gauthier, "The Other Korea," 108-112.

[45] For transcripts of meetings between North Korean and American representatives at Panmunjom, see National Archives II (College Park, MD), RG 333, 14A, UNCMAC, MMMAC, 07/28/1953-02/13/1981. Numerous American newspapers reprinted an Associated Press article with the "mad dog" quote. See, for example, "The Ship That Went Out in the Cold" and "Panmunjom: Mad Dogs

Bark at Moon" in *The Progress* (Clearfield, PA), November 14, 1969, 14 and *The Lawton Constitution* (OK), November 11, 1969, 9. Before delving into the archives, I originally learned about the "mad dog" quote through Martin's *Under the Fatherly Leader*, 129.

[46] For North Korea's version of history, see Kim Jun Hyok, *DPRK-US Showdown* (Pyongyang: Foreign Languages Publishing House, 2014). For a review of this work, see Brandon K. Gauthier, *"DPRK-US Showdown* – a book review," September 11, 2014:
https://web.archive.org/web/20200116053505/https://www.nknews.org/2014/09/dprk-us-showdown-a-book-review/
Accessed June 20, 2021.

[47] Lankov, *The Real North Korea*, 9.

[48] Christopher Hitchens would observe as much. See "Christopher Hitchens: How Religion Is Like North Korea":
https://youtu.be/eefS0gayKFc
Accessed July 28, 2021; idem., *God Is Not Great: How Religion Poisons Everything* (New York: Hatchette, 2007), 247-248.

[49] Portraits of Kim Jong-il and Kim Jong-suk later joined those of Kim Il-sung. For more on the portraits as well as the connection between religion and the Kims' cult of personality, see Barbara Demick, *Nothing to Envy: Ordinary Lives in North Korea* (New York: Spiegel & Grau, 2010), 45-48.

[50] The same is true of portraits of Kim Jong-il and Kim Jong-suk. Lankov, *The Real North Korea*, 51; Lee Hyeonseo and David John, *The Girl With Seven Names: A North Korean Defector's Story* (London: HarperCollins, 2015), xv-xvi.

[51] Baik Bong, *KIM IL SUNG: Biography (III): From Independent National Economy To 10-Point Political Programme*, trans. Committee for Translation (Tokyo: Miraisha, 1970), 1.

[52] Emphasis in original. Martin, *Under the Loving Care of the Fatherly Leader*, 9. Martin watched this opera live as a journalist during a 1979 visit. He relates the experience in the opening of *Under the Loving Care of the Fatherly Leader*, 1-10. For a close analysis of North Korean propaganda—including an emphasis on its maternal symbolism, see B.R. Myers, *The Cleanest Race: How North Koreans See Themselves—and Why It Matters* (New York: Melville House, 2010).

[53] See Hyeonseo Lee's story when she was first told historical truths about North Korea after she went to China in *The Girl With Seven Names*, 107-109.

[54] A good example of this is the story of Charles Robert Jenkins's family. Jenkins defected to North Korea in 1965 and remained there until he was finally allowed to leave in 2004. One of his daughters born there, Mika, largely embraced the regime's propaganda and ideological views even as her father did his best to quietly discourage as much. See Charles Robert Jenkins and Jim Frederick, *The Reluctant Communist: My Desertion, Court-Martial, and Forty-Year Imprisonment in North Korea* (Berkeley, CA: University of California Press, 2008), 110, 162, 170, 178.

[55] See the United Nations Human Rights Council's 372-page report on human rights violations in North Korea in "Report of the Commission of Inquiry on Human Rights in the Democratic People's Republic of Korea," February 7, 2014: https://web.archive.org/web/20210726073621/https://www.ohchr.org/en/hrbodies/hrc/coidprk/pages/reportofthecommissionofinquirydprk.aspx Accessed July 28, 2021.

[56] The regime investigated every citizen's background from December 1958 until the end of 1960 before creating the *Songbun* categories. For an overview of *Songbun*'s origins, see Balázs Szalontai, "The Evolution Of The North Korean Socio-Political System, 1945–1994" in *Routledge Handbook of Contemporary North Korea*, ed. Adrian Buzo (New York: Routledge, 2021), 25-28.

[57] Szalontai, "The Evolution Of The North Korean Socio-Political System, 1945–1994," 25.

[58] Ibid.

[59] On North Korea's human rights violations, see The Committee for Human Rights in North Korea's publications: https://web.archive.org/web/20210608135405/https://www.hrnk.org/publications/hrnk-publications.php Accessed July 28, 2021.

[60] Hwang Jang-yop, "The Problem of Human Rights in North Korea (2).

[61] Ibid.

[62] See Bernd Schaefer, "'North Korean 'Adventurism' and China's Long Shadow, 1966-1972," *Cold War International History Project*, WP #44, 10; Martin, *Under the Loving Care of the Fatherly Leader*, 125; Gauthier, "Other Korea," 163, FN 84.

[63] Martin described Kim Il-sung and Kim Jong-il's "Mansions Special Volunteer Corps" based on his numerous interviews with defectors in *Under the Loving Care of the Fatherly Leader*, 198-201, 309-310, 312-316, 318-320, 525, 808-809, EN 54-58.

[64] On discussion of as much, see Martin, *Under the Loving Care of the Fatherly Leader*, 188-189, 192, 370-373.

[65] Hwang Jang-yop's words in "The Problem of Human Rights in North Korea (2); idem., "The Problem of Human Rights in North Korea (1).

[66] Fred Hiatt, "North Korea's Isolation Seen Dangerous for Its Foes," *Washington Post*, February 23, 1988, A17; Gauthier, "The Other Korea," 256-257.

[67] Gauthier, "The Other Korea," 252-268.

[68] Lankov, *The Real North Korea*, 75-82; Cha and Sohn, *Exit Emperor Kim Jong Il*, 58.

[69] A reference to *Juche*—North Korea's pseudo state ideology. See B.R. Myers, *North Korea's Juche Myth* (Busan, ROK: Sthele Press, 2015).

[70] North Korea changed fundamentally as many of its citizens resorted to grassroots capitalism to avoid starvation; see Lankov, *The Real North Korea*, 77-91.

[71] See the experience of Kang Hyok's family in the mid-1990s in *This is Paradise! My North Korean Childhood*. Also see Jang Jin-sung's experiences in the famine-ravaged town of Sariweon in 1999—his friends, who had experienced extraordinary hardship, expressed awe that he had dined with Kim Jong-il and wanted to believe that the "Dear Leader" ate porridge and rice balls as stated by propaganda. Jang Jin-sung, *Dear Leader: Poet, Spy, Escapee—A Look Inside North Korea* (New York, Atria, 2014), 57; see also Brandon K. Gauthier, "An Individual Transformed: Review of Jang Jin-sung, *Dear Leader: Poet, Spy, Escapee—A Look Inside North Korea*," *Yonsei Journal of International Studies* 6, no. 2 (Winter 2015): 372-376.

[72] Stephen Haggard and Marcus Noland, *Famine in North Korea: Markets, Aid, and Reform* (New York: Columbia University Press, 2007), 58.

[73] On potential damage of renewed war, see Joel S. Wit, Daniel B. Poneman, and Robert L. Gallucci, *Going Critical: The First North Korean Nuclear Crisis* (Washington, D.C.: Brookings Institution Press, 2004), 180-181; for portrayals of the nuclear crisis in the American media, see Gauthier, "The Other Korea," 298-335.

[74] Don Oberdorfer and Robert Carlin, *The Two Koreas: A Contemporary History* (New York: Basic Books, 1997, 2014), 268; Cha and Sohn, *Exit Emperor Kim Jong Il*, 71.

[75] Mark Barry, "Meeting Kim Il Sung in His Last Weeks," *NKNews.org*, April 15, 2012.
https://web.archive.org/web/20120529013141/https://www.nknews.org/2012/04/meeting-kim-il-sung-in-his-last-weeks/
Accessed July 28, 2021.

[76] Ibid.

[77] Quoted in Marion Creekmore, Jr., *A Moment of Crisis: Jimmy Carter, the Power of a Peacemaker, and North Korea's Nuclear Ambitions* (New York: PublicAffairs, 2006), 72.

[78] Cha and Sohn, *Exit Emperor Kim Jong Il*, 71; Martin, *Under the Loving Care of the Fatherly Leader*, 506.

[79] Martin, *Under the Loving Care of the Fatherly Leader*, 506.

[80] The ensuing famine in North Korea killed at least 3% to 5% of the population (between 600,000 and 1,000,000 people) from 1995 to 1998; see Haggard and Noland, *Famine in North Korea*, 1. Other estimates of the death toll are far higher. The North Korean defector Hwang Jang-yop, a former mentor to Kim Jong-il, estimates that 3 million died. Ven. Pomnyun of the Korean Buddhist Sharing Movement, which conducted extensive interviews with refugees along the PRC-DPRK border, estimates 3.5 million. Former aid official Andrew Natsios—who helped lead the famine relief effort in 1997—thinks these estimates are far more accurate than Haggard and Noland's. Telephone interview with Professor Andrew Natsios by the author, June 19, 2015; cited in Gauthier, "The Other Korea," 300, FN 7. For other famine estimates, see Lankov, *The Real North Korea*, 78-79.

Chapter 7 (Lenin)

[1] For an overview of the family having servants (and on Soviet censorship of this), see Nikolai Valentinov, *The Early Years of Lenin* (Ann Arbor: University of Michigan Press, 1969), 16-17.

[2] Philip Pomper, *Lenin's Brother: The Origins of the October Revolution* (New York: W.W. Norton & Company, 2010), 19.

[3] Service, *Lenin*, 23.

[4] Leon Trotsky, *The Young Lenin*, trans. Max Eastman (London: David and Charles Publishers, 1972), 20. The family had subscriptions to journals from St. Petersburg that, as Trotsky put it, "beat the pulse of the libertarian movement of the times."

[5] Ul'yanova, *Detskie I shkol'nye gody Il'icha*, 18-21, 62-63; Pomper, *Lenin's Brother*, 17-18; Valentinov, *The Early Years of Lenin*, 26; Service, *Lenin*, 34-35.

[6] Valentinov, *The Early Years of Lenin*, 27. Lenin sent Christmas greetings as late as 1912, writing his mother and sister that year: "I sent holiday greetings to all of you. I wish you joy, good health and spirits for the holidays." See ibid., 29.

[7] As Isaac Deutscher stated, "Paraphrasing Tolstoy, one may say that unhappy children are unhappy each in his own way, each suffering his own particular misfortune, whereas the happy ones are almost all alike. Volodya's childhood was

so happy that it need hardly be described in detail…it must have contributed to the character of the future revolutionary, to the self-confidence, inner balance, and fullness of his personality." See idem., *Lenin's Childhood* (London: Oxford University Press, 1970), 25; Trotsky, *The Young Lenin*, 86.

[8] On Lenin's paternal grandparents, see Service, *Lenin*, 21-22; Deutscher, *Lenin's Childhood*, 3-4; Volkogonov, *Lenin: A New Biography*, 4, 7.

[9] Ibid.; emphasis added, quoted in Valentinov, *The Early Years of Lenin*, 21-22.

[10] Deutscher, *Lenin's Childhood*, 7-8; Trotsky, *The Young Lenin*, 14-15; Pomper, *Lenin's Brother*, 11.

[11] Pomper, *Lenin's Brother*, 14-16; Deutscher, *Lenin's Childhood*, 11-12, 18.

[12] Deutscher, *Lenin's Childhood*, 10.

[13] Maria, however, would never be very religious. See Ibid., 25.

[14] Volkogonov, *Lenin: A New Biography*, 6.

[15] Deutscher, *Lenin's Childhood*, 11; Hélène Carrère d'Encausse, *Lenin* (New York: Holmes & Meier, 2001), 6.

[16] Two other children died in infancy, a first daughter named Olga (1868) and Nikolai in (1873), much to the family's despair; see Pomper, *Lenin's Brother*, 19.

[17] Ibid., 15; Service, *Lenin*, 25-26; Deutscher, *Lenin's Childhood*, 22-24. As Pomper notes, Ilya initially had the responsibility of overseeing 70-80 schools a year as well as 526 poorly educated teachers. By the end of his time in the position, he would administer 434 schools—most of which he helped establish—with some 20,000 students. He was busy.

[18] Deutscher, *Lenin's Childhood*, 19-20; Valentinov, *The Early Years of Lenin*, 63; Tariq Ali, *The Dilemmas of Lenin: Terrorism, War, Empire, Love, Revolution* (London: Verso, 2017), 59-60. As Deutscher stated: "…[Ilya] did not see how the oppressed could gain anything through disobedience or rebellion." Trotsky hedged: Ilya's "approachability and unaffected manner earned him the malicious and partly ironical nickname 'The Liberal.'….On the other hand, a government official, paterfamilias and loyal citizen could not, of course, form ties with the suspected circles of the radical intelligentsia." See idem., *The Young Lenin*, 21.

[19] Pomper, *Lenin's Brother*, 21; Trotsky, *The Young Lenin*, 21; Deutscher, *Lenin's Childhood*, 24.

[20] Pomper, ibid; Ul'yanova, *Detskie I shkol'nye gody Il'icha*, 17.

[21] Ronald W. Clark, *Lenin* (New York: Harper & Row, 1988), 9.

[22] Pomper, *Lenin's Brother*, 21; Trotsky, *The Young Lenin*, 21.

[23] Valentinov, *The Early Years of Lenin*, 26-27; Deutscher, *Lenin's Childhood*, 24.

[24] Quoted in Service, *Lenin*, 111.

[25] Philip Pomper's words in "The Family Background of V.I. Ul'ianov's Pseudonym, 'Lenin,'" *Russian History*, Vol. 16, No. 2/4 (1989): 214; idem., *Lenin's Brother*, 65.

[26] Ul'yanova, *Detskie I shkol'nye gody Il'icha*, 37.

[27] Ibid.; Trotsky, *The Young Lenin*, 72-73; Deutscher, *Lenin's Childhood*, 27; Lenin's need to imitate his brother ("like Sasha") is a core theme of Pomper's *Lenin's Brother*. Service states that "it is difficult to avoid the thought that within the sinews of confidence there lurked a streak of diffidence even in young Volodia." See idem., *Lenin*, 45.

[28] Deutscher, *Lenin's Childhood*, 27-28; Pomper, *Lenin's Brother*, 22-24; Valentinov, *The Early Years of Lenin*, 35; Service, *Lenin*, 35-37. On the two brothers' personalities, see Trotsky, *The Young Lenin*, 109.

[29] Pomper, *Lenin's Brother*, 207.

[30] Trotsky, *The Young Lenin*, 39.

[31] Ul'yanova, *Detskie I shkol'nye gody Il'icha*, 13-30; Service, *Lenin*, 34-35.

[32] Deutscher's words in *Lenin's Childhood*, 26.

[33] Ul'yanova, *Detskie I shkol'nye gody Il'icha*, 13-16; Pomper, "The Family Background of V.I. Ul'ianov's Pseudonym, 'Lenin,'" 214. As Lenin's parents and older siblings sought to stop the little boy from breaking his toys, he sometimes hid away with them *for the purpose of breaking them*, free from such interference. See Ul'yanova, *Detskie I shkol'nye gody Il'icha*, 16.

[34] Ul'yanova, *Detskie I shkol'nye gody Il'icha*, 13-14, 23-30; Valentinov, *The Early Years of Lenin*, 34; Service, *Lenin*, 35-36; Trotsky, *The Young Lenin*, 72.

[35] Service, *Lenin*, 37; Ul'yanova, *Detskie I shkol'nye gody Il'icha*, 31.

[36] Service, ibid., 36-37; Trotsky, *The Young Lenin*, 21.

[37] Service, ibid; Pomper, *Lenin's Brother*, 16.

[38] That being said, according to Anna, Ilya's decision to enroll Sasha (and then Volodia) in school sought to place "the boys as early as possible under masculine influence." This removed them from their mother's sphere and apparently caused problems between Ilya and Sasha. See Pomper, *Lenin's Brother*, 22.

[39] Service, *Lenin*, 37-38. His big sister records that he most liked Latin classics, history, and geography in Ul'yanova, *Detskie I shkol'nye gody Il'icha*, 55.

[40] Deutscher's words in *Lenin's Childhood*, 27.

[41] Ul'yanova, *Detskie I shkol'nye gody Il'icha*, 46; Service, *Lenin*, 38-39; Deutscher, *Lenin's Childhood*, 28.

[42] Ul'yanova, *Detskie I shkol'nye gody Il'icha*, 45; quoted in Deutscher, *Lenin's Childhood*, 28.

[43] Deutscher, ibid., 28. Any distractions had to go. He enjoyed ice-skating very much, for example, but soon came to believe that the frosty air made him too drowsy and took away time from his studies; no more ice-skating. "From early youth…[he] knew how to push aside anything that stood in his way," his future wife would remark of his immense self-discipline. See Trotsky, *The Young Lenin*, 79; Krupskaya quoted in same.

[44] Ul'yanova, *Detskie I shkol'nye gody Il'icha*, 56, 60; Clark, *Lenin*, 11.

[45] Ul'yanova, *Detskie I shkol'nye gody Il'icha*, 44. Big sister Anna noted that Ilya's refusal to shower his kids with praise—even when they made the very best grades—was ultimately a positive for Volodia in that it "undoubtedly reduced the arrogance [of Volodia], which outstanding children are prone to." Quoted in Pomper, *Lenin's Brother*, 206.

[46] Lenin likely did not begin to pursue the opposite sex directly until his twenties. See Service, *Lenin*, 100. For Lenin's most open airing of his views about sex, see Clara Zetkin, "Lenin on the Woman Question": "Sex and Marriage" and "Sexual Morality." One notable quote from Lenin is as follows: "I don't mean to preach asceticism.…Not in the least. Communism will not bring asceticism, but joy of life, power of life, and a satisfied love life will help to do that. But in my opinion the present widespread hypertrophy in sexual matters does not give joy and force to life, but takes it away. In the age of revolution that is bad, very bad."

[47] Ul'yanova, *Detskie I shkol'nye gody Il'icha*, 56; Service, *Lenin*, 41, 44-45; Deutscher, *Lenin's Childhood*, 29.

[48] Deutscher, ibid., 34; Valentinov, *The Early Years of Lenin*, 50.

[49] Valentinov, ibid., 50, 74-75.

[50] Lenin, "The Abolition of the Antithesis Between Town and Country. Particular Questions Raised by the 'Critics'" in *The Agrarian Question and the "Critics of Marx"*: https://web.archive.org/web/20201205095218/https://www.marxists.org/archive/lenin/works/1901/agrarian/index.htm
Accessed July 29, 2021.

[51] Service's words in *Lenin*, 51-52.

[52] Ibid.; Valentinov, *The Early Years of Lenin*, 53-60.

[53] Authorities—after Sasha was arrested—chastised school officials for awarding the gold medal to such a young man; they would not risk the same mistake with Lenin. Ul'yanova, *Detskie I shkol'nye gody Il'icha*, 70, 72.

[54] Deutscher, *Lenin's Childhood*, 32-33.

[55] Ibid., 35; Pomper, *Lenin's Brother*, 66-67.

[56] Deutscher, ibid., 41.

[57] Ibid., 36-37; Service, *Lenin*, 48; Clark, *Lenin*, 12. Sasha surely resented as much: "What after all," writes Pomper, "had caused all of this suffering [including a breakdown Maria would experience after Ilya's death] if not the regime that had forced Ilya Nikolaevich into retirement and undermined his life's work?" See idem., *Lenin's Brother*, 143.

[58] Deutscher, *Lenin's Childhood*, 42-43; Service, *Lenin*, 50.

[59] From *Simbirske Gubernske Vedomosti* [*News of Simbirsk Gubernia*] quoted in Deutscher, *The Young Lenin*, 22.

[60] Ibid., 23-24.

[61] Pomper, *Lenin's Brother*, 96.

[62] A fellow student's words quoted in Ibid., 97; Trotsky, *The Young Lenin*, 89.

[63] Pomper, *Lenin's Brother*, 97. Maria, along with Anna, knew that Alexander was reading extensively about political and economic issues, but did not have any inclination that he was getting directly involved as an activist. See Victor Sebestyen, *Lenin: The Man, The Dictator, and the Master of Terror* (New York: Pantheon, 2017), 43.

[64] Trotsky, *The Young Lenin*, 113; Service, *Lenin*, 50; Deutscher, *Lenin's Childhood*, 44.

[65] Quoted in Deutscher, *Lenin's Childhood*, 44; Sebestyen, *Lenin*, 44.

[66] Service, *Lenin*, 52, 85; Trotsky, *The Young Lenin*, 84-85.

[67] Anna became an atheist at the same time as Sasha; see Ali, *The Dilemmas of Lenin*, 64; Deutscher, *Lenin's Childhood*, 32.

[68] Lenin, "Socialism and Religion," *Novaya Zhizn*, No. 28, December 3, 1905: https://web.archive.org/web/20210527033555/https://www.marxists.org/archive/lenin/works/1905/dec/03.htm
Accessed July 29, 2021.

[69] Valentinov, *The Early Years of Lenin*, 69. Deutscher highlights Anna's point that his behavior was "a symptom of adolescent rebelliousness which led him to 'reject' the authority and moral values of the adult world; he already described himself as an atheist and kept sneering and scoffing at the narrow-mindedness and stupidity of some of his school masters." See idem., *The Young Lenin*, 50.

[70] Deutscher, *Lenin's Childhood*, 46-49; Valentinov, *The Early Years of Lenin*, 68; Ali, *The Dilemmas of Lenin*, 73; Pomper, *Lenin's Brother*, 208.

[71] "The brothers were at war in the summer of 1886," writes Pomper in *Lenin's Brother*, 208.

[72] Anna Ul'yanova notes that their father had imparted his appreciation for chess to his boys. See idem., *Detskie I shkol'nye gody Il'icha*, 34.

[73] Chess anecdote and quote in Trotsky, *The Young Lenin*, 114; also quoted by Service, *Lenin*, 50; Sebestyen, *Lenin*, 44.

[74] Deutscher, *Lenin's Childhood*, 30-33; Service, *Lenin*, 42-43.

[75] See Lenin's August 1918 telegram highlighted in the introduction—its call to "...hang (hang without fail, so that the public sees) at least 100 notorious kulaks, the rich, and *the bloodsuckers* [emphasis added]." Consider it in the context of Maxim Gorky's statement that Lenin was "a splendid human being, who had to sacrifice himself to hostility and hatred, *so that love might be at last realized* [Emphasis added]." See idem., *Days With Lenin*, no trans. listed (New York: International Publishers, 1932), 39.

Chapter 8 (Mussolini)

[1] Quoted in Ludwig, *Talks With Mussolini*, 35.

[2] BMOO, eds. Edoardo and Duilio Susmel (Florence: La Fenice-Firenze, 1961), Vol. XXXIII, 219; Philip Cannistraro, "Father and Son", in *Mussolini 1883-1915*, eds. Spencer M. Di Scala, Emilio Gentile (New York: Palgrave Macmillan, 2016), 39; Monelli, *Mussolini: An Intimate Life*, 20; Gaudens Megaro, *Mussolini in the Making* (Boston and New York: Houghton Mifflin Company, 1938), 21.

[3] Spencer M. Di Scala, "Making Mussolini" and Philip Cannistraro, "Father and Son" in *Mussolini 1883-1915*, 19, 39, 50; Monelli, *Mussolini: An Intimate Life*, 21.

[4] Cannistraro, "Father and Son" in *Mussolini 1883-1915*, 43.

[5] Ibid. Alessandro did, however, make an effort to read *Das Kapital* and (supposedly) recited parts of it to his kids; see Farrell, *Mussolini*, 11.

[6] Quoted in Megaro, *Mussolini in the Making*, 28-29.

[7] Monelli, *Mussolini: An Intimate Life*, 21-22.

[8] Alessandro also set up a local cooperative of which he was proud. See Cannistraro, "Father and Son" in *Mussolini 1883-1915*, 40-47; Renzo De Felice, *Mussolini il rivoluzionario* (Torino: Giulio Einaudi editore, 1965), 4-5; Bosworth, *Mussolini*, 39-41; Farrell, *Mussolini: A New Life*, 11. Mussolini would later claim that Alessandro had been mayor opposed to deputy mayor, see Megaro, *Mussolini in the Making*, 24; Margherita G. Sarfatti, *The Life of Benito Mussolini*, trans. Frederic Whyte (New York: Frederick A. Stokes Company Publishers, 1927), 26.

[9] Cannistraro, "Father and Son" in *Mussolini 1883-1915*, 45-47.

[10] Benito Mussolini, *My Autobiography* (New York: Charles Scribner's Sons, 1928), 3. Arnaldo Mussolini ghost-wrote the autobiography for his older brother, states De Felice in *Mussolini il rivoluzionario*, 8.

[11] Sarfatti states that she was a "bundle of nerves controlled by an indomitable will and disguised beneath a tranquil and smiling countenance…a woman of extraordinary energy." See idem., *The Life of Benito Mussolini*, 27.

[12] Cannistraro, "Father and Son" in *Mussolini 1883-1915*, 44-45, 48.

[13] Monelli, *Mussolini: An Intimate Life*, 21.

[14] Cannistraro, "Father and Son" in *Mussolini 1883-1915*, 47.

[15] BMOO, Vol. III, 276; quoted in ibid; Benito Mussolini, *My Autobiography*, 18.

[16] BMOO, Vol. III, 276.

[17] Cannistraro, "Father and Son" in *Mussolini 1883-1915*, 47; De Felice, *Mussolini il rivoluzionario*, 9. For the text of Rosa's letter asking for the bonus, see Megaro, *Mussolini in the Making*, 45-46.

[18] Farrell, *Mussolini: A New Life*, 10-11. Mussolini's full name was Benito Amilcare Andrea Mussolini. *Benito* Juárez was the liberal nationalist who became Mexico's president in 1858 and later stopped foreign Archduke Maximilian from ruling as an emperor; Juárez allowed Maximilian's execution by firing squad in 1867. *Amilcare* Cipriani was an Italian revolutionary who served with Garibaldi and then fought for the Parisian Commune. *Andrea* Costa was a revolutionary socialist from Romagna, though he later became a reformist and parliamentarian.

[19] Bosworth, *Mussolini*, 50 [for this well-known anecdote, Bosworth cites A. Gravelli, *Mussolini aneddotico* (Rome: Casa Editrice Latinità, 1951), 5]; De Felice, *Mussolini il rivoluzionario*, 9.

[20] "Austere and melancholy" quoted in Cannistraro, "Father and Son" in *Mussolini 1883-1915*, 48; on home life: ibid; Monelli, *Mussolini: An Intimate Life*, 23; Farrell, *Mussolini: A New Life*, 12.

[21] Sarfatti, *The Life of Benito Mussolini*, 62; Cannistraro, "Father and Son" in *Mussolini 1883-1915*, 50.

[22] Victor Hugo, *Les Misérables* (Philadelphia: John D. Morris & Company, Undated), Vol. 1, 103-105.

[23] Isaac Stanley-Becker, "Twitter is eroding your intelligence. Now there's data to prove it," *Washington Post*, May 30, 2019:
https://www.washingtonpost.com/nation/2019/05/30/twitter-hurting-intelligence-not-smart-study/?utm_term=.e5194fe8ca60

Accessed July 28, 2021.

[24] Hugo, *Les Misérables*, 104-105.

[25] BMOO, Vol. XXXIII, 220; Cannistraro, "Father and Son" in *Mussolini 1883-1915*, 48; Monelli, *Mussolini: An Intimate Life*, 25.

[26] Mussolini, *My Autobiography*, 3; Farrell, *Mussolini: A New Life*, 8; Sarfatti, *The Life of Benito Mussolini*, 78; on seduction, see Bosworth, *Mussolini*, 483, EN 107; Bosworth cites G D'Aurora, *La mascheia e la volta di Magda Fontages* (Milan, 1946), 15.

[27] BMOO, Vol. XXXIII, 220; Sarfatti, *The Life of Benito Mussolini*, 31.

[28] Mussolini, *My Autobiography*, 6.

[29] Ibid.

[30] BMOO, Vol. XXXIII, 220.

[31] Sarfatti, *The Life of Benito Mussolini*, 31-32; Cannistraro, "Father and Son" in *Mussolini 1883-1915*, 50.

[32] BMOO, Vol. XXXIII, 221; Mussolini, *My Autobiography*, 3.

[33] Article from *Rivendicazione*, May 25, 1889 quoted in Farrell, *Mussolini: A New Life*, 13.

[34] His brashness as a youngster, of course, in no way suggested a straight line from juvenile miscreant to tyrannical dictator. Spencer M. Di Scala critiques the biographical literature along these lines in "Making Mussolini," in *Mussolini 1883-1915*, 1-2.

[35] Quoted in Monelli, *Mussolini: An Intimate Life*, 27.

[36] Emphasis added; quoted in Ibid., 24.

[37] Sarfatti, *The Life of Benito Mussolini*, 345.

[38] Monelli's words in *Mussolini: An Intimate Life*, 20; quoted in Cannistraro, "Father and Son" in *Mussolini 1883-1915*, 48.

[39] Angelica Balabanoff, *My Life as a Rebel* (Bloomington, IN: Indiana University Press, 1973; originally published by Harper & Brothers, 1938), 45.

[40] Benito's autobiography claimed that Rosa convinced her husband the institution was secular, but that seems problematic considering that Alessandro himself delivered his son to the priests there.

[41] BMOO, Vol. XXXIII, 222; Cannistraro, "Father and Son" in *Mussolini 1883-1915*, 50-51.

[42] Ibid.; Cannistraro, "Father and Son" in *Mussolini 1883-1915*, 52.

[43] BMOO, Vol. XXXIII, 222-223; Cannistraro, "Father and Son" in *Mussolini 1883-1915*, 50.

[44] BMOO, ibid., 224.

[45] Ibid., 224-225. Consider the parallels with student meals at Petite Picpus in *Les Mis*: "…the food of even the children [was] scanty….The children ate and held their tongues, under the guardianship of the mother of the week, who, from time to time, if a fly dared to move or buzz contrary to regulation, nosily opened and closed a wooden book. The silence was seasoned with the "Lives of the Saints," read aloud from a little desk standing at the foot of the crucifix, the reader being one of the big pupils, appointed for the week…." See Hugo, *Les Misérables*, Vol. II, 214-215.

[46] Cannistraro, "Father and Son" in *Mussolini 1883-1915*, 52.

[47] BMOO, Vol. XXXIII, 225.

[48] Cannistraro, "Father and Son" in *Mussolini 1883-1915*, 52.

[49] BMOO, Vol. XXXIII, 224-226; Cannistraro, "Father and Son" in *Mussolini 1883-1915*, 52.

[50] BMOO, Vol. XXXIII, 226-227.

[51] Ibid.

[52] Ibid.

[53] Benito's words in Ibid., 228.

[54] Ibid.

[55] Ibid.

[56] A Petite Picpus boarding student—taught to fear the world outside of the convent—had something similar to say in *Les Misérables*, Vol. II, 208.

[57] BMOO, Vol. XXXIII, 228.

[58] Ibid., 229.

[59] Ibid., 230-231.

[60] Ibid. 230; Christopher Hitchens's words.

[61] BMOO, Vol. XXXIII, 231.

[62] Cannistraro, "Father and Son" in *Mussolini 1883-1915*, 53.

[63] Twenty years later, Mussolini remarked: "I will never forget these words." See BMOO, Vol. XXXIII, 231.

[64] Ibid., 231-232

[65] Ibid., 232.

Chapter 9 (Hitler)

[1] Alois's original last name was Schicklgruber, his mother's maiden name; but in 1876, he took the name of his foster father, which was Hiedler—though Alois used

the spelling "Hitler." On Alois's background, see Note 16 in Adolf Hitler, *Mein Kampf: Eine kritische Edition*, eds. Christian Hartmann, Thomas Vordermayer, Othmar Plöckinger, and Roman Töppel, Band I (München – Berlin: Instituts für Zeitgeschichte, 2016), 97; Franz Jetzinger, *Hitler's Youth*, trans. Lawrence Wilson (London: Hutchinson, 1958), 35-41; Kershaw, *Hitler: 1889-1936*, 3-10; Brigitte Hamann, *Hitler's Vienna: A Dictator's Apprenticeship*, trans. Thomas Thornton (New York: Oxford University Press, 1999), 7; succinctly summarized as well in Charles Bracelen Flood, *Hitler: The Path to Power* (Boston: Houghton Mifflin Company, 1989), 6.

[2] Kershaw, *Hitler: 1889-1936*, 9.

[3] Toland, *Adolf Hitler*, Vol. 1, 6-7.

[4] August Kubizek's memoir reproduces the request letter from the archives of the episcopate in Linz, Austria. See idem., *The Young Hitler I Knew*, 47-48; Fest, *Hitler*, 17.

[5] Kershaw, *Hitler: 1889-1936*, 9-10; Toland, *Adolf Hitler*, Vol. 1, 6-7; Longerich, *Hitler*, 8; Fritz Redlich M.D., *Hitler: Diagnosis of a Destructive Prophet* (Oxford: Oxford University Press, 1999), 8; Kubizek, *The Young Hitler I Knew*, 51, 137; Fest, *Hitler*, 17.

[6] Dr. Eduard Bloch, "'My Patient, Hitler,'" *Collier's*, March 15, 1941, 35.

[7] Kershaw, *Hitler: 1889-1936*, 4, 10-11; Kubizek, *The Young Hitler I Knew*, 23.

[8] With childhoods overshadowed by so much loss, Adolf and Kubizek "felt like the survivors of an endangered lineage," as the latter put it. See Kubizek, Ibid.

[9] Quoted in Hamann, *Hitler's Vienna*, 12.

[10] Jetzinger quotes Alois's full obituary, which presents a dissenting case in *Hitler's Youth*, 52-53.

[11] One of Alois's letters highlights this pride; contacting a relative of his mother, he wrote: "Since you last saw me 16 years ago…I have risen very high." See Eugene Davidson, *The Making of Adolf Hitler* (New York: Macmillan Publishing Co., Inc., 1977), 5.

[12] When it came to tending the bees, Alois supposedly wore no protective gear—he merely smoked a big cigar; as a result, he would come back to Klara with 45-50 bee-stings, apparently unperturbed. See Redlich, *Hitler: Diagnosis of a Destructive Prophet*, 8; Weinberg, ed. *Hitler's Table Talk, 1941-1944*, 459; Hamann, *Hitler's Vienna*, 7-8.

[13] However, he was apparently capable of occasional moments of kindness towards little daughter Paula. See Redlich, *Hitler: Diagnosis of a Destructive Prophet*, 14.

[14] Jetzinger quotes a family friend who challenges the notion that Alois was physically violent in *Hitler's Youth*, 51.

[15] A "hippopotamus whip" specifically. See Toland, *Adolf Hitler*, Vol. 1, 9; Flood, *Hitler: The Path to Power*, 7.

[16] Quoted in N. 30 in Hitler, *Mein Kampf: Eine kritische Edition*, eds. Hartmann et al., Band I, 102.

[17] Ibid.; Hamann, *Hitler's Vienna*, 7. Toland records that Alois "often beat the dog until the dog would cringe and wet the floor." See idem., *Adolf Hitler*, Vol. 1, 9.

[18] Quoted in Hamann, *Hitler's Vienna*, 10.

[19] Kubizek, *The Young Hitler I Knew*, 51.

[20] Domestic violence in Adolf's family, historians have pointed out over the years, was not unusual for the time period. "In the Austria of those days," one biographer wrote for instance, "severe beatings of children were not uncommon, *being good for the soul*." (Emphasis added Toland's words in *Adolf Hitler*, Vol. 1, 9). Such reminders challenge psycho-historical analyses of Adolf's personal history in which there is nothing to see but a monster's making, a Freudian sociopath rearing his ugly head from the swamps of childhood abuse. So many children—sober scholars remind us—were mistreated in Adolf's time (many unimaginably worse) and yet managed not to become megalomaniacal-mass-murderers. Why, that narrative continues, should we over-emphasize the abuse Adolf experienced and give it the credence of causality? That argument resonates, but also remains problematic in inferring that Adolf the adult dictator existed in a vacuum in which his relationship with his father cannot be considered in the broader tableau of his life. It risks diminishing the ugliness that helped shape Adolf's character from his earliest years and denies a child the empathy he deserved in 1900. Even if we don't know the extent to which physical abuse shaped Adolf's personality from a young age (and cannot psychologically discern as much with certainty), one should not dismiss the possibility that beatings at the hands of his father affected him deeply. Nor should one play down abuse because it was more common in the time. (Should we dismiss the suffering experienced by his mother, Klara, because infant mortality rates were higher in the nineteenth century?). Positive factors in Adolf's childhood, as this book attests, played an important role in who he became, but there is ample reason to recognize that his father subjected him to hardships that should provoke sympathy.

[21] Quoted in Toland, *Adolf Hitler*, Vol. 1, 13; Flood, *Hitler,* 7. This account comes from a post-World War II interview with Paula. Half-sister Angela (Kershaw

notes) also confirmed that Alois beat Adolf severely. See Hitler, *Mein Kampf: Eine kritische Edition*, eds. Hartmann et al., Band I, 102, N. 30; Kershaw, *Hitler: 1889-1936*, 13, 606 EN 60.

[22] Toland quotes Frau Hanfstaengl, who said Hitler told her this story and remarked that it took "a long time [for him] to get over the episode." See idem., *Adolf Hitler*, Vol. 1, 13.

[23] Jetzinger picked up on this point as well in idem., *Hitler's Youth*, 61.

[24] Toland, *Adolf Hitler*, Vol. 1, 13; Flood, *Hitler: The Path to Power*, 7.

[25] Quoted in Hitler, *Mein Kampf: Eine kritische Edition*, eds. Hartmann et al., Band I, 102, N. 30.

[26] Kubizek, *The Young Hitler I Knew*, 51.

[27] Quoted in Toland, *Adolf Hitler*, Vol. 1, 13.

[28] Hitler, *Mein Kampf: Eine kritische Edition*, eds. Hartmann et al., Band I, 125. See also Christa Schroeder, *Er war mein Chef: Aus dem Nachlaß der Sekretärin von Adolf Hitler* (München: Lagen Müller, 1985), 63; published in English as *He was My Chief: The Memoirs of Adolf Hitler's Secretary*. Kershaw also notes that Hitler told Goebbels that "his mother was 'a source of goodness and love' while describing his father to others as "fanatical"; see idem., *Hitler: 1889-1936*, EN 61; Hamann, *Hitler's Vienna*, 18.

[29] Hamann, *Hitler's Vienna*, 10. One schoolmate of Paula's who passed the Hitlers's residence everyday remembered that "Klara would always walk her 'to the fence door and gave her a kiss; I noticed that because that was not what typically happened to us farm girls, but I liked it a lot. I almost envied Paula a little.'" Quoted in ibid.

[30] Kubizek, *The Young Hitler I Knew*, Chapter 4: "Portrait of His Mother."

[31] Alois, Jr. recalled years later with simmering resentment that Klara spoiled Adolf "from early in the morning until late at night, and the stepchildren had to listen to endless stories about how wonderful Adolf was." Quoted in Hamann, *Hitler's Vienna*, 7.

[32] His teacher from the school remembered Adolf as "mentally very much alert obedient, but lively," see Jetzinger, *Hitler's Youth*, 57.

[33] Toland, *Adolf Hitler*, Vol. 1, 4, 18.

[34] Hitler, *Mein Kampf: Eine kritische Edition*, eds. Hartmann et al., Band I, 99; Jetzinger, *Hitler's Youth*, 58-59; Toland, *Adolf Hitler*, Vol. 1, 9; Hamann, *Hitler's Vienna*, 8.

[35] Toland's words in *Adolf Hitler*, Vol. 1, 9.

[36] See Jetzinger, *Hitler's Youth*, 74-76.

[37] Adolf claims to have enjoyed reading it and to have become fascinated with militarism and war thereafter. Hitler, *Mein Kampf: Eine kritische Edition*, eds. Hartmann et al., Band I, 100-101, N. 25, 27; Hamann, *Hitler's Vienna*, 10. Alois was too cheap to give his son money to buy books; but Adolf, just the same, apparently spent hours gazing at the pictures of that illustrated book and developed an early admiration for Bismarck. News of the Boer War also attracted his interest, and local kids, with whom Adolf played, quickly began to adopt the conflict into their everyday games outside, according to Toland, *Adolf Hitler*, Vol. 1, 14.

[38] Hitler, *Mein Kampf: Eine kritische Edition*, eds. Hartmann et al., Band I, 103. While Alois could have sent his son to a secondary school focusing more on the humanities—a *Gymnasium*—the father, always practical, opted for *Realschule* because of its emphasis on math and science. The Linz *Realschule* did, however, have a drawing course, and this must have made Adolf more amenable. See Kershaw, *Hitler: 1889-1936*, 16; Redlich, *Hitler: Diagnosis of a Destructive Prophet*, 15; Toland, *Adolf Hitler*, Vol. 1, 14.

[39] Kershaw, *Hitler: 1889-1936*, 16-17; Kubizek, *The Young Hitler I Knew*, 59-61.

[40] Hamann, *Hitler's Vienna*, 11; Fest, *Hitler*, 18.

[41] Hitler, *Mein Kampf: Eine kritische Edition*, eds. Hartmann et al., Band I, 109 and N. 38 on 108; Victor and Mildred Goertzel, *Cradles of Eminence* (Boston: Little, Brown and Company, 1962)/idem., Ted George Goertzel, and Ariel Hansen *Cradles of Eminence* (Scottsdale, AZ: Great Potential Press, 2004), Chapter 10, 250-280; Kershaw, *Hitler: 1889-1936*, 17-18; Bullock, *Hitler: A Study in Tyranny*, 26; Fest, *Hitler*, 19. Toland characterizes Hitler's failure at the Linz *Realschule* more charitably, giving his later explanation more credence; he states that in addition to the possibility of laziness, his poor grades were "just as likely a form of revenge against his father, some emotional problem, or simply unwillingness to tackle uncongenial subjects." See idem., *Adolf Hitler*, Vol. 1, 15.

[42] Hitler's former teacher offered this testimony at the request of Hitler's lawyer in 1923. Quoted in N. 38 in Hitler, *Mein Kampf: Eine kritische Edition*, eds. Hartmann et al., Band I, 108.

[43] See Goertzel, *Cradles of Eminence*, Chapter Ten, 249-263.

[44] Hitler, *Mein Kampf: Eine kritische Edition*, eds. Hartmann et al., Band I, 99, 105. Hitler puts it lightly in the opening of *Mein Kampf* when he states: "Though I hardly had any serious thoughts over my future career at that time, I had decidedly no sympathy for the career path my father had taken."

[45] Quoted in Fest, *Hitler*, 19.

[46] *Hitler's Table Talk, 1941-1944*, 270.

[47] Hitler, *Mein Kampf: Eine kritische Edition*, eds. Hartmann et al., Band I, 108, N. 38.

[48] *Hitler's Table Talk, 1941-1944*, 528.

[49] Hitler, *Mein Kampf: Eine kritische Edition*, eds. Hartmann et al., Band I, 116-117, N. 62-63.

[50] Ibid., FN 62. After 1933, the former teacher grew "distant" as Hitler moved to seize Austria—declaring him an enemy of the country in 1937 and declining to visit him with former Linz students that year—but Pötsch ultimately visited Hitler in 1941, and the German dictator held a state funeral for him after the teacher died the following year.

[51] Kershaw, *Hitler: 1889-1936*, 17; Bullock, *Hitler*, 27; Davidson, *The Making of Adolf Hitler*, 11.

[52] He had a gruff exterior, read a local obituary, but a "good heart"—it is unclear whether the latter characterization was thrown in as a courtesy. See note 74 in Hitler, *Mein Kampf: Eine kritische Edition*, eds. Hartmann et al., Band I, 122.

[53] Jetzinger, *Hitler's Youth*, 52-53; Kershaw, *Hitler: 1889-1936*, 19.

[54] Kershaw, *Hitler: 1889-1936*, 19-20.

[55] Toland, *Adolf Hitler*, Vol. 1, 20.

[56] Kershaw, *Hitler: 1889-1936*, 609, EN 109.

[57] Hitler, *Mein Kampf: Eine kritische Edition*, eds. Hartmann et al., Band I, 123 N. 75; Jetzinger, *Hitler's Youth*; 89; Kershaw, *Hitler: 1889-1936*, 20. Dr. Bloch states on the lung ailment: "I cannot understand the many references to his lung troubles as a youth. I was the only doctor treating him during the period in which he is supposed to have suffered from this. My records show nothing of the sort." idem., "'My Patient, Hitler,'" 36.

[58] Kubizek witnessed this first-hand; see idem., *The Young Hitler I Knew*, 34.

[59] Kershaw, *Hitler: 1889-1936*, 20; Hamann, *Hitler's Vienna*, 21.

[60] Hamann, for example, cites evidence of anti-Semitic language from the Christian-Social *Linzer Post* and the *Linzer Fliegenden* [the latter of which Adolf supposedly read]. See idem., *Hitler's Vienna*, 22.

[61] *Hitler's Table Talk, 1941-1944*, 150; Hamann, *Hitler's Vienna*, 21. He recalled in a late night dinner in 1942 that—at the showing of the proto-pornographic film— "I found myself cheek by jowl with a teacher named Sixtel. He said...laughing: 'So you, too, are a keen supporter of the Red Cross!'' This remark seemed to me shocking." Quoted in *Hitler's Table Talk, 1941-1944*, 150.

[62] Kershaw, *Hitler: 1889-1936*, 20; Hamann, *Hitler's Vienna*, 27.

[63] Hitler, *Mein Kampf: Eine kritische Edition*, eds. Hartmann et al., Band I, 125; Dr. Eduard Bloch, "'My Patient, Hitler,'" 35.

[64] A succinct summary in ibid., *Mein Kampf*, 124, N. 76.

[65] Kubizek, *The Young Hitler I Knew*, 51.

[66] Ibid.

[67] Hitler, *Mein Kampf: Eine kritische Edition*, eds. Hartmann et al., Band I, 125.

Chapter 10 (Stalin)

[1] Dictated memoirs of Keke Jughashvili, *My Dear Son: The Memoirs of Stalin's Mother* (e-book published by Ministry of Internal Affairs of Georgia from Archive of the Central Committee of the Communist Party of Georgia, f.8, op.2, d.15); Suny, *Stalin: Passage to Revolution*, 13, 19; Aleksandr V. Ostrovskii, "Predki Stalin," *Genealogicheskii vestnik*, no. 1 (2001) Accessible at:
https://web.archive.org/web/20210224092547/https://baza.vgd.ru/11/5695 3/?pg=all
Accessed December 9, 2021, 2021; Montefiore, *Young Stalin*, 22-23. Keke was a teenager when she gave birth to her first son, Mikhail, who died a week later; the second son, Georgi, also passed away after six months. See Suny, *Stalin: Passage to Revolution*, 708, EN 5. Keke, historian Roy Medvedev noted, never forgot those earlier losses; when Soviet officials came to congratulate her on Stalin's birthday, she "would often remark that her first born, Mikhail, was the most-clever, the most beautiful of the three." One can imagine that such officials were not keen to pass on such comments to Stalin in Moscow. See idem., "Stalin's Mother," in *The Unknown Stalin: His Life, Legacy, and Death*, trans. Ellen Dahrendorf (New York: I.B. Tauris, 2003), 313.

[2] Keke Jughashvili, *My Dear Son: The Memoirs of Stalin's Mother*. The record book of the Cathedral of the Assumption in Gori, however, recorded Stalin's birth date as December 6, 1878; see Suny, *Stalin: Passage to Revolution*, 13; Aleksandr V. Ostrovskii, "Predki Stalin," *Genealogicheskii vestnik*.

[3] Suny, *Stalin: Passage to Revolution*, 20; Aleksandr V. Ostrovskii, *Kto stoial za spinoi Stalina?* (Moscow: Tsentropoligraf-Mim, 2004), Chapter 1, First Ten Years.

[4] Jughashvili, *My Dear Son*; quoted in Montefiore, *Young Stalin*, 23.

[5] Kotkin, *Stalin: Paradoxes of Power*, 20; Suny, *Stalin: Passage to Revolution*, 21.

[6] Neither did Keke and Beso's loss of a fourth child; the birth of a fourth child—a second Georgi—is listed in the archives, but there is no record of his death. He

might have been stillborn or died immediately after birth; see Suny, *Stalin: Passage to Revolution*, 708, EN 5.

[7] Jughashvili, *My Dear Son*; Suny, *Stalin: Passage to Revolution*, 17-19; Montefiore, *Young Stalin*, 21.

[8] Ibid.; Keke's words quoted in Suny, *Stalin: Passage to Revolution*, 19.

[9] Jughashvili, *My Dear Son*.

[10] Ibid.

[11] Ibid.; Suny, *Stalin: Passage to Revolution*, 19.

[12] Ibid.; Ostrovskii, *Kto stoial za spinoi Stalina?*, Chapter 1, First Ten Years.

[13] Jughashvili, *My Dear Son*.

[14] Ibid.

[15] Stalin told this story to Khrushchev, claiming his father had taught him how to drink from an early age. See Nikita Sergeevich Khrushchev, *Memoirs of Nikita Khrushchev: Reformer 1945-1964*, ed. Sergei Khrushchev (University Park, PA: The Pennsylvania State University Press, 2006), 131.

[16] Jughashvili, *My Dear Son*.

[17] Montefiore, *Young Stalin*, 25.

[18] Ibid.; Jughashvili, *My Dear Son*.

[19] Suny, *Stalin: Passage to Revolution*, 20; Kotkin, *Stalin: Paradoxes of Power*, 20; Ostrovskii, *Kto stoial za spinoi Stalina?*, Chapter 1, First Ten Years.

[20] Service, *Stalin*, 17; Kotkin, *Stalin: Paradoxes of Power*, 20; Ostrovskii, *Kto stoial za spinoi Stalina?*, Chapter 1, First Ten Years; Montefiore, *Young Stalin*, 31. During this domestic turmoil, there was even gossip that Beso was not Soso's real father. Such stories, historians have speculated, might have encouraged Beso's repugnant behavior and further damaged the family's social standing. Kotkin notes of Keke's alleged infidelity, for instance: "Keke, still young and pretty, may have been the cause of the trouble by flirting with married men....Whether Keke was flirtatious, let alone promiscuous, is unclear She had been ambitious in marrying Beso the artisan, and she may have moved on to more prestigious men. Perhaps they targeted *her* [emphasis in the original]. Reliable evidence about the possible liaisons of the future Stalin's mother is lacking."

[21] Montefiore, *Young Stalin*, 29.

[22] Suny, *Stalin: Passage to Revolution*, 26.

[23] Quoted in Montefiore, *Young Stalin*, 29-30.

[24] Jughashvili, *My Dear Son*; Suny, *Stalin: Passage to Revolution*, 20.

[25] Svetlana Alliluyev, *Twenty Letters to a Friend* (New York: HarperColins, 1967), 153; cited in Suny, *Stalin: Passage to Revolution*, 30.

[26] Montefiore, *Young Stalin*, 30.

[27] His daughter, Svetlana Alliluyev, recalls this incident in Thames TV Production, "Stalin":

https://youtu.be/TZw3sN4XeNo?t=2m31s

Accessed July 29, 2021; Robert Service, *Stalin*, 19; Suny, *Stalin: Passage to Revolution*, 27; Montefiore, *Young Stalin*, 30.

[28] Jughashvili, *My Dear Son*.

[29] Jughashvili, *My Dear Son*; quoted in Montefiore, *Young Stalin*, 31. Though Keke's memoirs infer that Stalin experienced a multitude of domestic abuse incidents, Kotkin writes: "...the most that could be claimed about the young Jughashvili was that he might have seen his father once come after his mother with a knife." Even if this was the only incident—and it wasn't unless other accounts of domestic violence in the home by Josef Iremashvili, Josef Davrichewy, and his daughter Svetlana Alliluyev (as told to her by Stalin himself) are fabrications—it was undoubtedly a traumatic one for a little boy to witness. See Kotkin, *Stalin: Paradoxes of Power*, 27.

[30] Suny, *Stalin: Passage to Revolution*, 31-37; Montefiore, *Young Stalin*, 38-42.

[31] Suny, ibid., 28. Stalin also used "Besoshvili (son of Beso)" as a revolutionary nickname for a time; see Suny, ibid., 27, 310.

[32] Quoted in J. V. Stalin, "Talk With the German Author Emil Ludwig December 13, 1931," *Works 13* (Moscow: Foreign Languages Publishing House, 1955), 115; Kotkin, *Stalin: Paradoxes of Power*, 10, 24, 27; Suny, *Stalin: Passage to Revolution*, 26-27. Kotkin writes: "Too much has been made of Beso's failings. Too much has been made out of the violence in Soso Jughashvili's early life....The trope of the traumatic childhood...came to play an outside role. It is too pat, even for those with genuinely traumatic childhoods."

[33] Josef Iremashvili, *Stalin und die Tragödie Georgiens* (Berlin: Verfasser, 1932); Suny, *Stalin: Passage to Revolution*, 26.

[34] See Tucker, *Stalin as Revolutionary 1878-1929*, 74. If too many writers over the decades blamed Soso's later cruelty on Beso's abuse, historians have gone too far in downplaying it in recent years. Princeton historian Stephen Kotkin (see note 32) emphasizes that historical figures like Peter the Great suffered unimaginably worse childhood abuse. To be sure, overemphasizing childhood abuse as the primary cause of adult monstrosity is problematic, but so, too, is suggesting that

the severity of one's abuse alone is the ultimate factor in its lasting impact; there is no uniform measure of psychological damage when it comes to childhood trauma. Nor should an adult's lack of willingness to talk about abuse necessarily suggest a lack of inner pain (a point acknowledged by Suny). See Kotkin, *Stalin: Paradoxes of Power*, 10, 24, 27; Suny, *Stalin: Passage to Revolution*, 26-27.

[35] "Why did you beat me so often?" Stalin asked Keke decades later as dictator. Keke's response: "You seem to have turned out alright [*sic*]." Quoted in Medvedev, "Stalin's Mother," in *The Unknown Stalin*, 315; Montefiore, *Young Stalin*, 30.

[36] Jughashvili, *My Dear Son*; Suny, *Stalin: Passage to Revolution*, 22.

[37] Jughashvili, *My Dear Son*.

[38] Ibid.; Suny, *Stalin: Passage to Revolution*, 22; Montefiore, *Young Stalin*, 33.

[39] Jughashvili, *My Dear Son*; Kotkin, *Stalin: Paradoxes of Power*, 21-22; Montefiore, *Young Stalin*, 35.

[40] Kotkin, *Stalin: Paradoxes of Power*, 22, 742, EN 44; Ostrovskii, *Kto stoial za spinoi Stalina?*, Chapter 1, First Ten Years.

[41] Jughashvili, *My Dear Son*. Note that Keke does not describe this incident as happening after the carriage accident; Kotkin, however, suggests that this incident occurred after the carriage incident in 1890—or, if not, perhaps the year before. See Kotkin, *Stalin: Paradoxes of Power*, 22.

[42] Jughashvili, *My Dear Son*; Kotkin, *Stalin: Paradoxes of Power*, 23.

[43] Ibid.

[44] Keke's words in Jughashvili, *My Dear Son*.

[45] Kotkin, *Stalin: Paradoxes of Power*, 26.

[46] Kotkin describes Yakov Egnatashvili—nicknamed "Koba"—as Stalin's "surrogate father." See idem., *Stalin: Paradoxes of Power*, 16, 20, 24, 28; Ostrovskii, *Kto stoial za spinoi Stalina?*, Chapter 1, First Ten Years and In a Spiritual School.

[47] Ibid., 16, 20; Ostrovskii, *Kto stoial za spinoi Stalina?*, Chapter 1, First Ten Years and In a Spiritual School.

[48] Quoted in Kotkin, *Stalin: Paradoxes of Power*, 25-26.

[49] Ibid., 41.

[50] Ibid., 52-53.

[51] On Stalin's time at the seminary, see Montefiore, *Young Stalin,* Chapter 6-7; Suny, *Stalin: Passage to Revolution*, Chapters 3-4; Ostrovskii, *Kto stoial za spinoi Stalina?*, Chapter 2, At the Seminary. The Tiflis seminary was the highest educational institution in Georgia at the time.

[52] Jughashvili, *My Dear Son*; quoted in Montefiore, *Young Stalin*, 52.

[53] Suny, *Stalin: Passage to Revolution*, 55-56.

[54] Ibid. Keke claimed this, and emphasized that she read her son's letters repeatedly, even sleeping with them in bed. A peer remembers Stalin from the first days of the seminary as quiet, helpful, bashful, and shy according to Ostrovskii, *Kto stoial za spinoi Stalina?*, Chapter 2, At the Seminary.

[55] Trotsky writes that the seminaries of the time were "notorious for the savagery of their customs, medieval pedagoguery, and law of the fist." Montefiore elaborates as follows: "This seminary…was worse than most: 'utterly joyless,' reported one pupil….Two inspectors were deployed full time in 'constant unremitting supervision'….[Stalin learned] exactly the repressive tactics—'surveillance, spying, invasion of inner life, violation of feelings,' in Stalin's own words—that he would re-create in his Soviet police state." See idem., *Young Stalin*, 55, 74. Seminary students, Kotkin records, perceived the priests as "'despots, capricious egotists who had in mind only their own prospects [of someday becoming bishops]'"; he adds that "Stalin would vividly recall the seminary's 'spying, penetrating into the soul, humiliation.'" Yet rejecting Trotsky's views as "too pat," Kotkin goes on to imply that what Stalin and other seminarians really learned from such institutions—more than fear—was "hard work, dignified poverty, devotion to others, and above all, a sense of moral superiority." See idem., *Stalin: Paradoxes of Power*, 36-37.

[56] Stalin, "Talk With the German Author Emil Ludwig, December 13, 1931," *Works 13*, 115-116.

[57] Montefiore, *Young Stalin*, 62-63; Kotkin, *Stalin: Paradoxes of Power*, 37, 42-44. On a number of other works that influenced Stalin during this time, see Suny, *Stalin: Passage to Revolution*, 86.

[58] Suny, *Stalin: Passage to Revolution*, 66-71; Kalder, *The Infernal Library*, 41-42.

[59] Iremashvili, *Stalin und die Tragödie Georgiens*, 18-19; Montefiore's translation from *Young Stalin*, 63; Suny, *Stalin: Passage to Revolution*, 66.

[60] Robert Conquest, *Stalin: Breaker of Nations* (New York: Penguin, 1991), 14. On Stalin's writings about nationalism, see "Marxism and the National Question," in Stalin, *Works 2: 1907-1913*, 300-381; Kalder, *The Infernal Library*, 49-55.

[61] Montefiore, *Young Stalin*, 69; Suny, *Stalin: Passage to Revolution*, 94.

[62] Jughashvili, *My Dear Son*.

[63] Ibid.

[64] Ibid; quoted in Montefiore, *Young Stalin*, 71.

[65] Suny, *Stalin: Passage to Revolution*, 90.

[66] Jughashvili, *My Dear Son*.

[67] Ibid.

[68] Kalder makes this same point in *The Infernal Library*, xiv.

[69] "If only fate had let me be born in the hovel of some unknown Georgian cobbler!"—his daughter, Svetlana Alliluyev, stated of the father she might have had; being born to an unknown cobbler would have allowed her to hate Stalin the ruler. See idem., *One More Year*, trans. Paul Chavchavadze (New York: Harpers & Row, Pub., 1969), 142.

[70] Thames TV production, "USSR | Joseph Stalin | Svetlana Alliluyeva interview | 1980's":

https://youtu.be/TZw3sN4XeNo?t=183

Accessed July 29, 2021.

[71] Alliluyev, *Twenty Letters to a Friend*, 154; partially quoted in Hiroaki Kuromiya, *Stalin* (New York: Routledge, 2013), 2.

Chapter 11 (Mao)

[1] Quoted in Dick Wilson, *Mao: The People's Emperor* (London: Hutchinson & Co., 1979), 19; Chang and Halliday, *Mao: The Unknown Story*, 6.

[2] Lucian W. Pye, *Mao Tse-tung: The Man in the Leader* (New York: Basic Books, Inc., 1976), 116. On a visit to his hometown after his rise to power, Mao said as much before his personal doctor, stating: "'My father was tough....He always beat us....I told him that an unkind father will have an unfilial son." See Li, *The Private Life of Chairman Mao*, 303.

[3] This is not to suggest, by any means, that Mao's relationships with his father was the central factor behind who he became; but it is to say that it was undeniably an important part of who he was. For a work that strongly emphasizes the impact of Yichang on Renzhi's life, see Lucian W. Pye, *Mao Tse-tung: The Man in the Leader*.

[4] Pang Xianzhi and Jin Chongji (CCCPC Party Literature Research Office), *Mao Zedong: A Biography*, Volume 1 1893-1949, trans. Foreign Languages Press (Cambridge: Cambridge University Press, 2020), 4; Edgar Snow, *Red Star Over China* (New York: Random House, 1938, 1944), 124-125; Emi Xiao, *Mao Tse-Tung: His Childhood and His Youth*, no trans. listed (Bombay, India: People's Publishing House, 1953), 3 [This is a translation of Xiao San, *Mao Tse-tung t'ung-chih te ch'ing-shaonien shih-tai* (Guangzhou: Xinhua, 1950)]; Pantsov and Levine, *Mao: The Real Story*, 13-14; Chang and Halliday, *Mao: The Unknown Story*, 3-5; Jerome Ch'en, *Mao and the Chinese Revolution*, trans. by Michael Bullock and Jerome

Ch'en (New York: Oxford University Press, 1965), 19; Karl, *Mao Zedong and China in the Twentieth-Century World*, 7.

[5] Emi Xiao, *Mao Tse-Tung: His Childhood and His Youth*, 5-6.

[6] Mao stated in his funeral oration for Qimei that "She was clear in thinking, adept in analyzing matters"; see "Mao Zedong's Funeral Oration in Honor of His Mother," *Mao's Road to Power: Revolutionary Writings, 1912-1949*, Vol. 1, 419; Karl, *Mao Zedong and China in the Twentieth-Century World*, 5.

[7] Quoted in Chang and Halliday, *Mao: The Unknown Story*, 5. Contrasts between Renzhi's parents were not particularly unusual for the cultural expectations of the time; the father often took on the role of the stern, demanding disciplinarian and the mother that of the affectionate nurturer; see Ch'en, *Mao and the Chinese Revolution*, 19.

[8] Karl, *Mao Zedong and China in the Twentieth-Century World*, 5; see also Pang and Jin, *Mao Zedong: A Biography*, 5-6.

[9] Ibid.

[10] Emphasis added. "Mao Zedong's Funeral Oration in Honor of His Mother," *Mao's Road to Power: Revolutionary Writings, 1912-1949*, Vol. 1, 419-420; see also Pang and Jin, *Mao Zedong: A Biography*, 6-7.

[11] His brother Zétán, twelve years younger, was executed by the Kuomintang in 1935. His brother Zemin, younger by three years, was executed by a warlord in 1943. His cousin and adopted sister, Zejian, was executed by the Kuomintang at age 23 in 1929. For a list of Mao's relatives, see Pantsov and Levine, *Mao: The Real Story*, 591-592. Jonathan Spence notes that eventually Mao sought to discourage his closest family members from participating in politics—yet "he was not so protective of his brothers' families..." See idem., *Mao Zedong*, 156.

[12] Pang and Jin, *Mao Zedong: A Biography*, 9; Chang and Halliday, *Mao: The Unknown Story*, 5; Zhao Zhichao, *Mao Zedong he ta de fu lao xiang qin* [*Mao Zedong and His Fellow Villagers*] (Changsha: Hunan wenyi chubanshe, 1992), 271-272, 274.

[13] Pang and Jin, *Mao Zedong: A Biography*, 9; Karl, *Mao Zedong and China in the Twentieth-Century World*, 4. After Mao was dismissed from school at age 13, he became a "full-time peasant," as Halliday and Chang put it in *Mao: The Unknown Story*, 6.

[14] Karl, *Mao Zedong and China in the Twentieth-Century World*, 5-6; Snow, *Red Star Over China*, 124.

[15] Xiao, *Mao Tse-Tung: His Childhood and His Youth*, 9.

[16] Zhao, *Mao Zedong he ta de fu lao xiang qin*, 103-105; Pantsov and Levine, *Mao: The Real Story*, 15.

[17] Snow, *Red Star Over China*, 124-125; Zhao, *Mao Zedong he ta de fu lao xiang qin*, 105.

[18] Xiao, *Mao Tse-Tung: His Childhood and His Youth*, 9.

[19] Snow, *Red Star Over China*, 126.

[20] Ibid.; Pang and Jin, *Mao Zedong: A Biography*, 5.

[21] Xiao, *Mao Tse-Tung*, 14-15.

[22] Pang and Jin, *Mao Zedong: A Biography*, 10; Zhao, *Mao Zedong he ta de fu lao xiang qin*, 110; Edwin Lowe, "Introduction" in Shi Naian, *The Water Margin: Outlaws of the Marsh*, trans. J.H. Jackson (North Clarendon, VT: Tuttle, 2010), xxviii.

[23] Pang and Jin, ibid.; Jon Fitzgerald, "Continuity Within Discontinuity: The Case for Water Margin Mythology," *Modern China*, Vol. 12, No. 3 (July 1986): 381; Lowe, "Introduction" in Shi, *Water Margin*, xxx.

[24] Shi, *The Water Margin: Outlaws of the Marsh*, 195; "Mao Cult of Personality (Propaganda) [Footage from Cultural Revolution Rally in Tiananmen square]": https://www.youtube.com/watch?v=Vk6m7cZDgiA
Accessed December 8, 2021.

[25] *Water Margin*—it's important to note though—did not call for the destruction of any ruling order, but rather a correction of its faults and a restoration of the proper order between ruler and ruled. The novel, as one of Renzhi's most apt biographers put it in this regard, "encouraged him at best to be a rebel within the framework of tradition." See Schram, *Mao Tse-Tung*, 21.

[26] Quoted in Pantsov and Levine, *Mao: The Real Story*, 46.

[27] As Stuart R. Schram states: "...for all the changes which Mao's ideas underwent during the decade after 1912, his personality (or cast of mind) remained strikingly consistent. In particular, *the focus on the individual will or consciousness, and on the role of the hero, stands out in all of Mao's early writings* [emphasis added], and indeed throughout his entire life. The emphasis on military heroism, and on the martial ethos, is also a recurrent trait." See idem., ed., *Mao's Road to Power: Revolutionary Writings, 1912-1949*, Vol. 1 (Armonk, NY: M.E. Sharpe, 1992), xxii.

[28] Snow, *Red Star Over China*, 127. Mao read works by Kang Youwei and Zheng Guanying, for instance, describing the desperate need for China to modernize to overcome foreign imperialism. See Pantsov and Levine, *Mao: The Real Story*, 21-24; Karl, *Mao Zedong and China in the Twentieth-Century World*, 6.

[29] Pang and Jin, *Mao Zedong: A Biography*, 5; Snow, *Red Star Over China*, 145; Pantsov and Levine, *Mao: The Real Story*, 26-27; Han Suyin, *The Morning Deluge: Mao Tsetung and the Chinese Revolution, 1893-1954* (New York: Little, Brown, 1972), 26.

[30] Schram, ed., *Mao's Road to Power: Revolutionary Writings, 1912-1949*, Vol. 1, "The Question of Ms. Zhao's Personality, November 18, 1919," 423.

[31] On the suggestion that the young wife became Yichang's concubine, see Short, *Mao: A Life*, 29.

[32] Xiao, *Mao Tse-Tung*, 11; Pantsov and Levine, *Mao: The Real Story*, 27.

[33] Pang and Jin, *Mao Zedong: A Biography*, 12; Xiaoyu notes that he brought *Water Margin* (*Shui Hu*) in idem., *Mao Tse-Tung and I were Beggars* (Syracuse, NY: Syracuse University Press, 1959), 12-23; on distance, see Chang and Halliday, *The Unknown Story*, 7.

[34] Xiao, *Mao Tse-Tung*, 18-19; Snow, *Red Star Over China*, 132.

[35] Xiaoyu, *Mao Tse-Tung and I were Beggars*, 21; Schram, *Mao Tse-Tung*, 26.

[36] Xiao, *Mao Tse-Tung*, 18-19; Pantsov and Levine, *Mao: The Real Story*, 28-29.

[37] Snow, *Red Star Over China*, 132.

[38] Ibid.; Pantsov and Levine, *Mao: The Real Story*, 29.

[39] Pang and Jin, *Mao Zedong: A Biography*, 14; Xiao, *Mao Tse-Tung*, 19-21; Snow, *Red Star Over China*, 134; Schram, *Mao Tse-Tung*, 25.

[40] A reference to Kang Yuwei and Liang Qichao; see Snow, *Red Star Over China*, 133; Pantsov and Levine, *Mao: The Real Story*, 29-30

[41] On July 4, 1944, Mao's *Liberation Daily* noted—ironically and humorously enough—"The work which we Communists are carrying on today is the very same work which was carried on earlier in America by Washington, Jefferson, and Lincoln [*sic*]..." See Schram, *Mao Tse-Tung*, 226. Mao's emphasis on the role of heroic leaders—alongside discussions about the peasantry and their need for "correct leadership"—came across strongly in his thinking about Chinese history. As Mao wrote in 1939, "In the many thousand-year history of the Chinese people, *many national heroes and revolutionary leaders* have emerged [Emphasis added]. China has given birth to many revolutionary strategists, statesmen, men of letters and thinkers." Such statements infer that heroic agency has its place alongside Marx's historical materialism. See Schram, *The Thought of Mao Tse-Tung*, 75.

[42] Pang and Jin, *Mao Zedong: A Biography*, 14.

[43] Snow, *Red Star over China*, 135-136; Pang and Jin, *Mao Zedong: A Biography*, 15.

[44] Snow, ibid.; Pang and Jin, ibid., 15-16; Pantsov and Levine, *Mao: The Real Story*, 33-34.

[45] Pang and Jin, *Mao Zedong: A Biography*, 16; Pantsov and Levine, *Mao: The Real Story*, 35.

[46] Pang and Jin, ibid.

[47] Ibid., 17; Xiao, *Mao Tse-Tung*, 34-35; Pantsov and Levine, *Mao: The Real Story*, 35; Chang and Halliday, *The Unknown Story*, 11.

[48] Pang and Jin, ibid.; Emi Xiao, ibid., 36; Chang and Halliday, ibid., 11.

[49] Xiao, ibid., 36.

[50] Pang and Jin, ibid., 17-18. Though how much of this geographical knowledge stuck is unclear, because—as Julia Lowell has noted—Mao once admitted during a meeting with Brazilian diplomats that he had no idea where Brazil was. See idem., *Maoism: A Global History*, 34.

[51] Snow, *Red Star over China*, 141-142; Xiao, *Mao Tse-Tung*, 35-37.

[52] Snow, *Red Star over China*, 142.

[53] Xiao, *Mao Tse-Tung*, 37; Pang and Jin, *Mao Zedong: A Biography*, 19.

[54] Pantsov and Levine, *Mao: The Real Story*, 37.

[55] Pang and Jin, *Mao Zedong: A Biography*, 19. The branch of the school he initially attended was technically the Fourth Normal School, but it soon merged with the First Normal School in March 1914.

[56] Xiao, *Mao Tse-Tung*, 38; Pantsov and Levine, *Mao: The Real Story*, 38; Li Jui, *The Early Revolutionary Activities of Comrade Mao Tse-Tung*, trans. Anthony W. Sariti (White Plains, NY: M.E. Sharpe, Inc., 1977), 22; this is a translation of Li Jui, *Mao Tse-tung t'ung-chih ti ch'u-ch'i ko-ming huo-tung* (Peking: Chung-kuo ch'ing-nien ch'u-pan-she, 1957).

[57] Snow, *Red Star Over China*, 143.

[58] Pang and Jin, *Mao Zedong: A Biography*, 20-21; Pantsov and Levine, *Mao: The Real Story*, 39.

Chapter 12 (Kim)

[1] Suh, *Kim Il Sung*, 5; Cumings, *North Korea: Another Country*, 105.

[2] Kim Il-sung, *With the Century*, Vol. 1 (Pyongyang: Foreign Languages Publishing House, 1998), 6.

[3] Ju Jin-o, "Gidokgyo, Kim Il-Sung eotteon yeonghyangeul michyeonna?", Vol. 20 (August 1992): 322-323; Martin, *Under the Loving Care*, 13.

[4] I witnessed this during a trip to North Korea in August 2015; it was adorable, and bizarre.

[5] Ju, "Gidokgyo, Kim Il-Sung eotteon yeonghyangeul michyeonna," 322-323; Choe Yeong-ho, "Christian Background in the Early Life of Kim Il-Song," *Asian Survey*, Vol. 26, No. 10 (Oct., 1986): 1087.

[6] Christianity had spread into Korea in the late 19th century and attracted the ire of Japanese occupiers. See Lankov, *From Stalin to Kim Il Sung*, 51; Martin, *Under the Loving Care*, 14-15.

[7] Ch'oe, "Christian Background in the Early Life of Kim Il-Song," 1083; Michael D. Shin, *Korean National Identity under Japanese Colonial Rule: Yi Gwangsu and the March First Movement of 1919* (New York: Routledge, 2018), 32, 34.

[8] Kim's later memoirs dropped anti-American language about the institution, but still claimed that Hyong-jik led a strike for better conditions (and supposedly encouraged his peers to "Believe in a Korean God, if you believe in one!") Nothing in the school's records corroborates that Kim's father led a strike. Quoted in Ch'oe, "Christian Background in the Early Life of Kim Il-Song," 1084; Kim, *With the Century*, Vol. 1, 20-21.

[9] Kim, *With the Century*, Vol. 1, 20-23.

[10] Quoted in Wada Haruki, *Bukan Hyeondaesa* (Paju, ROK: Changbi Publishers, Inc., 2012), 24.

[11] Financial reasons, one historian has suggested, do not solely explain his withdrawal; the institution offered tuition assistance. Ch'oe, "Christian Background in the Early Life of Kim Il-Song," 1085. Kim claimed his entire family struggled to pay his tuition in *With the Century*, Vol. 1, 9.

[12] Hyong-jik did not play a leading role as Song-ju's regime spuriously claims; see Ch'oe, "Christian Background in the Early Life of Kim Il-Song," 1085-1086; Wada, *Bukan Hyeondaesa*, 24.

[13] Ch'oe, ibid.; Lankov, *From Stalin to Kim Il Sung*, 51.

[14] Lankov makes the point that we do not know for certain that Hyong-jik—though mentioned in Japanese police files—was actually imprisoned. See idem., *From Stalin to Kim Il Sung*, 51.

[15] Kim, *With the Century*, Vol. 1, 31-32.

[16] Ch'oe, "Christian Background in the Early Life of Kim Il-Song," 1087; for more on cousin Kang Yang-uk's involvement in North Korean politics, see Ju, "Gidokgyo, Kim Il-Sung eotteon yeonghyangeul michyeonna," 323 and— fascinatingly—"Carrots and Radishes," *Time*, November 13, 1950, 30-33.

[17] Ch'oe, ibid.; Ju, ibid., 322.

[18] This account is from Rev. Shungnak Luke Kim who left Korea in the 1920s and settled in the United States; he—historian Ch'oe Yeong-ho states—had known "Kim Il-song's family intimately." Rev. Kim visited Kim Il-sung in Pyongyang in June 1981, and the North Korean leader described Rev. Kim's father as "'a good leader of the country'" while Rev. Kim (after leaving North Korea) remembered that Kim Il-sung's father and mother were both "good Christian[s]."

[19] Kim, *With the Century*, Vol. 1, 104.

[20] Ibid.

[21] Ibid., 103.

[22] Ibid., 68.

[23] "Substantial Citizens," *Time*, October 30, 1950, 34; Martin, *Under the Loving Care*, 80.

[24] Kim, *With the Century*, Vol. 1, 102-103.

[25] See Ch'oe, "Christian Background in the Early Life of Kim Il-Song," 1090.

[26] Kim, *With the Century*, Vol. 1, 104.

[27] Ju, "Gidokgyo, Kim Il-Sung eotteon yeonghyangeul michyeonna," 325-326.

[28] For example, watch: Amnesty International, "North Korea: Life in the camps": https://www.youtube.com/watch?v=JF4R6wwA4C4&t=6s Accessed July 30, 2021.

[29] Arcade Fire, "Intervention," *Neon Bible* (Rough Trade Records, 2007).

[30] Kim, *With the Century*, Vol. 1, 63; Martin, *Under the Loving Care*, 17.

[31] Kim, *With the Century*, Vol. 1, 63; Lankov, *From Stalin to Kim Il Sung*, 51. Fluency in Mandarin, as Chapter 18 emphasizes, enabled Song-ju to work closely with—and under the command of—Chinese guerillas in years to come. That language proficiency also enabled him as a dictator to communicate closely with his Chinese allies during periods of diplomacy, war, and disaster in Korea.

[32] Kim, *With the Century*, Vol. 1, 78.

[33] Ibid.; Martin, *Under the Loving Care*, 18.

[34] Kim, *With the Century*, Vol. 1, 80-82.

[35] Ibid., 83.

[36] Kim discusses his maternal uncle in ibid., Vol. 1, 63-65, 83. Controversially, the Republic of Korea's National Assembly conferred an award on Kim's maternal uncle Kang Jin-sok, as well as Kim's fraternal uncle Kim Hyung-kwon; see "Honoring Kim Il-sung's kin," *The Korea Times*, July 1, 2016: http://www.koreatimes.co.kr/www/opinion/2019/07/202_208411.html Accessed July 30, 2021.

[37] For essays describing a greater complexity behind Japanese colonialism in Korea—including economic development—see Lee Hong Yung, Yong-Chool Ha, and Clark W. Sorensen, eds., *Colonial Rule & Social Change in Korea, 1910-1945* (Seattle, WA: University of Washington, 2012).

[38] As historian Chong-sik Lee put it plainly, "Obviously, Song-ju was raised in a highly politicized environment with strong currents of nationalism and Communism....A sensitive child could very well have been drawn into any of the [nationalist and communist] organizations [fighting Japanese colonialism]." See idem., "Kim Il-Song of North Korea," *Asian Survey*, Vol. 7, No. 6 (June 1967): 375.

[39] Kim, *With the Century*, Vol. 1, 123.

[40] Ibid., 128-129.

[41] Ibid., 158.

[42] The kid could handle hunger—he allegedly told a peer—as long as he had lots of books. Ibid., 210.

[43] Ibid., 210-212; Sung-chul Yang, *Korea and Two Regimes: Kim Il Sung and Park Chung Hee* (Cambridge, MA: Schenckman Publishing Company, Inc., 1981), 79.

[44] Suh, *Kim Il Sung*, 8.

[45] Either way, Song-ju was never an intellectual. As one preeminent writer for Song-ju's regime stated (just before he was purged) in an anti-elitist vein in 1962: "The General is not such a man as would overestimate his brain and would be so snobbish as to pride himself on it....He is a type of genius who goes into the people, absorbs nourishments from them..." See Han Sorya, "Hero General Kim Il Sung," *Chosun Shinbo-sa* (1962), 43; Brian Myers, *Han Sorya and North Korean Literature: The Failure of Socialist Realism in the DPRK* (Ithaca, N.Y.: East Asia Program, Cornell University, 1994), 146-147.

[46] Lankov, *From Stalin to Kim Il Sung*, 51. Perhaps less reliably, Won Tai Sohn claims Song-ju enjoyed reading as a kid and read books like Sun Tzu's *Art of War* in preparation for guerilla war against Japan. See idem., *Kim Il Sung and Korea's Struggle: An Unconventional Firsthand History* (Jefferson, N.C.: McFarland & Company, Inc., 2004), 57, 83.

[47] *With the Century*, Vol. 1, 207-208; quote from a letter sent to Bradley K. Martin, *Under the Loving Care*, 22.

[48] *With the Century*, Vol. 1, 215.

[49] Wada, *Bukan Hyeondaesa*, 25; Suh, *Kim Il Sung*, 6. Note: Kim attended a Korean middle school (Hwasong School) before; Kim's years there are described from the North Korean perspective in *With the Century*, Vol. 1, 138-198.

[50] On Shang Yue's work, see idem., *Zhongguo lishi gangya* [*Outline of Chinese History*] (Beijing: Renmin chubanshe, 1954); for Shang Yue's recollections of Kim Il-sung as Song-ju, see idem., *Lishi huímóu: Shàng yuè xiansheng* [*Looking back at history: Mr. Shang Yue*] (Beijing: Zhōngguó Rénmín Dàxué Lìshi Xuéyuàn, 2011), 83-90. Special thanks to Sam Duan for helping with this source.

[51] Shang Yue, *Lishi huímóu: Shàng yuè xiansheng*, 86-87. The teacher writes: "I taught them how to analyze and distinguish comrades and friends from enemies based on class analysis. I made them clarify their boundaries with people in the class-society, [made them] hate [their] enemies, [made them] hate selfish and self-interested grey people, and hinted to them the heinous plots of reactionaries." Ibid., 87.

[52] Ibid., 88.

[53] Ibid.

[54] Ibid., 85.

[55] Ibid., 89. Kim Il-sung, the teacher remembered, wrote "descriptive essays, [in which] he sharply exposed the extreme exploitation and asphyxiating oppression by the Japanese imperialists; and the piteous life of the Korean people who were trapped in poverty, forced out of their country, and struggled on the verge of death because of their persecuted status. Thus, in some other essays, he praised the Korean national hero Yi sun-sin, and adventurist An Jung-geun." See Ibid.

[56] *With the Century*, Vol. 1, 225, 229, 233; Shang Yue, *Lishi huímóu: Shàng yuè xiansheng*, 88-89. Shang Yue, as noted, specifically recalled teaching about Lenin and Gorky.

[57] Shang Yue, *Lishi huímóu: Shàng yuè xiansheng*, 86-87. (Political circumstances in Mao-era China, of course, might have led the teacher to make his memories of the North Korean dictator more glowing.) Kim, Shang Yue records further, "interacted with normal progressive Han and Korean classmates very well. He interacted very harmoniously with all classmates in the class, and every time he came to my dorm, he was usually with the progressive students, which made [Shang Yue] feel that there were no obstacles between him and the Chinese students. One aspect of that was definitely because of the education from the Party or the Youth League, but another aspect of it demonstrates his ability to unite the masses, and that he was essentially eliminating these primitive boundaries from his young heart." Ibid., 86.

[58] Ibid., 90. Shang's daughter, in an interview with Reuters in 1994, stated that "her late father had remembered Kim as a star pupil in Jilin, 'diligent, putting good questions [forward], both inside and outside the class.'" Quoted in Martin, *Under the Loving Care*, 23 from Mark O'Neill, "N. Korea's Dead Dictator Remembered as Star Pupil According to Chinese Teacher's Daughter," (Reuters Dispatch from Beijing), *Korea Times*, September 10, 1994.

[59] Shang Yue, *Lìshǐ huímóu: Shàng yuè xiansheng*, 89-90. North Korea continued to host Shang Yue's relatives in Pyongyang after his death and sometimes referenced Shang Yue when discussing Kim Il-sung's years in China. See "Meeting for Remembering Kim Il Sung Held in China," KCNA [Korea Central News Agency], April 8, 2014; "Families of Those Related to Anti-Japanese Revolutionary Struggle Leave," KCNA, September 12, 2018; "Families of Those Related to Anti-Japanese Revolutionary Struggle," July 5, 2019. Link to these articles are in the bibliography.

[60] "Whenever I miss this man who left a lasting impression on me in my youthful days, I take a stroll in my heart in the garden of Yuwen Middle School," records Kim in *With the Century*, Vol. 1, 236; Martin, *Under the Loving Care*, 23. At age 79, Kim Il Sung brought up Shang Yue, among other individuals from Jilin, to Won Tai Sohn during a 1991 visit; the teacher came to the dictator's mind when he remembered those days. See idem., *Kim Il Sung and Korea's Struggle*, 134.

[61] Kim, *With the Century*, Vol. 1, 227; Shang Yue, *Lìshǐ huímóu: Shàng yuè xiansheng*, 85.

[62] Kim, ibid., 227.

[63] Lee, *The Girl With Seven Names*, 22, 71.

[64] Sohn, *Kim Il Sung and Korea's Struggle*, 49.

[65] Ibid., 57; Kim, *With the Century*, Vol. 1, 308, 354-355; Martin, *Under the Loving Care*, 25-26.

[66] Suh, *Kim Il Sung*, 7; Suh, *The Korean Communist Movement, 1918-1948*, 266-267.

[67] See, for example, David Hawk, *The Hidden Gulag: The Lives and Voices of 'Those Who are Sent to the Mountains'* (Washington, D.C.: Committee for Human Rights in North Korea, 2012) Second Edition, 130-131:

https://web.archive.org/web/20210109092738/https://www.hrnk.org/uploads/pdfs/HRNK_HiddenGulag2_Web_5-18.pdf

Accessed July 30, 2021; James Brooke, "N. Koreans Talk of Baby Killings," *New York Times*, June 10, 2002, 1:

https://web.archive.org/web/20210430025052/https://www.nytimes.com/
2002/06/10/world/n-koreans-talk-of-baby-killings.html

Accessed December 8, 2021.

[68] Yodok was a horrific concentration camp run by the North Korean state from 1970 to 2014. See Hawk, *The Hidden Gulag: The Lives and Voices of 'Those Who are Sent to the Mountains'*, 53-69; Kang Chol-hwan and Pierre Rigoulot, translated by Yair Reiner, *The Aquariums of Pyongyang* (New York: Basic Books, 2001).

[69] Suh, *The Korean Communist Movement, 1918-1948*, 267; Adrian Buzo, *The Guerilla Dynasty: Politics and Leadership in North Korea* (New York: I.B. Taurus & Co Ltd., 1999), 3. Lankov states that Kim served only several months in *From Stalin to Kim Il Sung*, 52. Kim, *With the Century*, Vol. 1, 346-347, 354.

[70] Kim, *With the Century*, Vol. 1, 360-361; Martin, *Under the Loving Care*, 27-28.

Chapter 13 (Lenin)

[1] Valentinov's words, *The Early Years of Lenin*, 94.

[2] Deutscher, *Lenin's Childhood*, 31. Sasha and big sister Anna—still young teenagers—offered no sympathy for the assassins. They apparently remained silent while trying to make sense of the first major political event of their lives.

[3] Ibid., 32.

[4] Anna stated: "I read together with Sasha all of Pisarev's works from cover to cover; they had a strong impact on us. These books were banned from libraries, but we borrowed them from an acquaintance....These were the first forbidden books we read. We were so absorbed in them that when we finished the last volume[,] we were deeply saddened to have to part from our beloved author." Quoted in Ali, *The Dilemmas of Lenin*, 63; see also Pomper, *Lenin's Brother*, 33.

[5] Quoted in Pomper, *Lenin's Brother*, 33. On Pisarev's influence, see ibid., 33-38. On Pisarev, see Frederick Copleston, *Philosophy in Russia: From Herzen to Lenin and Berdyaev* (Notre Dame, IN: University of Notre Dame Press, 1986), 113-115.

[6] Nikolai Chernyshevsky, *What Is to Be Done?*, trans., Michael R. Katz (Ithaca, N.Y.: Cornell University Press, 1989), 279, 288; Pomper, *Lenin's Brother*, 38-39. See also Richard Peace, "Nihilism" in *A History of Russian Thought*, ed. William Leatherbarrow, Derek Offord (Cambridge: Cambridge University Press, 2010), 212.

[7] Pomper notes, however, that Sasha also embraced sexist views about women, writing: "Sasha's opinions about women sound odd for a socialist sensitive to

history's victims, and they seem to contradict the Russian socialists' commitment to equality for women; see idem., *Lenin's Brother*, 54-57.

[8] Future conspirator, Govorukhin, was surprised by Sasha's admission in the fall of 1885 that he had already read these works. See Pomper, *Lenin's Brother*, 98.

[9] Ibid., 95-96.

[10] Ibid., 96, 99.

[11] Ibid., 96-98; Service, *Lenin*, 56-57.

[12] Pomper, *Lenin's Brother*, 114-116; Deutscher, *Lenin's Childhood*, 50-51. Sasha's response to that day's events, Derek Offord notes, was not "exceptional: anger at the treatment meted out to the demonstrators was widespread. Many students began to talk of another act of terrorism…" see idem., *The Russian Revolutionary Movement in the 1880s* (Cambridge: Cambridge University Press, 1986), 70-71.

[13] Pomper, *Lenin's Brother*, 119-122; Deutscher, *Lenin's Childhood*, 50-53.

[14] Ibid. Pomper records Anna's painful reflection that Sasha seemed to know that what he was doing for political ideals would cause his mother to suffer; yet he argues that: "Her perception of his agitated state may have been correct but her diagnosis wrong. He may have been unhappy with the way things were going—with the hasty and sloppy work of the conspirators, with their immaturity and recklessness, and even perhaps with his own. Sasha was still trying to be a perfect nihilist hero—a person whose ideas and actions were perfectly rational….Sasha played the role presumably assigned by the historical moment with the merciless consequentiality required of a developed person." See idem., *Lenin's Brother*, 144.

[15] Pomper, ibid., 122, 144-148.

[16] Ibid., 119-122, 126-127.

[17] Quoted in Ibid., 128; see also 123-132.

[18] Ibid., 154.

[19] Sasha did, however, use Anna's address as the destination for a coded letter relating to the conspiracy; she had no idea what it meant. Sasha also asked his oblivious sister to let a member of the conspiracy from Vilnius stay at her place for a night. These facts did not initially help Anna's case with police. See Ibid., 57, 63.

[20] Quoted in Ibid., 189.

[21] Ul'yanova, *Detskie I shkol'nye gody Il'icha*, 70; quoted in Deutscher, *Lenin's Childhood*, 56. Lenin, his big sister reflected, became an adult in that moment.

[22] Valentinov, *The Early Years of Lenin*, 113, 232.

[23] Ul'yanova, *Detskie I shkol'nye gody Il'icha*, 70.

[24] Deutscher, *Lenin's Childhood*, 57.

[25] Quoted in Valentinov, *The Early Years of Lenin*, 95-97; Valentinov cites A.S. Poliakov, *Vtoroe l-e marta: Pokushenie na imperatora Aleksandra III v 1887 g. (Materialy)* (Moscow, 1919), 54-56.

[26] Quoted in Ibid., 98.

[27] Ibid.; Pomper, *Lenin's Brother*, 192.

[28] Quoted in Valentinov, *The Early Years of Lenin*, 98.

[29] Deutscher, *Lenin's Childhood*, 57.

[30] Pomper, *Lenin's Brother*, 169-171.

[31] Pomper's words in ibid., 169.

[32] Deutscher, *Lenin's Childhood*, 58; Louis Fischer, *Life of Lenin* (New York: Harper & Row, 1964), 14.

[33] Quoted in Fischer, *Life of Lenin*, 15-16; Pomper, *Lenin's Brother*, 44.

[34] Quoted in Deutscher, *Lenin's Childhood*, 58.

[35] Two additional conspirators were sentenced to death but had their sentences commuted to life imprisonment as a result of their clemency petitions to the Tsar; see Pomper, *Lenin's Brother*, 196-197.

[36] Quoted in Valentinov, *The Early Years of Lenin*, 100.

[37] Pomper, *Lenin's Brother*, 192. If he had done otherwise, and the Tsar spared his life, would authorities have amnestied him during the 1905 Revolution, allowing him to later witness October 1917? Others received amnesties in 1905. See ibid., 59.

[38] Quoted in *Lenin's Brother*, 194.

[39] Deutscher, *Lenin's Childhood*, 61; Pomper records Maria's last words (through Anna) as "Courage!" in *Lenin's Brother*, 193.

[40] Pomper, *Lenin's Brother*, 1-4, 196-197; Valentinov, *The Early Years of Lenin*, 103-104; Sebestyen, *Lenin: The Man, The Dictator, and the Master of Terror*, 43.

[41] Deutscher, *Lenin's Childhood*, 61; Ali, *The Dilemmas of Lenin*, 68.

[42] Deutscher, *Lenin's Childhood*, 64; Service, *Lenin*, 61. "His academic performance," Service states, "...in the circumstances...was almost inhumanly impressive."

[43] Ibid. A classmate wrote of the exam: "We were all terribly agitated...only Vladimir Ulyanov, seated behind his desk, wrote calmly and unhurriedly....We were given only six hours for doing our papers....Vladimir Ilyich finished and delivered his work earlier than the rest of us and was the first to leave the examination hall."

[44] Deutscher, *Lenin's Childhood*, 65; Clark, *Lenin*, 15.

[45] A.I. Ul'yanova, *Detskie I shkol'nye gody Il'icha*, 70; Deutscher, *Lenin's Childhood*, 64; Fischer, *Life of Lenin*, 18; Valentinov, *The Early Years of Lenin*, 113-114; Service, *Lenin*, 61; Sebestyen, *Lenin*, 47; Clark, *Lenin*, 15.

[46] Ibid.

[47] Quoted in Nadezhda K. Krupskaya, *Memories of Lenin*, trans. E. Verney (New York: International Publishers, 1930), 5; see also Valentinov, *The Early Years of Lenin*, 93.

[48] Ul'yanova, *Detskie I shkol'nye gody Il'icha*, 70.

[49] Service, *Lenin*, 60; Valentinov, *The Early Years of Lenin*, 112.

[50] Valentinov, *The Early Years of Lenin*, 116-117.

[51] Ibid., 111-138.

[52] Chernyshevsky, *What Is to Be Done?*, 281-284.

[53] Ibid., 188-196.

[54] See the future paradise Chernyshevsky describes after the revolution in ibid., 369-372.

[55] This is the central argument of Valentinov's *The Early Years of Lenin*, discussed in detail in chapters VI-XII.

[56] Ibid., 135-136.

[57] Ul'yanova, *Detskie I shkol'nye gody Il'icha*, 72; Service, *Lenin*, 63.

[58] Trotsky summed it up well: "The political shadow of Alexander followed unrelentingly at Vladimir's heels for a number of years. 'Isn't this the brother of that Ulyanov?' wrote a high-ranking bureaucrat on the margins of an official document. Everybody saw him in this light. 'Brother of the Ulyanov who was hanging,' the young radicals would whisper with reverence. *Le mort saisit le vif.*" See idem., *The Young Lenin*, 159.

[59] Ul'yanova, *Detskie I shkol'nye gody Il'icha*, 72; Service, *Lenin*, 61-66 (Kerensky quoted 61-62); Deutscher, *Lenin's Childhood*, 62-63; d'Encausse, *Lenin*, 8; Sebestyen, *Lenin*, 58-59.

[60] Ul'yanova, *Detskie I shkol'nye gody Il'icha*, 72-73.

[61] Lenin quoted in Ali, *The Dilemmas of Lenin*, 72. Pisarev said this about the Tsarist system in his Ballod pamphlet, as noted in Peace, "Nihilism" in *A History of Russian Thought*, 131.

[62] The young man, his big sister explains, became "a revolutionary, courageous, convinced, not afraid of any difficulties, devoting all his strength to the struggle for the cause of the working people"; see Ul'yanova, *Detskie I shkol'nye gody Il'icha*, 74.

[63] Valentinov, *The Early Years of Lenin*, 122-123.

[64] Kotkin makes a similar point in *Stalin: Waiting for Hitler*, 6.

[65] Valentinov argues that Lenin's "ends justified the means" approach took inspiration from Chernyshevsky; see idem., *The Early Years of Lenin*, Chapter XII.

[66] Quoted in ibid., *The Early Years of Lenin*, 170-174; Service, *Lenin*, 87-88.

[67] Consider this cruelty alongside Krupskaya's perspective that "…his brother's fate whetted his brain, brought out in him an usual sobriety of thought, the capacity to look truth straight in the face, not for one moment to be carried away by phrases or illusions. It developed in him an extremely honest approach to all problems." See idem., *Memories of Lenin*, 6.

[68] Valentinov, *The Early Years of Lenin*, 43, 56; idem., *Encounters with Lenin* (Oxford: Oxford University Press, 1968), xvi.

[69] Lenin said this when a proclaimed socialist spoke of his past involvement in the 1905 revolution before the Soviet leader; quoted in Albert Rhys Williams, *Lenin: The Man and His Work* (New York: Scott and Seltzer, 1919), 85.

[70] Emphasis in original and quoted in Valentinov, who claims Lenin said this in 1919, see idem., *The Early Years of Lenin*, 77. Lenin also said this—in a moment of grim humor or not—in 1907 when asked what would happen when the revolution arrived. Quoted in Adam B. Ulam, *The Bolsheviks: The Intellectual and Political History of the Triumph of Communism in Russia* (New York: Macmillan Publishing Company/Harvard University Press, 1968, 1998), 201.

[71] As the younger brother's own radical convictions grew, he came to lament that Sasha had given up his life so easily. If one must be absolutely willing to die for the cause, Volodia quickly grasped that the purpose of revolutionary means is revolutionary ends—to overthrow the existing power structure. Martyrdom for martyrdom's sake was fatuous. Better to be smart and preserve one's ability to continue the struggle until one might actually succeed in bringing the revolution to fruition. See Pomper, *Lenin's Brother*, 201-202.

Chapter 14 (Mussolini)

[1] Farrell, *Mussolini: A New Life*, 15.

[2] BMOO, Vol. XXXIII, 234-236; Cannistraro, "Father and Son" in *Mussolini 1883-1915*, 54; Farrell, *Mussolini: A New Life*, 15-16.

[3] BMOO, Vol. XXXIII, 234-236; Bosworth, *Mussolini*, 52; Cannistraro, "Father and Son" in *Mussolini 1883-1915*, 54; Gregor, *Young Mussolini and the Intellectual Origins of Fascism*, 33. Benito bragged in *La Mia Vita* that he would become the best student

in his class; see BMOO, Vol. XXXIII, 242. De Felice records that he was a relatively normal student in *Mussolini il rivoluzionario*, 14.

[4] Mussolini, *My Autobiography*, 11.

[5] Ibid.

[6] BMOO, Vol. XXXIII, 238; on this stabbing, see also Monelli, *Mussolini: An Intimate Life*, 29.

[7] Monelli, *Mussolini: An Intimate Life*, 29; Cannistraro, "Father and Son" in *Mussolini 1883-1915*, 54; De Felice, *Mussolini il rivoluzionario*, 17. Until that time, Mussolini stayed nearby with an old woman who remembered him as irritating and exhausting. (Maybe he practiced the trumpet too often?) Even after they let Mussolini back into the dorms, he was eventually kicked out again for breaking curfew.

[8] BMOO, Vol. XXXIII, 239; Farrell, *Mussolini: A New Life*, 16-17.

[9] BMOO, ibid.; quoted in De Felice, *Mussolini il rivoluzionario*, 17.

[10] BMOO, Vol. XXXIII, 239-240; Farrell, *Mussolini: A New Life*, 16-17, 29; on the clap, Farrell cites Fabrizio Castellini, *Il ribelle di Predappio Amori e giovinezza di Mussolini: Testimonianze fra cronaca e storia* (Milan: Mursia, 1996), 94-95. Mussolini believed himself dying of syphilis for a time, which proved untrue—see A. James Gregor, *Young Mussolini and the Intellectual Origins of Fascism* (Berkeley, CA: University of California Press, 1979), 35-36, FN 15.

[11] He also scribbled trite poetry. Farrell, *Mussolini: A New Life*, 17; BMOO, Vol. XXXIII, 240.

[12] Bosworth, *Mussolini*, 53, 197; Cannistraro, "Father and Son" in *Mussolini 1883-1915*, 51. Mussolini, as a dictator, read that poet sage "again and again," notes Emil Ludwig in *Talks With Mussolini*, trans. Eden and Cedar Paul (Boston: Little, Brown, and Company, 1933), 215; quoted in Farrell, *Mussolini: A New Life,* 18. On Le Bon's work, Benito would reference him for years to come as he took the thinker's thoughts to heart about winning over a crowd through emotional discourse and straight-forward language; see Farrell, *Mussolini: A New Life,* 18. On Mussolini's first encounter with socialism, see De Felice, *Mussolini il rivoluzionario*, 15.

[13] On socialist politics as common place, see Gregor's words in *Young Mussolini and the Intellectual Origins of Fascism*, 33.

[14] BMOO, Vol. XXXIII, 242; Gregor, *Young Mussolini and the Intellectual Origins of Fascism*, 33; De Felice, *Mussolini il rivoluzionario*, 14; Megaro, *Mussolini in the Making*, 44.

[15] Quoted in Bosworth, *Mussolini*, 52.

[16] De Felice plays down the importance of the speech in idem., *Mussolini il rivoluzionario*, 14.

[17] In the months that followed the speech, Benito submitted an article to *Avanti!* and regularly attended—and occasionally spoke at—socialist meetings in Forlimpopoli and Forli (though those gatherings also doubled as dance parties, bringing to mind distinctly apolitical reasons for Benito's attendance). Ibid., 16-17. He started to attend socialist meetings in the town as early as 1898, see Cannistraro, "Father and Son" in *Mussolini 1883-1915*, 56.

[18] BMOO, Vol. XXXIII, 243.

[19] Ibid.; De Felice, *Mussolini il rivoluzionario*, 19.

[20] Quoted in Cannistraro, "Father and Son" in *Mussolini 1883-1915*, 57.

[21] Farrell, *Mussolini: A New Life*, 19.

[22] Ibid.; Cannistraro, "Father and Son" in *Mussolini 1883-1915*, 57.

[23] See Farrell, *Mussolini: A New Life*, 19-20.

[24] BMOO, Vol. XXXIII, 245.

[25] Ibid.

[26] BMOO, Vol. XXXIII, 246; Sarfatti, *The Life of Benito Mussolini*, 78; De Felice, *Mussolini il rivoluzionario*, 20; Monelli, *Mussolini: An Intimate Life*, 33; Ivon De Begnac, *Trent'Anni Di Mussolini, 1883-1915* (Roma: Menaglia, 1934), 51.

[27] BMOO, Vol. XXXIII, 246-247; Bosworth, *Mussolini*, 55; Monelli, *Mussolini: An Intimate Life*, 36; Farrell, *Mussolini: A New Life*, 23. The landlady, perhaps having seen that trick of leaving town before, actually followed the kid to the train station and forced him to hand over his black cloak as payment before he departed.

[28] BMOO, Vol. XXXIII, 246.

[29] Ibid.

[30] See Farrell, *Mussolini: A New Life*, 22 for more on this incident.

[31] BMOO, Vol. XXXIII, 247.

[32] Bosworth's words in *Mussolini*, 59.

[33] De Felice, *Mussolini il rivoluzionario*, 21; Farrell, *Mussolini: A New Life*, 23.

[34] BMOO, Vol. XXXIII, 247; Ludwig, *Talks With Mussolini*, 37. Mussolini wrote a friend in a June 6, 1902 letter that he had a job lined up with a railroad company. See BMOO, Vol. I, 210.

[35] BMOO, Vol. XXXIII, 247; Ludwig, *Talks With Mussolini*, 37.

[36] BMOO, Vol. I, 211-212; Ludwig, *Talks With Mussolini*, 37; Megaro, *Mussolini in the Making*, 50.

[37] De Felice's words in *Mussolini il rivoluzionario*, 24.

[38] BMOO, Vol. I, 210, 212; quoted in Megaro, *Mussolini in the Making*, 51.

[39] Ibid.

[40] BMOO, Vol. XXXIII, 248.

[41] BMOO, Vol. I, 212; quoted in Megaro, *Mussolini in the Making*, 51.

[42] Ludwig, *Talks With Mussolini*, 38.

[43] BMOO, Vol. I, 212; BMOO, Vol. XXXIII, 248-249; Megaro, *Mussolini in the Making*, 52-53, 56; Farrell, *Mussolini: A New Life*, 24-25; Bosworth, *Mussolini*, 58; Monelli, *Mussolini: An Intimate Life*, 35.

[44] Quoted in Ludwig, *Talks With Mussolini*, 35.

[45] Sarfatti, *The Life of Benito Mussolini*, 91-92; Farrell, *Mussolini: A New Life*, 24.

[46] Quoted in Ludwig, *Talks With Mussolini*, 38.

[47] Mussolini remarked in 1932: "They [a word suggesting a monolithic enemy] began by locking me up. Now I pay them back in their own coin." See Ibid., 39; Sarfatti, *The Life of Benito Mussolini*, 93; Farrell, *Mussolini: A New Life*, 24.

[48] BMOO, Vol. XXXIII, 250; De Felice, *Mussolini il rivoluzionario*, 29, 31; Farrell, *Mussolini: A New Life*, 25; Monelli, *Mussolini: An Intimate Life*, 36.

[49] Angelica Balabanoff, *My Life as a Rebel* (Bloomington, IN and London: Indiana University Press, 1938, 1973), 42.

[50] Ibid., 43.

[51] Ibid.

[52] Ibid., 42-43.

[53] Ibid., 45-47. It is uncertain whether Benito and Angelica slept together, though a biographer of Balabanoff has suggested as much. Mussolini's later declaration to his wife, Rachele, that he would rather "fuck a female monkey" than sleep with Balabanoff sounds like the words of a philandering husband seeking to (callously) dismiss the possibility of an extra-marital affair. Other comments by Mussolini (noted by biographer Maria Lafont) seem to signal a more intimate knowledge of Angelica's person as, for instance, when he wrote to his sister that Angelica "knows and understands a lot of things; she's read all the Marxists texts. But while her body is full of juice, her mind is full of dried ideas." The latter statement, as Lafont put it soberly, "implied much more than friendship." See idem., *The Strange Comrade Balabanoff: The Life of a Communist Rebel* (Jefferson, N.C.: McFarland & Company, Inc., Publishers, 2016), 87.

[54] Ibid., 44-45.

[55] Quoted in Yvon De Begnac, *Taccuini mussoliniani*, ed. Francesco Perfetti (Bologna: Società editrice il Mulino, 1990), 5.

[56] BMOO, Vol. XXXIII, 257; quoted in De Felice, *Mussolini il rivoluzionario*, 47.

[57] Long after the two fell out, a fawning 1925 biography of Benito—written by his mistress Margherita Sarfatti—mocked Balabanoff as "small, misshaped hunchbacked...[a] strange hysterical creature with a flashing mind." It added further: "The saving grace of humor failed her completely. She lacked a sense of beauty even more. This was fortunate for her. Otherwise she probably would have thrown herself down the nearest well. As things were, she had the slightest possible acquaintance with water [!]." See idem., *The Life of Benito Mussolini*, 114.

[58] Balabanoff, *My Life as a Rebel*, 46.

[59] Ibid., 47.

[60] Quoted in Ludwig, *Talks With Mussolini*, 36.

[61] Ibid., 46.

[62] Simone Visconti's words in "A Romagnol in Switzerland: Education of a Revolutionary," in *Mussolini 1883-1915*, 66.

[63] See Angelica Balabanoff, *Il Traditore: Mussolini e La Conquista Del Potere* (1943).

Chapter 15 (Hitler)

[1] Kubizek, *The Young Hitler I Knew*, 25-27; Kershaw, *Hitler: 1889-1936*, 21. Kershaw corrects Kubizek, who incorrectly remembers the date as in 1904.

[2] Kubizek, *The Young Hitler I Knew*, 27-28.

[3] Ibid., 37-39.

[4] Heinrich Hoffman, Hitler's long-time photographer, recalls that "...I always had to photograph him in private in new garments; only if he were completely satisfied with the resultant photograph would he then take them into public use." See idem., *Hitler Was My Friend* (London: Burke, 1955), 197.

[5] Kubizek, *The Young Hitler I Knew*, 36, 39, 62, 70.

[6] "I think I can say with certainty:" recalled Kubizek, "Adolf never met a girl either in Linz or Vienna, who actually gave herself to him." See idem., *The Young Hitler I Knew*, 214, 212-221; Kershaw, *Hitler: 1889-1936*, 44-46; Longerich, *Hitler: A Biography*, 23.

[7] One of Hitler's doctors recorded a direct examination of his genitals and found "no abnormalities." Quoted in Werner Maser, *Adolf Hitler - Legende- Mythos- Wirklicheit* (Munich: Bechtle Verlag, 1971), 390. Cited by Linge, *With Hitler to the End*, 171. Kubizek, for his part, stated: "...I must assert categorically that Adolf, in physical

as well as sexual respects, was absolutely normal. What was extraordinary in him was not to be found in the erotic or sexual spheres, but in quite other realms of his being"; see idem., *The Young Hitler I Knew*, 214. For an example of debates about Hitler's penis, see Ishaan Tharoor, "All right, let's talk about Hitler's penis," *Washington Post,* February 23, 2016: https://web.archive.org/web/20160223204402/https://www.washingtonpost .com/news/worldviews/wp/2016/02/23/all-right-lets-talk-about-hitlers-penis/

Accessed July 31, 2021.

[8] Kubizek, *The Young Hitler I Knew*, 27-28. Kershaw describes Kubizek as "highly impressionable....compliant, weak-willed, subordinate" and teenage Adolf as "superior, determining, dominant." See idem., *Hitler: 1889-1936*, 21.

[9] Kubizek, *The Young Hitler I Knew*, 29-30.

[10] Ibid., 31-35, 65.

[11] Ibid., 31-35.

[12] Ibid., 32.

[13] Ibid, 32-33.

[14] Ibid., 33.

[15] Machtan offers an intriguing discussion of circumstantial evidence suggesting Hitler was gay in *The Hidden Hitler*. During the Second World War, a fascinating, if flawed, psychological appraisal of Hitler's life by the U.S. Office of Strategic Services stated: "There is a possibility that Hitler has participated in a homosexual relationship at some point." For part of the report, see Walter C. Langer, *The Mind of Adolf Hitler: The Secret Wartime Report* (New York: Basic Books, Inc., 1972), 179. Dean Haycock notes that Langer's "conclusions are not surprising given his training as a Freudian psychologist and the limited, sometimes untrustworthy information Langer had available. Later studies have cast doubt on these conclusions. No one, obviously, can disprove them but there is just no convincing evidence to support them." See Haycock, *Tyrannical Minds*, Chapter One: Hitler's Bedfellow, "Psychoanalysis From A Distance."

[16] Machtan argues that Kubizek used this anecdote to distance Hitler from homosexuality. See idem., *The Hidden Hitler*, 44-45; Kubizek, *The Young Hitler I Knew*, 219-220; Hamann, *Hitler's Vienna*, 362.

[17] Kubizek, ibid., 33-34; Werner Maser, *Hitler's Letters and Notes*, trans. Arnold Pomerans (London: Heinemann, 1973), 4.

[18] Kubizek, ibid.

[19] Ibid., 212-213.

[20] Reinhold Hanisch, a friend of Hitler's during his time in Vienna, claimed that the future dictator told him this story as an example of his "discipline" with women. "The milkmaid behaved rather foolishly," Hitler told Hanisch. See idem., "I Was Hitler's Buddy," *New Republic*, April 19, 1939, 297; Toland, *Adolf Hitler*, Vol. 1, 25; Kershaw, *Hitler: 1889-1936*, 45.

[21] Kubizek, *The Young Hitler I Knew*, 66-75; Ian Kershaw's introduction, *The Young Hitler I Knew*, 13; Hamann, *Hitler's Vienna*, 24-25, 56. Machtan contends that the relationship with Stefanie was a fiction but accepts the scholarly consensus that Stefanie was indeed a real person in Linz during Hitler's time there; see *The Hidden Hitler*, 42.

[22] Kubizek, *The Young Hitler I Knew*, 66.

[23] Ibid., 69; Jetzinger, *Hitler's Youth*, 105-108; Davidson, *The Making of Adolf Hitler*, 20; Kershaw, *Hitler: 1889-1936*, 22.

[24] Kubizek, *The Young Hitler I Knew*, 67.

[25] Consider Hitler gazing at Speer's architectural models as Soviet artillery shells rained on Berlin in April 1945.

[26] Kubizek, ibid., 66-74.

[27] Ibid., 71.

[28] Ibid., 69-71. Jetzinger suggested the flower-throwing event never happened based on the dates given by Kubizek; Stefanie didn't remember the incident either. See idem., *Hitler's Youth*, 108.

[29] Kubizek, ibid., 73.

[30] Jetzinger, *Hitler's Youth*, 107; Hamann, *Hitler's Vienna*, 30. Kubizek recalls that Hitler—as he left for Vienna the third time—raised the possibility of writing Stefanie. See idem., *The Young Hitler I Knew*, 147.

[31] See Hamann, *Hitler's Vienna*, 362-363, 377. Hamann notes that, years later in Munich, Hitler spoke to his then-roommate Rudolf Häusler about Stefanie.

[32] Kubizek, *The Young Hitler I Knew*, 111-115; Kershaw, *Hitler: 1889-1936*, 22.

[33] Emphasis added. Kubizek, *The Young Hitler I Knew*, 114.

[34] Toland, *Adolf Hitler*, Vol. 1, 17.

[35] "All friends of the family [knew this]" stated Bloch in "'My Patient, Hitler,'" 36.

[36] Kubizek, *The Young Hitler I Knew*, 96. Kubizek states that Hitler's early water colors were "a simple pencil drawing coloured with tempera."

[37] Alan Bullock's words in *Hitler and Stalin: Parallel Lives* (New York: HarpersCollins, 1991), 9.

[38] Ibid., 7; Kubizek, *The Young Hitler I Knew*, 62; Bloch, "'My Patient, Hitler,'" 35. Hitler would go on, Alan Bullock notes, to re-read the entire Karl May series after coming to power; he loved to bring up May's books during evening dinners.

[39] Kubizek, ibid., 179.

[40] Ibid., 180; Davidson, *The Making of Adolf Hitler*, 18; Kershaw, *Hitler: 1889-1936*, 41; Flood, *Hitler: The Path to Power*, 8; Bloch, "'My Patient, Hitler,'" 35.

[41] Davidson cites Speer on the point about only reading the last chapter of a book in idem., *The Making of Adolf Hitler*, 18.

[42] As Kubizek notes: "I never felt, and particularly not in those days when we were lodging together in Vienna, that he was seeking anything concrete in his piles of books, such as principles and ideas for his own conduct; on the contrary, he was only looking for confirmation of those principles and ideas he already had." See idem., *The Young Hitler I Knew*, 182. Sebastian Haffner states of this: "True…he read a lot but – on his own admission – absorbed only what he thought he already knew. See idem., *The Meaning of Hitler*, trans. Edwald Osers (Cambridge: Harvard University Press, 1979), 5; see also, Kershaw, *Hitler: 1889-1936*, 41.

[43] Kershaw supports this assessment, writing: "Hitler was certainly not unintelligent, and possessed a sharp mind which could draw on his formidably retentive memory. He was able to impress…cool, critical, seasoned statesmen and diplomats with his rapid grasp of issues…" See idem., *Hitler: 1889-1936*, xxiv. Speer also notes Hitler's remarkable ability to recall architectural details in idem., *Inside the Third Reich*, 39-40, 115. Kubizek remembered further: "His memory was prodigious: it never failed him and was, of course, a great advantage in his work [studying architecture on his own during his youth]." See idem., *The Young Hitler I Knew*, 177.

[44] Davidson, *The Making of Adolf Hitler*, 18.

[45] See N. 14 in Hitler, *Mein Kampf: Eine kritische Edition*, eds. Hartmann et al., Band I, 130.

[46] Kubizek, *The Young Hitler I Knew*, 105.

[47] This willingness to tear down and reconstruct buildings on paper was not absolute, however. As a dictator in later decades, Hitler would prove willing to defer to select architects whom he held in the highest esteem; in almost every other area of life, he never yielded—he detested "experts." Perhaps the dictator's depth of knowledge about architecture opened his eyes to his intellectual limitations with the topic; see Speer, *Inside the Third Reich*, 41.

[48] Quoted in Kershaw, *Hitler: 1936-1945 Nemesis*, 181, 231.

[49] Kershaw, *Hitler: 1889-1936*, 22-23; Longerich, *Hitler: A Biography*, 19.

[50] Kubizek remembered that Dr. Bloch was "known in the town as the 'poor people's doctor', an excellent physician and a man of great kindness who sacrificed for his patients." See idem., *The Young Hitler I Knew*, 133; Toland, *Adolf Hitler*, Vol. 1, 24.

[51] Bloch, "'My Patient, Hitler,'" 36.

[52] Bloch, ibid.; N. 75 in Hitler, *Mein Kampf: Eine kritische Edition*, eds. Hartmann et al., Band I, 122-123.

[53] Bloch, ibid.; quoted in Toland, *Adolf Hitler*, Vol. 1, 24.

[54] Hitler, *Mein Kampf: Eine kritische Edition*, eds. Hartmann et al., Band I, 122-123, N. 75.

[55] Bloch, "'My Patient, Hitler'", *Collier's*, March 15, 1941, 39.

[56] Ibid. Klara, recalled Dr. Bloch, "was soft-spoken, patient; more concerned about what would happen to her family than she was about her approaching death. She made no secret of these worries; or about the fact that most of her thoughts were for her son."

[57] Hitler, *Mein Kampf: Eine kritische Edition*, eds. Hartmann et al., Band I, 129; Kershaw quotes a different translation of this line in idem., *Hitler: 1889-1936*, 24.

[58] Quoted in Bulloch, *Hitler*, 30; Kershaw, *Hitler: 1889-1936*, 24.

[59] Quoted in Hitler, *Mein Kampf: Eine kritische Edition*, eds. Hartmann et al., Band I, 131.

[60] Hitler remarked on as much in ibid.

[61] Kershaw, *Hitler: 1889-1936*, 24; Longerich, *Hitler: A Biography*, 19-20.

[62] See N. 13 in Hitler, *Mein Kampf: Eine kritische Edition*, eds. Hartmann et al., Band I, 130; see also Longerich, *Hitler*, 22.

[63] Kubizek, *The Young Hitler I Knew*, 132. Gustl notes: "The little one [Paula, age 11] had to go to school every day, Angela [her daughter in law] had enough worries...(she was expecting a second baby), and she could not rely on her son-in-law Raubal at all. Since she [Klara] had taken Adolf's side and supported him in his decision to go to Vienna, Raubal had been angry with her and now never showed up; had even prevented his wife Angela from looking after her."

[64] Kubizek, ibid., 134.

[65] Quoted in Rudolph Binion, *Hitler Among the Germans* (New York: Elsevier, 1976), 17.

[66] Ibid., 18.

[67] Bloch, "'My Patient, Hitler,'" 39.

[68] Hamann, *Hitler's Vienna*, 377. One of Hitler's valets, Karl Wilhelm Krause,

recalled the dictator saying: "My mother died on a Christmas Eve [*sic*] under the Christmas tree."

[69] Hitler, who initially considered going to Stefanie's home, declined an invitation from Kubizek to join his family for Christmas. See *The Young Hitler I Knew*, 140.

[70] Hamann, *Hitler's Vienna*, 377.

[71] Eduard Bloch, "'My Patient, Hitler'"; N. 78 in Hitler, *Mein Kampf: Eine kritische Edition*, eds. Christian Hartmann et al., Band I, 124; Toland, *Adolf Hitler*, Vol. 1, 29; Kershaw, *Hitler: 1889-1936*, 24.

[72] Bloch, "'My Patient, Hitler,'" 39. For more on Dr. Eduard Bloch, see Brigitte Hamann, *Hitlers Edeljude: Das Leben des Armenarztes Eduard Bloch* (Munich: Piper, 2008).

[73] *Hitler's Table Talk, 1941-1944*, 36.

[74] Kubizek, *The Young Hitler I Knew*, 143.

[75] Kubizek, ibid., 143-144; Kershaw, *Hitler: 1889-1936*, 25. On the offer to become a baker, see Kubizek, ibid., 125.

[76] Paula quoted in N. 78 in Hitler, *Mein Kampf: Eine kritische Edition*, eds. Hartmann et al., Band I, 124.

[77] Kubizek, *The Young Hitler I Knew*, 146-147.

[78] Hitler convinced their landlord to give up her own room so they could share it and fit in a piano for August; they had to pay double-rent. Kubizek, *The Young Hitler I Knew*, 154-155; Toland, *Adolf Hitler*, Vol. 1, 33-34; Kershaw, *Hitler: 1889-1936*, 47.

[79] Ibid.

[80] Kubizek, *The Young Hitler I Knew*, 158, 168-169, 189-203.

[81] Ibid., 200.

[82] Ibid., 194.

[83] Ibid., 156-157.

[84] Ibid., 212-213.

[85] Ibid., 152-153.

[86] Ibid., 157-158; Kershaw, *Hitler: 1889-1936*, 36-37, 44; Longerich, *Hitler: A Biography*, 23.

[87] N. 17 in Hitler, *Mein Kampf: Eine kritische Edition*, eds. Hartmann et al., Band I, 130.

[88] Ibid., 130, N. 11.

[89] Kubizek, *The Young Hitler I Knew*, 117.

[90] Ibid., 118.

Chapter 16 (Stalin)

[1] Childhood friend Joseph [Ioseb] Iremashvili declares that Stalin as a revolutionary ultimately had little in common with the literary "Koba." See idem., *Stalin und die Tragödie Georgiens*, 38.

[2] Quoted in Anton Antonov-Ovseyenko, *The Time of Stalin: Portrait of a Tyranny*, trans. George Saudners (New York: Harper & Row, Publishers, 1981), 249.

[3] Montefiore, *Young Stalin*, 35; Kotkin, *Stalin: Waiting for Hitler*, 887.

[4] Molotov, *Molotov Remembers*, 164, 174; Edvard Radzinsky, *Stalin: The First In Depth Biography...* (New York: Doubleday, 1997), 63; Montefiore, *Young Stalin*, 208. The immense evil of Stalin's crimes as a dictator have not deterred internet commentators from emphasizing his youthful good looks. For instance, A Tumblr blog from 2013-2015—named "Fuck Yeah Young Stalin"—emphasized the young revolutionary's attractiveness with forlorn, counterfactual cognizance of his extreme cruelty later in life, stating: "Here, Young Stalin is not the same as the evil, mass murdering dictator he grew up to be. He's simply a hot young Russian poet with a revolutionary streak. With emphasis on hot. Red hot." More recently, a Nov. 2021 tweet from a teacher about his students' fixation on young Stalin's good looks ["Help, my students are referring to Joseph Stalin as Joseph the Stallion after I showed them pictures of young Stalin."] received over 203,600 likes. Such posts—if in poor taste from the perspective of some—remind us that the dictator's youthful appearance mattered, then and now. See:
https://web.archive.org/web/20210216025415/https://fuckyeahyoungstalin.tumblr.com/
https://twitter.com/JacobDisagrees/status/1465415594648522753
Accessed December 8, 2021.

[5] Eugene Lyons, in an early biography, put it well: "Only the toughest, the most fanatic—and the most ambitious—remained in the hard, dangerous, and unprofitable career [of rebellion and revolution]," see idem., *Stalin: Czar of all the Russians* (New York: JB Lippincott Company, 1940), 75.

[6] Quoted in Suny, *Stalin: Passage to Revolution*, 334.

[7] Ibid. See how Stalin treated a fellow Bolshevik who slept too much in Montefiore *Young Stalin*, 141.

[8] "The rose bud had blossomed out," went one such poem by Stalin. "Reaching out to touch the violet. The lily was waking up. And bending its head in the breeze." Professor Donald Rayfield, who has translated and analyzed Stalin's youthful poems, offers guarded praise—"one might even find reasons not purely political

for regretting Stalin's switch from poetry to revolution." See idem., "Stalin as Poet," *PN Review* 11, 1 (1984): 45-47.

[9] Radzinsky put it cogently: "Koba killed people."; see idem., *Stalin*, 63. Emil Ludwig described him in power as a "man without nerves....utterly serene and self-confident" in *Stalin* (New York: G.P. Putnam's Sons, 1942), 5-6.

[10] The name Koba (from Kazbegi's *The Patricide*) lent young Stalin the Robin Hood allure of his country's "favorite romantic brigand who robs the rich for the sake of the poor." See Montefiore, *Young Stalin*, 63; Kalder, *The Infernal Library*, 41. "Koba" was also the nickname of Stalin's patron and "surrogate father" as a boy; see Kotkin, *Stalin: Paradoxes of Power*, 24, 28.

[11] Kotkin, *Stalin: Paradoxes of Power*, 105; Service, *Stalin*, 64; Montefiore, *Young Stalin*, 140-141; Suny, *Stalin: Passage to Revolution*, 334.

[12] Joseph Stalin, *Works 1: 1901-1907* (Moscow: Foreign Languages Publishing House, 1952), 191, 194.

[13] Alex De Jonge's words in *Stalin: And the Shaping of the Soviet Union* (New York: William Morrow and Company, Inc., 1986), 68.

[14] Leon Trotsky notes how rare this was of communist revolutionaries at the time, stating: "There was hardly a single case of a revolutionary intellectual marrying a believer." See idem., *Stalin: An Appraisal of the Man and His Influence* trans. Charles Malamuth (London: Hollis and Carter, Ltd, 1947), 86; quoted in Radzinsky, *Stalin*, 63.

[15] Iremashvili, *Stalin und die Tragödie Georgiens*, 39; Montefiore, *Young Stalin*, 140.

[16] Montefiore, *Young Stalin,* 159; Service, *Stalin*, 64; Kotkin, *Stalin: Paradoxes of Power*, 105.

[17] One early biography, in reductive contrast, described Kato as "scarcely more than a shadow on his [Stalin's life]. A meek, deeply devout girl, oriental in her submission to a man's world, she did not inquire into her husband's preoccupations." See Lyons, *Stalin: Czar of all the Russians*, 76.

[18] Kotkin, *Stalin: Paradoxes of Power,* 105; Service, *Stalin*, 64; Montefiore, *Young Stalin*, 141.

[19] Suny, *Stalin: Passage to Revolution*, 334.

[20] Montefiore, *Young Stalin*, 160.

[21] Kotkin, *Stalin: Paradoxes of Power,* 105; Service, *Stalin*, 64; Montefiore, *Young Stalin*, 141. Kamo quoted in Suny, *Stalin: Passage to Revolution*, 335; Ostrovskii, *Kto stoial za spinoi Stalina?*, Chapter 5, From Stockholm to London.

22 Quoted in Rosemary Sullivan, *Stalin's Daughter: The Extraordinary and Tumultuous Life of Svetlana Alliluyeva* (New York: HarpersCollins, 2015), 17; Montefiore notes that this quote comes from an interview with Svetlana Alliluyeva; see idem., *Young Stalin*, 159, 408, EN 7.

23 Montefiore, *Young Stalin*, 159.

24 Quoted in Ibid., 160; Kotkin, *Stalin: Paradoxes of Power*, 105.

25 Stalin, *Works 1: 1901-1907*, 297-372.

26 As Montefiore stated in summary: "There was no honeymoon."; see idem., *Young Stalin*, 160.

27 Iremashvili, *Stalin und die Tragödie Georgiens*, 39; quoted in H. Montgomery Hyde, *Stalin: The History of a Dictator* (London: Rupert Hart-Davis, 1971), 60.

28 Montefiore writes: "The Svanidze memoirs show that, far from being innocently oblivious to Stalin's double life, Kato was perfectly aware that she was married to the godfather of bank robberies." See idem., *Young Stalin*, 180.

29 Montefiore, *Young Stalin*, 166-167; Suny, *Stalin: Passage to Revolution*, 335-336; Kotkin, *Stalin: Paradoxes of Power*, 106.

30 Ibid.

31 Montefiore, *Young Stalin*, 167; Kotkin, *Stalin: Paradoxes of Power*, 106.

32 Quoted in Montefiore, ibid.

33 Montefiore, ibid., 167-177.

34 Stalin, of course, never admitted to having anything to do with the robbery. When writer Emil Ludwig asked him in 1931, in so many words, whether he had anything to do with it, Stalin "began to laugh in that heavy way of his, blinked several times, and stood up...walked over, with his somewhat dragging footsteps to the writing desk, and brought me a pamphlet of about thirty pages, his [official] biography...but there was nothing in it, of course, about my question. 'You will find all the necessary information in here,' he said, and laughed slyly..." See idem., *Stalin*, 42.

35 Suny, *Stalin: Passage to Revolution*, 365-368; Montefiore, *Young Stalin*, 180-181.

36 Ibid.; Kotkin, *Stalin: Paradoxes of Power*, 113-114; Ostrovskii, *Kto stoial za spinoi Stalina?*, Chapter 5, In the Baku Underground. Iremashvili references the robbery in *Stalin und die Tragödie Georgiens*, 32-33. Stalin later used the phrase "How r-r-revolutionary" in "Dizzy with Success: Concerning Questions of the Collective-Farm Movement, *Pravda*, March 2, 1930" in J. V. Stalin, *Works*, Vol. 12 (Moscow: Foreign Languages Publishing House, 1955), 197-205.

37 Suny, Montefiore, Kotkin, Ostrovskii, ibid.

[38] Quoted in Montefiore, *Young Stalin*, 179.

[39] Later, in 1941, Stalin executed Kato's brother Alyosha (along with his wife) and her sister Mariko; her sister Sashiko perhaps avoided the same end by dying of cancer in 1936. Stalin initially offered Alyosha a pardon if he—a former comrade from the early days—would ask forgiveness for being a Nazi spy. Kato's brother refused, stating: "What am I supposed to ask forgiveness for? I have committed no crimes." Stalin had him shot, remarking: "See how proud he is: he died without asking forgiveness." Quoted in in Robert Conquest, *The Great Terror: A Reassessment* (Oxford: Oxford University Press, 1990, 2008), 68; Montefiore, *Young Stalin*, 9.

[40] Montefiore, *Young Stalin*, 180; Suny, *Stalin: Passage to Revolution*, 378.

[41] Ostrovskii, *Kto stoial za spinoi Stalina?*, Chapter 5, In the Baku Underground.

[42] Ibid.; Radzinsky, *Stalin*, 64; Montefiore, *Young Stalin*, 186; Suny, *Stalin: Passage to Revolution*, 378.

[43] Joseph Stalin, "The Dispersion of the Duma and the Tasks of the Proletariat," in *Works 2: 1907-1913*, 46.

[44] "This *was* a cause: socialism and social justice, alongside the project of his own advancement," Kotkin writes. "Nothing—not the teenage girls, the violence, the camaraderie—diverted him from what became his life mission. See idem., *Stalin: Paradoxes of Power*, 9-10.

[45] As Kato's brother-in-law, Mikheil Monoselidze stated: "Soso would go early in the morning and return late at night while Kato sat home with a tiny baby terrified that he would be arrested. Bad diet, little sleep, the heat, and stress weakened her, and she fell ill. Surrounded by strangers, she had no friends around her. Soso was so busy he forgot his family!" Quoted in Suny, *Stalin: Passage to Revolution*, 398.

[46] Montefiore, *Young Stalin*, 190.

[47] Quoted in Suny, *Stalin: Passage to Revolution*, 398.

[48] Montefiore, *Young Stalin*, 190-191.

[49] Kato's family said she died of typhus and hemorrhagic colitis, but disagreements remain. Montefiore states she "almost certainly...suffered intestinal or peritoneal TB..." See idem., *Young Stalin*, 191.

[50] Iremashvili notes that she insisted that Soso give her a religious burial; see idem., *Stalin und die Tragödie Georgiens*, 40; quoted in Brackman, *The Secret File of Joseph Stalin*, 72.

[51] Stalin read Dostoevsky during his seminary days—though there is no evidence he read *The Idiot* in particular. The seminary library's copy of Dostoevsky's *Demons*— which somehow made its way into the institution's library—was supposedly

heavily marked up by the young student. See Donald Rayfield, *Stalin and His Hangmen: An Authoritative Portrait of a Tyrant and Those Who Killed for Him* (New York: Random House, 2004), 23; Montefiore, *Young Stalin*, 63.

[52] Fyodor Dostoyevsky, *The Idiot*, trans. Henry and Olga Carlisle (New York: Signet Classic, 1969, 2002), 22-23.

[53] The opposite of "The devil is not so terrible as he is painted."—a saying Stalin used in his first major speech to the Soviet people after Nazi Germany invaded the USSR. See "Speech at the Red Army Parade on the Red Square, Moscow, November 7, 1941," J.V. Stalin Archive, Works by Decade:
https://web.archive.org/web/20210419231336/https://www.marxists.org/reference/archive/stalin/works/1941/11/07.htm
Accessed July 30, 2021.

[54] Montefiore, *Young Stalin*, 192; Iremashvili, *Stalin und die Tragödie Georgiens*, 39-40.

[55] Iremashvili, ibid. Kato's funeral announcement in the newspaper stated the time of the funeral; Ostrovskii, *Kto stoial za spinoi Stalina?*, Chapter 5, In the Baku Underground.

[56] Iremashvili, *Stalin und die Tragödie Georgiens*, 40; quoted in Trotsky, *Stalin*, 87.

[57] Trotsky, *Stalin: An Appraisal of the Man*, 87.

[58] Quoted in Montefiore, *Young Stalin*, 192; Suny, *Stalin: Passage to Revolution*, 466.

[59] Ibid., 193.

[60] Ostrovskii, however, notes that it is not certain where Stalin was from late November to December 1907. See idem., *Kto stoial za spinoi Stalina?*, Chapter 5, In the Baku Underground.

[61] Quoted in Montefiore, *Young Stalin*, 193.

[62] Though, as Montefiore notes, "Sometimes Stalin managed to show brisk affection: he sent him [for example] one of his books, *The Conquest of Nature*, inscribing it: "Yasha read this book at once. J. Stalin." See idem., *Stalin: Court of the Red Tsar*, 117.

[63] The first K presumably stood for Koba. Joseph Stalin, *Works 2: 1907-1913* (Moscow: Foreign Languages Publishing House, 1953), 131, 168, 294. In October 1917, he signed a *Rabochy Put* piece as "K. Stalin"—did the K stand for Koba or Kato? See Joseph Stalin, *Works 3: 1917 March - October* (Moscow: Foreign Languages Publishing House, 1953), 382. Montefiore notes his use of K. Kato in idem., *Young Stalin*, 193.

[64] Iremashvili, *Stalin und die Tragödie Georgiens*, 40.

[65] Ibid.; Hyde's translation in *Stalin*, 91.

[66] Alliluyev, *One More Year*, 142.

Chapter 17 (Mao)

[1] Xiaoyu, *Mao Tse-Tung and I were Beggars*, 32. Xiaoyu [Xiao Zisheng] contradicts himself on this, writing "I should say not [on whether Mao had a good foundation in the classics and philosophy]! He never did read much from the classics and he never cared for studying from books [*sic*]; yet he then writes just 13 pages later: "He spent most of his time reading old classical essays and history." See Ibid., 54, 67.

[2] Ibid., 31-33.

[3] Ibid., 4-5. "Me? I'm not afraid of the devil himself!"—went the saying in Hunan; see ibid., 4.

[4] Ibid., 31.

[5] Li, *The Private Life of Chairman Mao*, 99, 102-103.

[6] Mao's words in response to entreaties for dental hygiene; quoted in ibid., 102.

[7] Xiaoyu, *Mao Tse-Tung and I were Beggars*, 69.

[8] Ibid., 68-69. Xiaoyu's statement on sweeping is a reference to the Chinese saying: "if one does not sweep his room, how might he sweep the world?" The original Chinese is "一屋不扫何以扫天下," literally: "[If one] does not sweep a room, how [is one] to sweep the world." There is a little play on the word "sweep" here: in Chinese, it can mean either to sweep with a broom, or to conquer.

[9] On other teachers that influenced Mao in these years, see Pang and Jin, *Mao Zedong: A Biography*, 23-24.

[10] Ibid., 38; Pang and Jin, *Mao Zedong: A Biography*, 21-22. Yang, as the writer Ross Terrill put it memorably, "was a vessel of old China in the grip of the currents of new China."; see idem., *Mao: A Biography* (New York: Harper & Row Publishers, 1980), 29.

[11] Yang on will and cold water quoted in Xiaoyu, *Mao Tse-Tung and I were Beggars*, 41.

[12] Xiao, *Mao Tse-Tung: His Childhood and His Youth*, 40-41.

[13] See Mao's lecture notes from a November 1, 1913 lecture by Yang—"November 1 Self-Cultivation," in Schram, ed., *Mao's Road to Power: Revolutionary Writings, 1912-1949*, Vol. 1, 14-15.

[14] Quoted in Li, *The Early Revolutionary Activities of Comrade Mao Tse-Tung*, 28.

[15] Snow, *Red Star Over China*, 146.

[16] Schram, *Mao Tse-Tung*, 41-42. The "three bonds"—ruler to ruled; father to son; husband to wife—did not obviate the need for individual struggle. In such

arguments, Yang particularly drew on the teachings of Wang Fuzhi and Tan Sitong, thus bringing those thinkers to Mao's attention; see Li, *The Early Revolutionary Activities of Comrade Mao Tse-Tung*, 17.

[17] Snow, *Red Star Over China*, 143; Pang and Jin, *Mao Zedong: A Biography*, 22.

[18] Terrill, *Mao: A Biography*, 29-31.

[19] "Letter to a Friend," in Schram, ed., *Mao's Road to Power: Revolutionary Writings, 1912-1949*, Vol. 1, 67-69. Mao went on to suggest that Xiao Zhisheng was capable of grasping Yang's teachings and potentially even expanding on them. Schram notes that "Already he has learned from the Chinese admirers of the nineteenth-century European liberal tradition (including Yang Ch'ang-chi) that the energy for making a nation rich and powerful is hidden within each member of society, and can be released only by stimulating individual initiative." See idem., *Mao Tse-Tung*, 42.

[20] Terrill's words in *Mao: A Biography*, 31.

[21] Quoted in Li, *The Early Revolutionary Activities of Comrade Mao Tse-Tung*, 18. On the impact of such thinking, see Pantsov and Levine, *Mao: The Real Story*, 40.

[22] "Letter to Xiao Zisheng," in Schram, ed., *Mao's Road to Power: Revolutionary Writings, 1912-1949*, Vol. 1, 72-74.

[23] Li, *The Early Revolutionary Activities of Comrade Mao Tse-Tung*, 18.

[24] Schram, ed., *Mao's Road to Power: Revolutionary Writings, 1912-1949*, Vol. 1, 250; different translation quoted in Chang and Halliday, *Mao: The Unknown Story*, 15.

[25] See Mao Zedong, "ON NEW DEMOCRACY, January 1940," *Selected Works of Mao Tse-tung*:

https://web.archive.org/web/20210418175334/https://www.marxists.org/reference/archive/mao/selected-works/volume-2/mswv2_26.htm

Accessed July 31, 2021. On the Buddhist origins of this phrase, see Lu Dadong, "The Sound of One Hand: Between Meaning and No-Meaning," in *New Thoughtfulness in Contemporary China: Critical Voices in Art and Aesthetics*, Jörg Huber and Zhao Chuan, eds. (New Brunswick: Transaction Publishers, 2011), 29-30.

[26] Quoted in Chang and Halliday, *Mao: The Unknown Story*, 22; see also Pang and Jin, *Mao Zedong: A Biography*, 22-23.

[27] Pang and Jin, ibid.; Li, *The Early Revolutionary Activities of Comrade Mao Tse-Tung*, 16-17.

[28] Xiaoyu, *Mao Tse-Tung and I were Beggars*, 40-45.

[29] Ibid., 43-44, 62; Chang and Halliday, *Mao: The Unknown Story*, 23-25. As Xiaoyu notes, Mao also had a serious relationship with Tao Szu-yung in 1920; he states

that he fell in love with her first and then became involved with Kaihui. Chang and Halliday argue that this relationship continued during his involvement with Kaihui.

[30] Chang and Halliday, *Mao: The Unknown Story*, 81-82. Mao's personal physician noted, in contrast, that the leader never spoke of her [in front of the doctor at least] and was wholly lacking in empathy and feeling altogether. "Perhaps," the doctor reflected, "he had seen so many people die that he had become inured to human suffering….As for those who had died, he would simply say that 'lives have to be sacrificed for the cause of revolution.'" See Li, *The Private Life of Chairman Mao*, 121.

[31] Mao Zedong, "REPLY TO LI SHU-YI, May 11, 1957," *Selected Works of Mao Tse-Tung*:

https://web.archive.org/web/20210730012124/https://www.marxists.org/reference/archive/mao/selected-works/poems/poems24.htm

Accessed July 31, 2021.

[32] Pang and Jin, *Mao Zedong: A Biography*, 27-28.

[33] Xiaoyu, *Mao Tse-Tung and I were Beggars*, 76.

[34] Snow, *Red Star Over China*, 144; Pantsov and Levine, *Mao: The Real Story*, 43.

[35] Xiaoyu, *Mao Tse-Tung and I were Beggars*, 151-154.

[36] Ibid., 130.

[37] Ibid., 129-133; some of this argument is quoted in Pantsov and Levine, *Mao: The Real Story*, 43.

[38] Schram, ed., *Mao's Road to Power: Revolutionary Writings, 1912-1949*, Vol. 1, xxxi, 263-264.

[39] Ibid.

[40] Pantsov and Levine, *Mao: The Real Story*, 45-46.

[41] For more on the "New People's Study Association [*Xinmin Xuehui*]," see Museum of the Chinese Revolution and Hunan Provincial Museum, eds., *Xinmin Xuehui Ziliao* [Sources for the New Citizen Study Society] (Beijing: People's Press, 1980).

[42] Snow, *Red Star Over China*, 146-147; Xiaoyu, *Mao Tse-Tung and I were Beggars*, 56-60; Li, *The Early Revolutionary Activities of Comrade Mao Tse-Tung*, 75-77, 163-164; Robert A. Scalapino, "The Evolution of a Young Revolutionary—Mao Zedong in 1919-1921," *The Journal of Asian Studies* Vol. 42, No. 1 (Nov., 1982), 31, FN 3. Some of the first members, for example, were Cai Hesen, Li Weihan, He Shuheng—early members of the CCP.

[43] Li, *The Early Revolutionary Activities of Comrade Mao Tse-Tung*, 76-78. Cai Hesen and He Shuheng, for instance, were both executed by the KMT in 1928.

[44] For Xiaoyu's description of their falling out, see *Mao Tse-Tung and I were Beggars*, 188-206. Mao said little about Xiaoyu to Edgar Snow, beyond acknowledging his Hunan travels with him. He ended his thoughts on his former friend by stating: "Hsiao Yu...later became a Kuomintang official in Nanking....Hsiao Yu [was] appointed to the office of custodian of the Peking Palace Museum. Hsiao sold some of the most valuable treasures in the museum and absconded with the funds in 1934. See Snow, *Red Star Over China*, 144.

[45] Pang and Jin, *Mao Zedong: A Biography*, 32-33.

[46] Schram, ed., *Mao's Road to Power: Revolutionary Writings, 1912-1949*, Vol. 1, 187-190.

[47] Ibid., 200-201.

[48] Ibid., 251. Quoted in Pantsov and Levine, *Mao: The Real Story*, 40-41.

[49] Schram, ibid., 252.

[50] Mao reflected: "Whether or not the soul remains immortal...does not depend on the length of life, but on the amount of one's achievement, which is really immortal." See Schram, *Mao's Road to Power: Revolutionary Writings, 1912-1949*, Vol. 1, xxvi.

[51] Xiaoyu, *Mao Tse-Tung and I were Beggars*, 55.

Chapter 18 (Kim)

[1] Kim, *With the Century*, Vol. 2, 4; Sohn, *Kim Il Sung and Korea's Struggle*, 12-13, 131-204. Savior quote in Sohn, ibid., 34.

[2] The inability to maintain a Korean Communist Party on the Korean peninsula—as well as widespread factionalism in the Korean communist movement, among other significant problems—led to the dissolution of the party in July 1928. As Buzo states: "[Thereafter,] the Korean communist movement...functioned as a collection of different movements, each possessing distinct organizations, hierarchies, histories and personal networks." See idem., *The Guerilla Dynasty*, 7; Suh, *The Korean Communist Movement, 1918-1948*, 178. On Kim Il-sung amid the aftermath of the Korean Communist Party's dissolution, see Wada, *Bukan Hyeondaesa*, 26.

[3] Quoted from Kim, *With the Century*, Vol. 2, 67.

[4] Buzo, *The Guerilla Dynasty*, 3; Yang, *Korea and Two Regimes*, 81.

[5] Suh, *The Korean Communist Movement, 1918-1948*, 132; quoted in Gauthier, "The Other Korea," 26-27.

[6] Suh, *Kim Il Sung*, 12.

[7] Hallett Abend, "Stolen Plum Came Near Causing War," *New York Times*, February 22, 1931, 47; quoted in Gauthier "The Other Korea," 26. Korean and Chinese communists lent each other armed support for years—most significantly, during the Chinese Civil War and the Korean War.

[8] Wada, *Bukan Hyeondaesa*, 27; Lankov states that he first began to use the name around 1935; see idem., *From Stalin to Kim Il Sung*, 53.

[9] Suh, *Kim Il Sung*, 11. For Kim's explanation of how he came to go by the name, see *With the Century*, Vol. 2, 104-105.

[10] Suh, *The Korean Communist Movement, 1918-1948*, 259; cited by Martin, *Under the Loving Care*, 730, EN 5.

[11] Suh, *Kim Il Sung*, 1-54; Suh, *The Korean Communist Movement, 1918-1948*, 256-257; Martin, *Under the Loving Care*, 29-30.

[12] Kim, *With the Century*, Vol. 2, 297-315; Wada, *Bukan Hyeondaesa*, 27; Suh, *Kim Il Sung*, 12.

[13] Yang, *Korea and Two Regimes*, 81; Suh, *The Korean Communist Movement, 1918-1948*, 268; Buzo, *The Guerilla Dynasty*, 3.

[14] Quoted in Yang, *Korea and Two Regimes*, 80. This is an old anecdote that Kim also told Anna Louise Strong before the Korean War; see Strong, *Inside North Korea: An Eye-Witness Account*, 18.

[15] Yang, *Korea and Two Regimes*, 81-82.

[16] As Dae-sook Suh stated: "Kim's accomplishments are impressive...but what is most damaging to his record is his exaggerated claims." See idem., *Kim Il Sung*, 30.

[17] Han Hongkoo, "Wounded Nationalism: The Minsaengdan Incident and Kim Il Sung in Eastern Manchuria," Ph.D. diss., University of Washington (1999), 177-178.

[18] Ibid., 182-183, 185, 347; Cumings, *North Korea: Another Country*, 111. For more on the Minsaengdan Incident, see Hongkoo Han, "Colonial Origins of Juche: The Minsaengdan Incident of the 1930s and the Birth of the North Korea-China Relationship" in J.J. Suh ed., *Origins of North Korea's Juche, Colonialism, War, and Development* (Lanham: Lexington Books, 2013), 33-62; cited by James Person, "Chinese-North Korean Relations: Drawing the Right Historical Lessons," The Woodrow Wilson International Center for Scholars, October 19, 2017: https://web.archive.org/web/20210215043543/https://www.wilsoncenter.org/article/chinese-north-korean-relations-drawing-the-right-historical-lessons Archived December 8, 2021.

[19] Suh, *Kim Il Sung*, 34.

[20] Buzo, *The Guerilla Dynasty*, 9; Han, "Wounded Nationalism: The Minsaengdan Incident and Kim Il Sung in Eastern Manchuria," 351-352.

[21] His division was in the Second Army of the CCP-led Northeast Anti-Japanese United Army. Kim never commanded more than several hundred guerillas at most. See Suh, *Kim Il Sung*, 20-22; Suh, *The Korean Communist Movement, 1918-1948*, 431; Lankov, *From Stalin to Kim Il Sung*, 53; Han, "Wounded Nationalism," 328.

[22] Quoted in Han, "Wounded Nationalism," 333-334; Cumings, *North Korea: Another Country*, 105-106.

[23] Han's words in ibid., 335-336.

[24] Ibid., 336, 340, 358.

[25] Suh, *Kim Il Sung*, 36.

[26] Ibid. 38.

[27] Ibid., 34-36, 38.

[28] Ibid.; Lankov, *From Stalin to Kim Il Sung*, 53-54. Take a look at North Korean elementary school books in the Republic of Korea's "North Korea Resource Center" (Tongilbu Bukan-jaryosenteo) at the ROK National Library (Guglibjung-angdoseogwan) in Seoul.

[29] Suh, *Kim Il Sung*, 38-39.

[30] Emphasis added. Quoted in full in Dae-sook Suh, *Documents of Korean Communism, 1918-1945* (Princeton, N.J.: Princeton University Press, 1970,) 449; Martin, *Under the Loving Care*, 40. Kim Il-sung's name is not signed to this note or others; but it is signed from the same army group and division that included the bulk of North Korea's future leaders, including Kim Il-sung, and phrases from it would reappear in Kim Il-sung's writings.

[31] Note: this letter is not from Kim's exact unit; see Suh, *Documents of Korean Communism, 1918-1945*, 450-451; Martin, *Under the Loving Care*, 41.

[32] The future dictator, one popular writer concludes as a result, became "a thug with a cause." See Blaine Harden, *The Great Leader and the Fighter Pilot* (New York: Viking, 2015), 26.

[33] Suh, *Kim Il Sung*, 38-39.

[34] Ibid., 39. The difficulty of procuring salt, and its regular absence, caused Kim and his men untold miseries; it was an especially cherished item; see Kim, *With the Century*, Vol. 7, 188.

[35] Even Kim's memoirs admit that such villages existed. *With the Century*, however, goes on to explain how Kim Il-sung and his men supposedly won over such a village *with musical theater*—a "mouthorgan concert," to be exact. See Ibid., Vol. 3, 371-389.

[36] Han states: "...Kim Il Sung and Wei Zhengmin were able to minimize the negative impact of the devastating purge and successfully restore the international united front. No doubt, it was an amazing achievement." See idem., "Wounded Nationalism," 313-317, 321, 324, 340, 352; Wei Zhengmin—Kim Il-sung's memoirs noted—told Kim that Moscow's Comintern supported the Korean struggle for independence and that the Korean communists would be responsible for it; see Kim Il Sung, *With the Century*, Vol. 4, 241; cited in Han, "Wounded Nationalism," 313.

[37] Kim, *With the Century*, Vol. 8, 81.

[38] Ibid.

[39] Ibid., 84.

[40] Such a perspective led North Korean worker Ko Tuman in 1961 to enter a boiler smokestack to clear a clog of ash while the smokestack was in operation. Rather than shutting it down and losing a few days of production, Ko voluntarily clad himself in a water-soaked heavy garment, along with a hat, mask, and goggles, and entered the working smokestack, fighting the clog amid a temperature of 572 degrees Fahrenheit while holding his breath. After five such efforts, Ko succeeded in clearing the ash, prompting the state to award him the title of labor hero. "Life is valuable," Ko recalled of his actions, "but it's not as valuable as the future of the fatherland." See Kim, *Heroes and Toilers: Work as Life in Postwar North Korea, 1953–1961*, 190.

[41] For a reference to Wei's white horse, see Kim, *With the Century*, Vol. 8, 96.

[42] Kim, *With the Century*, Vol. 8, Chapter 5, 81-99; Suh, *Kim Il Sung*, 10. For more on Wei, see Zhaoqing Guo, *Kang Ri ying xiong Wei Zhengmin*. (Shenyang: Liaoning ren min chu ban she, 1959).

[43] Han, "Wounded Nationalism," 341-343; Cumings, *North Korea: Another Country*, 106. That Song-ju let kids sleep in his bed raised a disagreement between historian Bruce Cumings and journalist Bradley K. Martin about whether that practice was the innocent continuation of an "ancient Korean custom" (Cumings's words) or an opportunity for pedophilia that resonated with Kim's later affinity for teenage girls (Martin). See Cumings ibid; in disagreement, see Martin, *Under the Loving Care*, 43-44, 809, EN 58.

[44] Kim, *With the Century*, Vol. 2, 96; quoted in Martin, *Under the Loving Care*, 41.

[45] Suh, *Kim Il Sung*, 51.

[46] Kim, *With the Century*, Vol. 3, 120-121; Martin relates the same incident in *Under the Loving Care*, 41-42.

[47] Suh, *Kim Il Sung*, 51.

[48] Quoted in Martin, *Under the Loving Care*, 204.

[49] Ibid., 204-205. Apparently Kim Jong-suk continued to defeather chickens personally even after Kim Il Sung took power.

[50] Kim, *With the Century*, Vol. 8, 83-85.

[51] Ibid., 84; Suh, *Kim Il Sung*, 47.

[52] Kim, *With the Century*, Vol. 8, 90; Vol. 2, 318.

[53] Kim, ibid., Vol. 8, 90-91; Suh, *Kim Il Sung*, 28-29.

[54] See Brandon K. Gauthier, "The Day Kim Jong Il Was Born," NKnews.org, February 15, 2013:

https://web.archive.org/web/20130224044503/https://www.nknews.org/2013/02/the-day-kim-jong-il-was-born/

Accessed July 31, 2021.

Conclusion

[1] Bloch, "'My Patient, Hitler'", 36.

[2] The U.S. genocide of Native Americans helped inspire the German dictator's *lebensraum* policy in Eastern Europe. For a summary of books on as much, see Alex Ross, "How American Racism Influenced Hitler," *The New Yorker*, April 23, 2018.

[3] On Stalin's appreciation for Russian historian R. Vipper's biography of Ivan the Terrible, see Service, *Stalin*, 341; on Stalin's notes on Napoleon's *Thoughts*, see Volkogonov, *Stalin: Triumph and Tragedy*, 101; excerpted in Robert V. Daniels, ed., *The Stalin Revolution* (New York, Houghton Mifflin Co., 1997), 14. As Montefiore previously emphasized of Stalin: "My lord was he well read; he had read his Balzac; he had read his *Forsyte Saga*; he had read Goethe; he had read his Victor Hugo." Montefiore, in response to a question on Stalin's passion for Dostoevsky, paraphrased Stalin as follows: "Dostoevsky was a genius; he really understood the psychology of the human soul, and that's why I banned him." See Interview with Simon Sebag Montefiore, Charlie Rose, May 31, 2005:

https://web.archive.org/web/20171121055020/https://charlierose.com/videos/14532

Accessed December 8, 2021.

4 On the influence of another Chinese classic in Mao's life—*Journey to the West*—see Lowell, *Maoism: A Global History*, 55.

5 GWF Hegel, *Lectures on the Philosophy of History*, trans. Ruben Alvarado (Aalten, Netherlands: WordBridge Publishing, 2011), 6.

6 Ibid.

7 Yuval Noah Harari, *Sapiens: A Brief History of Humankind* (New York: Random House, 2014), 310.

8 Hegel—whose ideas deeply influenced Marx—equates natural law and "reason" and, in doing so, suggests that universal laws—like gravity—govern all human and social events in ways that one can discover in the teleological pursuit of knowledge. Beginning his argument that "reason directs the world," he notes: "The movement of the social system takes place according to unchangeable laws. These laws are reason, implicit in the phenomena in question. But neither the sun, nor the planets which revolve around it according to these laws, can be said to have any consciousness of them. A thought of this kind—that nature is an embodiment of reason; that it is unchangeably subordinate to universal laws, appears nowise striking or strange to us. We are accustomed to such conceptions, and find nothing extraordinary in them." See GWF Hegel, *Lectures on the Philosophy of History*, 11.

9 Ibid. 19-20.

10 Ibid.

WORKS CITED

INTRODUCTION, CONCLUSION, AND MISC.

St. Augustine. *The Confessions*. Translated by Edward B. Pusey. New York: Pocket Books, Inc., 1954.

Adamovich, Ales. *Khatyn*. London: Glagoslav Publications, 2012.

Arcade Fire. *Neon Bible*. London: Rough Trade Records, 2007.

Arendt, Hannah. *The Origins of Totalitarianism*. New York: Harcourt, Inc., 1948, 1976.

Ben-Ghiat, Ruth. *Strongmen: Mussolini to the Present*. New York: W. W. Norton & Company, 2020.

Benton, Gregor and Lin Chun, eds. *Was Mao Really A Monster?: The Academic Response to Chang and Halliday's Mao: The Unknown Story*. New York: Routledge, 2009.

Browning, Christopher R. *The Path to Genocide: Essays on Launching the Final Solution*. Cambridge: Cambridge University Press, 1992.

Chaucer, Geoffrey. *The Poetical Works of Geoffrey Chaucer*. London: Routledge, 1868.

Cook, L.C. "Cardiazol Convulsion Therapy in Schizophrenia." *Proceedings of the Royal Society of Medicine*, Vol. XXXI, January 11, 1938, 567-577.

Cooper, Kathryn and Max Fink. "The chemical induction of seizures in psychiatric therapy: were flurothyl (indoklon) and pentylenetetrazol (metrazol) abandoned prematurely?" *Journal of Clinical Psychopharmacology*, Vol. 34, No. 5 (October 2014): 602-607.

Deaf Center. "Pale Ravine." UK: Type Records, 2005.

"Owl Splinters." UK: Type Records, 2011.

Defalque, Ray J. and Amos J. Wright. "Scophedal (SEE) was it a fad or a miracle drug?" *Bulletin of Anesthesia History*, Vol. 21, No. 4 (2003): 12-14.

Dikötter, Frank. *How to Be a Dictator: The Cult of Personality in the Twentieth Century*. New York: Bloomsbury, 2019.

Disasterpeace. "Hyper Light Drifter." Disasterpeace, 2016.

Dutton, Kevin. *The Wisdom of Psychopaths: What Saints, Spies, and Serial Killers Can Teach Us About Success*. New York: Scientific American/Farrar, Straus and Giroux, 2012.

Gaddis, John Lewis. *George F. Kennan: An American Life*. New York: Penguin, 2011.

Garbarino, James. *Lost Boys: Why Our Sons Turn Violent and How We Can Save Them*. New York: The Free Press, 1999.

Ghaemi, S. Nassir. *A First-Rate Madness: Uncovering the Links Between Leadership and Mental Illness*. New York: Penguin, 2012.

Gilbert, G. M. "The mentality of SS murderous robots." *Yad Vashem Studies*, Vol. 5 (1963): 35-41.

Goertzel, Victor and Mildred. *Cradles of Eminence*. Boston: Little, Brown and Company, 1962.

and Ted George Goertzel, and Ariel Hansen. *Cradles of Eminence*. Scottsdale, AZ: Great Potential Press, 2004.

Greenwood, Jonny. "There Will Be Blood (Original Motion Picture Soundtrack)." New York: Nonesuch, 2007.

"The Master (Original Motion Picture Soundtrack)." New York: Nonesuch, 2012.

"You Were Never Really Here (Original Motion Picture Soundtrack)." Los Angeles, CA: Lakeshore Records, 2018.

"Phantom Thread (Original Motion Picture Soundtrack)." New York: Nonesuch, 2018.

Harari, Yuval Noah. *Sapiens: A Brief History of Humankind*. New York: Random House, 2014.

Steve Hauschildt. "Tragedy & Geometry." Chicago, IL: Kranky, 2011.

"Sequitur." Chicago, IL: Kranky, 2012.

"S/H." Vienna: Editions Mego, 2013.

Haycock, Dean A. *Tyrannical Minds: Psychological Profiling, Narcissism, and Dictatorship*. New York: Pegasus, 2019.

Hegel, GWF. *Lectures on the Philosophy of History*. Translated by Ruben Alvarado. Aalten, Netherlands: WordBridge Publishing, 2011.

Hugo, Victor. *Les Misérables*. Philadelphia: John D. Morris & Company, Undated.

Hume, David. *A Treatise of Human Nature*. New York: E.P. Dutton & Company, Inc., 1936.

Hutchens, Robert Maynard, ed. *Great Books of the Western World: Montesquieu, Rousseau*. Chicago: William Benton, 1952.

Interview with Simon Sebag Montefiore, Charlie Rose, May 31, 2005.
https://web.archive.org/web/20171128175227/https://charlierose.com/videos/14532
Accessed December 8, 2021.

John F. Kennedy Presidential Library and Museum. "Commencement Address at American University, Washington, D.C., June 10, 1963."

https://web.archive.org/web/20210716100551/https://www.jfklibrar
y.org/archives/other-resources/john-f-kennedy-speeches/american-
university-19630610
Accessed July 28, 2021

Kalder, Daniel. *The Infernal Library: On Dictators, the Books They Wrote, and Other Catastrophes of Literacy*. New York: Henry Holt and Company, 2018.

Kershaw, Ian. "The Human Hitler." *Guardian.com*, September 17, 2004.
https://web.archive.org/web/20210610070124/https://www.theguar
dian.com/film/2004/sep/17/Germany
Accessed December 5, 2021.

Klimov, Elem. *Come and See* [*Idi i smotri*]. Moscow: Sovexportfilm, 1985.

Lewis, David Levering. *W. E. B. Du Bois, 1919-1963: The Fight for Equality and the American Century*. New York: Henry Holt and Company, 2000.

Library of Congress. "Revelations from the Russian Archives: Hanging Order, p. 1-2."
https://web.archive.org/web/20200122201840/http://www.loc.gov/
exhibits/archives/coll.html
Accessed December 5, 2021.

Loscil. "Submers." Chicago, IL: Kranky, 2002.

"Plume." Chicago, IL: Kranky, 2006.

"Endless Falls." Chicago, IL: Kranky, 2010.

"Clara." Chicago, IL: Kranky, 2010.

Malanowski, Jamie. "Human, Yes, But No Less A Monster." *New York Times*, December 22, 2002, Section 2, Page 1.
https://web.archive.org/web/20210126214557/https://www.nytimes
.com/2002/12/22/movies/human-yes-but-no-less-a-monster.html

Accessed December 5, 2021.

Martin, Benjamin G. *The Nazi-Fascist New Order for European Culture*. Cambridge, MA: Harvard University Press, 2016.

MSD Animal Health:
https://web.archive.org/web/20210121075956/https://www.msd-animal-health.co.in/products/tonophosphan-vet/
Accessed July 28, 2021.

Oneohtrix Point Never. "Replica." Brooklyn, NY: Software, 2011.

"Rifts." Brooklyn, NY: Software, 2012.

"The Fall into Time." Brooklyn, NY: Software, 2013.

Reinhardt, Jonas. "Mask of the Maker." Los Angeles, CA: Not Not Fun Records, 2013.

"Ganymede." Oakland, CA: Constellation Tatsu, 2014.

"Conclave Surge." Lucian Lift, 2017.

Reinhardt, Jonas and Jurgen Miller. "The Encyclopedia of Civilizations Vol. 1 Egypt." Lucian Lift, 2017.

Reznor, Trent and Atticus Ross. "The Social Network (Original Motion Picture Soundtrack)." Null, 2010

"Gone Girl (Original Motion Picture Soundtrack)." New York: Columbia Records, 2010

Ross, Alex. "How American Racism Influenced Hitler." *The New Yorker*, April 23, 2018.
https://web.archive.org/web/20211006104229/https://www.newyorker.com/magazine/2019/10/14/nietzsches-eternal-return

Accessed December 5, 2021.

"Nietzsche's Eternal Return." *The New Yorker*, October 14, 2019. https://web.archive.org/web/20211006104229/https://www.newyorker.com/magazine/2019/10/14/nietzsches-eternal-return Accessed December 6, 2021.

Ross, Atticus, Leopold Ross, and Claudia Sarne. "Dispatches from Elsewhere (Music from the Elsewhere Society)." Beverly Hills, CA: Lakeshore Records, 2020.

"Dispatches from Elsewhere (Music from the Jejune Institute)." Beverly Hills, CA: Lakeshore Records, 2020.

Shafer-Landau, Russ, ed. *Oxford Studies in Metaethics*, Vol. 3. New York: Oxford University Press, 2008.

Stanley-Becker, Isaac. "Twitter is eroding your intelligence. Now there's data to prove it." *Washington Post*, May 30, 2019: https://www.washingtonpost.com/nation/2019/05/30/twitter-hurting-intelligence-not-smart-study/?utm_term=.e5194fe8ca60 Accessed December 8, 2021.

Stannard, David E. *Shrinking History: On Freud and the Failure of Psychohistory*. Oxford: Oxford University Press, 1980.

Thucydides, *History of the Peloponnesian War*.

Waller, James. *Becoming Evil*. Oxford: Oxford University Press, 2002.

Weiss, Deborah. "Suffering, Sentiment, and Civilization: Pain and Politics in Mary Wollstonecraft's 'Short Residence.'" *Studies in Romanticism* Vol. 45, No. 2(Summer 2006): 199-221.

Wollstonecraft, Mary. *Letters Written During a Short Residence in Sweden, Norway, and Denmark* (1796).

https://web.archive.org/web/20210426071718/https://www.gutenbe
rg.org/files/3529/3529-h/3529-h.htm
Accessed December 5, 2021.

Zick, W. "[Experiments in therapy of mental diseases (psychoses) with the narcotic Quadro-nox]." *Therapie der Gegenwart*, Vol 93, No. 11 (1954): 432-433.
https://pubmed.ncbi.nlm.nih.gov/13226303/
Accessed July 28, 2021.

LENIN

Ali, Tariq. *The Dilemmas of Lenin: Terrorism, War, Empire, Love, Revolution*. London: Verso, 2017.

Baschet, Eric. *The Revolutionary Years: Russia 1904-1924*. Zug: Swan, 1989.

Bonch-Bruevich, V.D. "Smert' i pokhorony Vladimira Il'icha." ["Death and funeral of Vladimir Ilyich."]
https://web.archive.org/web/20210117170321/https://leninism.su/
memory/913-smert-i-poxorony-vladimira-ilicha.html
Accessed December 9, 2021.

Chernyshevsky, Nikolai. *What Is to Be Done?*. Translated by Michael R. Katz. Ithaca: Cornell University Press, 1989.

Clark, Ronald W. *Lenin*. New York: Harper & Row, 1988.

Copleston, Frederick. *Philosophy in Russia: From Herzen to Lenin and Berdyaev*. Notre Dame, IN: Search Press, 1986.

Davis, R.W., Mark Harrison, and S.G. Wheatcroft, eds. *The Economic Transformation of the Soviet Union, 1913-1945*. New York: Cambridge University Press, 1994.

D'Encausse, Hélène Carrère. *Lenin*. New York: Holmes & Meier, 2001.

Deutscher, Isaac. *Lenin's Childhood*. London: Oxford University Press, 1970.

Fischer, Louis. *Life of Lenin*. New York: Harpers & Row, 1964.

Gorky, Maxim. *Days With Lenin*. No translator listed. New York: International Publishers, 1932.

Krupskaya, Nadezhda K. *Memories of Lenin*. Translated by E. Verney. New York: International Publishers, 1930.

"Poslednie polgoda zhizni Vladimira Il'icha."
https://web.archive.org/web/20210303184903/https://leninism.su/memory/1401-poslednie-polgoda-zhizni-vladimira-ilicha.html
Accessed December 9, 2021.

Lenin, V.I. *Lenin: Collected Works*. Volume 23. Moscow: Progress Publishers, 1964.

Lenin: Collected Works. Volume 31. Moscow: Progress Publishers, 1965.

Selected Works. Volume 2. Moscow: Progress Publishers, 1975.

Selected Works. Volume 3. Moscow: Progress Publishers, 1975.

V.I. Lenin Archive. "Works by Decade":
"Socialism and Religion." *Novaya Zhizn*, No. 28, December 3, 1905:
https://web.archive.org/web/20210527033555/https://www.marxists.org/archive/lenin/works/1905/dec/03.htm
Accessed December 8, 2021.

"Lecture on the 1905 Revolution." January 9 (22), 1917.
https://web.archive.org/web/20210523173501/https://www.marxists.org/archive/lenin/works/1917/jan/09.htm
Accessed December 9, 2021

"Speech At A Meeting At The Former Michelson Works, August 30, 1918."
https://web.archive.org/web/20211101005656/https://www.marxists.org/archive/lenin/works/1918/aug/30a.htm

Accessed December 9, 2021

"Letter to the Congress [Lenin's Testament]."
https://web.archive.org/web/20210603205703/https://www.marxist
s.org/archive/lenin/works/1922/dec/testamnt/congress.htm
Accessed December 9, 2021.

"Our Foreign and Domestic Position and Party Tasks: Speech Delivered To
The Moscow Gubernia Conference Of The R.C.P.(B.), November 21,
1920."
https://web.archive.org/web/20210610004832/http://www.marxists.
org/archive/lenin/works/1920/nov/21.htm
Accessed December 5, 2021

Mark, Karl. "Marx's Mathematical Manuscripts 1881: On the Differential."
https://web.archive.org/web/20210616101220/https://www.marxist
s.org/archive/marx/works/1881/mathematical-manuscripts/
Accessed July 27, 2021.

Moynahan, Brian. *Rasputin: The Saint Who Sinned*. New York: Da Capo Press, 1997,
1999.

Montefiore, Simon Sebag. *The Romanovs: 1613-1918*. New York: Knopf, 2016.

Offord, Derek. *The Russian Revolutionary Movement in the 1880s*. Cambridge:
Cambridge University Press, 1986.

and William Leatherbarrow, eds. *A History of Russian Thought*. Cambridge:
Cambridge University Press, 2010.

Osipov, V.P. "Bolezn' i smert' Vladimira Il'icha Ul'iãnova-Lenina." ["Illness and
death of Vladimir Ilyich Ulyanov-Lenin."]
https://web.archive.org/web/20210303181033/https://leninism.su/
memory/910-bolezn-i-smert-vladimira-ilicha-ulyanova-lenina.html
Accessed July 27, 2021

Poliakov, A.S. *Vtoroe 1-e marta: Pokushenie na imperatora Aleksandra III v 1887 g. (Materialy)*. Moscow, 1919.

Pomper, Philip. *Lenin's Brother: The Origins of the October Revolution*. New York: W.W. Norton & Company, 2010.

"The Family Background of V.I. Ul'ianov's Pseudonym, 'Lenin.'" *Russian History*, Vol. 16, No. 2/4 (1989): 209-222.

Reed, John. *Ten Days That Shook The World*. New York: Modern Library, 1935.

Sukhanov, N.N. *The Russian Revolution 1917: Eyewitness Account, Volume I*. Translated by Joel Carmichael. New York: Harper & Brothers, 1962.

The Russian Revolution 1917: Eyewitness Account, Volume II. Translated by Joel Carmichael. New York: Harper & Brothers, 1962.

Service, Robert. *Lenin: A Biography*. Cambridge, MA: Harvard University Press, 2000.

A History of Twentieth-Century Russia. Cambridge, MA: Harvard University Press, 1998.

Sebestyen, Victor. *Lenin: The Man, The Dictator, and the Master of Terror*. New York: Pantheon, 2017.

Trotsky, Leon. *The Young Lenin*. Translated by Max Eastman. London: David and Charles Publishers, 1972.

On Lenin: Notes Towards a Biography. London: George G. Harrap & Co Ltd, 1971.

Turgenev, Ivan. *Smoke*. Translated by Michael Pursglove. Middletown, DE: Alama Classics, 2016.

Ulam, Adam B. *The Bolsheviks: The Intellectual and Political History of the Triumph of Communism in Russia*. New York: Macmillan Publishing Company/Harvard University Press, 1968, 1998.

Ul'yanova, A.I. *Detskie I shkol'nye gody Il'icha*. Moscow, 1990.

Ul'ianova, M. I. "O Vladimire Il'iche poslednie gody zhizni." *Izvestiia TSK KPSS*, No. 2 (1991): 125-140.

"O Vladimire Il'iche poslednie gody zhizni." *Izvestiia TSK KPSS*, No. 3 (1991): 183-200.

"O Vladimire Il'iche poslednie gody zhizni." *Izvestiia TSK KPSS*, No. 4 (1991): 177-191.

Valentinov, Nikolai. *The Early Years of Lenin*. Ann Arbor, MI: University of Michigan Press, 1969.

Volkogonov, Dmitri. *Lenin: A New Biography*. Translated by Harold Shukman. New York: The Free Press, 1994.

Williams, Albert Rhys. *Lenin: The Man and His Work*. New York: Scott and Seltzer, 1919.

Wilson, Edmund. *To the Finland* Station: *A Study in the Writing and Acting of History*. New York: Farrar, Straus, Giroux, 1940, 1987.

Zetkin, Clara. "Lenin on the Woman Question." https://web.archive.org/web/20211203233454/https://www.marxists.org/archive/zetkin/index.htm Accessed December 7, 2021.

MUSSOLINI

"Dictator's Birthday." *Time*, August 9, 1926, Vol. 8, Issue 6.

"One Man Majority." *Time*, December 31, 1928, Vol. 12, Issue 27.

Balabanoff, Angelica. *My Life as a Rebel*. Bloomington, IN: Indiana University Press, 1973; originally published by Harper & Brothers, 1938.

Il Traditore: Mussolini e La Conquista Del Potere. 1943. http://palmm.digital.flvc.org/islandora/object/fau%3A32634 Accessed December 8, 2021.

Baldoli, Claudia and Marco Fincardi. "Italian Society Under Anglo-American Bombs: Propaganda, Experience, And Legend, 1940-1." *The Historical Journal*, Vol. 52, No. 4 (December 2009): 1017-1038.

Bosworth, R.J.B. *Mussolini*. New York: Oxford University Press, 2002.

Mussolini's Italy: Life Under the Fascist Dictatorship, 1915-1945. New York: Penguin, 2006.

Claretta: Mussolini's Last Lover. New Haven, CT: Yale University Press, 2017.

Ciano, Galeazzo. *The Ciano Diaries, 1939-1943*. New York: Doubleday & Company, 1945.

Ciano, Edda Mussolini as told to Albert Zarca. *My Truth*. Translated by Eileen Finletter. New York: William Morrow and Company, Inc., 1977.

Ciano, Fabrizio. *Quando il nonno fece fucilare papà* (ed. Dino Cimagalli). Milan: Mondadori, 1991.

De Begnac, Yvon. *Taccuini mussoliniani*, ed. Francesco Perfetti. Bologna: Società editrice il Mulino, 1990.

De Felice, Renzo. *Mussolini il rivoluzionario*. Torino: Giulio Einaudi editore, 1965.

Di Scala, Spencer M. and Emilio Gentile, eds. *Mussolini 1883-1915*. New York: Palgrave Macmillan, 2016.

WORKS CITED

Falasca-Zamponi, Simonetta. *Fascist Spectacle*. Berkeley and Los Angeles, CA: University of California Press, 1997.

Farrell, Nicholas. *Mussolini: A New Life*. London: Phoenix, 2003.

Fermi, Laura. *Mussolini*. Chicago, IL: University of Chicago Press, 1961.

Gadda, Carlo Emilio. *Eros e Priapo (da furore a cenere)*. Milan: Garzanti, 1967.

Gerald R. Ford Presidential Library. National Security Adviser Trip Briefing Books and Cables for President Ford, 1974-1976, (Box 19). "Mao Book, December 1975." https://web.archive.org/web/20210413033128/https://www.fordlibrarymuseum.gov/library/document/0358/035800388.pdf Accessed December 8, 2021.

Gravelli, A. *Mussolini aneddotico*. Rome: Casa Editrice Latinità, 1951.

Gregor, A. James. *Young Mussolini and the Intellectual Origins of Fascism*. Berkeley, CA: University of California Press, 1979.

Harvey, Stephen. "The Italian War Effort and the Strategic Bombing of Italy." *History*, Vol. 70, No. 228 (1985): 32-45.

Hemingway, Ernest. "Mussolini, Europe's Prize Bluffer." *The Toronto Daily Star*, January 27, 1923.

"[Letter] to Ezra Pound, 23 January [1923]." https://web.archive.org/web/20151018152114/http://assets.cambridge.org/97805218/97341/excerpt/9780521897341_excerpt.pdf Accessed July 27, 2021.

Johnson, Bruce. ed. *Transnational Studies in Jazz: Jazz and Totalitarianism*. New York: Routledge, 2017.

Raymond Klibanksy, ed. *The Mussolini Memoirs 1942-1943: with Documents Relating to the Period*. Translated by Frances Lobb. London: Phoenix Press, 1949, 2000.

Lafont, Maria. *The Strange Comrade Balabanoff: The Life of a Communist Rebel*. Jefferson, N.C.: McFarland & Company, Inc., Publishers, 2016.

Ludwig, Emil. *Talks With Mussolini*. Translated by Eden and Cedar Paul. Boston: Little, Brown, and Company, 1933.

Luzzatto, Sergio. *The Body of Il Duce: Mussolini's Corpse and the Fortunes of Italy*. Translated by Frederika Randall. New York: Picador, 2006.

Megaro, Gaudens. *Mussolini in the Making*. Boston and New York: Houghton Mifflin Company, 1938.

Monelli, Paolo. *Mussolini: An Intimate Life*. London: Thames and Hudson, 1953.

Morewood, Steven. *The British Defence of Egypt, 1935-1940: Conflict and Crisis in the Eastern Mediterranean*. London: Frank Cass, 2005.

Morgan, Philip. *The Fall of Mussolini*. New York: Oxford University Press, 2007.

Mussolini, Benito. *My Autobiography*. New York: Charles Scribner's Sons, 1928.

> *Opera Omnia di Benito Mussolini*. Edited by Edoardo and Duilio Susmel. Florence: La Fenice-Firenze, 1951-1963.
> Vol. I
> Vol. XIV
> Vol. XXIV
> Vol. XXXIII

> *My Rise and Fall*. New York: De Capo, 1998.

Mussolini, Rachele as told to Albert Zarca. *Mussolini: An Intimate Biography by His Widow*. New York: William Morrow & Company, Inc., 1974.

Mussolini, Romano. *My Father, Il Duce: A Memoir By Mussolini's Son*. Translated by Ana Stojanovic. Carlsbad, CA: Kales Press, 2006.

O'Brien, Paul. *Mussolini in the First World War: The Journalist, the Soldier, the Fascist*. New York: Bloomsbury, 2005.

Rossato, A. *Mussolini: colloquio intimo*. Milan: Modernissima Casa Editrice Italiana, 1923.

Rosenthal, Bernice Glatzer. *New Myth, New World From Nietzsche to Stalinism*. University Park, PA: the Pennsylvania State University Press, 2010.

Saluppo, Alessandro. "Violence And Terror: Imaginaries And Practices Of Squadrismo In The Province Of Ferrara, 1914-1922." Ph.D. diss. Fordham University, 2016.

Sarfatti, Margherita G. *The Life of Benito Mussolini*. Translated by Frederic Whyte. New York: Frederick A. Stokes Company Publishers, 1927.

Schuster, Cardinal Ildefonso. *Saint Benedict and His Times*. Translated by Gregory J. Roettger. St. Louis: B. Herder Book Co., 1951.

Scurati, Antonio. *M: Il Figlio Del Secolo*. Milan: Bompiani, 2018.

　　M: L'Uomo Della Provvidenza. Milan: Bompiani, 2020.

　　M: Son of the Century. Translated by Anne Milano Appel. London: 4th Estate, 2021.

Smith, Denis Mack. *Mussolini: A Biography*. New York: Vintage Books, 1983.

Swan, Alessandra Antola. "The iconic body: Mussolini unclothed." *Modern Italy*, Vol. 21, No. 4 (2016): 361-381.

　　Photographing Mussolini The Making of a Political Icon. London: Palgrave Macmillan, 2020.

United Press. "Il Duce's Duelist Dies in Argentina." *Spartanburg Herald*, September 15, 1937, 2. https://news.google.com/newspapers?id=3kUsAAAAIBAJ&sjid=z8oEA AAAIBAJ&dq=duel%20swords&pg=3684%2C1474948 Accessed July 27, 2021.

HITLER

"Uneven Romance." *Time*, June 29, 1959. Vol. 73, Issue 26.

Aly, Götz, Peter Chroust, and Christian Pross. *Cleansing the Fatherland: Nazi Medicine and Racial Hygiene*. Baltimore, MD: Johns Hopkins University Press, 1994.

Binion, Rudolph. *Hitler Among the Germans*. New York: Elsevier, 1976.

Bloch, Eduard. "'My Patient, Hitler': A Memoir of Hitler's Jewish Physician." *Collier's*, March 15, 1941, 35-37; March 22, 1941, 69-73.

Bullock, Alan. *Hitler: A Study in Tyranny*. New York: Odhams Press, 1952.

   Hitler and Stalin: Parallel Lives. New York: HarpersCollins, 1991.

Burleigh, Michael. *Death and Deliverance: "Euthanasia" in Germany c. 1900-1945*. Cambridge: Cambridge University Press, 1994.

Childers, Thomas. *The Third Reich: A History of Nazi Germany*. New York: Simon & Schuster, 2017.

   ed. *The Formation of the Nazi Constituency*. Chapel Hill, N.C.: University of North Carolina Press, 1986.

   The Nazi Voter. Chapel Hill, N.C.: University of North Carolina Press, 1983.

Davidson, Eugene. *The Making of Adolf Hitler*. New York: Macmillan Publishing Co., Inc., 1977.

WORKS CITED

Eck, Dr. National. "Hitler's Political Testament." *Yad Vashem*, 12-19.
    https://web.archive.org/web/20210107222521/https://www.yadvash
    em.org/yv/pdf-drupal/en/eichmann-
    trial/hitlers_political_testament.pdf
    Accessed July 28, 2021.

Evans, Richard J. *The Third Reich in Power*. New York: Penguin, 2005.

    The Third Reich at War. New York: Penguin, 2009.

Fest, Joachim C. *Hitler*. Translated by Richard and Clara Winston. New York:
    Harcourt Brace, 1974.

Geary, Dick. "Who Voted for the Nazis?" *History Today*, October 19, 1998.

German History in Documents and Images.
    "Decree of the Reich President for the Protection of the People and State."
    https://web.archive.org/web/20210703110729/https://ghdi.ghidc.org
    /sub_document.cfm?document_id=2325
    Accessed July 28, 2021.

Görtemaker, Heike B. *Eva Braun: Life with Hitler*. Translated by Damion Searls. New
    York: Vintage Books, 2011.

Flood, Charles Bracelen. *Hitler: The Path to Power*. Boston: Houghton Mifflin
    Company, 1989.

Friedlander, Saul. *Nazi Germany and the Jews: Volume 1: The Years of Persecution 1933-
    1939*. New York: Harper Perennial, 1998.

Haffner, Sebastian. *The Meaning of Hitler*. Translated by Edwald Osers. Cambridge,
    MA: Harvard University Press, 1979.

Hamann, Brigitte. *Hitler's Vienna: A Dictator's Apprenticeship*. Translated by Thomas
    Thornton. Oxford: Oxford University Press, 1999.

Hitlers Edeljude: Das Leben des Armenarztes Eduard Bloch. München: Piper, 2008.

Hanisch, Reinhold. "I Was Hitler's Buddy." *New Republic*, April 5, 12, 19, 1939.

Hartmann, Christian. *Operation Barbarossa: Nazi Germany's War in the East, 1941–1945*. Oxford: Oxford University Press, 2013.

Hitler, Adolf. *Mein Kampf: Eine kritische Edition*. Edited by Christian Hartmann, Thomas Vordermayer, Othmar Plöckinger, and Roman Töppel (München–Berlin: Instituts fur Zeitgeschichte, 2016), Band I-II.

"My Political Testament," Jewish Virtual Library https://web.archive.org/web/20210418035432/https://www.jewishvi rtuallibrary.org/hitler-s-political-testament-april-1945 Accessed July 28, 2021.

Hoffman, Heinrich. *Hitler Was My Friend*. London: Burke, 1955.

Jetzinger, Franz. *Hitler's Youth*. Translated by Lawrence Wilson. London: Hutchinson, 1958.

Junge, Traudl. *Hitler's Last Secretary*. Edited by Melissa Müller. Translated by Anthea Bell. New York: Arcade Publishing, 2002, 2011.

Katz, Ottmar. *Prof. Dr. Med. Theo Morell, Hitler's Leibarzt*. Bayreuth: Hestia, 1982.

Kershaw, Ian. *Hitler: 1889-1936 Hubris*. New York: W.W. Norton & Co., 2000.

Hitler: 1936-1945 Nemesis. New York, W.W. Norton & Company, 2001.

The "Hitler Myth": Image and Reality in the Third Reich. Oxford: Oxford University Press, 1987, 2010.

The End: The Defiance and Destruction of Hitler's Germany, 1944-1945. New York: Penguin, 2011.

Kubizek, August. *The Young Hitler I Knew: The Memoirs of Hitler's Childhood Friend.* London: Greenhill Books, 2006.

Langer, Walter C. *The Mind of Adolf Hitler: The Secret Wartime Report.* New York: Basic Books, Inc., 1972.

Levi, Primo. *If This Is a Man [Survival in Auschwitz].* Translated by Stuart Woolf. New York: Orion Press, 1959.

Linge, Heinz. *With Hitler To The End: The Memoirs of Hitler's Valet.* Yorkshire, UK: Frontline Books, 2009.

Longerich, Peter. *Hitler: A Biography.* New York: Oxford University Press, 2019.

Machtan, Lothar. *The Hidden Hitler.* Translated by John Brownjohn. New York: Basic Books, 2001.

Maser, Werner. *Adolf Hitler - Legende- Mythos- Wirklicheit.* München: Bechtle Verlag, 1971.

   Hitler's Letters and Notes. Translated by Arnold Pomerans. London: Heinemann, 1973.

Misch, Rochus with Michael Stehle, Ralph Giordano, and Sandra Zarrinbal. *Hitler's Last Witness The Memoirs of Hitler's Bodyguard.* London: Scribe, 2014.

Ohler, Norman. *Blitzed: Drugs in the Third Reich.* Boston: Houghton Mifflin Harcourt, 2017.

Redlich M.D., Fritz. *Hitler: Diagnosis of a Destructive Prophet.* Oxford: Oxford University Press, 1999.

Schroeder, Christa. *Er war mein Chef: Aus dem Nachlaß der Sekretärin von Adolf Hitler.* München: Lagen Müller, 1985.

He was My Chief: The Memoirs of Adolf Hitler's Secretary. New York: Frontline Books, 2009.

Shalom, Yael Katz Ben. *The Last Witness* (Alma Films).

Speer, Albert. *Inside the Third Reich: Memoirs by Albert Speer*. Translated by Richard and Clara Winston. New York: MacMillan Company, 1970.

Tharoor, Ishaan. "All right, let's talk about Hitler's penis." *Washington Post*, February 23, 2016.
https://web.archive.org/web/20160223204402/https://www.washingtonpost.com/news/worldviews/wp/2016/02/23/all-right-lets-talk-about-hitlers-penis/
Accessed July 31, 2021.

Toland, John. *Adolf Hitler*. Vol. 1-2. Garden City: Doubleday & Co., Inc., 1976.

Ullrich, Volker. *Hitler: Ascent, 1889-1939*. Translated by Jefferson Chase. New York: Vintage Books, 2017.

United States Holocaust Memorial.
"Goebbels speaks at Sportpalast."
https://web.archive.org/web/20200327064431/https://collections.ushmm.org/search/catalog/irn1001951
Accessed July 28, 2021.

"Hitler's Aufruf an das deutsche Volk" ["Hitler's call to the German People"/Hitler's first speech as Chancellor, Berlin Sportpalast.]
https://web.archive.org/web/20210523012934/https://collections.ushmm.org/search/catalog/irn1001952
Accessed July 28, 2021.

"Nazi Party Platform."
https://web.archive.org/web/20210328101123/https://www.ushmm.org/learn/timeline-of-events/before-1933/nazi-party-platform
Accessed July 28, 2021.

WORKS CITED

von Papen, Fran. *Memoirs*. Translated by Brian Connell. London: Andrew Deutsch, 1952.

Weinberg, Gerhard L. ed. *Hitler's Table Talk, 1941-1944: His Private Conversations*. Translated by Norman Cameron and R.H. Stevens. New York: Enigma Books, 2008.

STALIN

"Central Executive Committee, On the Amendment of the Criminal Procedural Codes of the Union Republics. December 1, 1934." http://soviethistory.msu.edu/1934-2/the-kirov-affair/the-kirov-affair-texts/decree-following-kirovs-murder/ Accessed July 28, 2021.

Alliluyev, Svetlana. *Twenty Letters to a Friend*. New York: HarperColins, 1967.

One More Year. Translated by Paul Chavchavadze. New York: Harpers & Row, Pub., 1969.

Thames TV production, "USSR | Joseph Stalin | Svetlana Alliluyeva interview | 1980's" https://youtu.be/TZw3sN4XeNo Accessed July 31, 2021.

Antonov-Ovseyenko, Anton. *The Time of Stalin: Portrait of a Tyranny*. Translated by George Saudners. New York: Harper & Row, Publishers, 1981.

Applebaum, Anne. *Red Famine: Stalin's War on Ukraine*. New York: Penguin Random House, 2017.

Aranovich, Semyon. *I Served in Stalin's Guard: an Experiment in Documentary Mythology* [*I was Stalin's Bodyguard: Interviews with A.T. Rybin*]. Moscow: 1989.

Barnes, Steven A. *Death and Redemption: The Gulag and the Shaping of Soviet Society*. Princeton, N.J.: Princeton University Press, 2011.

Brackman, Roman. *The Secret File of Joseph Stalin: A Hidden Life.* London: Frank Cass, 2001.

Butler, Susan. *Roosevelt and Stalin: Portrait of a Partnership.* New York: Knopf, 2015.

Conquest, Robert. *The Great Terror: A Reassessment.* Oxford: Oxford University Press, 1990, 2008.

    Stalin: Breaker of Nations. New York: Penguin, 1991.

Crankshaw, Edward, Strobe Talbott, eds. *Khrushchev Remembers.* New York: Little, Brown, 1970.

Daniels, Robert V. ed. *The Stalin Revolution: Foundations of the Totalitarian Era.* New York: Houghton Mifflin Company, 1997.

De Jonge, Alex. *Stalin: And the Shaping of the Soviet Union.* New York: William Morrow and Company, Inc., 1986.

Dostoyevsky, Fyodor. *The Idiot.* Translated by Henry and Olga Carlisle. New York: Signet Classic, 1969, 2002.

Du Bois, W. E. B. "Stalin and American Negroes." Unpublished article for Pravda discussing race relations after Stalin's death, March 1953. https://credo.library.umass.edu/view/full/mums312-b214-i052 Accessed December 9, 2021.

    "On Stalin." *National Guardian*, March 16, 1953. https://web.archive.org/web/20210712041942/https://www.marxists.org/reference/archive/stalin/biographies/1953/03/16.htm Accessed December 9, 2021.

Getty, J. Arch and Oleg V. Naumov. *The Road to Terror: Stalin and the Self-Destruction of the Bolsheviks, 1932-1939.* New Haven: Yale University Press, 2010.

Gromyko, Andrei. *Memoirs.* New York: Doubleday, 1989.

WORKS CITED

Hyde, H. Montgomery. *Stalin: The History of a Dictator*. London: Rupert Hart-Davis, 1971.

Jughashvili, Keke. *My Dear Son: The Memoirs of Stalin's Mother*. E-book published by Ministry of Internal Affairs of Georgia, 2012; from Archive of the Central Committee of the Communist Party of Georgia, f.8, op.2, d.15

Khlevniuk, Oleg. *Stalin: New Biography of a Dictator*. Translated by Seligman Favorov. New Haven, CT: Yale University Press, 2015.

Kotkin, Stephen. *Stalin: Paradoxes of Power, 1878-1928*. New York: Penguin, 2015.

Stalin: Waiting for Hitler, 1929-1941. New York: Penguin, 2017.

Kuromiya, Hiroaki. *Stalin*. New York: Routledge, 2013.

Khrushchev, Nikita. *Memoirs of Nikita Khrushchev: Volume 1: Commissar, 1918–1945*, ed. Sergei Khrushchev. State College, PA: Penn State University Press, 2013.

Iremashvili, Joseph. *Stalin und die Tragödie Georgiens*. Berlin: Verfasser, 1932.

Lenoe, Matthew E. *The Kirov Murder and Soviet History*. New Haven: Yale University Press, 2010.

Ludwig, Emil. *Stalin*. New York: G.P. Putnam's Sons, 1942.

Lyons, Eugene. *Stalin: Czar of all the Russians*. New York: JB Lippincott Company, 1940.

McMeekin, Sean. *Stalin's War: A New History of World War II*. New York: Basic Books, 2021.

Medvedev, Roy. *The Unknown Stalin: His Life, Legacy, and Death*. Translated by Ellen Dahrendorf. New York: I.B.Tauris, 2003.

Let History Judge: The Origins and Consequences of Stalinism. New York: Columbia University Press, 1989.

Molotov, V. M. with Felix Chuev. *Molotov Remembers: Inside Kremlin Politics*. Chicago: Ivan R. Dee, Inc., 1993, 2007.

Montefiore, Simon Sebag. *Stalin: Court of the Red Tsar*. New York: Knopf, 2003.

Young Stalin. New York: Knopf, 2007.

Ostrovskii, Aleksandr V. "Predki Stalin." *Genealogicheskii vestnik*, no. 1 (2001). https://web.archive.org/web/20210224092547/http://baza.vgd.ru/1 1/56953/?pg=all
Accessed December 9, 2021

Kto stoial za spinoi Stalina?. Moscow: Tsentropoligraf-Mim, 2004.

Radzinsky, Edvard. *Stalin: The First In-depth Biography Based on Explosive New Documents from Russia's Secret Archives*. New York: Doubleday, 1997.

Rayfield, Donald. *Stalin and His Hangmen: An Authoritative Portrait of a Tyrant and Those Who Killed for Him*. New York: Random House, 2004.

"Stalin as Poet." *PN Review*. Vol. 11, No. 1 (1984): 44-7.

Roberts, Geoffrey. *Stalin's Library: A Dictator and His Books*. New Haven, CT: Yale University Press, 2022.

Rubenstein, Joshua. *The Last Days of Stalin*. New Haven: Yale University Press, 2016.

Stalin, Joseph. *Works*. Moscow: Foreign Languages Publishing House, 1952-55.
Volume 1: 1901-1907
Volume 12: 1929-1930.
Volume 13: 1930-1934.

WORKS CITED

J.V. Stalin Archive. Works by Decade:
    "Speech at Celebration Meeting of the Moscow Soviet of Working People's
    Deputies and Moscow Party and Public Organizations, November 6,
    1941."
    https://web.archive.org/web/20210420044555/https://www.marxist
    s.org/reference/archive/stalin/works/1941/11/06.htm
    Accessed July 31, 2021.

    "Speech at the Red Army Parade on the Red Square, November 7, 1941."
    https://web.archive.org/web/20210419231336/https://www.marxist
    s.org/reference/archive/stalin/works/1941/11/07.htm
    Accessed July 31, 2021.

Sullivan, Rosemary. *Stalin's Daughter: The Extraordinary and Tumultuous Life of Svetlana
    Alliluyeva.* New York: HarpersCollins, 2015.

Suny, Ronald Grigor. *Stalin: Passage to Revolution.* Princeton, N.J.: Princeton
    University Press, 2020.

    and Arthur Adams, eds. *The Russian Revolution and Bolshevik Victory.*
    Lexington: D.C. Heath & Company, 1990.

Taubman, William. *Khrushchev: The Man and His Era.* New York: W.W. Norton &
    Company, 2003.

Trotsky, Leon. *Stalin: An Appraisal of the Man and His Influence.* Translated by Charles
    Malamuth. London: Hollis and Carter, Ltd., 1947.

    Stalin: A Critical Survey of Bolshevism. New York: Alliance Book Corp.
    Longman, Green and Co., 1939.
    https://web.archive.org/web/20180715215506/https://www.marxist
    s.org/history/etol/writers/souvar/works/stalin/ch09.htm
    Accessed July 28, 2021.

Tucker, Robert C. *Stalin as Revolutionary 1878-1929: A Study in History and
    Personality.* New York: W.W. Norton & Company, 1973.

Volkogonov, Dmitrii A. *Stalin: Triumph and Tragedy*. Rocklin, CA: Prima, 1992.

Zhukov, Georgy. *Marshal of Victory: The Autobiography of General Georgy Zhukov*. 1974; South Yorkshire: Pen & Sword Books, 2013.

MAO

"Mao Cult of Personality (Propaganda) [Footage from Cultural Revolution Rally in Tiananmen square]":
https://www.youtube.com/watch?v=Vk6m7cZDgiA
Accessed December 8, 2021.

Becker, Jasper. *Hungry Ghosts: Mao's Secret Famine*. New York: Henry Holt and Company, 1996.

Chang, Jung and Jon Halliday. *Mao: The Unknown Story*. New York: Knopf, 2005.

Chang, Cai. "Huiyi Xinmin xuehui de huodong" ["Reflections of the activities of the New Citizen Association"] in *Xinmin xuehui ziliao* (*Documents Collection and Memories of the New Citizens' Study Society*). Edited by Zhongguo geming bowuguan and Hunan sheng bowuguan [The Editorial Committee of the Archives of Chinese Revolution and Hunan Provincial Archives]. Beijing: Renmin chubanshe, 1980.

Chang, Jung. *Wild Swans: Three Daughters of China*. New York: Simon & Schuster, 1991, 2003.

Ch'en, Jerome. *Mao and the Chinese Revolution*. Translated by Michael Bullock and Jerome Ch'en. New York: Oxford University Press, 1965.

Dao, Qing. *Wang Shiwei and Wild Lilies Rectification and Purges in the Chinese Communist Party 1942-1944*. Translated by Nancy Liu and Lawrence R. Sullivan. Armonk, NY: M.E. Sharpe, 1994; New York: Routledge, 2015.

Dikötter, Frank. *Mao's Great Famine: The History of China's Most Devastating Catastrophe, 1958-1962*. New York: Bloomsbury, 2010.

The Tragedy of Liberation: A History of the Chinese Revolution, 1945-1957. New York: Bloomsbury, 2015.

The Cultural Revolution: A People's History, 1962-1976. New York: Bloomsbury, 2016.

Domes, Jürgen. *P'eng Te-huai: The Man and the Image.* Stanford, CA: Stanford University Press, 1985.

Fitzgerald, Jon. "Continuity Within Discontinuity: The Case for Water Margin Mythology." *Modern China*, Vol. 12, No. 3 (July 1986): 361-400.

Guinn, Jeff. *The Road to Jonestown: Jim Jones and Peoples Temple.* New York: Simon & Schuster, 2017.

Karl, Rebecca. *Mao Zedong and China in the Twentieth-Century World.* Durham, N.C.: Duke University Press, 2010.

Han, Suyin. *The Morning Deluge: Mao Tsetung and the Chinese Revolution, 1893-1954.* New York: Little, Brown, 1972.

Hinton, Carma. dir. *Morning Sun.* 2003.

History and Public Policy Program Digital Archive, The Woodrow Wilson International Center for Scholars. "Summary of the Conversation between Comrade Peng Zhen and Romanian Ambassador in China Barbu Zaharescu." March 28, 1961. PRC FMA 109-03792-03, 6-13. Translated by Lu Sun.
https://web.archive.org/web/20210214164827/https:/digitalarchive.wilsoncenter.org/document/120005
Accessed December 8, 2021.

Hollingworth, Clare. *Mao and the Men Against Him.* New York: Jonathan Cape, 1985.

Huber, Jörg and Zhao Chuan, eds. *New Thoughtfulness in Contemporary China: Critical Voices in Art and Aesthetics.* New Brunswick: Transaction Publishers, 2011.

Leung, John K. and Michael Y.M. Kau, eds. *The Writings of Mao Zedong, 1949-1976*. New York: M.E. Sharpe, 1992.

Li, Jui, *The Early Revolutionary Activities of Comrade Mao Tse-Tung*. Translated by Anthony W. Sariti. White Plains, NY: M.E. Sharpe, Inc., 1977.

Li, Min. *Moi otets Mao Tszedun [My Father Mao Zedong]*. Beijing: Izdatel'stvo literatury na inostrannykh iazykakh, 2004.

Li, Zhisui. *The Private Life of Chairman: The Memoirs of Mao's Personal Physician*. Translated by Tai Hung-chao. New York: Random House, 1994.

Liu, Liyan. *Red Genesis The Hunan First Normal School and the Creation of Chinese Communism, 1903-1921*. Albany, NY: SUNY Press, 2012.

Lowell, Julia, *Maoism: A Global History*. New York: Knopf, 2019.

MacFarquhar, Roderick and Michael Schoenhals, *Mao's Last Revolution*. Cambridge, MA: Belknap Press of Harvard University Press, 2006.

Mao, Zedong. *Selected Works of Mao Tse-tung*.
https://web.archive.org/web/20211028152204/https://www.marxists.org/reference/archive/mao/selected-works/index.htm
Accessed December 9, 2021.

"Report On An Investigation Of The Peasant Movement In Hunan, March 1927."
https://web.archive.org/web/20210607155939/https://www.marxists.org/reference/archive/mao/selected-works/volume-1/mswv1_2.htm
Accessed July 28, 2021.

"OPPOSE BOOK WORSHIP, May 1930."
https://www.marxists.org/reference/archive/mao/selected-works/volume-6/mswv6_11.htm
Accessed April 5, 2020.

On Guerilla Warfare (1937).
https://web.archive.org/web/20210420094413/https://www.marxist
s.org/reference/archive/mao/works/1937/guerrilla-warfare/ch01.htm
Accessed July 28, 2021.

"ON NEW DEMOCRACY, January 1940."
https://web.archive.org/web/20211016075755/https://www.marxist
s.org/reference/archive/mao/selected-works/volume-
2/mswv2_26.htm
Accessed December 8, 2021.

"REPLY TO LI SHU-YI, May 11, 1957."
https://web.archive.org/web/20211203131539/https://www.marxist
s.org/reference/archive/mao/selected-works/poems/poems24.htm
Accessed December 8, 2021.

"Speech At The Chinese Communist Party's National Conference On
Propaganda Work, March 12, 1957."
https://web.archive.org/web/20210611061607/http://www.marxists.
org/reference/archive/mao/selected-works/volume-5/mswv5_59.htm
Accessed July 28, 2021

"Interview With Andre Malraux."
https://web.archive.org/web/20210514140437/https://www.marxist
s.org/reference/archive/mao/selected-works/volume-
9/mswv9_50.htm
Accessed July 28, 2021.

Chapter 8: People's War in *Quotations from Mao Tse Tung*.
https://web.archive.org/web/20210419164804/https://www.marxist
s.org/reference/archive/mao/works/red-book/ch08.htm
Accessed June 18, 2021.

"Speech At The Supreme State Conference 28 January, 1958."

https://web.archive.org/web/20210619063524/https://www.marxist
s.org/reference/archive/mao/selected-works/volume-
8/mswv8_03.htm
Accessed July 28, 2021

Masuda, Hajimu. *Cold War Crucible: The Korean Conflict and the Postwar World*. Cambridge: Harvard University Press, 2015.

Museum of the Chinese Revolution and Hunan Provincial Museum. Edited by *Xinmin Xuehui Ziliao* [*Sources for the New Citizen Study Society*]. Beijing: People's Press, 1980.

New Economic Thinking. "Understanding China's Cultural Revolution [Talk with Frank Dikötter]."
https://youtu.be/N9iVDCzGyiE?t=360
Accessed December 8, 2021.

Paine, S. C. M. *The Wars for Asia, 1911–1949*. Cambridge: Cambridge University Press, 2012.

Pang, Xianzhi and Jin, Chongji (CCCPC Party Literature Research Office). *Mao Zedong: A Biography*, Volume 1 1893-1949. Translated by Foreign Languages Press. Cambridge: Cambridge University Press, 2020.

Pantsov, Alexander V. and Steven I. Levine. *Mao: The Real Story*. New York: Simon and Schuster, 2012.

Pye, Lucian W. *Mao Tse-tung: The Man in the Leader*. New York: Basic Books, Inc., 1976.

Scalapino, Robert A. "The Evolution of a Young Revolutionary—Mao Zedong in 1919-1921." *The Journal of Asian Studies*, Vol. 42, No. 1 (Nov., 1982): 29-61.

Schram, Stuart. *Mao Tse-Tung*. Middlesex, UK: Penguin Books, 1966.

WORKS CITED

The Political Thought of Mao Tse-Tung. Cambridge: Cambridge University Press, 1989.

ed. and Timothy Cheek. *Mao's Road to Power: Revolutionary Writings, 1912-1949*, Vol. 1. Armonk, NY: M.E. Sharpe, 1992.

and Timothy Cheek. *Mao's Road to Power: Revolutionary Writings*, Volume VIII. New York: Routledge, 2015.

Schoppa, R. Keith. *The Columbia Guide to Modern Chinese History*. New York: Columbia University Press, 2000.

Schuman, Michael. *Confucius: And the World He Created*. New York: Basic Books, 2015.

Shi, Naian. *The Water Margin: Outlaws of the Marsh*. Translated by J.H. Jackson. North Clarendon, VT: Tuttle, 2010.

Short, Philip. *Mao: A Life*. New York: Henry Holt & Co., 1999.

Snow, Edgar. *Red Star Over China*. New York: Random House, 1938, 1944.

Spence, Jonathan. *The Search for Modern China*. New York: W.W. Norton & Company, 1990.

Mao Zedong. New York: Viking, 1999.

Tanner, Harold M. *Where Chiang Kai-shek Lost China: The Liao-Shen Campaign, 1948*. Bloomington, IN: Indiana University Press, 2015.

Terrill, Ross. *Mao: A Biography*. New York: Harper & Row Publishers, 1980.

Madame Mao: The White Boned Demon. Stanford, CA: Stanford University Press, 1999.

de Ven, Hans van. *China at War: Triumph and Tragedy in the Emergence of the New China.* Cambridge, MA: Harvard University Press, 2018.

Wang Rongfen Interview. "Dear Chairman Mao, Please Think About What You Are Doing.'" Radio Free Asia, May 16, 2016. https://web.archive.org/web/20210409045914/https://www.rfa.org/english/news/china/china-cultrev-05162016173649.html Accessed July 28, 2021.

Wemheuer, Felix. *A Social History of Maoist China Conflict and Change, 1949-1976.* Cambridge: Cambridge University Press, 2019.

Wile, Douglas. *Art of the Bed Chamber: The Chinese Sexual Yoga Classics Including Women's Solo Meditation Texts.* Albany, N.Y.: SUNY Press, 1992.

Williams, Sue, dir., *China: A Century of Revolution.* Ambrica Productions, Inc. and WGBH Educational Foundation, 1994.

Wilson, Dick. *Mao: The People's Emperor.* London: Hutchinson & Co., 1979.

Xiao, Zisheng [Xiaoyu]. *Mao Tse-Tung and I were Beggars.* Syracuse, NY: Syracuse University Press, 1959.

Xiao, Emi. *Mao Tse-Tung: His Childhood and His Youth.* No translator listed. Bombay, India: People's Publishing House,1953.

Xiao, San. *Mao Tse-tung t'ung-chih te ch'ing-shaonien shih-tai.* Guangzhou: Xinhua, 1950.

Zhao, Zhichao. *Mao Zedong he ta de fu lao xiang qin.* Changsha: Hunan wenyi chubanshe, 1992.

KIM IL-SUNG

"Chajusongul Onghohaja." *Rodong Sinmun*, August 12, 1966.

"Supplement to the Pyongyang Times: Let Us Defend Independency: Article of the *Rodong Sinmun*, August 12, 1966." *The Pyongyang Times*, 68, no. 68, August 18, 1966.

"Diplomatic Front." *Time*, July 9, 1951, 23.

"Carrots and Radishes." *Time*, November 13, 1950, 30-33.

"Letters: Plump Puppet." *Time*, May 31, 1948, 8.

"Substantial Citizens." *Time*, October 30, 1950, 34.

"Honoring Kim Il-sung's kin." *The Korea Times*, July 1, 2016.
http://www.koreatimes.co.kr/www/opinion/2019/07/202_208411.html
Accessed August 15, 2019.

"Right Way to the Left." *New York Times*, March 3, 1946, 32.

"YOU SAY POTATO, I SAY DPR KOREA." *Tampa Bay Times*, June 15, 2010:
https://www.tampabay.com/archive/2010/06/15/you-say-potato-i-say-dpr-korea/
Accessed December 8, 2021

Abend, Hallett. "Stolen Plum Came Near Causing War." *New York Times*, February 22, 1931, 47.

Armstrong, Charles K. *The North Korean Revolution*. Ithaca, N.Y.: Cornell University Press, 2003.

"Centering the Periphery: Manchurian Exile(s) and the North Korean State." *Korean Studies*, Vol. 19 (1995): 1-16.

Associated Press. "Asiatic Paul Bunyan: 'Legendary' Hero Returns to Korea Leading Army." *Salt Lake Tribune* (Salt Lake, UT), January 27, 1946, 6.

Barry, Mark. "Meeting Kim Il Sung in His Last Weeks." NKNews.org, April 15, 2012.
https://web.archive.org/web/20120529013141/https://www.nknews.org/2012/04/meeting-kim-il-sung-in-his-last-weeks/
Accessed July 28, 2021.

Bong, Baik. *KIM IL SUNG: Biography (III): From Independent National Economy To 10-Point Political Programme*. Translated by Committee for Translation. Tokyo: Miraisha, 1970.

Brooke, James. "N. Koreans Talk of Baby Killings." *New York Times*, June 10, 2002, 1.
https://web.archive.org/web/20210430025052/https://www.nytimes.com/2002/06/10/world/n-koreans-talk-of-baby-killings.html
Accessed December 8, 2021.

Buzo, Adrian. *The Guerilla Dynasty: Politics and Leadership in North Korea*. New York: I.B. Taurus & Co Ltd., 1999.

Politics and Leadership in North Korea: The Guerilla Dynasty, second edition. New York: Routledge, 2018.

Cha, John H. and K.J. Sohn. *Exit Emperor Kim Jong Il: Notes From His Former Mentor*. Bloomington, IN: Abbott Press, 2012.

Choe, In Su. *Kim Jong Il: The People's Leader*, Vol. 1. Pyongyang: Foreign Languages Publishing House, 1983.

Ch'oe, Yeong-ho. "Christian Background in the Early Life of Kim Il-Song." *Asian Survey*, Vol. 26, No. 10 (Oct., 1986): 1082-1091.

Committee for Human Rights in North Korea Publications.
https://web.archive.org/web/20210608135405/https://www.hrnk.org/publications/hrnk-publications.php
Accessed July 28, 2021.

WORKS CITED

Creekmore, Jr., Marion. *A Moment of Crisis: Jimmy Carter, the Power of a Peacemaker, and North Korea's Nuclear Ambitions*. New York: PublicAffairs, 2006.

Cumings, Bruce. *Origins of the Korean War: Liberation and the Emergence of Separate Regimes, 1945-1947*. Vol. 1 Princeton, N.J.: Princeton University Press, 1981.

    Korea's Place in the Sun: A Modern History. New York: W.W. Norton & Company, 1997.

    North Korea: Another Country. New York: The New Press, 2004.

    The Korean War: A History. New York: Modern Library, 2010.

Demick, Barbara. *Nothing to Envy: Ordinary Lives in North Korea*. New York: Spiegel & Grau, 2010.

Desmond, Edward W. "The Hard Way Out." *Time*. November 7, 1994, 53.

Gauthier, Brandon K. "The Other Korea: Ideological Constructions of North Korea in the American Imagination, 1948-2000." Ph.D. diss. Fordham University (2016).

    "Hope By Itself Is Not Enough: The Soft Power of North Korean Defectors." *Journal of East Asian Affairs*, Vol. 29, No. 2 (Fall/Winter 2015), 106-111.

    "An Individual Transformed: Review of Jang Jin-sung, Dear Leader: Poet, Spy, Escapee—A Look Inside North Korea." *Yonsei Journal of International Studies*, Vol. 6, no. 2 (Winter 2015): 372-376.

    "The Day Kim Jong Il Was Born." NKnews.org, February 15, 2013. https://web.archive.org/web/20200116072809/https://www.nknews.org/2013/02/the-day-kim-jong-il-was-born/ Accessed December 8, 2021.

"This Day in History: When Kim Il Sung Took Power." *NKnews.org*, October 9, 2012.
https://web.archive.org/web/20130208021124/https://www.nknews .org/2012/10/this-day-in-history-when-kim-il-sung-took-power/
Accessed July 28, 2021.

"The day South Korea faced the merciless reality of extinction." NKnews.org, June 25, 2013.
https://web.archive.org/web/20130704071746/https://www.nknews .org/2013/06/the-day-south-korea-faced-the-merciless-reality-of-extinction/
Accessed July 28, 2021.

"This Day in the History of the DPRK: June 18, Juche 41 (1953)." NKnews.org, June 17, 2012.
https://web.archive.org/web/20140222234939/https://www.nknews .org/2012/06/this-day-in-the-history-of-the-dprk-june-18-juche-41-1953/
Accessed July 28, 2021.

"Book Review: Cheehyung Harrison Kim, *Heroes and Toilers*." *Journal of American-East Asian Relations*, Vol. 26 (2019), 325-328.

"*DPRK-US Showdown* – a book review." September 11, 2014.
https://web.archive.org/web/20200116053505/https://www.nknews .org/2014/09/dprk-us-showdown-a-book-review/
Accessed June 20, 2021.

"What It Was Like to Negotiate With North Koreans 60 Years Ago." TheAtlantic.com, July 26, 2013.
https://web.archive.org/web/20211209044439/https://www.theatlan tic.com/international/archive/2013/07/what-it-was-like-to-negotiate-with-north-koreans-60-years-ago/278130/
Accessed December 28, 2021.

Telephone interview with Professor Andrew Natsios by the author, June 19, 2015.

WORKS CITED

Guo, Zhaoqing. *Kang Ri ying xiong Wei Zhengmin*. Shenyang: Liaoning ren min chu ban she, 1959.

Haggard, Stephen and Marcus Noland. *Famine in North Korea: Markets, Aid, and Reform*. New York: Columbia University Press, 2007.

Halberstam, David. *The Coldest Winter: America and the Korean War*. New York: Hachette Books, 2007.

Han, Sorya. "Hero General Kim Il Sung." *Chosun Shinbo-sa* (1962), 43.

Han, Hongkoo. "Wounded Nationalism: The Minsaengdan Incident and Kim Il Sung in Eastern Manchuria." Ph.D. diss., University of Washington (1999).

Harden, Blaine. *The Great Leader and the Fighter Pilot*. New York: Viking, 2015.

Hastings, Max. *The Korean War*. New York: Simon & Schuster, 1987.

Hawk, David. *The Hidden Gulag: The Lives and Voices of 'Those Who are Sent to the Mountains'* (Washington, D.C.: Committee for Human Rights in North Korea, 2012) Second Edition, https://www.hrnk.org/uploads/pdfs/HRNK_HiddenGulag2_Web_5-18.pdf
December 8, 2021.

Hiatt, Fred. "North Korea's Isolation Seen Dangerous for Its Foes." *Washington Post*, February 23, 1988, A17.

Hitchens, Christopher. *God Is Not Great: How Religion Poisons Everything*. New York: Hatchette, 2007.

FORA.tv: "Christopher Hitchens: How Religion Is Like North Korea." https://youtu.be/eefS0gayKFc
Accessed August, 14, 2019.

Hunt, Michael H. and Steven I. Levine. *Art of Empire: America's War in Asia from the Philippines to Vietnam*. Chapel Hill, N.C.: University of North Carolina, 2012.

Hwang Jang-yop (Former International-Secretary of KWP). "The Problem of Human Rights in North Korea (1)." Translated by the Network for North Korea Rights and Democracy.
https://web.archive.org/web/20030626015154/http://www.nknet.or g/en/keys/lastkeys/2002/7/03.php
Accessed July 28, 2021.

"The Problem of Human Rights in North Korea (2)." Translated by the Network for North Korea Rights and Democracy.
https://web.archive.org/web/20030202184515/www.nknet.org/en/k eys/lastkeys/2002/8/04.php
Accessed July 28, 2021.

Naneun Yeoksaui Jillireul Boatda [*I Saw the Truth of History*]. Seoul: Sidaejeongsin, 2010.

Jager, Sheila Miyoshi. *Brothers At War: The Unending Conflict in Korea*. New York: W. W. Norton & Company, 2013.

Jang, Jin-sung. *Dear Leader: Poet, Spy, Escapee—A Look Inside North Korea*. New York: Atria, 2014.

Jenkins, Charles Robert and Jim Frederick. *The Reluctant Communist: My Desertion, Court-Martial, and Forty-Year Imprisonment in North Korea*. Berkeley, CA: University of California Press, 2008.

Johnston, Richard J .H. "Communist Issue Growing in Korea." *New York Times*, April 27, 1946.

Ju, Jin-o. "Gidokgyo, Kim Il-Sung eotteon yeonghyangeul michyeonna." *Yeogsa Pip'yong*, Vol. 20 (August 1992): 321-326.

Kang, Chol-hwan and Pierre Rigoulot. *The Aquariums of Pyongyang*. Translated by Yair Reiner. New York: Basic Books, 2001.

Kang, Hyok and Philippe Grangereau. *This is Paradise! My North Korean Childhood*. Translated by Shaun Whiteside. London: Abacus, 2005.

Karig, USN Captain Walter, USN Commander Malcolm W. Cagle, and USN Commander Frank A. Manson, *Battle Report*. Vol. VI. *The War in Korea*. New York: Rhinehart and Company, 1952.

Kim, Cheehyung Harrison. *Heroes and Toilers: Work as Life in Postwar North Korea*. New York: Columbia University Press, 2018.

Kim, Il Sung. *With the Century*. Volumes 1-8. Pyongyang: Foreign Languages Publishing House, 1992-1998.

"Speech at the Conference of Activists from the Agricultural Cooperatives in North Hwanghae Province," December 20, 1957." *Works*, Vol. 11 Pyongyang: Foreign Languages Publishing House, 1982.

"On Effecting a New Revolutionary Turn in Socialist Economic Construction, Concluding Speech at a Consultive Meeting of the Senior Officials in the Economic Sector." *Works*, Vol. 44 December 1992-July 1994. Pyongyang: Foreign Languages Publishing House, 1999.

"Kanglian diyi lujun lueshi." ["Brief history of the First Anti-Japanese United Army."] in *Dongbei kangri lianjun shiliao* [*Historical materials of the Northeast United Anti-Japanese Army*]. Beijing: Zhonggongdang sheziliao chu-banshe, 1987. Vol. 2.

Kim, Jodi. *Ends of Empire: Asian American Critique and the Cold War*. Minneapolis, MN: University of Minnesota Press, 2010.

Kim Jun Hyok. *DPRK-US Showdown*. Pyongyang: Foreign Languages Publishing House, 2014.

Korean Central News Agency (KCNA). "Meeting for Remembering Kim Il Sung Held in China, April 8, 2014. https://web.archive.org/web/20141011173903/http://www.kcna.co.jp/item/2014/201404/news09/20140409-42ee.html Accessed December 8, 2021.

"Families of Those Related to Anti-Japanese Revolutionary Struggle Leave." September 12, 2018. https://web.archive.org/web/20191124041436/http://www.kcna.co.jp/item/2018/201809/news12/20180912-34ee.html Accessed December 8, 2021.

"Families of Those Related to Anti-Japanese Revolutionary Struggle," July 5, 2019. https://web.archive.org/web/20191124000030/http://www.kcna.co.jp/item/2019/201907/news05/20190705-13ee.html Accessed February 15, 2022.

Latham, William C. *Cold Days in Hell: American POWs in Korea*. College Station, TX: Texas A&M University Press, 2012.

Lankov, Andrei. *From Stalin to Kim Il Sung: The Formation of North Korea, 1945-1960*. New Brunswick, NJ: Rutgers University Press, 2002.

The Real North Korea: Life and Politics in the Failed Stalinist Utopia. New York: Oxford University Press, 2013.

Lee, Chong-sik. "Kim Il-Song of North Korea." *Asian Survey*, Vol. 7, No. 6 (June 1967): 374-382.

Lee, Hong Yung, Yong-Chool Ha, and Clark W. Sorensen, eds., *Colonial Rule & Social Change in Korea, 1910-1945*. Seattle, WA: University of Washington, 2012.

Lee, Hyeonseo. *The Girl With Seven Names*. London: William Collins, 2015.

Lee, Ki-baik. *A New History of Korea*. Translated by Edward W. Wagner and Edward J. Shultz. Seoul: Ilchokak Publishers, 1984.

Liem, Ramsay. "History, Trauma, and Identity: The Legacy of the Korean War for Korean Americans." *Ameriasia Journal*, Vol. 29, No. 3 (2003-4): 111-130.

Loh, Jules and Richard E. Myer (Associated Press). "The Ship That Went Out in the Cold" and "Panmunjom: Mad Dogs Bark at Moon."
     Lawton Constitution (OK), November 11, 1969, 9.
     The Progress (Clearfield, PA). November 14, 1969, 14.

Martin, Bradley K. *Under the Loving Care of the Fatherly Leader: North Korea and the Kim Dynasty*. New York: St. Martin's Press, 2004.

Myers, B.R. *Han Sorya and North Korean Literature: The Failure of Socialist Realism in the DPRK*. Ithaca, N.Y.: East Asia Program, Cornell University, 1994.

  The Cleanest Race: How North Koreans See Themselves—and Why It Matters. New York: Melville House, 2010.

  North Korea's Juche Myth. Busan, ROK: Sthele Press, 2015.

National Archives II (College Park, MD). Record Group 333, 14A.
  United Nations Command Military Armistice Commission, Minutes of Meetings of the Military Armistice Commission, 07/28/1953-02/13/1981.

Natsios, Andrew. *The Great North Korean Famine: Famine, Politics, and Foreign Policy*. Washington, D.C.: United States Institute of Peace, 2001.

Oberdorfer, Don and Robert Carlin. *The Two Koreas: A Contemporary History*. New York: Basic Books, 1997, 2014.

O'Neill, Mark. "N. Korea's Dead Dictator Remembered as Star Pupil According to Chinese Teacher's Daughter" (Reuters Dispatch from Beijing). *Korea Times*, September 10, 1994.

Pape, Robert A. *Bombing to Win: Air Power and Coercion in War*. Ithaca, N.Y.: Cornell University Press, 1996.

Person, James. "Chinese-North Korean Relations: Drawing the Right Historical Lessons." The Woodrow Wilson International Center for Scholars, October 19, 2017.
https://web.archive.org/web/20210428154312/https://www.wilsonc enter.org/article/chinese-north-korean-relations-drawing-the-right-historical-lessons
Accessed December 8, 2021.

Republic of Korea National Library (Gungnipjungangdoseogwan), Seoul, ROK North Korea Resource Center (Bukanjaryosenteo)

Scalapino, Robert and Chong-sik Lee. *Communism in Korea*. Vol. 1. Berkeley, CA: University of California Press, 1973.

Schaefer, Bernd. "'North Korean 'Adventurism' and China's Long Shadow, 1966-1972." *Cold War International History Project*, WP #44.

Shang, Yue. *Zhongguo lishi gangya* [*Outline of Chinese History*]. Beijing: Renmin chubanshe, 1954).

    Lìshi huímóu: Shàng yuè xiansheng [*Looking back at history: Mr. Shang Yue*] Beijing: Zhongguó Rénmín Dàxué Lìshi Xuéyuàn, 2011.

Shin, Michael D. *Korean National Identity under Japanese Colonial Rule: Yi Gwangsu and the March First Movement of 1919*. New York: Routledge, 2018.

Sohn, Won Tai. *Kim Il Sung and Korea's Struggle: An Unconventional Firsthand History*. Jefferson, N.C.: McFarland & Company, Inc., 2004.

Strong, Anna Louise. *Inside North Korea: An Eye-Witness Account*. Montrose, CA, 1947.

Suh, Dae-Sook. *The Korean Communist Movement, 1918-1948*. Princeton, N.J.: Princeton University Press, 1967.

Documents of Korean Communism, 1918-1945. Princeton, N.J.: Princeton University Press, 1970.

Kim Il Sung: The North Korean Leader. New York: Columbia University Press, 1988.

Suh, J.J. ed. *Origins of North Korea's Juche, Colonialism, War, and Development.* Lanham: Lexington Books, 2013.

Sung-chul Yang. *Korea and Two Regimes: Kim Il Sung and Park Chung Hee.* Cambridge, MA: Schenckman Publishing Company, Inc., 1981.

Szalontai, Balázs. "The Evolution Of The North Korean Socio-Political System, 1945–1994" in *Routledge Handbook of Contemporary North Korea.* Edited by Adrian Buzo. New York: Routledge, 2021.

United Nations Human Rights Council. "Report of the Commission of Inquiry on Human Rights in the Democratic People's Republic of Korea," February 7, 2014.
https://web.archive.org/web/20210726073621/https://www.ohchr.org/en/hrbodies/hrc/coidprk/pages/reportofthecommissionofinquirydprk.aspx
Accessed July 28, 2021.

Wada, Haruki. *The Korean War: An International History.* Translated by Frank Baldwin. Lanham, MD: Rowman & Littlefield, 2014.

Bukan Hyeondaesa. Paju, ROK: Changbi Publishers, Inc., 2012.

Weathersby, Kathryn. "'Should We Fear This?' Stalin and the Danger of War in Korea," Cold War International History Project Working Paper No. 39 (July 2002); and "Korean War Origins, 1945-1950," The Woodrow Wilson International Center for Scholars Digital Archive.
https://web.archive.org/web/20210423121437/https://digitalarchive.wilsoncenter.org/collection/134/korean-war-origins-1945-1950
Accessed July 28, 2021.

Wit, Joel S., Daniel B. Poneman, and Robert L. Gallucci, *Going Critical: The First North Korean Nuclear Crisis*. Washington, D.C.: Brookings Institution Press, 2004.

Yang, Sung-chul. *Korea and Two Regimes: Kim Il Sung and Park Chung Hee*. Cambridge, MA: Schenckman Publishing Company, Inc., 1981.

INDEX

Gratitude

I went on a walk in July 2018, unsure of what to write next. Called my friend Carter Mitchell, talked about anything and everything. Then I came up with an idea for a book. Went home and started writing immediately. The death of Stalin's first wife—I knew that story. It, like so many other historical moments of feeling, ricocheted around my mind, like a bullet searching for a target. It was almost cathartic, for me, to write about that event in a way that expressed the feelings it evoked—feeling what we weren't supposed to feel for tyrants. So I went deeper. Started doing research at Dartmouth's Baker-Berry Library that summer. Long and joyful work in windowless basement stacks followed, surrounded by tomes, the smell of old books—all thanks to Kate Krecker and Curtiss Clark who helped with childcare.

Completed two rough chapters by September 2018: Stalin and Hitler. I sought feedback. Shared the drafts with librarian Betty Jipson at Derryfield and my trusted teaching comrade Beth Knobel at Fordham. Appreciated their support and suggestions. Found a literary agent in Douglas Grad that October. And we sent off a proposal and the Stalin chapter to the big-hitters. Alice Mayhew (Rest in Peace) at Simon & Schuster gave good feedback. Cool. Mitchell Lerner at Ohio State University read early chapter drafts and offered helpful thoughts (*why leave out Kim Il-sung?*); I appreciated that. Same goes for Kirsten Swinth and Daniel Soyer at Fordham University, my alma mater, as well as Michael Latham at Punahou School. Charlotte Labbe at Fordham's Interlibrary loan office helped track down a number of crucial sources.

I worked steadily throughout 2019, expanding the project— writing one chapter at a time, two to three a season, when not teaching. On many long afternoons, when colleagues and students had gone home, I sat in a classroom alone, drinking green tea, listening to music, researching and writing. The pleasure of intellectual labor, unimpeded mental sweat.

Derryfield helped tremendously. Day to day, students provided joyful encouragement. Alumnus Emma Abate, a very good writer in her own right, stood out in that regard. Thank you to Mary Carter and Pete Brandt for the support of a Nancy S. Boettiger and Nancy Kamborean Faculty Enrichment Fund grant in the summer of 2019. Much obliged to DS teaching mentor Karen Whitmore, who not only read rough drafts of five of these chapters and offered encouragement, but put me into contact with Ann McGreevy, who suggested I read *Cradles of Eminence*. That got me thinking. Thank you as well to Lindley Shutz, Mary Karlin, Peter Talpey, and Diane Hotten-Somers. They read drafts of early chapters and offered support as well as thoughtful ideas.

By April 2020, through what felt like Herculean effort, I finished a draft of the manuscript. Fellow Fordham Ph.D. alums and dear friends—Alessandro Saluppo and Laurence Jurdem—offered feedback. Saluppo loved it. Offered thoughtful guidance on Italian sources. Jurdem had constructive criticisms. (I hope he has less now!) The hunt continued for the right publisher as a first-rate literary agent in Britain told me—unironically—that "20th-century history feels like a hard sell." An email to Adam Johnson at Stanford yielded timely encouragement—"keep working." Todd Brewster—my former boss at the West Point Center for Oral History—read some of the first draft in July 2020 (*This is good!*), and then put me in touch with his agent, who offered interesting counsel about the publishing world.

Three presses expressed interest by the fall of 2020. And how happy I was to be able to go with Gerald Brennan's Tortoise Books. In a market in which a small number of major publishers give readers increasingly homogenized styles from an ever-shrinking number of authors, Tortoise Books is doing something *interesting*. I am grateful to Brennan for believing in this project. He is not only a kind person and a great editor; he is an excellent writer. (Buy his books!) In December 2020, Brennan offered indispensable feedback on my manuscript. Suggested I add six opening chapters and reorganize the book. Due— at my insistence—by a deadline of July 2021.

January to June 2021 saw me work relentlessly. In every spare moment outside of the normal work day, I pounded away on my keyboard, surrounded by books in a small windowless office. Andy Myers—fine British bloke that he is—took an interest and read the first four chapters. Offered excellent editorial feedback (even if his doctorate is in biology)! My work ethic, I realized, was on point when I heard a colleague pass by my door on a late May afternoon and— much to my amusement—sigh: "I am worried this book is crushing him." *Onwards*.

Summer 2021 saw me working poolside, around the clock, finishing up this book with gratitude, with such appreciation that I, in addition to the privilege of teaching, continue to have the opportunity to research and write as a historian. With something approaching a final draft materializing by the end of July, Fordham doctoral student Kaitlin Shine and Boston University undergraduate Sam Duan graciously served as assistant editors. Kaitlin's keen editorial eye was much appreciated—so was Sam's help with Chinese sources.

Special thanks as well to Bryan Nickerson—my traveling compatriot from a trip to North Korea in August 2015—who allowed me to use his photo at the beginning of chapter six. Additional thanks to everyone who helped with proofreading, especially Betty Jipson, Bradley K. Martin (Check out GreatLeaderBooks.com), Curtiss Clark, David Lott, and Phoebe Gauthier. Special nod to Pieter Lott for advice on the cover.

My most important thank you goes out to Phoebe and Hadley. Phoebe helped me with an endless number of tasks relating to this manuscript and listened patiently as I talked about it for untold hours. Her intelligence, empathy, and excellence in everything she does remains a constant source of inspiration for me. How grateful I am to have her as my life partner. Hadley brought me joy throughout the process of writing this book—so often asking me to let her write her name on the keyboard in big letters! Thank you to my mother and father, Buddy and Nancy Gauthier, for their endless support and assistance over the years. Best to Keith Lockhart for being one of the coolest people alive.

In closing, I return to a dear friend I thanked in my dissertation acknowledgments (to the chagrin of a crank or two): Frannie, my beloved English Cocker Spaniel. ("She represents the innocence and beauty that surrounds us on a daily basis in even the most ordinary of circumstances.") Sadly, she passed away in July 2021, just as I was finishing this book. She was a dog. Not a human. But her loss, which upset me, left me more determined than ever to try and empathize with the experiences of all men and women, whoever they may be, whatever may be their experience.

Respect to Greta Lou.

ABOUT THE AUTHOR

Brandon K. Gauthier completed his doctorate in Modern History at Fordham University in New York City in 2016. He is the Director of Global Education at The Derryfield School and an Adjunct Professor of History for Fordham University. He speaks passionately, and loudly. He frequently asks his students to yell "WHO CARES?" and then tell him why he's wrong about everything. When not teaching and writing, he listens to music at loud volumes and walks long distances. Historical conundrums keep him up at night. He lives with his wife and two daughters in New Hampshire. *BEFORE EVIL* is his first book.

ABOUT TORTOISE BOOKS

Slow and steady wins in the end—even in publishing. Tortoise Books is dedicated to finding and promoting quality authors who haven't yet found a niche in the marketplace—writers producing memorable work that will stand the test of time.

Learn more at www.tortoisebooks.com or follow us on Twitter: @TortoiseBooks.

CPSIA information can be obtained
at www.ICGtesting.com
Printed in the USA
JSHW022116150322
23593JS00002BA/2

9 781948 954617